*I enthusiastically suggest that persons interested in Nativ̶̶̶̶̶̶̶̶̶̶̶̶̶̶
this new important book....It brings to the reader a cultur̶̶̶̶ ̶̶̶̶̶̶ ̶̶̶̶̶̶̶̶̶̶̶̶ ̶̶̶̶̶̶̶̶̶̶ ̶̶̶̶ ̶̶̶̶̶̶̶̶
from the original creation to contemporary times. It is a unique document.*
—**Lowell J. Bean**, Professor Emeritus of CSU Hayward, author of *Mukat's People:
The Cahuilla Indians of Southern California* and *California Indian Shamanism*

*This book offers rare insights into Kumeyaay tribal and family history.
It is both a well-researched text and a highly personal narrative that
significantly adds to our understanding of the past and present.*
—**Richard Carrico**, Department of American Indian Studies, SDSU

*Blood of the Band gives a detailed look into the origins of the San Pasqual Ipaay people....
Toler provides a rare glimpse into the internal conflicts regarding identity, "indian-ness"
and belonging....This book is a great addition into the family of Kumeyaay reference
material and stands to be a much cited reference in the years to come.*
—**Michael Connolly Miskwish**, Kumeyaay Historian

*I congratulate the author for bringing us not only a wealth of detail to set the record straight
on a difficult time in San Pasqual history, but also the rich personal stories that provide life
and substance to his story. Dave is to be commended for giving us the lives of real people,
too often lost in the broad generalizations of history.*
—**Ken Hedges**, Emeritus Curator, San Diego Museum of Man

*An authoritative, well-researched, and highly readable story of how a Nation adapted to the
difficult natural world of their ancestral homelands, to the cultural hierarchies of Spanish and
Mexican rule, and to displacement, removal, and assimilation by the US government—and
emerged stronger and richer as a Nation despite their immense challenges.*
—**James Mayfield**, Historian, Stanford University

*...Toler's book...is written by a Kumeyaay Citizen...who is also an elected member of
the Tribal Council....he is a man who follows the ancient cultural ceremonies of the
Kumeyaay people.... I believe this gives him insight that other authors of
Southern California Indian history have lacked....Blood of the Band is David's
legacy and his gift to generations of San Pasqual People not yet borne.*
—**Anthony Pico**, Former Chairman, Viejas Band of Kumeyaay Indians

*This unique work ties tribal pasts to the present, allowing us into significant elements
of Kumeyaay culture and history. Toler centers this account on Ipai bands and people who
continue their tribal sovereignty in the heart of San Diego County. This is a penetrating study by
a tribal leader and scholar willing to share details about the first people of Southern California.*
—**Clifford E. Trafzer**, Distinguished Professor of History and Rupert Costo Chair of
American Indian Affairs, University of California, Riverside

Blood of the Band
An Ipai Family Story

David L. Toler, Jr.

David L. Toler

2015

Sunbelt Publications, Inc
San Diego, California

Sunbelt Publications, Inc.
Copyright © 2015 by David L. Toler, Jr.
All rights reserved. First edition 2015

Cover and book design by Barry Age
Project management by Deborah Young
Printed in the United States of America

No part of this book may be reproduced in any form without permission from the publisher.
Please direct comments and inquiries to:

Sunbelt Publications, Inc.
P.O. Box 191126
San Diego, CA 92159-1126
(619) 258-4911, fax: (619) 258-4916
www.sunbeltpub.com

18 17 16 15   4 3 2 1

Library of Congress Cataloging-in-Publication Data

Toler, David L.
  Blood of the band : an Ipai family story / by David L. Toler, Jr.
     pages cm
  Summary: "The Ipai (also known as Kumeyaay) are the native people of northern San Diego County. This
book illustrates how one Ipai family's remarkable story forms part of the little-known, yet profoundly significant long-term history of human habitation in the land that only recently has come to be known as southern
California. Beginning with the ancestors' accounts of the creation of the world that link the Ipai with the unique
characteristics of our region's natural world, the journey then takes readers through the archaeological, historical, ethnographic and contemporary accounts of the dramatic transformations through which the Ipai have
persisted and ultimately prospered"–Provided by publisher.
  Includes bibliographical references and index.
  ISBN 978-1-941384-12-1 (softcover : alkaline paper) 1. Toler, David L.–Family. 2. Kamia Indians–California–
San Diego County–Biography. 3. Kamia Indians–California–San Diego County–Genealogy. 4. San Diego County
(Calif.)–Biography. 5. San Diego County (Calif.)–Genealogy. 6. San Pasqual Band of Diegueqo Mission Indians
of California. 7. Kamia Indians–California, Southern–History. 8. Kamia Indians–California, Southern–Social life
and customs. I. Title.
  E99.K18T65 2015
  979.4'9800497572–dc23
                              2015022239

Cover photo: *Trask Girls (Helen and Florence) Easter Sunday 1916, San Pasqual Reservation.*

Dedication

Blood of the Band is dedicated as a memorial to the original inhabitants of San Diego County, a testament to our peoples' courageous spirits, their brave and continued resistance in the face of invasion and colonizing forces, and their values and integrity, both individually and as a group. *Blood of the Band* is meant as an acknowledgment of the stamina, resilience, and perseverance of our region's native peoples, not only during prehistoric times, but also in the face of more recent adversities and, ultimately, successes.

Table of Contents

Preface

We are Ipai, meaning "the People" in the ancient language of our land. From our ancestors we learned the stories of the creation of every part of the world and the people, plants, and animals that live here. We see and feel our deep connection to this part of the earth in the places where the People lived, worked, sang, prayed, and left messages on the rocks and trails on the ground. We are still here, and we have a story to tell.

This history of our San Pasqual Ipai family describes how our ancestors lived in times past, when we were the only people on this part of the continent. We show how we adapted, survived, and managed to thrive through difficult times following the arrival of the invaders from other continents. Our family's story forms part of the little-known yet profoundly significant long-term history of human habitation in the land that only recently has come to be known as southern California. We pay special attention to the voices of our ancient ancestors, as well as those native people who managed to survive the turbulent historical periods and more recently, those of our relatives who lived during the last century. We also include a kaleidoscope of information from a variety of sources related to historical processes in California, the United States, and the world, since our people have long been active participants in all of these processes, and through their adaptability and persistence have managed to continue making history into the present.

This is also the story of the San Pasqual Band of Mission Indians, a people with roots that extend back thousands of years. This is the tale of the village and pueblo of San Pasqual that once sat astride the beautiful valley of the same name, a valley whose pleasant climate and abundant resources made it home to several Ipai villages and settlements. These were inhabited by people belonging to *shimulq* (named lineages or clans) who knew virtually every landform, traveled to places of wonder, and told and retold ancient stories of mythical creatures and important events. One of those clans, the La Chappa, called many places their home, including the desert village of San Felipe, the mountainous enclave of *Tekemuk* (Mesa Grande), the broad valley of *Pa'mu*, and the once serene

Opposite page: Angela Guachena La Chappa, Leonora La Chappa Trask's paternal grandmother.
Photo: E. H. Davis, San Diego History Center.

valley of *Mukalkal* (San Pasqual), where our ancestral village is today marked only by a small cemetery.

In this book we offer readers something that is rare in California history — a story of a people written on a large scale but also written as the personal story of a modern family from its roots thousands of years ago. This is also a narrative of many families and how those families comprised bands of people — bands that became tribes. In telling the story of the San Pasqual Band of Mission Indians it is necessary to take a broad view of the Ipai tribe. This is so because it is almost impossible to tell when bands or clans became a tribe and when those tribes and bands and clans became a cultural and political unit. In telling this story we hope that the reader will come to better understand who the native people of San Diego County were, and who they are today. An overall theme of the book is family, and ultimately the book is written for those families alive today and for those families who will inherit this earth from us.

The history and cultural traits of the Ipai of San Pasqual Valley, and more recently Valley Center, are the main focal points of *Blood of the Band*, but the history and cultural traits of our four neighboring groups — the Tipai (the native people who live to the south of the Ipai), the Luiseño, the Cupeño, and the Cahuilla peoples — are also part of our story, since our heritages are inextricably intertwined and interrelated. For thousands of years the ancestors of these tribes of what is now San Diego County interacted not only within their own bands and clans, but undoubtedly with each other as well, through marriage, trade, ceremonies, games, and other activities. All together, we are the People — a term that we have collectively called ourselves, and have currently re-adopted.

The Tipai are a special consideration in *Blood of the Band*, since their language and culture are closely related to those of our ancestors. Today, a concerted effort by Ipai and Tipai on both sides of the US-Mexican border is resulting in the frequent reuniting of these native bands, along with a renewal of strong, long-lasting cultural ties.

Since the first Spaniards arrived in San Diego in 1542, the Ipai and Tipai people (known collectively as Kumeyaay) have been the subject of great interest to many people. Most of the written histories of our region, beginning with European explorers in the 1500s and Spanish priests in the 1700s, while providing extremely valuable descriptions of native peoples during those periods, have tended to portray a biased version of events that served to justify the conquest and colonization of the original inhabitants and their lands. Historians in the 1800s and anthropologists in the 1900s also provided important glimpses into native cultures and the processes that affected them, but only rarely have native voices been able to provide indigenous perspectives. While it is impossible in one book to correct more than four centuries of mistakes and misunderstandings, one goal of *Blood of the Band* is to provide a fuller, more accurate story of the People.

The published literature on the native peoples of California in general, and on the Kumeyaay of San Diego County specifically, has virtually exploded in the last four decades. A thorough bibliography compiled in 1974 had approximately 400 sources that included historical accounts, solid anthropological studies, and general (often erroneous) overviews. An annotated bibliography published by Phillip White of San Diego State University in 1998 has almost 700 references. That same bibliography, if published today, would have more than 800 entries, and this does not include the massive (although unevenly professional) "gray" literature produced by cultural resource firms. Now in this second decade of the twenty-first century, persons wanting to know more about the rich and varied history and prehistory of the San Diego Kumeyaay have nearly unlimited access to the past.

Blood of the Band, written from the heart but based on years of primary research and dogged attention to detail, fills that gap for the bands and cultural groups of the Kumeyaay/Ipai/Tipai in San Diego County. We sincerely hope that this book will allow us to hear the voices of the People more easily and clearly, while moving us further along the journey toward a more extensive understanding and appreciation of the native people of San Diego County.

Very special thanks go to Welda Lou Johnson, who carried out extensive research and writing, making significant contributions to the formation of this book. Welda, a retired teacher whose career has included writing the book, *Brothers of the Earth*, has long worked with Indian students of the region. Her knowledge of local Ipai history and culture and her commitment to this project have provided invaluable perspectives throughout the text.

We would like to thank Richard Carrico and Mike Wilken for the time and effort they have devoted to this endeavor. Their input, suggestions, and direction have been valuable beyond description. We are grateful to David L. Toler III, a Trask family descendant, who has provided all of the government documents and much of the research used in *Blood of the Band*. Appreciation goes to all Trask family descendants who offered interviews and their encouragement as *Blood of the Band* was being written. Thanks go also to archivist Carl Shipek for his willingness to open for the Toler family's perusal his mother's archives at Kumeyaay Community College located at the Sycuan Band of the Kumeyaay Nation, and to Cindy Stankowski and her staff at the San Diego Archaeological Center for their aid in providing information about Malcolm Rogers.

In reading this book you will notice many variations in the spelling of names. We went to great lengths to preserve the way a name was used in its time. Please see page 227 for more information.

Introduction

The People have been known by many names, including Diegueño (because of their proximity to the San Diego Mission), Mission Indians, Native Americans, and indigenous people. In this work we will use the name *Ipai*, or native people, to describe ourselves. The names *Ipai* and *Tipai* designate two historically-related groups of native people who live in northern and southern portions of San Diego County, and who have slight language and cultural differences, but who share a closely related cultural history, which unites them from ancient times to the present. Together, these groups are often referred to simply as Kumeyaay.

As recently as two centuries ago, the Kumeyaay were still the majority population living in the territory extending from the San Luis Rey River as far south as Santo Tomas in Baja (Lower) California, Mexico, to the deserts, and perhaps as far as the Colorado

> *The names Ipai and Tipai designate two historically-related groups of native people who live in northern and southern portions of San Diego County, and who have slight language and cultural differences, but who share a closely related cultural history, which unites them from ancient times to the present. Together, these groups are often referred to simply as Kumeyaay.*

River on the east, and to the Pacific Ocean on the west. Though the Ipai lived in what are now the northern sections of San Diego County, and the Tipai in the southern sections as well as Baja California, both of these areas were once part of New Spain, and after 1821, Mexico. As a result of the war against Mexico, the United States government took control of California, Arizona, and other former Mexican territories in 1848, as established by the Treaty of Guadalupe Hidalgo.

Original Kumeyaay territory was bisected by the newly established international border, after which many of the Tipai traditional communities remained on the southern side of the border in Mexico. Those north of the border became part of the United States, albeit

Traditional songs, an enduring part of the native cultural heritage of our region. *Illustration: Robert Freeman.*

without the rights of citizenship and under rapidly changing conditions where a new language — English — was taking the place of Spanish, as cultural and political domination by Americans became the new challenge for the People.

The term Diegueño (also *Dieguino* or other alternate spellings; see Luomala 1978) is used here only in the historical contexts in which it may have been used prior to the adoption of Kumeyaay (or more specifically Ipai or Tipai after circa 1970). For many Kumeyaay, the term Diegueño is not only inaccurate, it also represents the worst case of an exonym, a name given to a people by outsiders including enemies. Though historical records may use the spelling San Pascual, especially during the Spanish and Mexican periods from 1769-1835, we will use the spelling San Pasqual.

Ipai territory included parts of what is now north San Diego County, from the San Diego River to as far northeast as Lake Henshaw, from the Pacific Coast up to the mountains and down to the desert. However, the main focus of this book will be the Ipai of the San Pasqual Valley. They lived in the area around the San Dieguito River for thousands of years before the arrival of invaders to their territories, and, since 1909, have lived in Valley Center, six miles north of their traditional lands in San Pasqual Valley.

We use the term "band" when talking about groups of families related by blood or inter-marriage, and who live and work together as a social unit. In the past, bands often moved throughout their traditional territories in annual cycles, depending on the availability of animal or plant resources. Tribes are made up of many bands who share similar languages and cultures, and who have reasons (such as the need to defend against common enemies) to identify themselves as part of the larger group.

It is the goal of *Blood of the Band* to present a history of the Ipai of San Diego County throughout time, with the structure moving chronologically in a compelling, comprehensive, accurate, and truthful manner. The People's territory — within the San Pasqual Valley, Mesa Grande, Santa Ysabel, Volcan Mountain, the San Felipe Valley, the Santa Maria Valley near Ramona, and areas extending to the coastal regions, the inland valleys, and the mountains and eastern desert — can be envisioned by considering the ancient traces of their inhabitants. The voices of those natives who were displaced, and their descendants, are coming to light, and are being more frequently presented — through ancient pictographs, petroglyphs, discovered artifacts, evidences of mortars, metates, pestles, pottery, burial remains, and hearths, along with a resurgence and more thorough perusal of creation stories, historic myths and legends, interviews, personal writings, and informant recordings chronicling the oral histories of the People. All of these remind the observer that we are still here.

Most histories of San Diego County's native population, and the native peoples' journeys through time, have been told from the viewpoints of the invaders — be they Spanish colonists, Mexican rancheros, American capitalists, or modern non-Indian anthropologists and historians. Diaries, journals, artists' renderings, and, later, photographs and movies, have been extensively presented as evidence portraying how the original inhabitants of the county lived at the time of first contact with Europeans. But these conclusions usually are from the perspectives and viewpoints of those chronicling the histories — members of the colonizing society.

Today, the "new" San Pasqual Indian Reservation in Valley Center can claim continued inhabitance by the native people for over a century. Within those more than hundred years, many cultural traits and characteristics of the Ipai have been retained, and have been faithfully passed on to new generations, both orally and using writings, illustrations, photographs and artistic drawings. The San Pasqual Band of Mission Indians have been told of their ancestors' struggles to keep their traditional lands for themselves and their families, from 1769 forward, in spite of the occupation by hostile forces from the Spanish, Mexican, and American cultural groups, with many native people perishing, many resisting the onslaught of injustices, and many surviving to fight for their rights another day.

That the native people of San Diego County were the targets of genocide, extermination, murder, tracking, killing, rape, decimation, and enslavement are facts that have been documented by non-Indians and Indians alike throughout the centuries. Official historical records give positive evidence that the United States government and much of the

Eagle Dancers. Five men stand in a row, each holding up a staff with feathers on top in their right hand. The men are (possibly) from left to right: Joe Burro Waters, Rafael Charley, Narciso Lachappa, Quero Santo, and Antonio Maces. *Photo: E. H. Davis, San Diego History Center.*

Tipai woman in front of her traditional house at Campo, early 1900s. *Photo: Edward Curtis.*

American population not only condoned wiping out the existence of the San Diego County native population, but, also, that their means of extermination were cruel, inhumane, brutal, and senseless. In relying on the voices of the native people to tell the stories of San Diego County Indian history—in the actual words of those who lived and died in their traditional lands, and those who have survived to tell their stories today—this book includes as many available resources as possible to achieve that goal. It is with the greatest humility that we embark upon such an endeavor. May this book allow each of us to hear the voices of the People ever so much more easily and clearly.

I

Origins:
Creation of the People

"We are going to dig in the ground, and take mud, and make the Indians first."
And he dug in the ground, and took mud, and made of it first the men, and after
that the women *(Cinon Duro, Ipai Creation story recorded by DuBois in 1901).*

Then was begun the creation of people out of clay. They lay there sleeping,
and then began to come to life. This happened at the mountain Wikami
(LaChappa, in Curtis 1926:122).

Western science and archaeology cannot answer all of the questions of human origins,
or in this case the origins of the Kumeyaay people. To understand how a people came to be
we must combine timeless, ancient stories and ideas with the results of scientific inquiry.
Science and spiritual belief are not enemies or opponents, in direct opposition with each
other; they should be viewed as complementary.

Native peoples around the world have ways of understanding their origins based on
oral traditions passed on from generation to generation. Some groups have mythologies or
oral histories describing complex migrations, while other groups, such as the Kumeyaay,
trace our origins to the sacred geography within our own traditional territory and to the
Yuman homelands in the Colorado River desert directly to the east.

Ipai oral tradition, passed down from generation to generation, continued being transmitted in spite of the invasion of non-Indians and the introduction of the Roman Catholic
religion; in some cases the narratives have been creatively adapted to these new influences.
An account of the Ipai story of creation was told by Cinon Duro, the last hereditary chief or
kwapaay of the Mesa Grande Band and a keeper of knowledge.

Charles Russell Quinn described the Ipai people at Mesa Grande as "a people whose
boast it had been that 'when the hills were young they had danced upon them'" (1962:28-32).
Cinon Duro was born in 1816 and lived until 1906. He served at Mesa Grande as their

Opposite page: The creation of man and woman out of clay. *Painting: Robert Freeman*

1

spiritual leader and the last hereditary captain. The ceremonies which Cinon performed throughout his lifetime were taught to him by his father (DuBois 1904 and Ancestry.com 2014). Quinn noted that:

> The loss which the tribe suffered in the death of their last hereditary chief, old Cinon Duro, or to use his Indian name, Mata Whur [*Methuir*], "hard rock," will be readily understood, as he was, apart from his dignity as bearer of the hereditary title, the custodian of the sacred legends which were handed down from chief to chief, and leader in the ceremonials and rites of the primeval religion (Quinn 1962:28-32).

With Duro's passing, an unknown quantity of wisdom and ancient tradition went with him. Fortunately he told the story of creation that is provided below to anthropologist Constance DuBois in the late 1890s, and also sang the words of the creation songs that follow the story.

It should be noted that as is common with most cultures and peoples, there are differing versions of the Kumeyaay creation story. This is understandable given the thousands of years that have preceded any telling or transcription of the story and given that different clans or social units might have versions that vary one from another.

An Ipai Story of Creation, as Told by Cinon Duro

When Tu-chai-pai made the world, the earth was the woman, the sky was the man. The sky came down upon the earth. The world in the beginning was a pure lake covered with tules. Tu-chai-pai and his younger brother, Yo-ko-mat-is, sat together, stooping far over, bowed down by the weight of the sky. The Maker said to his brother, "What am I going to do?"

"I do not know," said Yo-ko-mat-is.

"Let us go a little farther," said the Maker.

So they went a little farther and sat down to rest. "Now what am I going to do?" said Tu-chai-pai.

"I do not know, my brother."

All of this time the Maker knew what he was about to do, but he was asking his brother's help. Then he said, "We-hicht, we-hicht, we-hicht," three times. He took tobacco in his hand, and rubbed it fine and blew upon it three times. Every time he blew, the heavens rose higher above their heads.

Younger brother did the same thing because the Maker asked him to do it. The heavens went higher and higher and so did the sky. Then they both did it together, "We-hicht, we-hicht, we-hicht," and both took tobacco, rubbed it, and puffed hard upon it, sending the sky so high it formed a concave arch.

Then they placed North, South, East, and West. Tu-chai-pai made a line upon the ground.

"Why do you make that line?" asked younger brother.

"I am making the line from East to West and name them so. Now you make a line from North to South."

Cinon Duro, spiritual leader
and captain of Mesa Grande.
*Photo: E. H. Davis, San Diego
History Center.*

Yo-ko-mat-is thought very hard. How would he arrange it? Then he drew a crossline from top to bottom. He named the top line North, and the bottom line South. Then he asked, "Why are we doing this?"

The Maker said, "I will tell you. Three or four Indians are coming."

The brother asked, "Do four men come from the North, and two or three men come from the South?"

Tu-chai-pai said, "Yes. Now I am going to make hills and valleys and little hollows of water."

"Why are you making all of these things?"

The Maker explained, "After a while when men come and are walking back and forth in the world, they will need to drink water or they will die." He had already made the ocean, but he needed little water places for the people.

Then he made the forests and said, "After a while men will die of cold unless I make wood for them to burn. What are we going to do now?"

"I do not know," replied younger brother.

"We are going to dig in the ground and find mud to make the first people, the Indians." So he dug in the ground and took mud to make the first men, and after that the first women. He made the men easily but he had much trouble making women. It took him a long time.

After the Indians, he made the Mexicans and finished all his making. He then called out very loudly, "People, you can never die and you can never get tired, so you can walk all the time." But then he made them sleep at night, to keep them from walking in the darkness. At last he told them that they must travel toward the East, where the sun's light was coming out for the first time.

The Indians then came out and searched for the light, and at last they found light and were exceedingly glad to see the Sun. The Maker called out to his brother. "It's time to make the Moon. You call out and make the Moon to shine, as I have made the Sun. Sometime the Moon will die. When it grows smaller and smaller, men will know it is going to die, and they must run races to try and keep up with the dying moon."

The villagers talked about the matter and they understood their part and that Tu-chai-pai would be watching to see that they did what he wanted them to do. When the Maker completed all of this, he created nothing more. But he was always thinking how to make Earth and Sky better for all the Indians (DuBois 1901:181-185).

The first creation song that Cinon Duro presented was a song sung by the Sky father, who begot the creator-gods Tu-cha-pai and Yo-ko-mat-is:

Yi-haw-ma-ya-a i
Yi-haw-ma-ya-a I (repeated six times)
(A long sigh repeated)
Ich-a-pa-wha-chi-ho
Yo-o-o
Ich-a-pa-wha-chi-yo
Yo-o-o
Ma-to Tu-chai-pa
Mai-i-i-Yo-ko-mat
Ich-a-pa-wha-chi-yo
(DuBois 1904:217-241).

The second song Duro presented was sung by the Earth mother, and describes the bringing forth of the creator-gods:

Chu-pa-chu-wha
W-i-i
Tu-chai-pa
Chu-pa-chu-wha
Wa
W-i-i-i
W-i-i-i
(DuBois 1904:217-241).

The Creation, as Told by Jose Bastiano LaChappa

Jose Bastiano La Chappa was born in 1839 at Mesa Grande and lived there until his death in 1889. His parents were Logario and Maria Jesusa La Chappa. Sometime before 1859 Jose Bastian married Angela Guachena, variously shown as born between 1819 (Census of Mesa Grande 1890), 1823, and 1833 (Census of 1894) and living until 1907. Together the couple had at least three children, Jose Antonio, Juan Diego, and Petra. Angela lived until 1907.

La Chappa narrated the following creation story, which was documented by Edward Curtis in his voluminous work, *The North American Indian*. The story provides additional details that again show the deep connections between the Ipai and their traditional territory, from the Pacific Ocean on the west to the Colorado Desert to the east.

Umut [earth] was a woman and Uhá [water] a man. Earth was beneath Water. She bore two sons, and she named them Chakopá and Chakomát. Chakopá was mutuwihl [Elder] and Chakomát was qusánk [younger]. They stood up and pushed with their hands, raising the water until it formed the sky. They were standing on the earth. The younger was blind.

First they made the sun, then the moon, then the stars. The younger brother rolled clay into a flat disc and threw it into the western sky. It slipped down twice. He tried it in the southern sky, but it slipped down twice. He tried it in the north, and again it slipped down twice. He tried it in the east, and it remained without slipping so rapidly. The elder brother said it felt too hot, and it was raised higher. Three times it was moved higher, until it felt right. In the same way the moon was finally fixed in place, but it was too cold, and three times it was moved higher until it was right. For the stars many small pieces of clay were scattered through the sky. Then was begun the creation of people out of clay. They lay there sleeping, and then began to come to life. This happened at the mountain Wikami.

The people planned a ceremony, and built a large enclosure of brush. Then they sent a messenger to bring the great serpent Umaihuhlya-wít ("sky moon") from the ocean. He came and coiled himself in the enclosure but he could not get his entire length inside. On the third morning, when he had coiled as much of his body as the enclosure would contain, the people set fire to it and burned him. His body exploded and scattered. Inside his body was all knowledge, comprising songs, magic secrets, ceremonies, languages, and customs. Thus these were scattered over the land and different people acquired different languages and customs.

The elder brother became sick. Huhlyá-kwuhl (approximately November) was the moon in which he fell sick. Before this there were no names for the moons: they had been concealed in the body of Umaihuhlya-wít. His sickness continued through the following moons: Huhlyá-nyumsáp, Huhlyá-tai, Huhlyá-pesiu, Huhlyá-mutiña, Huhlyá-nicha. In that moon he died.

They prepared to burn his body on a pile of wood, and Coyote was sent for the fire of the Fireflies in the west; for they feared he would make trouble. And while he was absent they began to make fire with the drill. He came back from the west

5

Rock art of the Kumeyaay territory. *Photo: Greg Erikson..*

unsuccessful, and was sent in turn to the south, to the north, to the east. While he was in the east, fire was at last kindled, and by the time he returned, the body was consumed, all except the heart. All the people stood around the fire, wailing. They would not let Coyote in. Round and round he ran, trying to find an opening. He wanted to be burned up, he said. Finally he jumped over Badger, who was a short man, seized the heart, jumped back over Badger, and ran away. All pursued him, but they could not catch him. He threw the heart away, and its blood became the red paint found in mineral springs.

The younger brother went up into the sky. He is now seen as ball-lightning. He carries away the spirits of people and so causes their death (Curtis 1926:121-122).

2

Twelve Thousand Years of Native Lifeways: The Archaeological Record of the People

According to Richard Carrico (2010), "The study of archaeology seeks to better document the origins of prehistoric people in the area, and to understand the evolution of technologies, people, and cultures." The discussion that follows provides a Western scientific approach to the people and cultures that have inhabited San Diego County for more than 10,000 years. This scientific narrative may or may not vary from the traditional Kumeyaay views of origins and cultural development. In many ways, the Western scientific approach and the traditional views complement each other and are not always at odds. Both narratives imbue the Kumeyaay with a long tenure on the land, both perceive the Kumeyaay as stewards of the land, and both celebrate the ability of the ancient cultures to persist and thrive, on their road to becoming the Ipai and Tipai of today.

Early Prehistoric Peoples: the Populating of Our Region

Recent reports based on DNA evidence address the issue of the antiquity of the native people of North America, lending credence to the idea that native people have populated North America for many millennia. DNA research that is being carried out with populations around the world supports the idea that the populating of the Americas began some time toward the end of the last Ice Age, by way of Siberia and Beringia. This approach has shown that the peoples of North and South America are related to the ancient ancestors in eastern Asia and the Steppes of Euro-Asia. Roughly 20,000-25,000 years ago, these prehistoric humans are believed to have carried their Asian genetic lineages up into the far reaches of Siberia, and eventually across the then-exposed Bering land mass into the Americas. Thus, the first Native Americans may be the descendants of the early peoples who emerged from the Altai region.

Dr. Theodore Schurr, from the University of Pennsylvania, focuses in particular on the region of "Altai" as an important part of this new information:

Opposite page: Rock art of the Ipai region. *Photo: Greg Erikson.*

Altai in southern Siberia sits right at the center of Russia. But the tiny, mountainous republic has a claim to fame unknown until now: Native Americans can trace their origins to the remote region. Recent DNA research revealed that genetic markers link people living in the Russian republic of Altai, southern Siberia, with indigenous populations in North America. A study of the mutations indicated a lineage shift between 13,000 and 14,000 years ago—when people are thought to have walked across the ice from Russia to America. This roughly coincides with the period when humans from Siberia are thought to have crossed what is now the Bering Strait and entered America. Altai is considered a key area because it is a place where people have been coming and going for thousands of years (Schurr 2012).

One conflict, however, between native peoples of California and many archaeologists is the way that non-native researchers have grouped or categorized past people and cultures. In general the model that has been used is one that came into use more than a hundred years ago; it categorizes people by artifact types/assemblages (material culture) and by time and space (spatial). While the original intent may have been to ascribe some mean-ingful name to ancient people, it has led to serious misunderstandings amongst native people. What is needed is a more comprehensive understanding and blending of the lan-guage of a people, their artifacts and material culture, their ideological beliefs, and their physical attributes.

While one may agree or disagree with the archaeological terminology, and even with the implications of separating San Diego County's past into somewhat artificial patterns, complexes, and horizons, some kind of categorization based on a synthesis of existing information is, nonetheless, a useful tool to aid in understanding what the technologies and lifeways of the pre-contact people were.

Malcolm Rogers and Early Efforts to Understand Our Region's Archaeological Record

Malcolm Rogers, an archaeologist who was influential in developing some of the for-mative theories regarding the populating of the southern California region, first described the ancient native people of the San Diego County area in 1929, when he called them the "Scraper Maker Culture." Rogers's findings were influenced by excavations from what became known as the Harris Site, located in the San Dieguito River Valley in north San Diego County, and one of the most important archaeological sites in the United Sates, now listed on the National Register of Historic Places.

Rogers first discovered his interest in archaeology as a boy in upper New York State. Well-educated at Syracuse University, he eventually worked as an assayer and mining geologist. When his family moved to Escondido in 1919 and acquired a citrus grove, Rogers—because his family had some level of affluence—was free to pursue looking for artifacts throughout San Diego County. He claimed that the same year he moved to Escondido he discovered twelve ancient stone tools intact, and a number of broken ones.

Table 1-1
Terminology for Culture History in the San Diego Area
(Adapted from Gallegos 2002)

Geologic Time	Period	Years Before Present	Other Names	Diagnostic Cultural Material
Late Holocene	Late Period	Present ... 1,300	Historic Late Prehistoric Yuman Cuyamaca Complex San Luis Rey I, II	Bow and arrow, small triangular and side-notched points, cremations, fish hooks, ceramics Obsidian Butte obsidian.
Late Holocene	Early Period (Archaic)	2,000 3,000		Stone bowls, triangular points fishing gorges, burials.
Middle Holocene	Early Period (Archaic)	4,000 5,000 6,000		Dart and atlatl, cogged stones, plummet stones, leaf-shaped points/knives, corner-notched and stemmed points, Coso Obsidian, burials.
Early Holocene	Early Period (Archaic)	7,000 8,000 9,000 10,000	Pauma Complex Encinitas Tradition La Jolla Complex San Dieguito Tradition/Complex	Spear, crescents, lanceolate and leaf-shaped points, leaf-shaped knives, Casa Diablo and Coso Obsidian, burials.

Terminology for Culture History in the San Diego Area (adapted from Gallegos 2002).

In 1927 a flood in the San Dieguito River Valley, on a farm near Lake Hodges and Rancho Santa Fe owned by C. W. Harris, exposed large projectile points and scrapers. The following year, Malcolm Rogers began excavation work there. With the Great Depression intervening, however, work at the site had to be put on hold (Hanna 1982).

In 1938 Rogers and a field crew returned to conduct further excavations, which led to Rogers concluding that cultural artifacts at the north San Diego County site could be divided into three separate categories. They were the San Dieguito Cultural Group, which existed at least 10,000-8,000 years before present (YBP); the La Jolla Culture Group, which existed 7,500-3,000 YBP; and the Late Prehistoric Culture Group—also called the Early Milling Horizon—which began about 1,300 YBP and ended with the beginning of permanent colonization by the Spanish in the region in 1769, with the establishment of Misión San Diego de Alcalá. (Carrico 1987:5-7).

Today the Harris Site sets next to a development of 443 homes called the Crosby Estates, ten miles west of the San Pasqual Valley; the site represents cultural evidence of native lifeways at least as far back as 9,500 YBP. It also offers consistent proof that the People used the resources within their environments, and that they were mobile groups, traveling during certain seasons to certain sites to access those resources. The Harris Site continues to be viewed as a place where other discoveries will most likely be revealed, and its date of 9,500 years before present continues to make it a most valuable resource for researchers (Carrico et al 1991).

Based on radiocarbon samples from the Harris Site, Carrico (1987) reports that 10,000-8,000 YBP the people of the San Dieguito Complex Phase I (the earliest peoples of the San Dieguito Cultural Group) probably lived east of the Laguna Mountains range, with the Imperial and Mojave deserts as part of their territory, which may have extended as far as Mono Lake. They were mostly hunters, also gathering acorns, nuts, seeds, and berries (Carrico 1987).

The San Dieguito Complex Phases II and III people lived in the San Diego County area. They were characterized by the use of heavy, "horse-hoof" planes, rounded end scrapers, side and end scrapers, choppers, knife-points, long-stemmed point knives with weak shoulders, crescents, hammerstones, macro-flakes, thick primary flakes, and thick trimming and finishing flakes (Carrico 1987). He adds that "... by 7,500 years ago, the San Dieguito people had been assimilated or possibly evolved into the La Jolla Culture Complex of the Early Milling Horizon" (Carrico 1987:7).

In 1929 Malcolm Rogers had called the people of the second division the "Shell Midden People," but later he called this period from 7,500-3,000 years ago "The La Jolla Culture," with Phases I and II. Other historians, however, later used the terms "Early Milling Horizon" and "The Encinitas Tradition" to describe the La Jolla Culture Complex, terms which all described the cultural ways of the native people of the southern California coast, who were increasingly using grinding tools to process plant foods.

Following the above designations, historical researchers collected information in the Pauma Valley of northeastern San Diego County, near the San Luis Rey River, and learned that this group possessed characteristics similar to the San Dieguito and La Jolla people, in that they used grinding stones and chipped stone tools. In addition to increased usage of plant foods, evidence supports the theory that the people of the La Jolla Cultural Complex consumed great amounts of shellfish and used fire hearths along with stone tools such as metates, pestles and manos, and stone bowls (Carrico, 1987).

Huge piles of shellfish remains — called "shell middens" — have been found along the southern California coast, lending credence to the theory that the native people utilized the nearby natural resources. Shell middens are actually deposits of refuse once used by ancient people and consist mainly of stacks of mollusk shells, also containing a complex mixture of debris that presents clues as to the lifeways of those who once inhabited the region. Animal bones, pieces of pottery shards, and other artifacts representative of the culture of the group are also often found in the middens. Archaeologists have been able to analyze and describe what the cultural traits of certain groups were, by comparing the day-by-day products unearthed in middens. Burial sites containing human remains and artifacts buried with the bodies are sometimes found in or near these same shell middens (Brinton 1866).

In a recent manuscript, Carrico (2010) offers information about what he believes may have happened with the people of the La Jolla Cultural Complex. He says that the following changes began to occur about 3,000 years ago:

> While still controversial, it is probable that the earlier Hokan-speaking people (La Jolla) were gradually displaced, or more likely assimilated, into a population of people that slowly migrated from the eastern desert lakes region and into San Diego County. This change in cultural and ethnic make-up may have begun as early as 3,000 years before present and was fully developed by 2,000 years ago. Charles Bull has suggested that the people of the La Jolla Pattern were Hokan-speaking people—linguistically, if not genetically, related to the people of the deserts to the east and to the people of the Santa Barbara region. Bull's hypothesis is important because if the people of the La Jolla pattern were Hokan-speaking, they may have been closely related, at least linguistically, to their chronological successors, the Hokan-Yuman-speaking Kumeyaay (Carrico 2010:TS).

Malcolm Rogers's third division, the Late Prehistoric Period, is known as the San Luis Rey Complex Phases I and II, and occurred about 1,300 years ago. With archaeologists finding more milling features from this era, it is believed that the people were processing an increasingly wider variety of plant resources as one of their staple foods, along with the use of the bow and arrow for hunting game. Small triangular projectile points, mortars and pestles, and flake scrapers are all indicative of this time period (Carrico 1987).

San Luis Rey Phase II attributes included all those found in Phase I, and about 1,000 years ago, added cremation, pottery-making, and particular styles of pictographs (rock paintings), and petroglyphs (rock carvings). The Kumeyaay peoples' rock art may have contained messages to travelers, or might have had religious meanings (Patterson 1992), however interpretations are problematic since it is not possible to consult with the artists.

Historian D. L. True recognized and defined the Cuyamaca Complex as occurring in eastern San Diego County during the same time as Phase II of the San Luis Rey Complex, and identified some of the differences that the Cuyamaca peoples' culture exhibited. Their cemetery areas were separate from their living areas, and they also used grave markers. Mortuary offerings included cremation urns holding the ashes of the deceased, miniature vessels, complex projectile points and shaft straighteners. The Cuyamaca people used a variety of scrapers, scraper planes, and other stone tools, along with an assortment of ceramic items, including pots and bowls, bow pipes, effigy forms and rattles (True 1970).

Carrico concluded that the native people of San Diego County:

Ancient grinding stones of the Ipai region.

... Can be considered as descended from the San Luis Rey and Cuyamaca cultural phases resulting in the Yuman-speaking Northern Diegueño (Ipai) and Southern Diegueño (Tipai) in southern San Diego and the Shoshonean-speaking Luiseño and Cahuilla in northern San Diego County. ... It was the most recent development stage of the pattern that was practiced by Indian inhabitants of San Diego County when the Spaniards first set foot here (Carrico 1987:10).

These language differences and variations in cultural traditions and artifacts partially account for the differences found at each of the varying archaeological sites throughout San Diego County. They also help differentiate characteristics of the five main groups of Indians who live in the region, who researchers say were already well-established and clearly defined when the first Spaniards arrived on the North American continent. Carrico elaborates on these concepts: "The Late Milling pattern of the Ipai, Tipai, Luiseño, Cahuilla, and Cupeño reflects cultural diversity, variable linguistic and dialectic groups, unique religious systems, and true ethnic consciousness" (Carrico 1987:10).

Ongoing Discoveries Increase Our Understanding

Recent archaeological discoveries also provide additional information about the Ipai ancestors of San Diego County. The San Pasqual Aquatic Treatment Facility on Highland Valley Road was excavated by archaeologists in 1994 and provided evidence that the area may have been the site of occupation by the native people as far back as 3,500 years ago, extending into current-day habitations (Carrico 2010).

Though vandals have partially destroyed an ancient example of Ipai rock art that exists above the treatment facility, observers can still see vertical and intersecting lines on the rock, a cross-type motif, a grid, and an elongated trapezoidal form. Hedges (1970) believes that the pictograph may have been created by a shaman, or that the message may have been made as part as a native ritual.

Turtle shell rattle fragments and a possible pipe mouthpiece were found within the site, lending credence to Hedges's theory. Other artifacts may indicate that the people living there were part of a vast trading network, which extended from the San Pasqual area to as far away as 110 miles to the east, near the Salton Sea, to a location called Obsidian Butte, and northeast as far as 215 miles, to a place called Coso Hot Springs. Also discovered at the site was a type of stone called Piedra de Lumbre chert, that is known to be found only near what is now Camp Pendleton (Carrico 2010).

Carrico offered evidence from the San Pasqual Aquatic Treatment Facility site that this vast trading network extended to the coastal regions as well, noting that an analysis of burned and cut bone from the site revealed that the prehistoric marine diet of the people included sheep head, Pacific barracuda, kelp bass, bat ray, cottontails, jackrabbits, pond turtles, and mule deer. The discovery of bean clams, spiny cockle, wavy turbans, and mussels also substantiated researchers' theories that the people of San Pasqual travelled to the rocky coastline and bays to collect shellfish.

Two types of stone materials used in the production of Ipai tools were found at the Aquatic Treatment Facility (Carrico 2010), with excavations producing two gun-flints associated with the early 1800s which may be remains of the campsite of General Andres Pico after the Battle of San Pasqual, but before his assault on General Stephen W. Kearny's forces at Mule Hill. Another group of items included Cottonwood Triangular points rather than the Desert Side-Notched Points that are more indicative of the southern Tipai (Pigniolo 2000). "This is further evidence for the cultural association of the San Pasqual Valley people with the more northern Ipai than with the Tipai or eastern Kumeyaay" (Carrico 2010).

Since the native people of San Diego County traversed the same paths over and over, the narrow brush trails soon became well-worn paths, and eventually developed into long-established routes of travel. Early Spanish explorers and later American road builders essentially followed the ancient paths of the native Ipai, leading to the establishment of El Camino Real, Highway 101, Highway 395, Old Campo Road and San Pasqual Valley Road. Granite outcroppings along some of these trails provided the canvas for some of the native peoples' artistic endeavors.

Rock Art: An Enduring Legacy from Our Ancient Ancestors

It is believed that petroglyphs were created by ancient native people of San Diego County when they tapped directly on large rocks with a chisel made of stone and used a "hammerstone" to carve the design on the rock surface. This artwork does not appear to

An important pictograph site seen under natural light (L) and using DStretch technology (R) to reveal remains of previously visible pigments. *Photos: Greg Erickson.*

be the same as hieroglyphics, which were symbols used to represent specific words, but instead may have been powerful cultural representations of symbols that reflected the complex cultural and religious beliefs of the tribe that created them. Context does seem to matter in the positioning of petroglyphs and pictographs, in terms of where the individual artwork is placed in relation to the landscape, horizon, and surrounding artwork of importance (Patterson 1992).

Pictographs were formed using natural materials found abundantly in the San Diego County region including minerals, pigments, and oils. The native people knew how to create the alchemy needed to sustain these long-lasting paintings. They used clay soils to produce gray and white colors, and manganese oxide or charcoal to produce black. Reds and oranges could be made using ochre, hematite, or ferric oxide from springs that contained iron. They extracted green from plants, as well as from oils of the abundant cactus plants nearby, or the seed of the native wild cucumber. The fixative that ensured that the colors remained throughout the centuries came from a variety of sources, with stink bug juice being one of the important ones (Carrico 2010).

Carrico has noted that many important rock art sites have been located in the heart of Ipai territory.

> These pictographs were important in Ipai life in the San Pasqual Valley. A major pictograph site is located several miles up Rockwood Canyon above the floor of San Pasqual Valley. The pictographs at this site are unusual; they have red and black designs with zigzags, diamond chains, and nets. More remarkably, there are two right hands painted on the right side of the rock somewhat beyond the major art work.

16

Several other rock painting sites in the San Pasqual Valley have faded red and black geometric designs painted on them (2010:TS)

Archaeology provides many clues regarding the ancient history of our land, but many questions remain about the ancestral peoples, their cultures and their history. Referring to archaeological excavations in Nevada in which he had participated, Mark Harrington noted in 1961 his feelings about the discoveries which his work had produced.

> The information here is but a group of clues — scarcely more than isolated words and phrases in the dramatic story of Man's Ice Age occupation of Western North America. The authors hope that the readers will find in these pages useful informative clues which will be helpful to others joining in the effort to wrest history from silent campfires of the past (Harrington 1961:138).

Future archaeological research will surely provide more clues about how humans lived and interacted with the diverse environments and cultures of our region, but we must also look beyond ancient remains to other lines of evidence such as historical documents, ethnographic descriptions and oral tradition to provide us with a more complete perspective of our Ipai cultural legacy.

3

The People and the Land

The archaeological discussion provided in the previous chapter is one way of explaining and understanding the culture and people known as Ipai. Archaeology is, however, only one tool and one approach to gaining knowledge of the past. Beginning with the voyage of Cabrillo in 1542, non-native observers began to describe in written documents the peoples and the cultures they encountered, providing valuable, though biased, perspectives of native lifeways (see chapter four). Ethnography, the study of both material and non-material culture, is another valuable method of gaining insights. Ethnography can be conducted from the inside by knowledgeable tribal members (emic view) or by outsiders who work closely with tribal elders and interested tribal people (etic view).

In the Kumeyaay region, much valuable information was preserved, thanks to the wisdom of native women and men and their collaboration with people who helped them to document their knowledge for future generations. Many of the descriptions of traditional lifeways presented in this chapter are available today thanks to these important efforts on the part of Ipai cultural authorities and the skilled ethnographers, activists, and other allies who understood the significance of keeping the knowledge alive, even as the world was changing dramatically before their very eyes.

With each elder that passes, many lifetimes of information may be lost. However, Kumeyaay culture has not disappeared even though many "experts" had predicted it would. Besides documented ethnographic information, knowledge also exists that has been passed on informally from generation to generation. Language, songs, stories, skills, philosophies, memories, and other traditional knowledge may be transmitted, and in some cases adapted, to fit the circumstances in which descendant communities find themselves.

However, it is important to remember that even the best ethnography cannot present all aspects of a culture:

> Readers are often led to believe the report of a scene is complete—that little of importance was missed. In reality, an ethnographer will always miss some aspect

Opposite page: Ipai and Tipai territory included coastal regions such as the areas known today as Torrey Pines and La Jolla.

Edward H. Davis (right) interviews Jose Antonio Morales (center) of San Pasqual with the help of an Indian interpreter (possibly Will Guassac). Morales, 98 years old, was born in Pauma Valley. *Photo: San Diego History Center.*

because they are not omniscient. Everything is open to multiple interpretations and misunderstandings ... What is depicted in ethnography is not the whole picture (Fine 1993:22).

Furthermore, some parts of culture that are considered secret or not appropriate to share with outsiders may also continue to circulate among tribal members. Nonetheless, even a partial view can help us reimagine and reconstruct the vital cultures and peoples that lived on this part of the continent for thousands of years.

Territory and Regional Connections

In the past few decades there has been a tendency to associate tribal units and people with where they are currently located. In part this is because many tribal units have adopted, or had forced on them, the name of a reservation or ranchería such as San Pasqual or Mesa Grande. The fallacy in this approach to land tenure is that it assumes that there has been minimal relocation and displacement of Indian people, either prehistorically or in the historic period.

It also mistakenly assumes that the People had the same concept of private property as that held in modern United States society, and that native people only belonged to one village or place within their traditional territory. In the following discussion we will examine traditional Kumeyaay concepts of land tenure and how the People have adapted to the changes imposed by Spanish, Mexican, and American legal systems.

Defining the cultural and ethnic boundaries of a given tribe or band spans two major concerns: where the tribe or band is now located and where they may have been at various points in the past (their traditional lands). In the case of the native people of southern California, this distinction between past and present has two elements to it — the pre-Hispanic period (prehistoric to AD 1769) and the post-Hispanic/American period (1769 to the present).

With a history and prehistory that extends back thousands of years, the traditional territory of the Ipai-Tipai has shifted, expanded, and contracted over the centuries. Bands moved throughout the year in annual cycles that took them from the coastal or inland areas up through interior valleys and plains to the mountains and deserts, based on generations of interacting with the plant and animal resources that became available during different seasons. It is important to note that the Ipai and Tipai had a very definite sense of localization. Specific clans and families were associated with settlements and territories; even after marriage and movement out of the home area, people were known from their

The Cuyamaca Mountains, part of the Peninsular Range stretching from southern California to the tip of Baja California.

Sunrise from the Anza-Borrego Desert State Park region.

geographical origins. With some of their clan bases in the deserts to the east, the People of San Pasqual and the mountains of San Diego County formed part of a larger group—the Yuman family of cultures and languages—that extends deep into what is now Arizona and northern Baja California.

Surrounded by an abundance of good things, the People have been able to survive and thrive, and to experience deeply rich and meaningful interpersonal relationships, spiritual belief systems, and continuing rituals and customs. These traditions were passed on to our children and grandchildren through personal experiences and oral reminders, along with recording our heritage in pictographs and petroglyphs. Thus it is evident that the Ipai and other native people of San Diego County did truly create our region's first real "living history," having far greater time-depth of history in the region than any of the non-Indian groups that arrived later, even if much of that history is not yet in written form.

According to Katharine Luomala, Tipai-Ipai territory extended "east of the mountain people to Salton Sea and into Imperial Valley of Imperial County and southwest into Mexico" (1963:282). In a later publication Luomala wrote that the Tipai territory extended from "the southern end of the Salton Sea, and irregularly fronted other Yuman speakers. ... The eastern-most Tipais lived along sloughs like New River and in the adjoining desert, not along the Colorado ..." (1978:593-594).

A demarcation is made between the lands of the Tipai and the nearby Cocopahs. Alfred Kroeber wrote that: "They [the Cocopah] have survived in some numbers, but have, and always had, their principal seats in Baja California." The Ipai have several well-documented names for locales and places in the desert region south of the Salton Sea, including *Hakeruwiyp* at Mountain Springs meaning "water lined up," *Matkusiyaay* at Table Mountain meaning "shaman's mountain," *Wii'ipaah* for Signal Mountain meaning "eagle's mountain," and *Wilkch* for Yaqui Well (Kroeber 1925).

Origins of the San Pasqual Ipai

The early travel stories and origin myths of the Ipai/Tipai reflect strong connections with the land from the Pacific Ocean to the Colorado River desert. Traditionally, many Tipai, including the desert group the "Kamia," believed that they originated somewhere to the northeast, usually at a mountain called *Wikami* or *Wikamee*. This mountain is known by the Yuma and Mohave as *Avikame* (Spirit Mountain); it is the highest peak of the Newbury Mountains near Loughlin, Arizona (Gifford 1931:12; Hinton and Watahomigie 1984). Edward Winslow Gifford's informants told him that in an ancient time, "The Kamia ancestors camped on the eastern side of the Salton Sea [Lake Cahuilla], from which they later scattered, some settling in Imperial Valley, others going to the mountains of San Diego County and becoming Diegueño. Other sacred peaks include Signal Mountain and Coyote Mountain" (Gifford 1931:12).

In her recordings of songs and myths of the Ipai/Tipai, Constance DuBois wrote that her informant from Manzanita, Sant (Santo Lopez), who lived as a child with "the desert Indians," considered the eastern desert Mojaves as the last born of related tribes who stayed in the "ancestral home" (1906:145). This would indicate a root or homeland in the desert for the people of Manzanita. In other words, at some time thousands of years ago, the Kamia/Tipai had a common desert root and then divided into sub-tribes or bands with some (the San Pasqual band included) going into the mountains of San Diego. Jay Von Werlhof (2004) suggested that the tribes split into smaller groups once the population surpassed the land's ability to support a given settlement. This fragmentation of larger culture units into smaller groups who then migrate out of the homeland is a standard interpretation of the development and expansion of prehistoric cultures across the landscape.

According to Richard Carrico (2010), the majority of tribes and bands in southern California have had their land tenure seriously disrupted. Tribes in Orange, Los Angeles, and Imperial counties perhaps have been the most affected, with the majority of these tribes currently being non-federally recognized and most having lost their land base. In present-day San Diego and Riverside counties, tribes and bands, most of which are federally recognized, have a legal land base as the result of federal reservation policies beginning in the mid-1870s, or as a result of later state and federal legislation setting lands (reservations and rancherias) aside for use by native people.

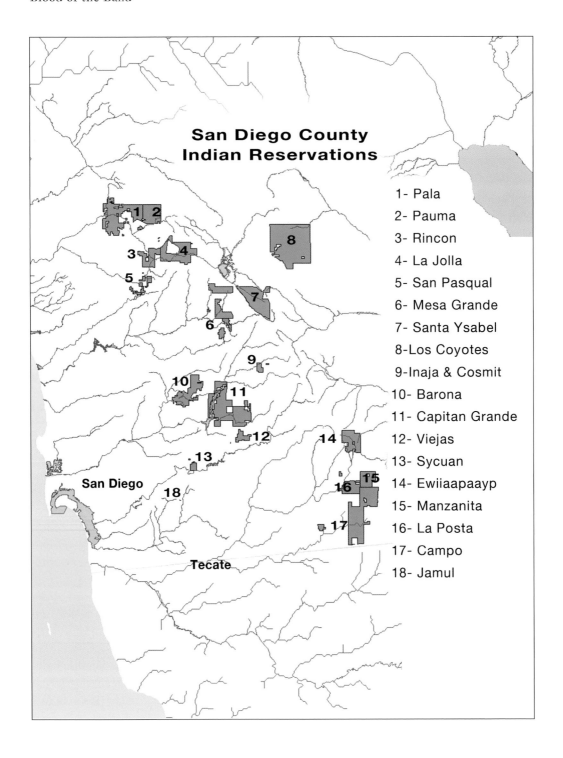

**San Diego County
Indian Reservations**

1- Pala
2- Pauma
3- Rincon
4- La Jolla
5- San Pasqual
6- Mesa Grande
7- Santa Ysabel
8- Los Coyotes
9- Inaja & Cosmit
10- Barona
11- Capitan Grande
12- Viejas
13- Sycuan
14- Ewiiaapaayp
15- Manzanita
16- La Posta
17- Campo
18- Jamul

San Diego

Tecate

Several reservations in San Diego County encompass lands and village sites that were traditionally occupied by the ethnic group currently living on those reservations. Others have resulted from bureaucratic decisions, the pressures of non-Indian settlers, the appropriation of valuable agricultural lands — with resettlement on less desirable lands — and even errors by officials with no understanding of native territories. Kroeber (1925:711) noted that for the prehistoric/pre-Hispanic settlements, "Most of these [places and place names] are little reservations now, but it seems as if many of the reservations constituted by the government in this region, as among the Luiseño and Cahuilla, had an ancient village community as their nucleus." Examples include Sycuan, Manzanita, Campo, and Santa Ysabel. Reservations that were established on non-traditional or ambiguously non-traditional lands include San Pasqual, Viejas, and Barona.

Tribal and Linguistic Nomenclatures

The Ipai and Tipai belong to the Yuman family of cultures and languages, which in turn is part of a larger American language group known as the Hokan phylum or stock (Hinton and Watahomigie 1984). Although some linguists have recently questioned the validity of the Hokan language group, there is still evidence for some kind of ancient historical linguistic relationship between most of the languages in the group, which are located all the way from Oregon in the United States south into Central America, along the west side of the continent. The Yuman languages make up one family of the Hokan group, and include the River languages (Mojave, Maricopa, and Quechan), the Pai languages (Paipai, Yavapai, Hualapai, and Havasupai), the Kiliwa branch (possibly related to extinct Cochimí languages of the Baja California peninsula) and the Delta-California Yuman languages — Cocopah, Ipai, and Tipai (Hinton and Watahomogie 1984:5).

Ipai was spoken from the Pacific Ocean throughout northern and central San Diego County. Those who lived at San Pasqual, Mesa Grande, Santa Ysabel, Barona, Inaja, and Cosmit were Ipai speakers. Those living at Jamul, Campo, Manzanita, and Cuyapaipe, and into the Imperial Valley, were Tipai speakers. Tipai, or possibly a southern variant of Tipai, is still spoken in several Kumeyaay villages in northern Baja California (Luomala 1978), including Juntas de Neji, San José de la Zorra, San Antonio Necua, and La Huerta. Ko'alh, A closely related Yuman language, is also spoken by some of the Paipai in Santa Catarina, Baja California, Mexico (Wilken 2012).

To the north and northeast of the Ipai region, the Luiseño, Cupeño, and Cahuilla spoke languages belonging to the Takic (sometimes referred to as Shoshonean) branch of the Uto-Aztecan language group. Although these languages are completely different from the Hokan-Yuman languages, there are many similarities between our cultures.

The term Diegueño, as adopted by anthropologists and historians, was originally derived from the Spanish, beginning in the 1770s, and was commonly utilized through the mid-twentieth century. The term was applied to those Indians under the jurisdiction of Mission San Diego and also connoted a generalized tribe differentiated from the

Wooly blue curls, a medicinal plant, grow in front of Kuchumaa, a sacred mountain of the Kumeyaay.

Takic-speaking people to the north (Luiseños), the Cocopah (Cucapá) to the east and the Paipai to the south. In this sense, the term Diegueño is an exonym, a name applied to a tribe by others, whereas the term Kumeyaay or Ipai/Tipai is an autonym, what the People choose to call ourselves. Similarly, some writers used the more generic name "Mission Indians" to refer to California native people, because of their proximity to and affiliation with the twenty-one missions that dotted the coastal landscape from southern to northern California.

Similar exonymic glosses for Diegueño or Dieguiño were used in the American period including "Diegeenos" in 1849 by A. Whipple (1961:31), Diegeno in 1850 by John Bartlett (1854:7), Diegueños by Benjamin Hayes in 1870 (Hayes 1934:140), and by the anthropologist John Harrington (1908:324) in 1908 when he noted that the Central Yuman Group included "Diegueño (Kamyá)," with the term Kamyá referring to the eastern Diegueños.

Those of us in groups previously known as the northern and southern Diegueño have more recently begun to call ourselves by our more traditional names—Kumeyaay, Ipai, and Tipai. While there is no universal agreement regarding nomenclature among the various Yuman-speaking bands and tribes, for this study the native groups north of the San Diego River basin are identified as Ipai, those to the south as Tipai.

In the 1970s some groups of what were previously called southern Diegueños adopted the term Kumeyaay for themselves (Hedges 1975). This group, based in the Campo and La Posta area of eastern San Diego County, was encouraged by anthropologist Florence Shipek in extending the term Kumeyaay well beyond the immediate area of the eastern mountain valleys. By the 1980s and well into the late 1990s, for many historians, anthropologists, and native peoples, the term Kumeyaay had come to encompass all of the people previously known as Diegueño, although the term has never been entirely accepted. Kumeyaay is still in wide use in the Campo region and into Baja California (there spelled *Kumiai*). While some people and groups still self-identify as Kumeyaay, the terms Ipai and Tipai reflect a more traditional, localized form of self identification and are used in this study of the San Pasqual Band and the roots of people now living on that reservation, while the term Kumeyaay is used here to refer to the whole of the Ipai-Tipai region.

Luomala noted that based on Gifford's studies and on her research in the late 1960s and into the 1970s, the term Tipai was used to denote "people" in southern San Diego County and northern Baja California. By contrast she provides the word Ipai for the people of northern San Diego County (Luomala 1978). In part, following Luomala, there has been a break from the practice of generalizing Kumeyaay to all Yuman-speaking people and cultures in San Diego County, with Ipai or Ipay becoming more common for northern Diegueño and Tipai or Tipay for the southern Diegueño.

Leslie Spier (1923:198) based on his 1920 fieldwork, may have been the first researcher to apply the term Tipaí to the southern Diegueño, and suggested that the northern Diegueño were Kumiai (Kumeyaay). Alfred Kroeber (1925:710) wrote that the speakers of the southern language variant in American California included Manzanita, Campo, La Posta, Guyapipe [Cuiapaipe], and La Laguna. William D. Hohenthal's *Tipai Ethnographic Notes*, based on 1948-1949 fieldwork conducted in Baja California, mentions that "the Indians refer to themselves as Ipai or Tipai people" (2001:37). That there are significant linguistic variations between the northern and southern people is well documented in the literature and acknowledged by contemporary speakers. For example, an important bird dance recorded by Constance DuBois was called Ee-sha at Manzanita (southern) and Ah-sha at Mesa Grande (northern) (1906:1).

In her introduction to *Let's Talk 'Iipay: An Introduction to the Mesa Grande Language*, the seminal book on Ipai language, Margaret Langdon noted that there are many variations of the 'Iipay language (her orthography) and stressed that the spellings and pronunciations were specific to Ted Couro and Mesa Grande people (Couro and Langdon 1975). Some linguists, such as Langdon, have suggested that Kumeyaay may actually be made up of three different language varieties.

In the early twentieth century, during his travels through the San Pasqual Valley, researcher J.P. Harrington referenced the close connections of the people there with other native people in the county, when he explicitly differentiated the existence of varying groups of Ipai living at varying locations, including the San Pasqual people, whom he called Kuwakapaj, and those who lived near the seashore, called the Kamijaj—near one another but with their own identities and names. Several of his handwritten field notes (Harrington 1913-1933:4_37. 6_15. 7_7. 9_5. 28_27), concern references to those differentiated sites and their identities, including remarks that the Mataguay, San Felipe, Vallecitos, Mesa Grande, and San Pasqual people are all Kuwakupaj, and that the San Felipe Indians formerly lived at Yaqui Well.

Angel Quilp working with plant fibers.
Photo: E. H. Davis, San Diego History Center.

Harrington said: "The Kamijaj are the people who lived at San Dieguito and the San Luiseños of the coast. ... The Mesa Grande people are not Kamijajs." Informant Ysidro Nejo also spoke of one of the designations, saying: "Kamijaj — the gente that lives where the sun sets." Harrington added further: "The people beyond Jacumba are Kwakapa. These people are very brave [fierce]. Angel [Kwilp or Quilp] knows no name for the Campo people except Abajenos. Cannot get him to translate it into Diegueño" (Harrington 1914:177-188).

To the south of the Tipai are the Paipai (a related Yuman-speaking people), and to the southeast, the Cocopah or Cucapá in Baja California (also a related Yuman-speaking group). Further to the east of both the Ipai and Tipai, with an area of concentration along the Colorado River, are the Quechan. The Kamia, a group of Yuman-speaking people identified by Gifford (1931) and others as living between the eastern Diegueño (Tipai) of the Laguna Mountains and the Colorado River, are now thought to have essentially been desert dwelling, agricultural Tipai who adapted to the desert environment and blended Quechan traits into their culture.

Gifford was aware of the strong cultural connection between the eastern Diegueño (Tipai) and the group known as Kamia. After his research with the "Kamia" in 1928-1929, he wrote, "The Kamia also call themselves Tipai, which means 'person'" (Gifford 1931:17). Linguistically, Luomala and others have noted that the language "shades into Tipai at communities like Jamul, Campo, Manzanita, and Cuyapaipe, and also in Imperial Valley" (1978:593).

Although Gifford treated the Kamia as a separate group, he noted: "The eastern Diegueño [Tipai] as regularly visited the [desert] Kamia as the Kamia visited them. The two groups spoke the same language and were 'one tribe,' having been created together in the north, informants said" (Gifford 1931:17). Gifford also wrote that, "It is assumed that they [the Kamia] are a people of Diegueño origin, who moved down into Imperial Valley and came under the influence of the Yuma, from whom they adopted agriculture" (1931:1). For this study, it is assumed that the so-called Kamia are essentially desert-dwelling eastern Tipai.

The Rumorosa, a Tipai landscape in Baja California, looking out onto the desert and Cucapá territory.

Social Organization

• Bands

The People lived and moved in bands made up of various extended families, usually composed of members of specific clans, together with those who had married in from other clans. The Spanish called this type of mobile social unit a *rancheria*, and in English it is referred to as a band or sometimes as a village. The bands were made up of approximately a hundred individuals, possibly varying between fifty and one hundred fifty (Laylander 1997). They were associated with specific band territory, some of it exclusive and some of it—such as pinyon gathering areas in the mountains—shared with other bands. Leadership of the bands was provided by the *kwaaypaay*, a headman or captain whose authority rested on his depth of knowledge and managerial capacities (Shipek 1982).

Bands were flexible, ongoing, and openly recognized; kinship was clearly identified; and relationships with neighboring bands were seriously considered for long-term effects and consequences. Luomala reported that there were thirty bands of Ipai and Tipai, with some of these groups friendly and others hostile toward one another. Each band was patrilineal—usually ruled by a male figure, autonomous—not subject to the control of

Coastal regions from the areas now known as Del Mar up to Carlsbad, California, form part of Ipai territory.

any other band of native people, and seminomadic — moving from place to place season by season. Bands that were friendly with one another often shared overlapping areas. However, hostile encounters were also a part of life, especially when traversing into enemy areas which were off limits to outsiders.

As bands moved seasonally through their territories, families built homes from willow branches, tules, rocks, and stones, depending on the materials that were available locally. In each locale, band members hunted a variety of animals, as well as harvesting and processing seeds, nuts, and acorns, all of which they prepared not only for their current use, but also for storage for the future. Some groups lived in the desert lands on the eastern side of the mountains during the winter, while others lived in the inland foothills to the west of the mountains, with movement toward higher altitudes in the spring and summer. Visits to the coast were regular occurrences, as the People enjoyed a varied and healthful diet of seafood. Marine resources such as shellfish, seaweed, fish, sea mammals, and seabirds provided a rich complement to their terrestrial diet.

• Kinship: Shumulq or Clans

Kinship among the Kumeyaay was based on *shumulq* or clans that traced their descent through the father's line (patrilineal) and that required members to marry outside their own clan (exogamy). This pattern of kinship and marriage reduced the potential for incest, assured alliances with other clans and bands, and led to identification with the territory and lands held by the clan members. It is said that each person told who he or she was by stating the clan they were from, where that clan lived, and who the male leaders of the families in that clan were.

The People knew that heritage and lineage would always be measured according to the father's line, and that boys and girls at certain ages would be initiated through specific ceremonies. When someone died, traditional rites of passage would be performed. Girls ready for marriage knew that they must find a partner from outside their own clan, so that would usually mean going to live with their husbands' families. Such relationships were forged by parents intentionally and consciously, with the results meant to strengthen each tribe, band and clan.

When talking about clans other than one's own, people would tell where the other group was located, such as "eastern" people, "western" people, or those who lived south of the Mexican border, called "Southern Water" people. A phrase such as, "He belongs to a different water," would let others know how the important component of water influenced a person's identity, an important consideration for native people as they moved from place to place in this arid land (Luomala 1978).

Leslie Spier, a highly observant anthropologist, noted in 1923 that a variety of clans were part of the southern Diegueño/Ipai populations during times before the arrival of invaders to San Diego County.

According to Kroeber, Diegueño clan names were chosen according to each clan's distinguishing feature, as were those from other southern California clans. Certain clans were associated with certain areas, including Kwitak at Campo; Hitlmawah at Manzanita; Kwamal at La Posta (meaning "wishing to be tall"), and Kwatl at Jacumba Valley. These clans included: *Kwaha* (unknown meaning); *Waipuk* ("kingsnake"); *Huhlwa* ("twined basket"); *Oswal* (unknown meaning); *Hlich* ("worthless"); *Kalyarp* ("butterfly"); *Hotum* ("drum"—learned from Spanish), and *Kwainyitl* ("black"). These clans had such names as Paipa, Nihkai, Tuman, Lyacharp, Neeihhawach, Hitlmiarp, Kwatl, Kwitark, Kwamai, Miskwis, Kwinehich, Hitlmawa, and Salkur.

Richard Carrico reminds us that kinships and clans were elaborate, functional, and flexible:

> The native people who lived in San Pasqual Valley from prehistoric times through the Mexican period, and even later, reflected a mixture of clans, families, and places of geographic origin. ... [T]hese were a people who traveled a great deal for food procurement, for trade, to continue family and clan alliances, and to attend fiestas and mourning ceremonies. Given this, it is not surprising that families and sibs would have intermarried and formed a village or ranchería made up of people from several geographic areas (Carrico 2010:TS).

The Ipai did not marry into their own clans. Rather, young girls would go through the puberty ceremonies and rites, preparing to have a relationship with someone from a differing clan. Each girl would then leave the village and move with her new husband to the region of the husband's clan. Subsequent gatherings and get-togethers among clans would provide opportunities for reuniting and creating memories among the groups. Since each clan was comprised of close-knit families, the regrouping of clans connected by intermarriage would most likely be close-knit too. Such groupings of people meant that relationships among families were well known by all those involved in the groups. With celebrations and get-togethers occasioning movement of people, and with seasonal migrations a normal occurrence, those who lived within the area of discussion would, naturally, come into close contact with each other from time to time.

Carrico has noted that the Ipai of San Pasqual Valley may have married predominantly with those from the west at San Dieguito (*Jelleagua*), which was close to Rancho Santa Fe and Rancho Bernardo (*Apta'*). Going east they most likely made marriages and alliances with those living in the villages of *Pa'mu* and *Tekemuk* (Mesa Grande).

During Mission times, beginning in 1769, neophytes (those who had been trained at the mission) were allowed to return to their villages from time to time when food shortages occurred at the mission, so they could provide for themselves through hunting and food gathering. In spite of the challenges faced by the Ipai during this dramatic period of change, the Ipai are believed to have maintained their traditional marriage routines as much as possible. Since it was apparently not unusual for Ipai from villages near one another—Santa Ysabel (*Jellpeacequa*), Rancho Bernardo (possibly *Apta'* or *Pelluqui*), or San Pasqual (*Jelleaqua*) to intermarry, it was also then common to find that some of these native people had lived at the San Diego Mission, and after the missions secularized, those same people may have relocated to the San Pasqual Valley.

Carrico concludes that:

> It is likely that the eastern and western villages were occupied by clans and families with strong ties to San Pasqual. Other villages represented by the occupants in the pre-1850 settlement at San Pasqual include *Pa'mu*, San Felipe, *Camojar* (near Santa Ysabel), *Viccumiay* (near Santa Ysabel), *Matamo*, near present-day Sycuan, and of course the neophyte settlement at Mission San Diego after secularization in 1835 but known originally as *Nipawai* (Carrico 2010).

In some cases, the marriage could be between an Ipai and a Luiseño to the north, as in the case of *Cucheu* (Luis Beltran) a Luiseño from the village of *Gequepa* near San Luis Rey. He married *Jomoguilc* (Antonia) from *Pelluhui* (associated with Rancho Bernardo) and settled at San Pasqual by at least 1838, when their child María de la Natividad was baptized and they were all listed as living at the Pueblo de San Pasqual (Carrico 2010:TS).

Carrico added:

> Overall, the clan, or family names that appear in the mission records (Kroeber 1925 and Carrico 2010) from 1821 to 1842 for females are (as they are written or transcribed)

Najuchal, Jomohuilc, Curriulp, Curarenal, Coaspulp and *Tajuil.* For males they are *Yiutanar, Cucheu* (Luiseño), *Cuerp, Jalan, Jalloi, Chujar,* and *Jatallap.* There were once at least twelve Ipai kin groups in northern San Diego County (Carrico 2010).

These sibs or clans (Carrico 2010:TS), and their meaning if known, included *Kukuro* ("dark or shady"); *Letcapa* ("short"); *Matuwir* or *Metehuir* ("strong or hard"); *Critcak* or *Shrichak* (a type of owl); *Kwilp* or *Kwitlp* (name of a shrub); *Xesil* or *Hestil* (type of small Manzanita); *Kwaha* (a type of wormwood); *U'u* (species of owl); Bapipa or Paipa; *Tumau* ("grasshopper"); Esun, and Hipuwach (unknown translation).

Several of these clan names have survived as family names. For example, Couro comes from Kukuro; La Chappa from Letcapa; Duro from Matuwir/Metehuir (meaning strong in both Ipai and Spanish); Paipa from Bapipa; Quilp from Kwilp, and Osuna from Esun or Osun.

The Mesa Grande Reservation was also home to several important clans and large families directly related to the San Pasqual people. The ancient village of Tekemuk at Mesa Grande was the summer and fall home to the people of Pa'mu and was well known to the San Pasqual people, some of whom had parents and grandparents living at this village.

Spier (1923) believed that it may have been a regular occurrence for mixed groups to spend the winter months together, as they lived in the eastern foothills, at the edge of the desert, and to spend the fall and spring months elsewhere, perhaps further to the west. He asserted that clans sometimes fought each other, and that each clan owned the eyries

Chaparral, hills, and inland valleys, a typical landscape in Ipai territory. *Photo: David L Toler Jr.*

(eagle nests on high places) and food products where they lived, but they didn't own the acorns. He records that there was no preferential marriage between certain clans, and that the clans had no animal icons (totems) associated with their groups.

While there was a great deal of flexibility and movement (and intermarriage) between clans or sibs Homer Aschmann (1959:27) noted that there would be a strong sense of identity and belonging associated with a district or an area comprised of more than one settlement or village, and, as did Jay Von Werhlof, suggested that as a settlement, or aggregate of settlements, became too large (more than two hundred occupants) some residents would split off and resettle at a new site.

The Land and Its Resources: From Coast to Mountains to Desert

From west to east the land forms coasts, mountains, and deserts (Luomala 1963). The coastal lands are flat or gently sloping, followed by plateaus of granite, rising ever higher, and separated by the Peninsular Range, with mountains as high as Cuyamaca and Laguna, more than 6,500 feet. Both the foothills and mountains have narrow canyons, rocky hills, and lands that are flat. The eastern slopes of the mountains have either rocky cliffs or slopes strewn with boulders, tilting down to the Colorado Desert, which is below sea level.

The San Pasqual Valley, home to many Ipai villages and part of the larger Ipai territory.
Photo: San Diego History Center.

Gathering acorns in oak woodlands. *Drawing: Robert Freeman.*

The arid Mediterranean climate, with winter rains rolling in from the Pacific Ocean and generally dry summers, meant that a wide variety of wild plants and raw materials were available to native people. With stair-like transitional regions, consisting of flat areas, hills, and canyons, each region to which the native people migrated had predictable habitats and environments. Along the coast, the intertidal zone; dune habitat; coastal sage scrub, and wetland ecosystems of estuaries provided an abundance of plant and animal resources. Further inland, the Ipai interacted with chaparral, chamise, wild lilac, manzanita, and other shrubs. Creeks and river valleys supported extensive woodlands of live oak, willow, sycamore, cottonwood, and elderberry, and broad plains were filled with grasslands, many of them now extinct. Mountain regions contained a variety of pines and black oaks, while desert areas provided important plant resources such as agaves, palms and mesquite.

Whereas the Ipai of the San Pasqual Valley were accustomed to spending much of their time in their traditional band territory of the San Pasqual Valley, they also traveled to the mountains for acorns in the fall of each year, and to the desert regions to gather plant and animal resources, including those used as food, medicine, clothing materials, and construction items.

Historical researchers (Luomala 1963) corroborate the fact that the native people of San Diego County interacted extensively, both intermarrying within the clans found at various sites, and gathering together regularly for socializing, ceremonials, rituals, harvests and trading. Spier also noted this seasonal movement:

> The Kumeyaay did not maintain permanent year-round villages. Instead, they moved between at least two semi-permanent villages, a summer village located in the mountains, and a winter village located on the coast or along the desert floor. The

occupancy of the gentile territories was seasonal. Winter found them living in groups of mixed gentile affiliation among the foothills on the edge of the Colorado Desert. In the spring they returned to the mountains, keeping pace with the ripening of the wild food staples, and passing the summer in their respective valleys. The whole territory was not occupied at one time: when a locality was hunted out or fruits ripened elsewhere, they moved on. In the course of a year or so, however, all of the recognized settlements had been occupied (Spier, 1923:306).

Allen E. Lawson, Jr., the eldest grandson of Helen Trask Lawson and great-grandson of Frank Trask and Leonora La Chappa Trask, has served as tribal chairman of the San Pasqual Band of Diegueño Mission Indians of California for many years. He shared in an interview his thoughts about how his Ipai ancestors in San Diego County lived during the times before the arrival of the Spanish, Mexican, and Americans:

> It is my understanding that there were over 100 village sites in the San Pasqual area, all the way out to Escondido and down through the valley. There wasn't just one village. Sometimes, the people talk of *the* village and I say, "There were multiple villages within this area and multiple families. There's no record of San Pasqual Indians living in a particular village. They lived in certain areas of the San Pasqual Valley. Some lived up in the canyon. Some lived on the side of the valley. Some lived over in the center of the valley." The problem is that there was no written history, so the Spanish came in and applied a written history that had a lot of misconceptions. Applying a written language to an oral culture can be a problem, especially when there are sounds that are parts of the words. When you don't use the proper sound, you get an improper meaning. I found in the last few years that there were quite a few families that had lived in San Pasqual, Santa Ysabel, and Mesa Grande. They had always lived here, there, back and forth, all over the place. I think they were like most of our families in San Diego County and in this Southern part of the United States — they moved around (Lawson Jr. 2011).

David L. Toler Jr., grandson of Helen Trask Lawson and great-grandson of Frank and Leonora Trask, noted that he finds it interesting to trace the activities of his Ipai ancestors who moved throughout the watersheds of Mesa Grande, Santa Ysabel, and other areas as they merged into the San Dieguito River that flows through San Pasqual Valley. On the eastern slope of this same mountain range San Felipe Creek drains into the Salton Sink, which has many Kumeyaay and Kamia village sites. The people connected by those waters often interacted and intermarried with those from neighboring watersheds (Toler Jr. 2011).

For the Ipai people, trips to the mountains and deserts alternated with time spent at the inland and coastal regions. The San Bernardo/San Dieguito River ran through the San Pasqual Valley and drained directly into the ocean. Following the waterways (Carrico 2010:TS), as well as adjacent estuaries, the native people could launch their tule canoes and rafts from a place near the mouth of the San Dieguito River and eventually fish along the coast to a point south, near La Jolla. Those canoes and rafts also enabled the native

The Ipai enjoyed shellfish such as mussels, seaweed, and many other marine resources in the coastal regions.

people to fish the deep waters of the Pacific Ocean and to reach the islands offshore. Sardines, mussels, starfish, shellfish, sea mammals, and seabirds (Palou 1769:101) were all available to the Ipai during their coastal ventures.

Salt was also a basic necessity that the Ipai gathered at the Pacific Ocean. They placed branches in the ocean at low tide—the branch would retain the salt which accumulated there from the water washing over it during high tide—then at the next low tide the branch could be removed, and the salt would be dried and stored for future use.

In the desert regions, native people dug Olivella or other univalve shells out of the ground in the eastern desert and made them into necklaces, called *ahchitl* (Spier 1923). These may have been living shells in the banks of New River, or may have been ancient remains from former lake beds or overflowed districts in the region below sea level.

Ipai women and their children were responsible for gathering the acorns and other plants, seeds, grasses, and resources found at the mountains and deserts. The women became proficient at leaching the bitter tannen from the acorns, accomplished by cracking the hard shell, grinding the inner pulp on a metate using a hand-held grinding stone, then pouring hot water over the acorn mush to remove the tannen. The women and children

Estevan Wypooke sits behind a pile of acorns which she shells by beating them with a paddle. *Photo: E. H. Davis, San Diego Historical Society.*

Tipai Norma Meza sifting acorn meal, one step in the process of preparing acorn mush.

also gathered plant materials for creating the baskets in which these processed acorns and other food products would be stored. These plant materials were also used to make clothing. The survival of their families depended on the women and children perfecting these abilities and skills that were handed down generation to generation.

Men, on the other hand, grew increasingly adept at killing and processing the wild animals found in these habitats. They developed creative and ingenious ways of capturing these rich sources of meat for their families, including the use of bows and arrows,

A view to Cuyamaca Lake near Yguai.

handcrafted nets with which to envelop the captured prey, and traps which were buried within pits dug into the ground and camouflaged, so that roaming animals would not realize they were the objects of prey until it was too late. A wide assortment of bugs, insects, and other small animals were also available for consumption, including crickets, grasshoppers, grubs, snails, snakes, and certain birds, though some animals, such as eagles, were usually not considered as food because of their sacred nature to the native people.

Yguai: A Treasured Gathering Place in the Mountains

An archaeological examination of Cuyamaca Rancho State Park (Cultural Resources Inventory 1981) provided a documented history of the Native American impact at the mountain site, located forty miles east of San Diego. Harrington called the peak of Cuyamaca Waqitjat, and the northern peak of Cuyamaca WiqiLyst (Harrington 1913-1933:4_38). Granted to Agustin Olvera in 1846 as a Mexican Land Grant (Fetzer and Redmond 2009), Cuyamaca Rancho State Park is bounded on the north, east, and west by the Cleveland National Forest, and on the south by the Descanso and Samagatuma valleys. Elevations range from 3,480 feet in Descanso to 6,512 feet atop Cuyamaca Peak.

The Indians came to Yguai, one of the villages in the Cuyamaca Mountains, from San Felipe and Santa Ysabel, representing desert and lower mountain environments. During acorn harvests, the oak groves of Cuyamaca Valley supported a large influx of people from the desert, who settled into the camps and villages around Cuyamaca Valley near Yguai. Pottery and chert [also called "flint"] materials from the desert are found throughout the mountains, supporting the theory that these locations were connected.

Today, the location of Yguai is made up of a midden (ancient heaps of shells and debris from daily life) deposit that is 820 feet by 984 feet and contains mountain-made brown and desert-made buff ware pottery, flaked stone artifacts, and other objects which show that the area was at one time occupied. Adjacent to the midden deposit is a bedrock ridge, covered with mortars, basins, and slicks. The ridge is terraced, with one of the terraces containing remains of rock architecture, and it descends to a spring. Yguai most likely also included several smaller sites that have been recorded nearby. All of these sites are located on the hills and ridges above drainages that empty into the upper end of Cuyamaca Valley.

In 1852 the Treaty of Santa Ysabel gave local native people a large reservation centered in the Cuyamacas; however, the US Senate never ratified the treaty. After Yguai was abandoned in 1869-1870 (Woodward 1934:146), the people went to Inaja.

Tom Lucas, who referred to himself as "Kwaaymii" a distinct tribal group from the Laguna Mountains, offered information on how his people lived in times past (Tom Lucas interview with Carrico, 1975). When an interviewer asked him in 1975 what the name Cuyamaca meant, he responded: "Cloud—cloud cover. Cuyamaca—well, you look at it and a lot of times in the wintertime when you see a cloud cap over it, you know... the cloud cover Cuyamaca—Cuy means cloud... Cmaca means thrown over."

Carmen Lucas, Kwaaymii, of the Laguna Band of Mission Indians has said: "This is where they lived and where they died and where they still live on, as far as memory is concerned" (Lucas 2004:1). Lucas has a map (Cuyamaca Village National Register Form Sections 7, 8, 9, 2013) that illustrates the locations of those living within the Cuyamaca Village and the Cuyamaca Mountains in times past, and they are connected with those from beyond those two locations. Lucas believes that the people of those areas still connect with one another, especially the people from the Salton Basin, San Felipe, Harper Flat, Vallecito, Canebreak, Kitchen Creek, Corte Madera, Descanso [Guatay], Los Conejos, Capitan Grande, Inaja, and Santa Ysabel. She believes that the native people from these villages were related, that they often intermarried, that they held ceremonials and rituals together, and that they traveled on well-known paths to visit one another regularly. Lucas (personal communication 2015) recalled that according to her father Tom Lucas, the word Kwaaymii refers to a beautiful magical bird, mentioned in mythology of the region that was seen only at special times in the Cuyamaca region.

E.H. Davis believed that the Indian name Cuyamaca denoted "water," which may have accounted for Jose Luchapa's choice of assuming that surname and other variations (Cuyamaca Village National Register Form 2013). Luchapa took Davis into his confidence and showed him a stash of hidden, sacred artifacts, stored in a cavern on Stonewall Peak. Davis related that a native person would stand or kneel in front of the area where the ceremonial, household, or family items had been buried, and would talk to the cave or cavern

The Ipai have long used white sage (*Salvia apiana*) for medicine and ceremonial purposes.

as though it was the person who had buried the treasures. The names of the ancestors who buried the artifacts were handed down through the generations and the person kneeling or standing would address his remarks and songs to that ancestor, since the native people believed that the spirit of the person who had buried the ceremonial items was hovering nearby, guarding the treasures.

Cho cal' was the legendary name of the person who took control of the head plumes, feather girdles, Toloache mortars, and drinking cups, among other items. He lived at the Rancheria Pilscha, halfway between Stonewall or Cuyamaca and Green Valley, and later moved to E-Wy' [Yguai].

Environmental Management Practices

Based on a review of the ethnographic literature and interviews with consultants from Campo and Manzanita reservations, Ruth Almstedt surmised that the use of native plants, bushes, shrubs, herbs, berries, and seeds offered a distinct advantage to the Kumeyaay in their quests to heal those who were ill or who were suffering from the repercussions of accidents or encounters with hostile forces. These natural plants provided relief for many maladies (Almstedt 1977).

There is strong evidence that the Kumeyaay planted or transplanted vegetation that was of particular importance or value to them. Examples of this include elderberry plants at village sites in settings that would not normally contain or sustain elderberries. Noteworthy

Common Name	Scientific Name	Primary Uses
Black Sage	*Salvia mellifera*	Food, medicinal
California buckwheat	*Erigonum fasciculatum*	Headaches, eye infections, stomach
California wild rose	*Rosa californica*	Diarrhea
Chia	*Salvia columbariae*	Eye infections, bruises, wounds
Coffee berry	*Rhamnus californica*	Laxative
Creosote bush	*Larrea tridentate*	Pains, stomach problems
Datura	*Datura meteloides*	Snake and tarantula bites
Desert tea	*Ephedra californica*	Coughs and colds
Elderberry	*Sambucus Mexicana*	Eye infections, coughs, colds
Holly-leaved Cherry	*Prunus illicifolia*	Colds
Live Oak	*Quercus agrifolia*	Food, Toothache
Miner's lettuce	*Claytonia perfoliata*	Food
Monkey flower	*Diplacus sp.*	Diarrhea
Sugar bush	*Rhus ovata*	Coughs, chest pains
Wormwood	*Artemisia californica*	Vaginal problems
White Sage	*Salvia apiana*	Muscle pains, stiff neck, colds
Yerba santa	*Eriodictyon crassiflium*	Headache

Important medicinal plants used by the Kumeyaay/Ipai in the San Pasqual Valley Area (based on Almstedt 1977).

examples of this have been found at the site of the village of Jamul in southeastern San Diego, and at a large settlement known today as Piedras Pintadas that existed for thousands of years near Lake Hodges. Not far from the Jamul site at the recorded location of the village of Jamacha, biologists reported mesquite completely out of context growing within the settlement (Beauchamp 1998: personal communication).

Anthropologist Florence Shipek promoted the idea that the Kumeyaay were farmers who tended orchards and fields of corn, squash, and beans, and that the Spanish were simply unable to recognize their agricultural practices. However, Don Laylander's 1995 review of the ethnographic literature dealing with the question of prehistoric agriculture found Shipek's claims to be unfounded:

Elderberry (*Sambucus nigra*) has long been used by the Ipai as a medicine as well as for food and drink. It is often found in association with archaeological sites in southern California.

As thus far published, Shipek's view in this matter has been based on assertion rather than evidence. Earlier ethnographers had consistently arrived at the opposite conclusions, as has been noted above. It seems improbable that any late twentieth century ethnographic testimony concerning mid-eigthteenth century conditions and practices could convincingly overrule the mass of earlier ethnographic and ethnohistoric evidence (Laylander 1995:200).

Kent Lightfoot and Otis Parrish (2007) make a strong case for not trying to force California Indians into an agricultural or proto-agricultural category, but rather recognizing that the highly specialized environmental management techniques developed over the millennia (such as prescribed burns and cultivation methods that create diversified regional landscapes) represent a unique adaptation that allowed Native Californians to support relatively dense populations.

Because the Indians lacked regimented, plowed fields and made use of seasonal native plants, the Europeans may have failed to perceive the depth and breadth of Kumeyaay plant husbandry. In part, this may help explain the fact that the Spanish often did not understand the natives' drive to return to the mountains and inland valleys. To the Spaniards, the areas away from the mission were wastelands, wild landforms with little potential. For the Kumeyaay, the coasts, mountains, and valleys were native gardens and pharmacies maintained through generations of interactions with native landscapes.

As European cultures spread across the continent, native peoples everywhere incorporated aspects of the new cultures they encountered. An early account from 1776 by Fernando de Rivera y Moncada documents the flexibility of the Ipai as they dealt with changing land management in their region. Traversing inland valleys, he came upon a valley near current-day Ramona, up the hill to the northeast from the San Pasqual Valley,

Beautiful examples of coil basketry made from the juncus plant by Kumeyaay artists of Baja California. *Photo: Photo Darkroom.*

and recorded that he found "a cut field of well-sown wheat with other nearby plantings" (Rivera y Moncada 1967; translation by Richard Carrico).

The desert Quechan near Yuma probably provided the seed for the wheat, rather than the friars at the San Diego Mission, since the mission at the time was struggling (Carrico 2010:TS) and had little contact with locations north of El Cajon Valley prior to 1778. Wheat was first planted at the San Diego Mission in 1773, and the crops were small and not of uniform quality. Carrico explains:

> There is no evidence in the mission records that the local Spaniards had produced a wheat crop of any size at this time and certainly not enough to be providing seeds to non-mission Indians of the inland valleys. It is also possible that Kumeyaay field workers appropriated some wheat seeds as fruits of their labor and passed them on to their cousins in the north. Whether from a local source or one to the east, the presence of wheat in the Santa Maria Valley (current day Ramona) reflects Kumeyaay adaptability (Carrico 2010).

Ipai Cosmology, Religion, and Healing

Holy men or shamans were seen as traditional doctors or healers for the native people. The *kuseyaay* could be either born into a family or band, or might be chosen once their

Narciso Lachapa holding a deer hoof rattle. He wears a feather headdress and net skirt with hanging condor feathers. *Photo: E. H. Davis, San Diego Historical Society.*

healing attributes had become obvious to those in power within the band. Usually the *kuseyaay* was a male, though females may have played a more major part in the healing process after the groups came into contact with those from the outside world. Native people also experienced accidents from time to time, including hunting injuries, animal bites, snake bites, poisonous spider bites, falls, cuts, scrapes, and accidental poisonings. Wounds and injuries resulting from ambushes, warfare, or other hostile encounters also needed to be treated.

Many attributed both illnesses and injuries to internal and external forces, believing in the power of evil and the existence of dark forces. Some Ipai believed that others might level a curse against them, and that some of those doing the leveling (Carrico 2010) might be a *kuseyaay*. Native herbs and other plants were used to target the offending agents of illness, along with the use of healing rituals that involved singing, chanting, dancing, cutting the injured site, and blowing tobacco smoke onto the injury or affected area.

In *Dreams and Dream Interpretation of the Diegueño Indians of Southern California*, G. Tofflemier and K. Luomala called the shaman the *kwisiyai*, and explained that a shaman initiation would be an important part of becoming a *kwisiyai*, because few people were recognized as such at birth. Such people reportedly discovered their abilities as *kwisiyai* by

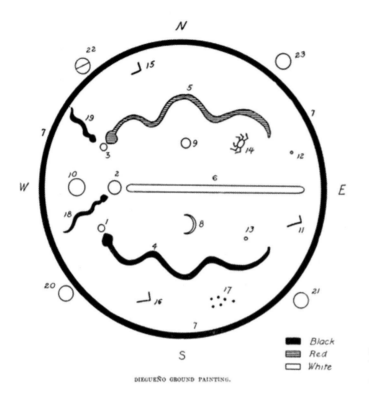

DIEGUEÑO GROUND PAINTING.

Black
Red
White

Ground Painting *created by Jose Waters and Antonio Maces (Waterman 1910).*

paying attention to what their dreams revealed. Those who already held the title of *kwisiyai* helped select other shamans "by choosing individuals with good health, intelligence, good sense, energy, and abundant sexuality" (Tofflemier and Luomala 1936:195).

The initiation ceremony involved spending the year prior to the initiation in training for the actual event. Learning how to diagnose disease, methods of curing, how to interpret dreams, introduction to specific professional and tribal ethics, learning the stories of the stars, communicating with spirits, secrets of hunting, and ways of learning to be successful at both love and gambling were part of the regimen required for someone being identified as ready for initiation as a shaman. Fasting, purification, and meditation were other prerequisites. By the end of the young peoples' completion of the puberty ceremony, the current shamans became aware of who might be suitable for future service.

One historian who studied the religious practices of the Ipai (Waterman, 1910:271-358) pointed out that: "Only individuals with special innate sensitivity were selected as shamans." He added: "Some people got to be witches or medicine-men (*kwisiyai*) and orators, but not many." In addition to the *kusesaay* (*kwisiyai*) there were other shamans who performed curative practices for the native people, including when people were bitten by rattlesnakes. These shamans (Carrico 2010:TS) were called *wikwisiyai* or *'ewikusesaay*, and they used sucking, blowing, chanting, dancing, and singing to cure, as well as herbs and medicines.

Joe Waters and Antonio Maces, from Mesa Grande (Waterman 1910), created the ground painting on the preceding page in the early 1900s. Waterman recorded the painting, and it is reproduced here. It was fifteen feet in diameter and represented the world as the Ipai knew it. Waterman believed that the symbols used in the world circle were consistent throughout the Mesa Grande, Santa Ysabel, Capitan Grande, Inaja, and Campo areas of San Diego County, and their meanings were the same for each group.

Material Culture

Leslie Spier (1923) outlined some of the customs of the Tipai of prehistoric times. He noted that when men wore clothing, they wore a braided girdle made of agave fiber meant to ease the burden of carrying an object, not to cover the body. Women wore a two-piece apron, with the back made of willow bark and the front perhaps of willow bark or close strings of milkweed, sometimes braided or netted. Sandals were worn only on rough ground, and were made of agave or yucca fibers, cushioned to half an inch or so.

Men and women both wore their hair long, with women letting it hang loose and often trimming it on the forehead, while men bunched their hair up on their crowns. Sometimes both the women and men wore a small basket on the crown of their heads. The women's caps were diagonally twined, while the men's caps were coiled. Men's tattooing consisted of two or three vertical lines on the chin, and sometimes the same pattern on the forehead, cheeks, arms, and chest. When girls were initiated into their adolescence ceremony, they were also tattooed. The method involved using a cactus thorn to prick charcoal into the skin.

Mountain and coastal houses, created in the winter (Spier 1923), were sometimes earth covered. Three posts planted in a row were connected by a short ridge log, on

Angel Quilp wears ceremonial regalia including a net skirt with hanging feathers, feather headdress, and wand. *Photo: E. H. Davis, San Diego History Center.*

47

A cache of ancient Ipai pottery in northern San Diego County.

which poles were then leaned from the sides. A layer of brush kept the soil that had been spread onto the frame from sifting or washing in.

The door was not oriented toward any certain direction, and there was an elliptical outline, a sharp roof, and an absence of walls. Sweat houses were smaller than dwellings, but were higher than houses. The sweat-house center rested on four poles set in a square. The roof was similar to that on a dwelling, and the indoor fire was placed between the posts and the house. Men sweated regularly in the evening. Women, however, never entered the sweat house. Wells were dug with sticks, and Spier (1923) said that the Tipai perfected this skill long before the arrival of the Europeans, since permanent springs are not numerous on the eastern slope of the mountains.

Spier (1923) explained that the Ipai made smoking pipes (*mukwin*) which were 6 to 8 inches long, were tubular, and were made of stone or pottery. Religious pipes were made of stone, and pottery was used to make pipes for every-day smoking. In addition, the Ipai also made pipes of cane. The Ipai had no drums, but used rattles called *ahnatl* made from a gourd or turtle shell. The old-time rattle was of deer hooves or clay, with gourds being

An Ipai hunter carries a willow bow. *Drawing: Robert Freeman.*

brought in from the Mohave Desert. The Tipai used a deer-hoof rattle in their mourning ceremony (Spier 1923).

Alfred Kroeber (1925) reported that Kumeyaay pottery was made with reddish clay and mixed with finely crushed rock, then coiled, shaped with a stone and a wooden paddle called *hiatutlt*, and fired. This pottery was without ornamentation. The Ipai used clay pottery as water jars, cooking pots, and plates, but they used baskets as bowls. They used milkweed for creating clothing and close-twined sacks, carrying nets and wallets. The sacks and carrying nets were created with the double loop or square knot, and were found only among the Tipai.

Kroeber (1925) described a war club that the Kumeyaay created, called a *hitlchahwai*, made of heavy mesquite wood, with a cylindrical enlargement at the head. Their metates were often unsquared, with the hollow being oval. They captured rabbits with a net, and took small rodents in a stone deadfall, baited with an acorn. Good blankets contained an average of twenty jackrabbit or forty cottontail skins. These blankets served mainly as bedding, but were also worn as ponchos. The men brought trees down using fire, never using wedges. Bows were made from willow or other flexible wood. Arrows were made from arrowweed, carrizo, or mulefat with detachable hardwood points, and arrowheads of stone were for large game only. They preferred soapstone arrow straighteners to those made of clay. The Kumeyaay calculated seasons by saying that the moons of the year had six months only, repeated, and apparently represented seasons not lunations.

Gaming

The Ipai engaged in several types and styles of games and gaming, including kickball, foot racing, shinny (a game similar to hockey, but played on dirt), soccer, ring and pin, stick and arrow, hoop games, stick games and dice. One dominant and enduring game has been the game of peon, known as *homarp* in the Kumeyaay language. Peon is a traditional hand game that includes guessing and gambling. It is played in and around southern California, northern Baja California, along the Colorado River, as far north as Fort Mojave, as far south as the Gulf of California, and on the Arizona side, along the Gila River. The game is as old as anybody can remember, and has been played traditionally at ceremonies and at social gatherings that are held on reservations throughout the region, mostly in the summertime.

Peon gaming pieces from Mesa Grande, circa 1890 (Culin 1907:325).

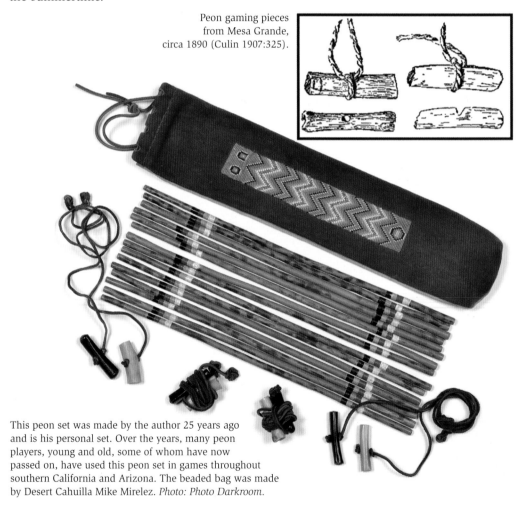

This peon set was made by the author 25 years ago and is his personal set. Over the years, many peon players, young and old, some of whom have now passed on, have used this peon set in games throughout southern California and Arizona. The beaded bag was made by Desert Cahuilla Mike Mirelez. *Photo: Photo Darkroom.*

Peon games in action. *Drawing: Robert Freeman.*

Fiesta at Santa Ysabel, 1900s. Peon would have been a major event and Ipai players from San Pasqual may have attended. *Photo: E. H. Davis, San Diego History Center.*

The game is played by two teams of four players each, with one player as the captain; both teams face each other across a bonfire. A *koime* serves as the referee. The koime has a set of gaming pieces which consists of fifteen *palitos* (counter sticks) and four sets of *peones*. Each set is made up of a white and black bone, with a hole drilled through the center, through which a leather strap is passed; one end has a loop for the players' wrists. The bone for the peones is usually the coyote leg bone, although some teams use other types. Each team also has a blanket, which is used when it is their turn to hide the peones. The objective of the game is to win all the palitos.

To start the game, the koime asks the captain of each team who is going to "fight the hand" (to decide which team will hide first) and gives them a set of peones. The captain "fights the hand" or designates one of his players to fight it. Whichever team sings a fighting song first will be recognized by the koime to start the "fighting of the hand." As the song is being sung, the team, when ready, pulls up the blanket so that the "fighting of the hand" player can hide his peones.

As the "hiding" team sings, they drop the blanket when ready. The player who is hiding the peones has them tucked up under his arms. The opposite team will call a shot, trying to guess which hand the set of peones is in. The hider will not disclose his position until the koime relays the shot. The player shows in which hand he has the peones; this process can go back and forth between the teams until one player prevails by outguessing the other.

Once this is decided by the "fighting of the hand," the winning team will receive a palito and the four sets of peones; each player receives a set with its white and black bone. As the team sings their peon song and pulls up the blanket to hide the peones, each player has either spoken with the other players of his team to decide which hand to place which color bone, or sometimes each player decides individually where they will hide their bones. Once the players have hidden their peones, and dropped the blanket, the song continues as they grunt and taunt, in an attempt to intimidate their adversaries. When the opposing (or "shooting") team decides on their shot, the shooter for the team addresses the koime with the shot.

For example, if the shooting team thinks that all the black bones are placed toward the center (with the center between the middle two players), they would point with two fingers to that center and address the koime with the shot that is called *aweta grande*. If two of the players have their black bone in the direction of the shot as called (the center), they have been guessed correctly and must surrender their peones to the two players across from them. The two players with their white bone facing in that direction (who were not guessed) each receive a palito for their team and get to hide again. Now the challenge for the shooter is to try to figure out if the "hiding" players will switch or stay or if one switches and one stays, or which one will switch and which one will stay. One advantage for the shooter is that he knows where the peones were last hidden, and he may recall how the players have hidden their peones earlier in the game and have had a tendency to hide in a particular way.

The koime relays the shot and the hiding team has to show their hand. The players who are guessed correctly toss their peones over the fire to the player opposite them. The players that are missed receive a palito for their team and hide again. The game continues with much singing, taunting, and excitement as the hiders receive palitos for each incorrect guess until all are guessed. At this point the other team takes their turn, singing their peon songs and hiding the peones until all are guessed. A game can last for a short time or can go on all night and into the next day.

Peon is a game of strategy, endurance, deception, skill, and, at times, luck. Teams are often made up of family members and

Running and foot races were popular pastimes among Native Californians. *Drawing: Robert Freeman.*

Coyote and Fire. *Drawing: Robert Freeman.*

band members; associates may also be added to form "pick-up teams" because there are times that a team may not have all members present. Today there are also women's and children's teams. Peon is a game that has been passed on through oral tradition from generation to generation. In the old days, and sometimes still today, teams and family members and those who wanted to support their team would put their money up in order to challenge another team with the amount they have accumulated for that game. The captain would approach the captain of another team and challenge them to a game, which requires a matching bet. If accepted, they will approach a koime who would hold the money in a bandana and give it to the winner. The winner in return would pay the koime for his services. The koime has a great responsibility, since it is necessary for him to be alert and know the intricacies of the game. Much depends on his ability to control the game.

Today many tribes put up a pot of money to draw a number of teams; this is called a peon tournament. The mens' teams come up with amounts to place a "buy-in" to add to the pot. There is a draw to see which teams will play each other. Many of the older players discuss playing the old way with no pot, but rather using their own resources instead, such as a horse, a belt buckle or something else of value, as was done originally. There are so many other details to the game that those who are interested should try to attend a gathering to experience the full impact. This game has kept an ancient tradition of our land alive, and has created relationships that continue to maintain a special bond between players.

Ipai games involved not only skill, but also chance, adding an element of surprise and anticipation to the encounters, and breaking up the monotony of daily survival routines. Men usually joined in playing the games, while the women sang and bet on the outcomes of the competitions. Foot racing, soccer, and shinny (sometimes called "Indian hockey"), a game using a stick and wooden ball, involved more physical aspects, as did stick and arrow and hoop games. Dice or stick games demanded that two sticks or dice be thrown on the grass or a flat surface, with points being gained each time a player reached a certain count or series of counts.

In the game of kick ball, Ipai team members most likely kicked a smooth, rounded stone ball around a predetermined path, or from one post to another. They ran with the ball, kicking it with their feet. The game of ring and pin used a string of large acorn cups and a pointed stick with which to gather the cups, with the person gathering the most cups on the pointed stick winning the game.

• Gambling in Myths and Legends of the Ipai of San Diego County

Some native people believe that gaming and betting have been a part of Ipai life since ancient times, brought to the People by a spirit or great power. Gaming certainly plays an important part in some of the native peoples' myths and legends, including the story of Chaup, a story that the Mesa Grande Indians told.

In the story, a group of Ipai played peon at a neighboring village, and lost to their competitors. Cuyahomarr, the hero in the story, told his grandfather that he would go to the neighboring village, and that he would be victorious over the competitors. Cuyahomarr's grandfather cautioned him that the neighboring villagers would kill him. The hero of the story, however, summoned the courage to travel to the neighboring village, beat the competitors at peon, and then, in revenge for the previous loss, burned the villagers' homes and fields.

The Tipai of the Manzanita Reservation told a similar version of the same myth (DuBois 1906). The ancient people of their band were believed to be coyotes before they were human, and in their version Cuyahomarr assisted his uncle, using magic, and helped him win a game of hoops and sticks, rather than peon. After Cuyahomarr's uncle won, Cuyahomarr's revenge was to take possession of all the most important food items, tools, metates, and manos of the losing tribe.

4

Historical Period:
Pre-Mission Historical Accounts

The historical period for San Diego County must be seen in the context of Spanish settlement of mainland Mexico and Baja California, since what is now California was at the time considered (at least by non-Indians) to be part of the Spanish empire. European explorers began to survey the region only fifty years after the arrival of Columbus. The establishment of the Jesuit missions began in 1697 in Loreto, in the southern Baja California peninsula, and from there the missionaries added missions to the south (toward the tip of the peninsula) and up into the northern peninsula.

Juan Rodriguez Cabrillo first arrived at the San Diego Bay in 1542, though Captain Sebastian Vizcaino reportedly gave the area its Spanish name in 1602 when he explored the Pacific Coast.

When some of the men with Cabrillo ventured onto the shore for the first time, Clarence McGrew (1922:2) said that they spent the night camping after getting lost, and after they returned safely to their two ships, the San Salvador and the Victoria, a group of native people appeared. Using hand signs the native people apprised the visitors that other white men were exploring the interior regions of the area on horseback.

Joel Hyer (2001) related how the Jesuits in Baja California established seventeen missions among the indigenous people, wreaking disease, abuse, and hunger on the people, to the point that though there were some 40,000 natives there in 1697, by 1768 the numbers of Indians in the Baja California peninsula had dropped to 7,000. Further information on native population numbers and their decline after contact with the Spanish, Mexican, American, and European invaders can be found later in this chapter.

By 1768 the Jesuits were expelled from the Americas and within a few years the Dominican Order took over the missions of Baja California while the Franciscans took over those of Alta (upper) California, beginning with San Diego.

McGrew (1922) related that before Father Junipero Serra accompanied the governor of the Californias, Gaspar de Portola, on the first overland expedition to San Diego, he

Opposite page: San Diego Mission. *Photo: San Diego History Center.*

officiated at the send-off of the supply ships that were part of the expedition by sea. The San Carlos, with Captain Vincente Vila in charge, sailed from La Paz, Mexico, January 9, 1769, and the San Antonio, with Captain Perez in charge, left San Jose del Cabo February 15, 1769.

The second ship to leave was the first to arrive. The San Antonio docked April 11, 1769, at Ballast Point in San Diego. Those on the San Antonio then waited on board for the San Carlos, which arrived April 29. Scurvy had broken out on both ships, and some of the crewmen had died, while others were seriously ill.

Captain Vila reported that on May 1, 1769, some of those from the group of newcomers at San Diego went onshore at Point Loma and came upon an Indian rancheria of thirty-five or forty families:

> The officers and the Missionary Fathers reported that they had walked about three leagues along the shore [of Point Loma and Dutch Flats] and at that distance had come to an Indian Rancheria on the banks of a river with excellent water; that the Indians inhabiting the village to the number of thirty-five or forty families scattered along the stream in small rude huts, were very friendly and gentle and that the country was pleasant and green, abounding in various odiferous plants, wild grapes and game (McGrew 1922:7).

Father Crespi later wrote a letter telling of the many rancherias he had seen as the group traveled northward by foot. The priest considered the native people to be "wretched," observing that the males wore no clothing, but that the women were "decently covered," wearing clothes made of fiber and animal skins. Men and women alike were "much painted," and the men wore a piece of shell through their pierced noses (McGrew 1922:8).

Portola and Father Serra arrived in San Diego in June 29, 1769. Portola's goal was to eventually travel up the Pacific Coast and find the bay at Monterey (McGrew 1922) so the area could be secured as the home of the second mission. It was Father Serra's intention to stay in San Diego and convert the native people to Christianity, and to bring them under the control of the missions with the help of soldiers and other colonists from Spain and New Spain who had come with him.

On July 16, 1769, Father Serra established and named the San Diego de Alcala Mission, the first of twenty-one missions in Alta California that were constructed along the El Camino Real (the King's Highway) from San Diego to Sonoma. The mission's patron saint, Saint Didacus of Alcala (circa 1400-1463), who was also called San Diego, was a Spanish hermit who entered the priesthood as a Franciscan friar, then became the Franciscan Pope Sixtus V in 1588. Serra also named the San Diego Presidio, the first Spanish fort in Alta California (Parks Canada 2009).

Spanish military authorities erected presidios at San Diego, Santa Barbara, Monterey, and San Francisco. Spanish, and other non-Indian colonists settled the lands that belonged to Native Californians, arrogantly displacing the area's original inhabitants and destroying the natural resources on which the native people had relied for survival.

During the Spanish and Mexican periods, the term *Californio* was used to identify the Spanish-speaking, generally Roman Catholic people of Latin American descent, who were born in Alta California starting with the arrival of the first Spanish colonies in 1769 through the Treaty of Guadalupe Hidalgo in 1848. The term distinguished the Spanish and later Mexican residents from local native peoples, since the Indians' first language was not Spanish. However, the Spanish-speaking *mestizo* or mixed-blood descendents of Native Californians and settlers would also be considered Californios.

Father Serra began his ministry with the Kumeyaay by employing a policy known as "*reducciones*," used by Catholic priests throughout Latin America. This meant congregating the Indians into one location—the mission—and attempting to indoctrinate and acculturate them into a new religion and a new way of life. The missions were envisioned as European-style settlements, based on agriculture and the grazing of livestock, with the newly-coerced native people serving as a labor force for the colony.

The invaders' attitudes toward any non-European person was that they were dark, uncivilized, immoral people. Plans included the building of a military installation known as a presidio (fort) near each mission, so Spanish soldiers could exert their authority as needed. Spanish citizens would then receive free lands in the region, though these were the lands on which the Kumeyaay had traditionally lived for thousands of years. The invaders planned to establish these settlements to provide further support to the missions, since they were convinced that their "right of discovery" entitled them to claim these lands in the name of Spain.

Contemporary Native American (Shawnee/Lenape) historian and author Steve Newcomb used history and cognitive theory to explain how the colonial powers of Europe, and later the United States, used concepts derived from Christianity to justify the taking of lands belonging to the native people. They also denied native people the independence to which they were entitled. Newcomb likened the commandeering of the rights of native people and their native lands to a "conqueror-based doctrine," which continues to affect United States policy both nationally and internationally.

> An explanation … is that for the Christian colonizers of the Americas, the Chosen People-Promised Land cognitive model was the basis for drawing an analogy between the lands of North America and the lands of Canaan in the Old Testament. This entails the lands of North America being conceived of as "land free to be taken" (Newcomb 2008:52).

On August 15, 1769 (McGrew 1922), a group of native men attacked the San Diego Presidio with bows and arrows after some of its soldiers had left the fort. The solders returned, wearing their leather jackets which withstood the arrows, and used their guns to kill several native men and wound a few more. The native men used their bows and arrows to kill Joseph Maria, a servant who tended to the friars' needs, and another arrow hit one of the friars, Father Vizcaino, in the hand, resulting in a disability which plagued him the rest of his life. Two soldiers were also slightly injured.

Gaspar de Portola sailed away from San Diego Bay with another of the friars, Father Crespi, in search of Monterey Bay and spent the next six months attempting to find the proposed site of the second California mission, but to no avail (McGrew 1922). They returned to San Diego to find those who had remained waiting for the San Antonio's return, since it had also left to fetch food and supplies. Though Portola wanted to return immediately to Mexico City, Fathers Serra and Crespi talked him into staying, and on March 19, 1770, the San Antonio appeared, saving the expeditionary teams from starvation.

In April 1770 Portola and a small group that included Father Crespi headed for Monterey on foot, while another group, including Father Serra, sailed north on the San Antonio in search of Monterey Bay. Portola's group arrived first, on May 24, 1770, and Father Serra's arrived the following week. On June 3, 1770, Father Serra established the second California mission. A short time later, Portola left on the San Antonio for Mexico City and designated Lieutenant Don Pedro Fages as governor of Alta California. Father Serra lived until August 28, 1784, when he died in Carmel, California at the age of 70.

By 1772 Father Luis Jayme (Hyer 2001), a Franciscan friar at the San Diego Mission, had called to account Spanish soldiers who were kidnapping and raping Kumeyaay women and girls. He admitted that it happened at all the existing California missions, and warned the soldiers that there was one village near the San Diego Mission where the native men were threatening to come and kill them all.

Twice within the first six years of its creation, attacks (Luomala 1963) on the San Diego Mission ended with fatalities. In 1775, a year after its relocation away from the presidio, about 800 native people from some seventy villages united to burn the mission to the ground.

On November 5, 1775, a group of Tipai attacked the San Diego Mission de Alcala. Father Luis Jayme responded by yelling, "Children, love God!" These 800 men were tired of the atrocities that had been leveled against them, their wives, and their children, and proceeded to kill three Spaniards, including Father Jayme. The Tipai who hoisted the large stone that crushed Father Jayme's skull responded, "No love God anymore!" Other attackers shot arrows into those who had fallen (Hyer 2001:30).

Joel Hyer reminded readers that: "Despite this violence, the attack on the San Diego Mission was not the mindless act of heartless savages; rather, it reflects a rational decision made by civilized peoples in response to soldiers who raped innocent Kumeyaay women and girls" (Hyer 2001:30). An excerpt of a letter from Father Luis Jayme read:

> No wonder the Indians here were bad when the mission was first founded. To begin with, they did not know why they [the Spanish] had come; unless they intended to take their lands away from them. Now they all want to be Christians because they know that there is a God who created the heavens and earth and

all things, that there is a Hell, and Glory, that they have souls, etc., but when the mission was first founded they did not know all these things; instead, they thought they were like animals, and when the vessels came at first, they saw that most of the crews died; they were very loathe to pray, and they did not want to be Christians at all, instead, they said that it was bad to become a Christian and then they would die immediately.

No wonder they said so when they saw how most of the sailors and [Baja] California Indians died, but now thanks be to the Lord, God has converted them from Sauls to Pauls. They all know the natural law, which so I am informed, they have observed as well or better than many Christians elsewhere. They do not have any idols; they do not go on drinking sprees; they do not marry relatives; and they have but one wife. The married men sleep with their wives only. The bachelors sleep together, and apart from the women and married couples. If a man plays with any woman who is not his wife, he is scolded and punished by his captains.

Concerning those from the Californias I have heard it said that they are given to sexual vices, but among those here I have not been able to discover a single fault of their nature. Some of the first adults whom we baptized, when we pointed out to them that it was wrong to have sexual intercourse with a woman to whom they were not married, told me that they already know that, and that among them it was considered to be very bad that, and so they did not do so at all. 'The soldiers,' they told me, 'are Christians and, although they know that God will punish them in Hell, do so, having sexual intercourse with our wives. We,' they said, 'although we did not know that God would punish us for that in Hell, considered it to be very bad, and we did not do it, and even less now that we know that God will punish us if we do so.' When I heard this, I burst into tears to see how these gentiles were setting an example for us Christians ... (Connolly Miskwish 2007:49).

Richard Carrico and Michael Connolly Miskwish noted that the attack involved several hundred Kumeyaay, just after midnight, and was planned as a coordinated strike of two groups, one to attack the San Diego Mission and the other the presidio, but the mission attackers struck before those assigned to the presidio were ready, with the result being that both groups struck the mission, demolishing the buildings there, while the presidio went unscathed. As those who lived at the mission awoke, they realized that the mission was ablaze. The Quechan had decided not to join in the attack, since their Chief, Palma, had become friends with Juan Bautista de Anza, and the Ipai-speaking Kumeyaay also declined, though forty Kumeyaay leaders sent troops to help with the battle.

Carrico expands on the story by delineating the village where the main Kumeyaay-Tipai warriors and their families had recently resided, called *Neti* or *Meti*, in the Spring Valley area, though they had even more recently abandoned the village as their homesite (Carrico 1987:30; Connolly Miskwish 2007:64).

A difference of opinion exists concerning how many native people actually were taken to the missions in California. Edward Castillo (1998), a Cahuilla-Luiseño, said that there were 81,586 baptized Indians at the twenty-one missions in California, and that more than one out of every twenty-four escaped, which would number at least 3,399 that were able to escape the forced slavery there.

Katharine Luomala wrote that in 1779 some native people lived near the mission of San Diego rather than at the actual mission site, and numbered those native people as 1,405. By 1811 the number had grown to 1,559. After 1818 the establishment of the Santa Ysabel branch mission permitted interior Indians to become affiliated with the San Diego Mission without moving away from their native villages (Luomala 1963).

California Indian agent Charles E. Kelsey (1913) drew on statistics and information from a 1906 investigation he had conducted regarding the number of Indians in California, and included the information in his final report of 1913 before retiring. This report came at the culmination of his ten to twelve years of service with the Office of Indian Affairs. He said:

> We do not know how many Indians there were in California at the time of the American occupation in 1846. The Census of 1850 estimated them at 100,000. The Anthropological Department of the University of California estimates the number as 150,000 at the time of the Spanish occupation, or practically the beginning of the 19th Century. C. Hart Merriam of the U. S. Biological Survey estimated 260,000 at that time. This is a matter of academic interest now, and yet it seems clear that at least 90 percent of the California Indians perished within the memory of men now living (Kelsey 1913:TS).

Hyer said: "Spanish missionaries intended not only to Christianize California's first people, but also to alter their lifestyles and obliterate their cultures." He added that the Spanish either lured the Indians in with food or European goods, or had the soldiers assist in bringing the native people in forcibly" (Hyer 2001:24).

It is in the context presented above that the health, diet, and treatment of Indian people at Mission San Diego must be understood. Assessment of the health and treatment of the Kumeyaay associated with the mission is based on three major avenues of research: 1) the written narratives of the priests and others, 2) the population and death records kept for the mission, and 3) the archaeological record as revealed by excavation and analysis of the human remains. Individually none of these approaches is very satisfying but when synthesized and compared, they offer a valuable although incomplete historical record.

While the Kumeyaay at Mission San Diego fared better in terms of death rates than natives at most other missions, the effects of missionization were still devastating. In particularly bad years, more Indians died at Mission San Diego than were baptized. For the years 1805-1806, 152 natives were baptized but 252 were laid to rest in the mission cemetery. In 1809 60 Indians were baptized and 75 died, and in the period from 1813-1816, 319 were baptized with 411 souls committed to the brown soil in the *camposanto* (graveyard) (Carrico 1987).

The neophytes lived in crowded, filthy rooms with little ventilation, resulting in outbreaks of smallpox, chicken pox, measles, diphtheria, and tuberculosis. Imported from

Comparison of Death Rate Per Thousand Mission San Diego vs California (Carrico 1987:29)			
Period	**San Diego**	**California**	**Difference**
1785-1789	65	91	-25
1790-1794	55	79	-24
1795-1799	57	88	-31
1800-1804	48	98	-50
1805-1809	65	91	-26
1810-1814	71	73	-02
1815-1819	67	81	-14
1820-1824	61	73	-12
1825-1829	74	75	-01
1830-1834	62	50	+12
Mean Death Rate	56	78	

Europe, these diseases were quickly transmitted to the native people, who had no resistance to the new diseases. Kumeyaay who lived in the interior regions and other areas of San Diego County contracted the diseases when they came into contact with either neophytes who had been at the mission, or with friars, soldiers, or other Spaniards connected with the invasion of Kumeyaay territories. The native populations also had no immunological defenses against the potent strains of syphilis that the Spanish brought to the missions and spread among the native population through sexual contact (Hyer 2001).

The mission records rarely provide the cause of death for Indian people, so details of morbidity are rare. However, historical records indicate that a measles epidemic spread throughout California in 1806 and again in 1827 (Jackson and Castillo 1995:41-42). Hubert Bancroft notes that an unnamed pestilence moved through California in 1825 (1886:551) and Sherburne F. Cook (1939:173) documents a smallpox epidemic in northern California in 1828-1829 with its effect being felt as far south as San Diego. Cook and others also note that a second smallpox epidemic raced through Alta California in 1838-1839 (Cook 1939:183; Preston 1996:16). Based on the historical records, one would expect a higher than normal incidence of mortality in the years 1806, 1825-1829, and 1838-1839.

The death records at Mission San Diego attest to the tragic effects of these scourges, even if the direct causes of death are not provided in the documentation. At San Diego, 167 Indians died in 1806, the second greatest number for any single year of the mission's history. With a population of 1,486 natives in 1806, the rate per thousand was 112, the second highest ever recorded at San Diego (Table 8-1). The 1825 pestilence, most likely smallpox, was even more devastating, the worst epidemic to strike the ill-prepared mission. In that year, 186 Indians died of a population of 1,728 for a death per thousand rate of 186, the highest in the mission annals. During the 1827 epidemic, a probable holdover from the 1825 scourge or a precursor to the 1828-1829 epidemics, 148 Indians died of a population of 1,630 for a death per thousand of 90 individuals (Carrico 1987).

A comparison of the death per thousand rates of 112 for 1806, 186 for 1825, and 90 for 1827, and at San Diego with an average of 56 per thousand for the years 1785-1834 bears testimony to the severity of the epidemics. It is suggested that the apparent mass graves or so-called "plague pits" discovered in the cemetery at Mission San Diego contain the remains associated with one or more of these terrible epidemics. This seems more than plausible given that in the 90 days between January 1806 and March 1806, 109 burials were completed including two adults and two children on one day, January 30 (Libro de los Difuntos 1774-1811).

In spite of devastating epidemics and outbreaks of pestilence, the narrative record from the mission priests and administrators for San Diego is strangely quiet on these matters. Between 1785 and 1834 the mean death rate for the California missions was 78 per thousand (Jackson and Castillo 1995:40). The San Diego mission over the same period experienced a rate of 56 per thousand, a significantly lower number. These data compare with a rate of 50 per thousand for typical hunter/gatherers and collectors. With the exception of the 1830-1834 era, San Diego maintained a consistently lower death rate than that for California but nonetheless, higher than might be expected in a pre-contact setting (Carrico 1987).

The reasons for this lower post-contact death rate at San Diego can be found in environmental and cultural factors. The climate of San Diego is generally less severe and more temperate than the colder, wetter regions to the north and, as suggested by Robert Jackson and Edward Castillo (1995:43), weather conditions, such as those in the San Francisco Bay area and Central Valley, can play a significant role in mortality rates (Carrico 1987).

However important climate may have been, in the case of the Kumeyaay, their ability, especially the males, to move freely in and out of the mission complex, may have also saved their lives. Jackson and Castillo (1995:48-50) and others have noted the role that poor sanitation, inadequate housing, and overcrowding played overall in Alta California mission Indian mortality. Elton Molto et al. (1998) has suggested a similar scenario for the Las Palmas people of Baja California with an emphasis on the deadly effects of the mission conversion system specifically. The mobility of the Kumeyaay at Mission San Diego may have decreased the incidence of disease and delayed the breakdown of immunological systems (Carrico 1987).

The other key to understanding the health and morbidity of the Indian population at the mission is the data derived from the two studies conducted on the human remains from the mission cemetery. The first study, by Patricia Mitchell, was conducted on human bone fragments generally associated with the cemetery. Because of the fragmentary nature of the bones, the analysis was severely hampered but not invalidated.

The second physical anthropological study was performed by Rose Tyson of the San Diego Museum of Man. Because of time constraints placed upon Ms. Tyson by local tribal members, her study was limited to a cursory examination of intact bones from articulated and disarticulated burials. Ms. Tyson concluded that many of the individuals suffered from varying degrees of malnutrition as evidenced by tooth enamel and bone porosity. Further, it appeared that arm bones and vertebrae had been adversely affected by stress from carrying heavy burdens or severe physical exertion. In several cases, this was particularly evident in young Indians who were in their growing cycle.

In a story that is probably more symbolic than factual, Rosalie Robertson (Costo and Costo 1987), born at Campo in 1918, said that when her people disobeyed the friars, soldiers would throw the native children off a nearby cliff. She said it was at "The Crying Rock," the name local native people gave to the San Diego County rock formation where this happened. Robertson did not give a detailed description of the location.

Magante, a Luiseño from Pauma, recounted how the Spanish soldiers made the Indians work as though they were beasts of burden, forcing them to build the missions at San Diego, San Luis Rey, and San Juan Capistrano using timbers cut at Palomar Mountain. He said the native people "carried logs on their shoulders, and they couldn't sit or drop the timbers on the ground until they reached the missions." He added that the Spanish overseers "severely whipped and punished" those who attempted to stop and take a break (Costo and Costo 1987:134). Marvin Amago (Costo and Costo 1987) told how the Spanish would separate families and force them to work without giving them enough to eat.

While the neophytes learned at the mission to tend horses, cattle, mules, donkeys, and sheep, the downside for the native people not at the mission was that these newly-introduced animals drove away local game and overgrazed the grasses and plants that the native people had always used as food (Hyer 2001).

A cultural bias that may have skewed the Spaniards' view was the perception of the Kumeyaay work ethic. To a people in tune with the rhythms of nature and for whom labor adhered to the schedule provided by the seasons, rainfall, and natural occurrences, the pattern of forced labor that the Spanish demanded from the native people must have seemed strange indeed. Anthropologist Robert F. Heizer noted that "The compulsion to labor and steady work was something new to the Indian, who was unused to forced and continuous energy exertion" (Heizer 1978:128).

Another factor to consider in any review of the Spanish accounts is that with some few exceptions, the documents reflect a view of the villages and lands along the coast adjacent to El Camino Real and infrequent entries into the inland valleys and meadows. In other words, the Spaniards are most often seeing and recording only the coastal plain and once-pristine areas undergoing rapid change from cattle and horse grazing.

The mission system at San Diego quite clearly could not, and did not, provide an adequate or steady diet to the Indians. As Father Serra himself noted in October 1776, "This San Diego Mission has nothing of its own in the matter of food for the Fathers, or for its converts, with the exception of the cattle" (Tibesar 1961:49). Serra continued, "As for the Indians, the Fathers have nothing to give them, nor any directions for their employment ..." (Tibesar 1961:51). Though the situation improved after 1776 and the food supply became less meager, although often uncertain, the Kumeyaay continued to come and go freely from the mission as the padres encouraged them to hunt and gather native foodstuffs.

As an example of the irregular food supply, in a six-day period in June 1776, Commandant Fernando de Rivera y Moncada twice sent a sergeant and a pack mule from the San Diego presidio to the neophyte village of San Buenaventura (along Rose Creek near present-day Pacific Beach) to trade for fish. The sergeant bartered fishhooks and glass beads that Moncada had purchased in Mexico. Moncada noted that he was "lacking entirely the ration of corn and had no flour with which to supply this lack, being minimal the stew that remains, it is not possible to give them a corresponding portion. The sergeant returned with the mule laden with very good fish ..." (Burrus 1967:267) [translation by R. Carrico].

That the native people, in their traditional state, were used to eating well is documented by Father Lausen. He wrote in 1782 that the rations offered by the priests were insufficient to "satisfy the voracious way of eating in which they were brought up. ... None would submit to the slightest discipline if were denied access to his hunting and fishing" (Kenneally 1965:81). Father Torrent wrote in 1788 that without some form of irrigation ditches, the wheat and barley crops would continue to be unsteady and there will never be enough surplus to feed even those Indians at the mission let alone those beyond the Spanish settlement (Torrent 1788). He noted that those Indians living beyond the mission in "their indigenous rancherías ... do not have food other than the wild seeds that they dry and eat as do the wild beasts" (Torrent 1788) [translation by R. Carrico].

To the north of Ipai territory, oral traditions tell of the Cupeño people going to secret hiding places in the hills, after first sighting a group of pale-skinned Spaniards who were part of Father Juan Mariner and Captain Juan Pablo Grijalva's expeditionary force (Mariner 1795). Mariner and Grijalva were in San Diego County to find a site for a new mission and presidio, and traveled as far north as San Juan Capistrano. Aware of the stories Indian traders from other bands had shared when traveling through this region, stories which related the newcomers' atrocities toward the native people, some Cupeño believed that the foreigners meant to kill them, and they responded by watching cautiously from a distance. After passing by the Luiseño village of Pala, the expeditionary group entered a lush valley to the northeast, and named it Valle de San Jose, (now known as Warner Springs), then passed the villages of Cupa (Agua Caliente) and Wilakalpa. When the Cupeño were assured that the Spaniards were gone, they sent a scout ahead to their villages, to make sure that the area was safe. Since the native people had heard that these men arrived by way of the water, they called them the "Ocean People."

In 1797 the first recorded visit by non-Indians to the valley of Temecula occurred (Castillo 1998) when Father Fermin Lasuen, the Franciscan padre who followed Father Serra as president of California's Franciscan missions, led an exploring party over the mountains, searching for a new mission site. In 1798 Fermin Lasuen (Castillo 1998) founded San Luis Rey, "The King of the Missions."

In 1810 Mexico declared its independence from Spain (Castillo 1998), after 300 years of being a Spanish colony, during which time its population dropped by half. The Chapel of San Antonio at Pala was founded in 1816 as an *asistencia* of San Luis Rey, and Santa Ysabel, south of Warner Springs, was founded as an *asistencia* of Mission San Diego with an inaugural mass in 1818 (Castillo 1998). In 1821, after a long struggle for freedom that had started in 1810, Mexico won its independence from Spain. The province of California and the missions then became part of the new Republic of Mexico. Friars often stayed with their mission and took Mexican citizenship. The first native Mexican governor was Jose Maria Echeandia, about whom Clarence McGrew said:

> The old Governor had some trouble with the Indians, and kept his troops busy much of the time in keeping them scared away from the port (of San Diego). The California soldiers brought in the ears of their victims, to show what the day's work had been. On one occasion a lieutenant is said to have brought in 20 pairs of ears from Indians slain in this section (McGrew 1922:32).

By 1822 a chapel and several buildings had been constructed at the *asistencia* of Santa Ysabel, further extending the mission influence to the Ipai. This led to more Ipais adopting the Catholic belief system, along with Spanish ways of agriculture, including the use of horses and other animals. On August 18, 1824, the Mexican Congress passed a general colonization law, which said that territorial governors were able to give away grants for vacant Lands, with the exception that if the land was occupied by Indians, "it must be returned to them, if the granting of such land [to non-Indians] would cause the Indians damage or injury" (Connolly Miskwish 2007:63).

Ipai raids were also becoming more effective, using more sophisticated strategies and improved warfare techniques, since those who escaped the missions were able to share with the native people of the backcountry the vulnerabilities of the friars and soldiers. Because of the loss of the coastal areas to the Spanish, many Ipai were unable to use their traditional winter camps, and were often forced to stay in the mountain areas year-round. Some Ipai adapted to these restrictions by trading with the missionized native people, as well as carrying out raids on mission cattle (Connolly Miskwish 2007).

The neophytes who remained at the missions were the economic backbone of the mission system, since it was the Indians who spun wool, tanned leather, herded animals, tended livestock, and made saddles, bricks, shoes, and candles. They learned about the Catholic religion, became adept at new crafts, tended crops, learned to use plows, and expanded irrigation techniques, and learned how to care for domestic animals, along with a multitude of other new skills (Phillips 1974).

According to Thorne, the Catholic Church's mission to remake the Indian in the European image was not realized. She supports the idea that there was often a lack of food, water, and arable land for use at the missions, which led the church to have to allow *paseos* or personal excursions of neophytes to their homelands to harvest wild foods for self-support. Those native people who chose not to be baptized Catholic were called gentiles. While the neophytes were visiting their native homes they were likely to resume their native customs, eating native foods, speaking their native languages, and, perhaps, integrating what they were learning and adopting from the Spanish, and later, Mexican cultures into their lives (Thorne 2012).

These Ipai had met the needs of the friars at the missions and had been responsible to the military personnel at the presidio. They offered their captors a vast array of services, often amidst brutal, harsh, and unendurable conditions, as evidenced by the 4,322 neophytes who died at the San Diego Mission between 1769-1834 while in the servitude of the friars and soldiers (Luomala 1978).

On July 25, 1826, Jose Maria de Echeandia issued an edict (Bancroft 1890), taking the first steps toward "secularization" or breaking up and giving away the lands which belonged to the twenty-one missions in Alta California. The *Provenciones de Emancipacion* stated that the native people connected with the missions, who qualified, would be set free and would be eligible to assume Mexican citizenship. Those who chose to stay at the mission would no longer have corporal punishment inflicted upon them, something which had been a longtime concern for many neophytes. Bancroft (1890) believed that the new decrees were not meant to benefit the native peoples, but were efforts to appease those Mexican Californians who wanted the mission lands for themselves.

California Indian agent B. D. Wilson later reported that at the time of secularization, the value of the missions and their property, not counting the lands, had been $5 million. Within six months, all those resources had been dispersed to non-Indians. Later, when a Congressional Appropriation of $120,000 for the Indians of California had been reduced to $20,000, Senator William M. Gwyn said, "If this is to be the policy of the government towards this people, it will form a dark page in our history, if it does not bring vengeance from heaven upon us as a nation" (Pourade 1963:N.p.)

With California being so far from Mexico City at a time when most communication was by boat, foot, or horseback, the process of secularization moved slowly, and in the meantime the missions continued to function. Father Zephyrin Englehardt noted that by 1828: "Persons who can definitely be identified as ancestral to present San Pasqual band members were being baptized at the San Diego Mission as San Pasqual people" (1913:638; 1922:92-93).

The Founding of the San Pasqual Pueblo

The Mexican government appointed General Jose Figueroa as the new governor of California in 1833, and after he arrived in the upper California region and began finalizing plans to secularize the missions, he announced on May 1, 1833, that, "Three new pueblos have been formed—San Dieguito, Las Flores, and San Juan Capistrano" (Smith 1982:346).

By 1834 Mexican authorities had turned the twenty-one missions of Alta California over to the secular clergy and to designated Indian neophytes. At that time the Mexican government gave Pablo Apis, a Luiseño and a former mission convert, 2,000 acres of Rancho land in Temecula. The Mexican government also created Rancho Temecula at the southern end of the valley, Rancho Pauba, to the east, and Rancho Santa Rosa, in the hills to the west. These lands, which had been stripped from the missions, were all given to private individuals (Van Horn 1974).

The San Pasqual Pueblo came into existence on November 16, 1835, with eighty-one native people. Though some historians believe that all the people had been at the San Diego Mission (Smith 1982), others claim that sixteen of the returnees had come from the San Luis Rey Mission (Rustvold 1968). In either case, there is no reason to assume that the settlement at San Pasqual was not already occupied by non-mission Indians whose ancestors had lived there for centuries. Bancroft described the eighty-one native people who comprised the returnees as "Indians selected for the ... missions for their intelligence, good behavior, industry, and fitness in all respects for earning their own living and managing their own affairs" (Bancroft 1885:11).

Californio Santiago Argüello

Santiago Argüello had entered the Spanish Army as a cadet in Yerba Buena (San Francisco) in 1805, and spent his Spanish and Mexican years at the presidios of San Francisco, Santa Barbara, and San Diego. By 1817 he was paymaster at the Presidio of San Diego. In 1825, as he was chasing horse thieves near Vallecito, he came upon the San Felipe Valley and followed it to San Gabriel and Los Angeles, a path which became a well-worn desert route with time. In 1829 he was granted the first of three ranchos — Rancho Tia Juana. In 1833 and 1834 Argüello served as the revenue officer of San Diego.

By 1841 he was granted Rancho Trabuco, and in 1846 he was granted the ex-Mission San Diego, from the secularized Mission San Diego de Alcala lands. During the Mexican-American War he was friendly to the Americans and helped them, and he and his brother-in-law, Juan Bandini, issued an appeal to others not to resist the Americans. US soldiers were quartered at his house and he held a commission as captain in the US California Battalion. He was a member of the US California Military Territory Legislative Council in 1847, and later was appointed Collector of the Port of San Diego. He died on his Rancho Tia Juana in Baja, California, Mexico, in 1862.

Trask family oral history concludes that the family's La Chappa, Guachena, Nejo, and other ancestors may have lived within their own village in the San Pasqual Valley. As documented in the National Archives and Records Administration (NARA), historian John P. Harrington lent credence to the idea when he noted that one of his informants told him about several families who lived in the San Pasqual Valley during the 1800s, including the information that some of the La Chappas and Guachenas had lived in the San Pasqual Valley, "... with Osuna when the Guachenos and La Chappas are at a different place" (Harrington 1914:177-188). Another journal notation stated that: "There was a Rancheria, side by side near the river, about two miles in the gachegcal (valley), more or less, to the south lived an Indian by the name of LaChap. This LaChap family was another type of

Ranchos of San Diego County

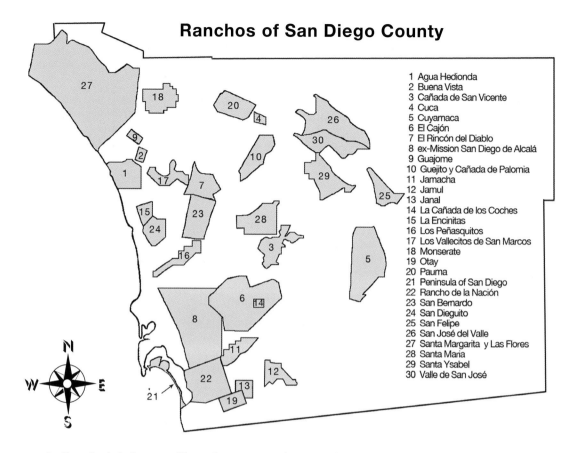

1 Agua Hedionda
2 Buena Vista
3 Cañada de San Vicente
4 Cuca
5 Cuyamaca
6 El Cajón
7 El Rincón del Diablo
8 ex-Mission San Diego de Alcalá
9 Guajome
10 Guejito y Cañada de Palomia
11 Jamacha
12 Jamul
13 Janal
14 La Cañada de los Coches
15 La Encinitas
16 Los Peñasquitos
17 Los Vallecitos de San Marcos
18 Monserate
19 Otay
20 Pauma
21 Peninsula of San Diego
22 Rancho de la Nación
23 San Bernardo
24 San Dieguito
25 San Felipe
26 San José del Valle
27 Santa Margarita y Las Flores
28 Santa Maria
29 Santa Ysabel
30 Valle de San José

Indian, had their own village, known as Selugpa. Selugpa meant to pull or to pluck, which was the name of their village" (Martinez N.d., N.p).

Mexican official Don Santiago Argüello was present in the San Pasqual Valley on that November day in 1835 when the Mexican government ceremonially presented the Ipai with the lands of the new civil pueblo and endowed them with Mexican citizenship, later writing a letter to the United States government describing the ceremony (Connolly Miskwish:2007).

Some of the neophytes who had been released from the missions went to work for the Californios, while others returned to their traditional lands. Some joined relatives and friends at locations that had been home to their people for thousands of years (Moyer 1969). George Phillips (1974) said that some of the native people refused to take the lands offered them after secularization because of the killings, exploitations, and abuses that they had suffered while in the servitude of the Spanish and Mexican mission authorities and soldiers. Instead, they returned to their native villages, desiring no further contact with those who had personally perpetrated or allowed the often-deadly mission abuses to occur.

The Kumeyaay people soon discovered that although the Mexican government assured them that these lands would remain theirs forever, official grants of huge tracts of land to other Mexican citizens would prove that the Indians had been much more loyal to their mission masters than the mission officials were going to be with them. San Diego County was the site of thirty of these huge ranchos. In 1836 Silvestre de la Portilla was given a land grant in Cupeño territory, at the southern half of their valley, which he named Rancho Valle de San Jose. In 1840 Jose Antonio Pico was given the northern half of the valley, which he called Rancho San Jose del Valle.

Michael Connolly Miskwish said:

> The implementation of the Secularization Act was one of utter betrayal to the spirit of the law and the faith of the Indian people. Instead of the Mexican government granting individual lands to the Kumeyaay, they created huge Ranchos across the lands by the Governor for his friends. Many of those lands had been promised to the converted Kumeyaay, while others were far into the areas under the direct control of the unconverted Kumeyaay. Some of the converts chose to stay and work as laborers on the ranchos or in towns. Others were forced to labor on the ranchos like slaves, or were hired out in slave gangs by cruel overseers. Many others fled the coastal areas to live in the mountains with their Kumeyaay relatives, who either had not left the San Diego backcountry, or who had chosen to return there. Those emancipated neophytes who chose to live within these more inland areas, brought their knowledge of how the missions had been operated, what the Mexican people were like, and the strengths and weaknesses of both. This helped the Kumeyaay to become much more effective in their resistance to the Mexican invaders, and more effective in how they strategized their resistances and raids. They also brought their Catholic religion with them to the mountains, and a population of Christianized Kumeyaay began to assimilate with the mountain Sh'mulqs (clans) (2007:65).

During the late 1830s local native people, unhappy with the way secularization and the granting of lands to Mexicans were affecting their lives, responded to the situation by carrying out rebellions of various types, including plundering ranchos at San Bernardo, Jamul, Tecate, and Tijuana during the years 1835-1837 and carrying out raids at Rancho Jamul (*San Diego Union* 1938; Carrico 2010:18).

Throughout the dramatic changes of the Spanish, Mexican, and American periods, Ipai people and their leaders had to organize themselves and make important decisions in order to survive and resist the invasion of non-Indian peoples and cultures throughout their traditional territory. How did Ipai people respond to these challenges through leadership and governance during these critical periods? Like clan structure, tribal leadership among the Ipai was flexible and pragmatic. During the Spanish and Mexican periods, leadership probably remained largely traditional, based on the authority of the headmen of local bands. One example was José Panto, an important leader and historical personality who led the people of San Pasqual during difficult times.

Panto signs the treaty of 1852. *Drawing: Robert Freeman.*

José Panto: Tribal Leadership during a Tumultuous Time

After secularization of the San Diego Mission, Mexican officials named Juan Cuerpo (Farris 1997) as the *alcalde* or leader at San Pasqual. Cuerpo may have been a former San Diego Mission neophyte and one of the eighty-one native people to be removed to the San Pasqual Valley in 1835. Sometime between 1835 and 1837, Jose Panto appeared upon the scene at San Pasqual, and replaced Cuerpo. Though it is not certain where or when Panto was born, he spent the next thirty-seven years as captain of the San Pasqual people. In 1854 Panto replaced Tomas as the captain of Mesa Grande and eventually served both reservations until his death in 1874. According to Glenn Farris, "The link with Mesa Grande is important because when the people of San Pasqual were forced out of their homes, many of them apparently migrated to Mesa Grande" (1997:149).

As to his involvement in the appointment of Panto to be captain of the Mesa Grande Indians, Cave Johnson Couts, Indian Subagent for San Diego County, wrote to Federal Indian Agent B.D. Wilson on May 7, 1854, saying, "I only sought the appointment of the San Luis Indians, and never meddled with the Diegueños until the most prominent Rancherias in their midst called twice, requesting the removal of Tomas and appointment of Panto" (Caughey 1952:TS).

Because it was not known conclusively whether Panto had ever been at the San Diego Mission, speculation (Spier 1923) has focused on the fact that Ipai captains did not have to be from the clan of the native people they were leading. Farris (1997) believed that Panto was baptized January 11, 1817, at the age of 14, with a group of native people from Santa Ysabel, and that he was from the village of Matamo, also called the Rancheria of San Juan de Matamo, possibly located between the land grants of El Cajon and Jamacha (Harlow 1987). Various other spellings of Panto's name include Ponto or Pontho (Carrico 2010).

By 1845, on the eve of the fall of California to the United States, Panto was well acknowledged by Mexican authorities as the captain of the San Pasqual village and was considered a highly respected leader. With the American takeover of California in 1848, Panto sought alliances and treaties with officials from the new government that he had aided. During the Garra Revolt of 1851, Panto refused to join the insurrection and remained loyal to the Americans. In January 1852, Panto was one of twenty-two important Ipai/Tipai leaders who signed the Treaty of Santa Ysabel. Panto, listed as Pantho of San Pasqual, made the trek to Santa Ysabel, no doubt seeking to ensure land rights and recognition for his people. The treaties of 1852, however, were never ratified by the United States Congress.

Censuses for the year 1860 for the San Pasqual and Mesa Grande villages show Panto as captain of both (Farris 1997), but Panto's age differs by ten years. George W. Barnes gathered the information for both sites, but the San Pasqual Census shows Panto as age fifty, while the Mesa Grande Census shows him as sixty. According to the 1860 Census of San Pasqual Valley, José Panto had 100 acres of improved land, with a cash value of his farm at $1,000. He also had farming equipment, horses, milk cows, oxen, sheep, and cattle valued at $2,200. With a total assessed value of more than $3,000, José Panto was one of the more prosperous men, white or Indian, in the region and a man of high status.

According to anthropologist Florence Shipek,

> All the people listed in the 1870 Census were classified as white, even Jose Panto, and his wife was shown as Dolores. In an additional 1870 Federal Census taken of the San Pasqual Valley Reservation, almost all the residents were identified as white. A few were Mexicans who are known from later records to have had children with San Pasqual Indian women (Shipek 2012:MS).

Throughout the thirty-seven years that Panto served as captain of both the San Pasqual and Mesa Grande people, he met with a near constant parade of American officials from federal and state governments. He consistently pleaded for the US government to recognize

Ysidro Nejo standing on the site of Panto's house at the San Pasqual village in 1927. *Photo believed to be by J. P. Harrington.*

Awi Kuesaay: The Witched Rock or Ringing Rock of San Pasqual

the Indian citizenship and land rights that had been conferred on the Ipai by the Mexican government in 1824.

José Panto may have led his people longer than any other Indian leader in San Diego County. Panto's time as captain spanned the Mexican era, the US-Mexican War, the Antonio Garra Uprising, the United States Treaties of 1852, the ill-fated and short-lived San Pasqual Reservation of 1870, and the dawn of the forced removal of his people from their homeland. Near the end of his life, Panto met with Judge Benjamin Hayes in San Diego to press the claims of his people and to ensure that he had the required paperwork needed to prove his peoples' claims to the lands. In 1874 he was preparing, along with Olegario Calac, a Luiseño leader from Rincon, to travel to Washington DC to meet with President U.S. Grant and present the president with Mexican documents that clearly recognized the San Pasqual Indians' citizenship and land rights. Tragically, on April 27, 1874, Panto was thrown from his horse and died at the San Pasqual village.

His place in local politics and history was reflected in a lengthy obituary that the *San Diego Union* published May 3, 1874, noting that Panto was of "polite manners and good character." With his death, an era drew to a close for the Ipai of San Diego County. Ominously, the *San Diego Union*, whose editors knew that whites had filed claims for all of the San Pasqual Valley, noted in his May 3, 1874, obituary that: "Now that Panto, who governed his people so well, is gone, it is believed that they will not linger long upon their old planting grounds."

Sadly, these words proved prophetic; within a few years the Ipai of San Pasqual Valley would be removed at gunpoint from their ancestral home.

Sometime in the decade between 1835 and 1846, a group of warriors from the east, probably Quechan from the Yuma region, attacked families at San Pasqual, stealing livestock and kidnapping at least one Ipai woman. This event and the ensuing Battle of the Nameless Hill were well remembered by the people of San Pasqual as late as the 1920s; the story was told to both the anthropologist J.P. Harrington and to a local pioneer resident of San Pasqual, Elizabeth Judson Roberts.

According to both stories, the intruding warriors were tracked down by headman Panto and his men, and chased to a point just south of the San Dieguito River and west of the current site of Lake Hodges. In addition to Captain Panto, the San Pasqual warriors who took part in the battle were Miguel Kwiskwis, known also as Kwalmitsis; Bautiste known also by his native name of Kujás; Pedro Duro; Carlos; and Santiago, also known as Tapuhuir.

The Quechan force was pursued and driven to a hillside east of present-day Interstate 15 and on the southern slope of the hills above what is now Lake Hodges. Panto ordered the hillside to be torched and with what was reported to be the aid of strong spirits that brought the eastern winds beckoned by the sounds from San Pasqual Valley's *awi kuesaay* (ringing rocks), all but one of the trapped men were burned to death. Later the charred bodies of the Quechan were covered with rocks to form cairns and were left there.

In 1925 one of Harrington's informants related that only a few years before that time, an Indian who still lived just below the burial cairns near the San Dieguito River said that human bones could still be seen among the rocks. Out of respect for the fallen foes, Panto ordered that stone memorials be constructed for each of the men and, when completed, tobacco was burned and war songs were chanted. This place where the stone cairns were constructed was known as *awisilut*, meaning "put the stones there" (Carrico 2010:TS).

While Panto was serving his long tenure as captain of the San Pasqual Valley, newcomers were attempting to secure the lands on which the Ipai lived. San Diegan Bonifacio Lopez took a petition to California Governor Pio Pico on September 10, 1845, and requested that the governor grant him the lands of the San Pasqual pueblo. Lopez said that the native people there were "disreputable, and had allowed the pueblo to go into decay" (Farris

An Indian woman washes at Warner Hot Springs (Agua Caliente), ca. 1901. *Photo: George P. Thresher, California Historical Society Collection, Doheny Memorial Library, University of Southern California.*

1997:N.p.). Pico responded by sending an official of the district of San Diego (possibly Santiago Argüello) to investigate conditions at the valley. The emissary reported on his visit of September 23, 1845, to the San Pasqual Valley:

> This settlement comprises sixty-one Christian souls, and forty-four unconverted Indians, with dwellings after their manner, huts of tule forming a kind of irregular Plazuela [a small square], the police thereof is under the care of an alcalde of the Christian residents appointed by the First Alcalde's Court of this place, and of the unconverted Capitan Panto (Farris 1997:N.p).

The report also told of the condition of the lands, which the chronicler said were in excellent shape, and he noted that agricultural pursuits were achieved as the result of the native people of San Pasqual Valley working together cooperatively to raise both stock and crops.

In December 1846, John S. Griffin, an assistant surgeon in the US Army, described the Ipai village at San Felipe (Griffin 1846), though he saw no Indians there. He did see cultivated cornfields and pea patches. When these intruders could find no wood for a fire, they burned the lodges of the Indians and used the wood for their campfires. This would be but the beginning of the Indians of San Diego County having to deal with the invasions of Americans from the eastern part of the United States. Bancroft (1884) documented that during this time the Mexican provincial governor in California passed resolutions that set aside funds to reward its citizens for killing native people.

In 1846 Warner's Trading Post was established (Moyer 1969), and an Indian named Felipe Castillo applied for and received a major land grant from the Mexican government

Felicita and her husband, Jose Morales. *Photo: Escondido History Center.*

Felicita, possibly the daughter
of Panto, lived until 1915.
Photo: Escondido History Center.

77

for a rancho in the San Felipe Valley. This fertile valley had traditionally been the home of the Ipai. A half century later, the US government would eventually eject the Ipai living there from their homes and forcibly remove them to Pala. There the Ipai would live alongside Luiseños of Pala and Cupeños, who had also been removed only a few months prior from their homes at Warner Springs (Agua Caliente).

Felicita La Chappa Morales: A Lasting Legend

There is a park in Escondido named after Felicita La Chappa, the woman some (Ryan 1980; Peet 1973) called the last Indian princess of San Diego County, and who was described as Captain Panto's eldest daughter. Some conjecture centers around whether Panto is actually Felicita's biological father, or whether as has been common in many Ipai families, the captain may have adopted her as part of his clan. Panto is sometimes shown as born in 1810 (Census of San Pasqual 1852) and Felicita as born in 1820 (Census of San Pasqual 1900 and Ryan 1980).

Frances Ryan (1980) noted that Felicita was twelve years old in 1832 when she was baptized by a Catholic priest in the San Pasqual Valley at the river near her home. According to Felicita, "at this time the tule huts of our village stood thick on either side of the river, for the mission at San Diego was no longer prosperous, and many Indians had come to our valley from that place" (Roberts 1994:90).

Captain Panto appeared on the 1852 Census of the San Pasqual Indians as forty-two years of age, which would mean he was born in 1810 and may have, in fact, taken Felicita as his daughter in name, though she might not have been his blood relative, since according to Ryan's and Elizabeth Roberts' accounts she would have been born in 1820.

The 1869 San Pasqual Census showed Felicita's age as forty, indicating that she would have been born in 1829. She was shown as having married in 1860, and living at the time of the census in the San Pasqual Valley with her husband, Jose (Jessie) A. Morales. Morales is thought to have been a north county Luiseño Indian.

The 1900 Census for San Pasqual showed Felicita as age eighty, married to Jesse A. Morales, age seventy-eight, and living in the San Pasqual Valley. Felicita and Morales were noted as being married forty years—since 1860. Felicita La Chappa Morales died October 29, 1915.

Mary Peet chronicled Felicita La Chappa's life and death, and told not only of attending the princess's funeral in the San Pasqual Valley, but included a song that one of the women there sang in honor of Felicita:

"The millionaires, the governors,
And the poor Indians,
All come to rest at last
In Mother Earth.
There is no difference" (Peet 1973:89-92)

The Battle of San Pasqual. *Drawing: Robert Freeman.*

Peet added:

> Thus she sang. When she had finished, a man stepped forward, removed the cover of the plain little County coffin and all drew near for a last look at Felicita La Chappa, oldest resident of San Pasqual and daughter of Pontho, the last of the hereditary chiefs of the San Pasqual Indians" (Peet, Mary Rockwood 1973:89-92).

At this time the question of Panto's and Felicita's relationship remains a mystery and a challenge for researchers.

The Americans Lose the Battle of San Pasqual but Win the War

As the Ipai in the Valley of San Pasqual were adjusting to continued abuses and changes in lifestyle, another group of invaders — Americans — were heading to San Diego County from the eastern United States. Under the command of General Stephen Watts Kearny, these "Dragoons" or soldiers of the Army of the West, had traveled on foot 1,200 miles from Ft. Leavenworth, Kansas.

These American soldiers would soon find themselves fighting with Mexican troops under the direction of Captain Andres Pico, in an important early military encounter of the Mexican-American War, the Battle of San Pasqual.

The Americans had learned on December 2, 1846 (Bibb 1976), as they camped at Warner Springs, that all of California, excepting San Diego, Monterey, and San Francisco, was in control of the Mexicans. General Kearny also learned that Mr. Stokes, an Englishman, lived at Santa Ysabel, fifteen miles away, and the general sent out Bill Marshall, who was

"We saw soldiers that were not Mexicans come riding down the mountainside. They looked like ghosts coming through the mist." *Drawing: Robert Freeman.*

Ysidro Nejo (also known as Isidro Nejo) standing on rocks at San Bernardo where the American soldiers under General Kearny were entrenched at the Battle of San Pasqual in 1846. *Photo: E. H. Davis, San Diego History Center.*

tending Warner's Ranch in the absence of its owner, to ask Stokes for a meeting. Stokes returned with Marshall to Warner's Ranch and confirmed all that Marshall had shared with Kearny. Stokes said he was neutral, but offered the Americans any information of which he was aware, agreeing to take a letter from General Kearny to Commodore Stockton in San Diego, since he was traveling there the next day. On December 4, 1846, in the midst of rain, the Americans took their mules and horses and went to Stokes's place at Santa Ysabel, where he fed them and provided some fresh though unbroken horses. It was still raining on December 5 when the Americans traveled to Ramona, where they met up with Captain Gillespie, Navy Lieutenant Edward Beale, and thirty-six men, all who came in response to the letter that Kearny had sent to Stockton via Stokes (Peet 1973).

The reinforcements had brought news that the Mexican forces were nine miles away in the San Pasqual Valley, and the Americans sent out a scouting party that same night. While patrolling the San Pasqual area the party dropped a US Army blanket, alerting the Mexican forces to the fact that the American troops were in the vicinity. At 2:00 a.m. eighty-five American men began their quest to surprise the Mexican troops, taking along two howitzers. Just before daybreak, on the north side of the San Pasqual Valley near the present-day bridge, close to the knoll where the native people had created their cemetery and their Ipai village, the battle with Pico and his eighty to one hundred-fifty Mexican forces began.

The Mexicans were well-fed and well-rested, as were their animals. The Mexicans also had long lances, in comparison with the Americans, who were at a disadvantage with their tired animals and short sabers, since the rain the night before had left their muzzle-loading guns useless. On December 6, 1846, the battle erupted on a cold, wet, and foggy morning. During the ensuing battle, the Mexicans saw American troops traveling down the hill to the east with the two howitzers and headed west, but the mules connected to the howitzer panicked, broke loose, and ran away. The Mexican troops captured the howitzer, turned back on the Americans, and according to a Mexican lad who lived his whole life in the valley, they lassoed the Americans, pulling them from their mules and stabbing them with the long lances. According to Peet, the battle of San Pasqual lasted about ten minutes (Peet 1973).

Dr. John S. Griffin, surgeon of the American expedition, wrote: "Captain Johnston who led the first charge was killed by a gunshot wound in the head. In all, 35 men were killed and wounded and I think there were not to exceed 50 men who saw the enemy" (Peet 1973:46).

Captain Panto's daughter, Felicita, about age twenty-six at the time of the battle, watched what was happening that day and later said:

> Early one rainy morning we saw soldiers that were not Mexicans come riding down the mountainside. They looked like ghosts coming through the mist, and then the fighting began. The Indians fled in fear to the mountains on the north side of the valley, from where they looked down and watched the battle. All day long they fought. We saw some Americans killed and knew they were in a bad way. That afternoon

Mule Hill, site of the Battle of San Pasqual, 1846. *Photo: San Diego History Center.*

Pontho, my father, called his men together and asked them if they wished to help the Americanos in their trouble. The men said they did. When darkness was near, Pontho sent a messenger to the Mexican chief telling him to trouble the Americans no more that night else the Indians would help the Americans. And the Mexican chief heeded the message and the Americans were left to bury their dead and to rest because of my father's message. The Americans do not know of this but my people know of it (Roberts 1994:90).

A Private Dunne, said to have taken part in the Battle of San Pasqual, wrote later (Roberts 1907) that he was an eyewitness to the fighting and one of the participants in the battle. He said that the troops under General Kearny retreated to a nearby knoll and were surrounded by the California forces. The knoll was later called Mule Hill and got its name after the wounded and near-starving American soldiers spotted a wayward mule leaving the enemy forces and quickly claimed it as their own. McGrew said that, "They captured a fat mule from Pico, shot him, cooked him and ate him" (McGrew 1922:49).

Dunne added that on the second evening:

An Indian from San Pasqual reached the hill, and no person in the command being able to talk to him, except Kit Carson in Spanish. This Indian guided Lieutenant Beale and Carson that night, from the hill, to San Diego. They passed through a strong guard of Mexicans right on the road — by the Indian directing them what way to take (Roberts 1907:220).

Larry Stirling said in a *Daily Transcript* article of 2007 entitled, *"Did We Ever Thank Chemuctah?"* that: "Three men agreed to go on what amounted to suicide missions: the redoubtable Kit Carson, Navy Lieutenant Edward Beale, and a Diegueño tribe member recorded as Chemuctah. What courage to undertake a long trek at night through hundreds of mounted enemies to get help!" (Stiring 2007:N.p.). Stirling wrote that all three men removed their shoes to avoid being detected by the Mexican forces that surrounded them. Malcolm Irving, however, cited *Tales of a Salty Sailor* as his source when he concurred with Stirling's view that the third man was the local native Chemuctah, adding that the native person had kept his shoes on when the other two travelers had removed theirs, managing to be the first to arrive in San Diego to procure reinforcements for the Americans trapped in the San Pasqual Valley (Irving, personal communication 1978).

William Smythe, however, believed that the native person accompanying Kit Carson and Edward Beale was Captain Panto of the San Pasqual Band. He noted that: "Alcalde Panto had arrived before Beale and Kit Carson arrived after." Smythe added that as Carson and Beale traveled barefoot through the Mexican lines, on the journey to San Diego:

> At one time Beale thought all was over. Pressing Carson's thigh to get his attention, and putting his mouth upon his ear, he whispered, "We are gone; let us jump and fight it out." Carson said, "No, I have been in worse places before and Providence saved me." His religious reliance encouraged the sinking hopes of Beale, and they got through (Smythe 1908:222).

Smythe concluded that the Indian arrived in San Diego first, then Edward Beale, and finally Kit Carson. He added further details as to how the three messengers secured reinforcements for those stranded at Mule Hill after the Battle of San Pasqual.

At 10:00 p.m. on the 9th a messenger arrived, who made the urgency of the situation unmistakable. This was Lieutenant Beale, bleeding, exhausted, reduced to a skeleton and scarcely recognizable. He was so weak that the pickets had to carry him in, and soon after telling his story he became delirious" (Smythe 1908:218). By December 11, 1846, at 2:00 p.m. reinforcements of two hundred fifteen sailors and marines who had been drilling on Presidio hill with one fieldpiece of artillery, under the command of Lieutenant Andrew F. V. Gray of the Congress, and Lieutenant Jacob Zeilin, also of the Congress, in charge of the marines, had reached Kearny's forces (Carrico 2010:TS).

The Ipai of San Pasqual Valley also aided the Americans who had survived by helping them bury their dead (Roberts 1994). The notes of John P. Harrington (Harrington 1925) showed that a San Pasqual Indian, Pedro La Chappa, had killed animals he owned and prepared food for those same surviving Americans. Informant Ysidro Nejo later pointed out Pedro La Chappa's house to Harrington as the two walked through the San Pasqual Valley, and noted that the residence was in the northeast section of the valley.

Related to the Battle of San Pasqual, the Pauma Massacre occurred in December 1846 when a group of eleven Californio lancers, who had been in the Battle at San Pasqual, traveled northeast to Rancho Pauma. Along the way they allegedly stole horses belonging to the Pauma Band of Luiseño Indians. That night Luiseño Captain Manuelito Cota captured the Californio lancers and took the eleven men to Rancho Potrero, an Indian ranchería, where they were executed (Hyer 2001).

General José María Flores was in Los Angeles in early January of 1847 (Miller and Ebbeling 2010), when he learned what had happened. He immediately sent Jose del Carmen Lugo, of San Bernardino, to Pauma. Mountain Cahuilla Captain Juan Antonio and some of his men met the Mexican forces as they were nearing Pauma, and the groups joined together. Jose Ramon Carrillo was at Mission San Luis Rey with additional Mexican forces, and when Lugo learned of their whereabouts, he recruited them too. Next, Lugo placed his three groups in strategic positions, with the goal being to deceive the Luiseños at Pauma as to their whereabouts. Captain Juan Antonio learned that the Luiseño forces were in a canyon east of Temecula, so he placed his men at a nearby meadow, while Lugo and his men joined at the opposite end of the valley, with both groups stationed on rolling hills.

When the Luiseños realized that Carrillo and his men were approaching, they came out attacking, and, as part of their plan, the Carrillo group turned and fled. As the Luiseño continued their attack, Lugo and the Cahuilla suddenly turned and came their way, capturing them with their strategy of surprise. Captain Juan Antonio and his men maintained their positions, eventually taking over custody of the Luiseños, and, finally, killing them all.

The number of Luiseño men who died that day is uncertain—some reports say from thirty-three to forty, but Jose Lugo said in later years that his forces killed a hundred Luiseños in the canyon, located where the Vail Lake Dam is presently situated. Due to sudden and severe rainstorms that occurred shortly after the attack, it would be three weeks before the families of the Luiseño men killed that day were able to retrieve the bodies. On January 25, 1847, the families were able to bury the casualties of the Temecula Massacre in a cemetery which is today located south of the Temecula Parkway.

On January 7, 1847, as the US-Mexican War was concluding in southern California (Hyer 2001), Commodore Robert F. Stockton's American troops fought with Californios under the direction of General José María Flores at San Gabriel. Two days later the Americans and Californios exchanged artillery fire near Los Angeles, at the Battle of San Gabriel, the last battle of the US-Mexican War. On January 10, Stockton and his troops raised the American flag over the small Mexican community of Los Angeles. By January 13 the Californios surrendered, and California came under the control of the Americans.

As plans were being made for the Americans to take over, the last Mexican governor of California, Pio Pico, was preparing to leave. Abel Stearns, next-in-charge, claimed that Pico gave out large land grants as gifts in Upper California right up to the minute that the Americans took over. These land grants were measured in the larger measurement of leagues rather than acres, and Stearns explained, "And that was the way things were … not as it is now, when they measure it off by the inch to you" (McGrew 1922:37).

On February 2, 1848, although there was not yet any military or civil rule in California, the United States and Mexico entered into the Treaty of Guadalupe Hidalgo (Castillo 1990), with Mexico ceding California and the Southwest to the United States. America took over certain claims of American citizens against the government of Mexico, and paid the defeated country $15 million.

In 1824 the Mexican Constitution had granted Mexican citizenship to Indians in California, and the United States promised to uphold the rights of Mexican citizens in the new American territory. The Americans had no right to take over Indian lands, and after one year the native people should have become American citizens, with their property rights protected under the United States Constitution. Hyer said: "In fact, in the treaty with Mexico all native peoples in the newly acquired territory are referred to as 'savage tribes'" (2001:207).

In 1849, soon after the Americans took control of California, the commissioner of Indian Affairs in Washington DC, wrote a letter to Adam Johnson, superintendent of Indian Affairs in California, stating that little was known about the population, condition, or situation of the Indians in the state. He could give no specific instructions relative to them and told Superintendent Johnson to "count, scrutinize and otherwise become knowledgeable of the various tribes, so that in the future, relations and treaties can be intelligently formulated" (Lea 1849:2).

1850s: Dealing with a New Government: The American Period

As Panto strived to ally with the Americans and gain justice for his people, a multitude of changes were occurring in California and San Diego County. The 1850s presented a variety of challenges for the Ipai. California had entered the Union in 1848 as a free state, but most of the California Legislature was made up of whites who immediately began passing laws that restricted the rights of anyone not belonging to the new American ruling society. Native people received none of the liberties that Americans and others claimed for themselves. Many native people refused to be victims, however, and continued to fight the invaders, committing themselves to keeping their traditional cultural ways.

During the American period, the Ipai and the Luiseño/Cahuilla to the north soon realized that a different type of leader was required—one that held more centralized power and could negotiate effectively with US government authorities. The Ipai noted that the American leaders did not want to deal with or negotiate with a series of "headmen" from multiple villages. They gradually adapted to the evolving American political power structure (Carrico 1987).

With the discovery of gold in northern California, thousands of miners and immigrants from the East, along with foreigners from other parts of the world, invaded California, treating those who had been here for thousands of years as inferior, second-class people—certainly not second-class citizens, because the United States government promptly refused to honor its promises to make the native-people citizens of America, though the Mexican government had bestowed citizenship on the native population of San Diego County in 1824.

In 1850 the California state government and the US federal government went head-to-head on the question of who had jurisdiction over the indigenous people in California. An 1832 US Supreme Court decision, *Worcester v. Georgia*, had ascertained that the federal government was the authority designated to deal with Indian Affairs. However, Hyer noted that when California passed its *Act for the Government and Protection of California Indians (California Statute Chapter 133)* on April 22, 1850, "In essence — the Federal Government, contrary to the wishes of the Founding Fathers, who instituted national control of Indian policy — initially allowed the state of California and its racist white residents to reign supreme in Indian affairs" (Hyer 2001:60). Most of the sections of this Act remained in effect until 1937. A brief overview of some of the sections in the act give clues as to how the lives of the native people must have changed during these times:

Section 1 placed Anglos in authority over native people, and local justices of the peace held jurisdiction in all cases involving them. This gave great power to the Americans at the municipal and county levels. Custody of Indian children, criminal cases, water rights, and land and property rights were routinely settled in favor of the anglos, by judges who detested the Indians.

Section 2 set aside lands stipulated as being sufficient for the necessary wants of the native people, so they could resettle in their traditional regions. Magistrates could give the rest of the land to whites, who claimed to own the property.

Section 3 assured that whites could gain legal custody of Indian children — and some were indentured for as long as ten years.

Section 5 guaranteed labor contracts between Indians and whites, though Indians often could not read or understand what they were signing.

Section 6 said that judges could not use any Indian testimony to convict whites. Their word was considered worthless in a court of law.

Section 10 prohibited native people from setting grasslands on fire, though they had managed their lands in this way for thousands of years in order to encourage the growth of plants and grasses used as food. Indians who lit such fires were subject to fines or punishment.

Section 14 said that if any Indian received a fine and couldn't pay, a white person could post bond and make the Indian work until the cost of the bail was covered.

Section 20 said that law enforcement officials could apprehend any Indian found to be loitering, strolling about or begging. The "vagrant" could then be hired out to the highest bidder for up to four months. Native people were also prohibited from selling or transferring guns (Hyer 2001:59).

An artist's depiction of Antonio Garra.
Drawing by Robert Freeman.

The increasing presence of non-Indians threatened Indian survival and traditional lifeways. Some tribal leaders put aside their long-standing differences and began to create alliances to resist the invaders. *Drawing: Robert Freeman.*

The Garra Revolt

Historian Herbert Lockwood described the notable Cupeño Captain Antonio Garra as follows:

> The chief of the tribe living in the vicinity of Warner's Ranch [Agua Caliente] was a remarkable man called Antonio Garra. He had received a good education at the San Luis Rey Mission and had a few ideas about taxation without representation; Indians, incidentally, were not allowed to vote in California (Lockwood 1967:76-77).

The *San Diego Union* newspaper called Garra "a man of energy, determination and bravery" (Hyer 2001:88). In the early 1850s, more of the native people of San Diego County perceived the true nature of the American invaders, increasingly realizing that their presence threatened not only their survival, but the traditional lifeways of those who did survive. Some native people who had not been friendly with other nearby native bands or clans now put aside their differences and long-standing enmities and began to create alliances with each other. At the same time, some of them responded to the invaders by disobeying their decrees, by avoiding entering into unfair legal contracts with them, and by working only for those who treated them fairly. In opposition to state laws, some of the native people continued to burn grasslands, and some refused to be a part of what they considered to be an immoral anglo system (Hyer 2001).

87

Ranch House at Warner's Ranch. *Photo: Philipp Rittermann, Library of Congress.*

The increased number of Americans who were passing through or settling in the San Jose Valley, the location of Warner Hot Springs [Agua Caliente], only increased the pressures felt by the native people in that region. The intruders not only killed the local game on which the native people relied for their sustenance, but allowed their animals to feed on the plant-life and grasses that were an important part of the native peoples' diets. Antonio Garra and others could clearly see that the Americans would take all of the land and resources that they could get.

By 1850 Garra had made alliances with some of the Americans in the Warner's Ranch area, including Bill Marshall, who was married to the daughter of Cupeño native Jose Noca. Marshall had been born about 1827 in Providence, Rhode Island, and had, according to his own account, arrived in San Diego via a whaling ship, possibly named Hope, in 1844 at the age of about 17. By 1846 when the United States had declared war upon Mexico, Marshall was working for Jonathan Trumball Warner at Warner's Ranch, taking care of the ranch and watching out for Mrs. Warner and the couple's children, since Warner had been taken into custody by the Americans for suspected disloyalty to the American cause (Bibb 1976).

When General Kearny arrived at Warner's Ranch on December 2, 1846, with a hundred troops, weary after their march from Ft. Leavenworth, Kansas, Marshall greeted them (Bibb 1976) and aided them, informing the Americans that the Mexicans still held control of the whole state, except the ports at San Diego, Monterey, and San Francisco. Marshall told Kearny about a Mr. Stokes, the Englishman mentioned earlier in this chapter, who lived fifteen miles from Warner's Ranch. Kearny responded by sending Marshall to summon Stokes back to their site. When Stokes returned, he agreed with all that Marshall had told the Americans and eventually aided the American forces in several ways, though he told them he was neutral. Stokes agreed to take a letter from Kearny to Commodore Stockton in San Diego the next day. When the Army forces arrived at his home December 4, he gave them food and fresh, though unbroken horses.

At this time, Bill Marshall would have only been about nineteen years old, perhaps considered by Kearny to be too young and inexperienced to help his cause, since the American general chose to send Mr. Stokes with letters to San Diego requesting reinforcements, resulting in troops from San Diego joining the Americans at Ramona on December 5.

Historian Herbert Lockwood said about Marshall: "A sometime clerk at the store at Warner's Ranch, Bill Marshall was a jump-ship sailor who lived with the Indians. Garra poured out his grievances into Marshall's ear ... " (Lockwood 1967:76). Leland Bibb (1976) noted that Benjamin Hayes made a journal entry saying that the store Marshall operated for Jonathan Trumball Warner was a saloon, a pawn shop, and a place where the native people could buy liquor for ten cents a drink or a dollar a pint.

In 1850, the county treasurer of San Diego (Hyer 2001) was assessing taxes of $600 per person on the native people of San Diego County, though they were not citizens of the country or the state. San Diego County Sheriff Agoston Haraszthy determined in September 1851 that he was going to enforce the assessment, and when native people refused to pay, he confiscated their lands and property.

General Joshua Bean, in charge of the state militia in southern California, came to San Diego in the summer of 1851 and advised the native people that they didn't have to pay the taxes. Sheriff Haraszthy notified the attorney general of the impasse, and the attorney general ruled that Haraszthy was, indeed, to collect the taxes. Haraszthy then demanded that the Cupeños pay $250 in tax money, along with 18 cows and 5 horses and mules to cover the taxes. Antonio Garra's people "grudgingly and only reluctantly" handed over the money and their animals (Hyer 2001:62).

Hyer observed:

> One must at least partially blame Juan Jose Warner for the increased friction. The man from Connecticut seems to have been a dishonest individual who improved his lot at the expense of others" (Hyer 2001:61). Known as a trapper, clerk and merchant, the American, whose original name was Jonathan Trumball Warner had immersed

Agua Caliente Indian houses at Warner's Ranch, circa 1900. *Photo: California Historical Society Collection, Doheny Memorial Library, University of Southern California. Photographer unknown.*

himself into the Mexican culture, learning to speak fluent Spanish and changing his name to the Spanish version. In 1844 he filled out paperwork requesting that Governor Manuel Micheltorena give him a land grant for the whole San Jose Valley, the location of Warner's Springs and the Indian village of Agua Caliente. He received his grant that same year (Hyer 2001).

In 1836 and 1840 two Mexican citizens, Silvestre de la Portilla and Jose Antonio Pico, had also been given Mexican land grants. By 1845, when Warner brought his family to the area, the Cupeños had already convinced the Portilla and Pico families that they were unwelcome neighbors of the native people who lived at Agua Caliente. Cupeño raids on the two ranchos and the commandeering of horses and other animals, along with supplies, had convinced the Portilla and Pico families to abandon their properties.

As Antonio Garra became increasingly aware of the Americans' influence on native peoples' lifeways, he came to believe that the invaders must be driven out. He consulted frequently with Bill Marshall (Pourade 1963), who encouraged Garra to believe that the Californios and Mexicans would surely join the side of the native people once a revolt had begun. Garra listened and sent runners between the Pacific Coast and the Colorado River, from the San Joaquin Valley south, and into the upper part of Baja California.

Garra devised a plan to wipe out the American garrison at Camp Independence on the Colorado River, then to go on to the coast in order to attack San Diego, Los Angeles, and Santa Barbara. He began sharing his plans with other groups of Indians, and with some Mexicans, including Jose Joaquin Ortega and Jose Antonio Estudillo. Garra sent messengers to Captain Panto at San Pasqual, to Luiseño leader Pablo Apis at Temecula, to Mountain Cahuilla Captain Juan Antonio in the San Bernardino area, to the native people from along the Colorado River, and to the Tipai south of the border, asking them to join him in his efforts to expel the Americans (Hyer 2001).

Garra pled with those he hoped would join him in his efforts by saying, "We have got to help with our lives, because we are invited to lose them" (Evans 1966:342). In his appeal to Captain Juan Antonio he stated: "If we lose this war all will be lost — the world! If we gain this war, then it is forever; never will it stop; this war is for a whole life" (Hyer 2001:63). In addition to support from Marshall, Garra managed to add the support of Ortega and Estudillo, but captains Panto, Apis, and Juan Antonio never joined with the Cupeño leader. As reported in a newspaper article (Hayes n.d.), "Confessions of William Marshall," the American said later before his execution that he had been threatened with death if he didn't join in supporting Antonio Garra's resistance movement.

By the middle of November 1851 (Hyer 2001), Garra and his followers had attacked Camp Independence at Yuma twice, on consecutive nights, shooting arrows into the stockade and attempting to crash through the wood and brush barrier surrounding the camp. They also attacked a group of Americans herding sheep nearby. Five whites were killed, along with ten of Garra's men. When Quechan Indians from the Colorado River quarreled with the Cupeños over how to divide the 3,000 sheep, the Quechan chose to leave the resistance group, and Garra and his allies headed home to the San Jose Valley.

On November 21, 1851, Pablo Apis, leader of the Luiseño Indians at Temecula, wrote to the *alcalde* of San Diego referring to the uprising that was taking place and said, "... We [the Temecula village] wish to leave here for the Mission of San Luis Rey ... until things are settled" (Rios 1851:Stearns Collection). According to a January 1, 1852, article in the *San Diego Herald*, Apis returned to Temecula with his group of Luiseños at the end of December.

As Garra was returning to Agua Caliente from Camp Independence in Yuma, he learned that some Cahuillas from Los Coyotes and some Agua Caliente Cupeños wanted to attack Warner's Ranch. On November 22, 1851, Garra was recuperating at his home from a personal illness, and Jonathan Trumball Warner had sent his family to San Diego to assure their safety. A hundred native men joined together and attacked Warner's Ranch that day. Warner and his hired hand held off the attackers and protected a small boy who had been left with Warner, until their ammunition ran out, then Warner escaped with the boy, amid a hail of gunfire, but the hired hand was killed (Lockwood 1967). The Cahuillas and Cupeños then drove off all the stock and burned the ranch (Hyer 2001), destroying all of Warner's belongings — including 250 cattle, five wagons, tools, rifles, and saddles, having a value of $59,000 (33rd Congress: Doc. 4). These native people had effectively evicted Jonathan Warner from the valley. From Warner Springs they went to Agua Caliente, where they killed four Americans who were at the hot springs.

While the native people were celebrating their successes, panic was becoming wide-spread in San Diego. Officials declared a state of martial law and the *San Diego Herald* of November 27, 1851, was documenting the heightened level of excitement among the people, noting that the city looked like a fortified camp. Watchmen scouted the outskirts of the city, preventing any Indian who could not explain his appearance there from entering the city. A group of volunteers under the authority of Major E. H. Fitzgerald were sent to Agua Caliente during this time. The *Alta California* newspaper of December 3, 1851, recorded for its readers that Fitzgerald and his men soon found Bill Marshall and two other men (his friend Juan Verdugo and his father-in-law Jose Noca) and immediately arrested them, accused them of helping Antonio Garra and his followers, and escorted them to San Diego to await their trials (Hyer 2001).

The court martials of Bill Marshall, Juan Verdugo, and Jose Noca began on December 9, 1851 (Bibb 1976), with the three charged with high treason, murder, and robbery. As reported in the *Alta California* edition of December 14, 1851, local residents in San Diego had already decided unanimously to convict Marshall and Verdugo and to hang them. Pourade (1963) believed that those who lived in San Diego had erected the gallows for the men before the trial began.

Marshall and Verdugo (Bibb 1976) were convicted of high treason but were found innocent of murder and robbery. It was determined that Jose Noca played no role in the events and he was released. The gallows had been erected near the Catholic burial ground near the southern end of San Diego, and Marshall chose to be baptized before his and Verdugo's execution by hanging. A priest handled the proceedings and gave both men final absolution. Marshall said he was innocent and that he hoped his friends and the people around him would forgive him. Marshall would have been twenty-four years old at the time. Verdugo said in Spanish that he was ready to give his life up as a result of his wickedness and crimes. According to a *San Diego Herald* article of December 18, 1851, neither man had a hood placed over his head, and both went to their final resting places in shirt sleeves.

Leland Bibb (1976) proposes that William Marshall may have been an innocent man, hanged for a crime he didn't commit. He adds that if that were true, Jonathan Warner could have likely saved him, but didn't come forward to defend the man he had known since 1846, and who had not only worked for him, but had watched over Warner's wife and children at the outbreak of the Mexican-American War, when Warner had been taken into custody and removed to San Diego for suspected disloyalty to the Americans. Bibb also surmises that Marshall may have been at an extreme disadvantage with the Americans in 1851 because he had married the daughter of Cupeño Jose Noca, and lived in the Indian village at Agua Caliente, an uncommon occurrence at that time, though it happened more frequently during the next decade. Marshall's relative isolation at the region of Agua Caliente naturally meant that he was not well known by the Americans, or a vital part of their culture, even though he had aided Kearny and his forces just before the outbreak of the Battle of San Pasqual. Marshall's close ties to the Indians during the Garra Revolt in 1851 would, most likely, lead to the American forces and population distrusting the man from Rhode Island.

Bibb expands upon these points:

> Further, the revolt was an extraordinary event. Not since 1775 had southern California Indians achieved sufficient unity to resist the white intruders effectively. We may assume that the Americans, far outnumbered by Indians in the county, would want to place responsibility for the revolt on someone other than the Indians because the Americans could not admit to themselves that the Indians had the capacity to plan and initiate such a movement. Once the charges had been made, the burden was placed on Marshall to prove his innocence. Because of his relative isolation from the American community this was virtually impossible. If Warner had come forward and supported Marshall, he would not have been hanged. Consequently, Warner's silence was to a great extent responsible for Marshall's conviction and death (Bibb 1976: N. p.).

As the ultimate consequences of retaliation by the Americans began to become more apparent to the native people, Antonio Garra and the Cupeños of Agua Caliente eventually removed from the Warner Springs area, north to Los Coyotes Canyon, to be with the Cahuillas there (Hyer 2001).

On either December 18, 1851 (Pourade 1963) or December 21, 1851 (Hyer 2001), American soldiers fought with the Cupeño and Cahuilla native men at Los Coyotes Canyon, with the *San Diego Herald* reporting on December 25 that eight Cahuilla natives, including two captains, had been killed. An American council, formed to investigate the charges against the native men, was led by Officer-in-Charge Major Samuel P. Heintzelman, who brought charges against four Indians that he believed were involved in the deaths of the four Americans at the hot springs at Agua Caliente. The newspaper account speculated that Francisco Mocate and Louis (Cupeños), Juan Bautista (Cahuilla) and Jacobo (either Cupeño or Cahuilla) were, "... the prominent actors in the murder of the Americans at Agua Caliente" (*San Diego Herald* 1851).

Oliver M. Wozencraft, the federal Indian commissioner, was at the proceedings, and recorded in his notes that Francisco Mocate, Louis, Juan Bautista, and Jacobo had been declared "... guilty of murder, arson and robbery" (Wozencraft 1852:212). The four had been immediately sentenced to execution, and American soldiers carried out the killings in front of approximately eighty native people on Christmas morning 1851. A January 10, 1852, *San Diego Herald* announcement called the executions a "most righteous punishment," and hailed Heintzelman for his "skill, prompt action and perseverance."

A few days before the American forces attacked the native Cupeños and Cahuillas at Los Coyotes Canyon (Hyer 2001), and the arrests of the four men suspected of the killings at Agua Caliente, Antonio Garra had approached his sometimes enemy, Mountain Cahuilla leader Juan Antonio, at San Bernardino a final time, still seeking his assistance in the

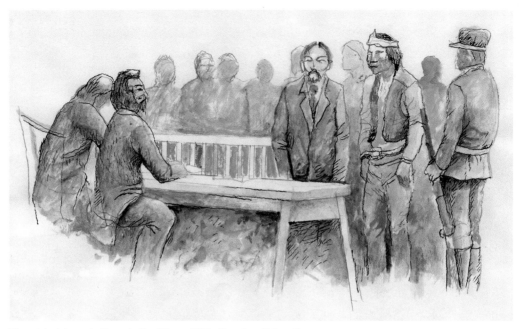

The trial of Antonio Garra in San Diego, 1852. *Drawing: Robert Freeman.*

revolt against the Americans. Juan Antonio seized that opportunity to have his men capture Garra, and notified General Bean in San Diego that the leader of the uprising was in his custody. Hyer reminds readers that although Juan Antonio was related to some of the Cahuillas at Los Coyotes, they were under the directorship of their own leaders and lived near the Cupeños from Agua Caliente. The *Alta California* newspaper of January 6, 1852, reported that General Bean met with Juan Antonio and convinced him to trade Antonio Garra for a batch of supplies.

General Bean was able to convince Garra to write a letter to his son, Antonino Garra, telling him and other Cupeños to surrender to Mountain Cahuilla Juan Antonio. The younger Garra did what his father asked, bringing ten other Indians with him, but while in custody, Juan Antonio kept insulting the younger Garra, who subsequently stabbed the older man with a knife, though Juan Antonio lived. Military officials soon convicted the younger Antonio Garra and executed him, along with a second Indian named Jose, at Chino in San Bernardino County.

On January 8, 1852 (Hyer 2001), Captain Antonio Garra was taken to San Diego as a captive of the Americans, and on January 10, 1852, the *Alta California* newspaper reported that the elder Antonio Garra had been convicted by a court on the charges "of levying war against the government, of murder and robbery" (Hyer 2001:66). They sentenced the Cupeño leader to death by a firing squad.

The execution of Antonio Garra. *Drawing: Robert Freeman.*

Though Garra had made two statements on December 13, 1851 (Garra Confession: NARA and *San Diego Herald*: December 18, 1851), saying that Bill Marshall and Juan Verdugo had not been involved in the attack at Warner's Ranch, he offered different testimony at the time of his trial, saying: "I told Bill Marshall that if he did not join us I would kill him. Bill M. said that it was all good that he had been then a long time [sic]. B. M was at that time at the Coyotes. I would not have killed B. M. if he had not joined us. What for?" (Garra 1852:MS).

Cave Couts, who in June 1853 would become San Diego County's first permanent Indian subagent, served as judge advocate for the proceedings for Garra, who was summarily convicted, then executed by firing squad that same afternoon (Pourade 1963). Lieutenant Sweeny, commanding officer of the Regular Army Unit in San Diego, refused to sit on the court martial for Garra, and would not let his soldiers carry out the execution. Herbert Lockwood (1967) noted that pioneer San Diegan Thomas Whaley accompanied Garra to the cemetery, and was a member of the firing squad. Oliver M. Wozencraft, the federal Indian commissioner, was also at Garra's trial.

Lockwood (1967) said that a priest was also with Garra that afternoon and encouraged him to pray. Garra responded: "What's the use?" but when the priest went on in Latin, Garra added: "You've got it all wrong!" and substituted the correct version for that erroneously presented by the Catholic priest (Lockwood 1976:77).

> *An Alta California article of January 15, 1852, quoted Antonio Garra as saying at the time of his execution: "Gentlemen, I ask your pardon for all my offenses, and expect yours in return" (Hyer 2001:66).*

Garra opposed the executioners covering his eyes, but then laughingly relented, still chuckling as he knelt next to his grave and the firing squad released their ten musket balls in his direction. Antonio Garra died instantly.

The January 15, 1852, *Alta California* article concluded that "... No man could have met his fate in a more grave and dignified manner, than did Antonio Garra" (Hyer 2001:66). Historian William Glum later queried in an online article: "How could an Indian who was not in the military, was not considered a citizen, be tried in a military court for treason?" Glum decided it took "a little stretching of the law" (Evans 1997). Clinton Linton, tribal consultant at Red Tail Monitoring and Research, has commented that his family is related to Antonio Garra (personal communication 2015).

Debbie Moretti, seventh great-granddaughter of Antonio Garra, and a lifetime resident of the Los Coyotes Indian Reservation, is also the granddaughter of Nelda Campagnoli Taylor and Banning Taylor, who served the Los Coyotes people as chairman for 53 years. She and her family are currently researching historical and genealogical records to learn more about their famous ancestor, who gathered native people together to mount resistance against the American invaders. Her grandmother turned 102 as *Blood of the Band* was being written, and is interviewed in the final chapter as she recalls long-ago memories, having been raised at Mesa Grande in Ipai territory, then following the traditional way of going to her husband's territory at Los Coyotes after she married Banning Taylor.

The Treaties of 1852

On January 7, 1852 (*San Diego Herald* 1852), Captain Panto headed a list of twenty-two "headmen" of the Diegueño Indians, and as captain of the San Pasqual Ipai represented local native people when he signed one of eighteen treaties crafted in California from 1851-53 and overseen by Dr. Oliver M. Wozencraft, who visited California to make the treaties. Two and a half million acres of land were promised to the California Indians, but the US Senate never ratified the treaties, leaving the native people, in many cases, landless.

Not being citizens (Kappler 1929 in Carrico 1987), the Ipai of San Diego County were also unable to homestead lands. Often, whites would move onto Indian lands and confiscate the native peoples' belongings and properties, or would move on and file a homestead, usurping the Indians' legal rights. Sometimes whites would simply burn the Indians off their lands and take over their houses, belongings, animals, and properties. A long history of murders, rapes, enslavement, and abuse toward the Indians of San Diego County was the order of the day in 1852 in San Diego County. The eighteen treaties of 1852 that were

TREATY WITH THE DIEGUINO, 1852.

TREATY MADE AND CONCLUDED AT THE VILLAGE OF SANTA YSABEL, CALIFORNIA, BETWEEN O. M. WOZENCRAFT, UNITED STATES INDIAN AGENT, AND THE CAPTAINS AND HEAD MEN OF THE NATION OF DIEGUINO INDIANS, JANUARY 7, 1852.

A treaty of peace and friendship made and concluded at the village of Santa Ysabel, California, between the United States Indian agent, O. M. Wozencraft, of the one part, and the captains and head men of the nation of Dieguino Indians, of the other part.

ARTICLE 1. The several tribes of the abovementioned nation do acknowledge the United States to be the sole and absolute sovereigns of all the soil and territory ceded to them by a treaty of peace made between them and the republic of Mexico.

ART. 2. The said nation of Indians and the several tribes thereof, acknowledge themselves, jointly and severally, under the exclusive jurisdiction, authority and protection of the United States, and hereby bind themselves hereafter to refrain from the commission of all acts of hostility and aggression towards the government or citizens thereof, and to live on terms of peace and friendship among themselves, and with all other Indian tribes which are now or may come under the protection of the United States; and, furthermore, bind themselves to conform to and be governed by the laws and regulations of the Indian bureau, made and provided therefor by the Congress of the United States.

ART. 3. To promote the settlement and improvement of said nations it is hereby stipulated and agreed that the following district of country, in the State of California, shall be and is hereby set apart forever, for the sole use and occupancy of the aforesaid nation of Indians, still reserving to the government of the United States all minerals found thereon, to wit: commencing at the southern line of the State at the eastern base of the Sierra Nevada mountain and on the desert, and running along the base northerly to the northeastern corner of the reservation set apart for the Kahwe-as, San Luis, and Co-con-cah-ra nations of Indians, thence following the southern lines of the same to the northwestern corner of the grant of the San Jose del Valle, thence following the boundaries thereof by south and east to the southeastern corner of it, thence on a right line to the northwestern corner of the San Felipe grant, thence on the western line of the same to the southwestern corner thereof, thence southerly to the southern line of the State at a point twenty miles from the place of beginning, thence along said southern line to the place of beginning: To have and to hold the said district of country for the sole use and occupancy of the said Indian nation forever: Provided, that there is reserved to the government of the United States the right of way over any portion of said territory, and the right to establish and maintain any military post or posts, public buildings, school-houses, houses for agents, teachers, and such others as they may deem necessary for their use or the protection of the Indians.

The said nations and tribes and each of them, hereby engage that they will never claim any other lands within the boundaries of the United States, nor ever disturb the people of the United States in the free use and enjoyment thereof.

ART. 4. To the said nation of Indians, in their subsistence while removing to and making their settlement upon the said reservation, the United States will furnish them, free of all charge, one thousand eight hundred head of beef cattle, to average in weight five hundred pounds each, within the term of two years from the date of this treaty.

ART. 5. As early as convenient after the ratification of this treaty by the President and Senate, in consideration of the premises, and with a sincere desire to encourage said nation in acquiring the arts and habits of civilized life, the United States will also furnish them the following articles, to be divided among them by the agent according to their respective numbers and wants in the different tribes, during each of the two years succeeding the said ratification, viz: one pair among pantaloons and one red flannel shirt for each man and boy, one linsey gown for each woman and girl, five thousand five hundred yards of calico, three thousand yards of brown sheeting, sixty pounds Scotch thread, four dozen pairs of scissors, fourteen dozen thimbles, five thousand needles, one 2½-point Mackinaw blanket for each man and woman over fifteen years of age; six thousand pounds of iron and five

thousand five hundred pounds of steel; and in like manner in the first year for the permanent use of said nation, and as the joint property of the several tribes thereof, viz: one hundred and twenty brood-mares and six stallions, five hundred young cows and thirty bulls, fifteen yoke working oxen with yokes and chains, sixteen work mules or horses, thirty ploughs assorted sizes, and sixteen grindstones, and the necessary seeds of various kinds.

The stock enumerated above and the product thereof; and no part or portion thereof shall be killed, exchanged, sold or otherwise parted with, without the consent and direction of the agent.

ART. 6. The United States will also employ and settle among said nation, at or near their towns or settlements, one practical farmer, who shall superintend all agricultural operations, with two assistants, men of practical knowledge and industrious habits; one wheelwright, one carpenter, one blacksmith, one principal school-teacher, and as many assistant teachers as the President may deem proper to instruct said nations in reading, writing, &c., and in the domestic arts upon the manual-labor system. All the above-named workmen and teachers to be maintained and paid by the United States for the period of five years, and as long thereafter as the President shall deem advisable.

The United States will also erect suitable school-houses, shops and dwellings for the accommodation of the school teachers, mechanics, agriculturists and assistants above specified, and for the protection of the public property.

In testimony whereof, the parties have hereunto signed their names and affixed, their seals, this seventh day of January, one thousand eight hundred and fifty-two.

[SEAL.]   O. M. WOZENCRAFT,
United States Indian agent.

For and in behalf of the Dieguino Indians:

SANTIAGO, of Ha-coom, his x mark.	[SEAL.]
KWA-PI, of Ta-cah-tay, his x mark.	[SEAL.]
SOLDADO, of Matirom, his x mark.	[SEAL.]
NE-CAH, by Coo-LIM, of Wah-ti, his x mark	[SEAL.]
SURDO, of Sa-quan, his x mark.	[SEAL.]
AT-CHU-CAL, of Ha-soo-male, his x mark	[SEAL.]
TAH-CA-PAN, of Coquilt, his x mark.	[SEAL.]
LEANDRO, of San Diego mission, his x mark	[SEAL.]
TADEO, of San Dieguito, his x mark.	[SEAL.]
LAZARO, of Santa Ysabel, his x mark	[SEAL.]
TOMAS, of Santa Ysabel, his x mark.	[SEAL.]
AS-SO-TORE, of How-wee Valleito, his x mark	[SEAL.]
PANTHO, of San Pascual, his x mark.	[SEAL.]
JOSE APAN, of To-co-mac, his x mark.	[SEAL.]
JUAN PABLO, of Ca-ma-jal, his x mark	[SEAL.]
MATEO (Co-mu-po-ip) of Tah-wee, his x mark	[SEAL.]
LOENZO, (Cho-lo-pe) of Prickaway, his x mark	[SEAL.]
TAMOUROO, of Too-weal, his x mark	[SEAL.]
HEPERERA, of Mel-co-to-nac,, San Felipe, his x mark	[SEAL.]
ELOO, of Inah-mak, La Puerta, his x mark	[SEAL.]
OON-AH-OON, of Lu-ah-pi, his x mark.	[SEAL.]
FELIPE, (Am-coo-si) of Matajuni, his x mark.	[SEAL.]

Signed, sealed and delivered, after being fully explained, in presence of—
DELAVIN DAVIDSON, Captain 2d infantry.
E. MURRAY, Lieutenant 2d infantry.
J. J. WARNER.

ADDENDA.—From the above district of country, set apart for the Indians, is reserved to the present owner thereof, the Hon. J. J. Warner, one square league at Aqua Caliente, to be selected by him for the purpose of improving the warm springs at said place, in case the said ownership be adjudicated in his (Warner's) favor by the land commissioners of California.[1]

J. HAMILTON,
Secretary of the Indian agency.

[1] Act referring claims of the California Indians to the Court of Claims, approved May 18, 1928 (45 Stat. 602)

The 1852 Treaty of Santa Ysabel.

never ratified by the United States Senate were placed in the Senate Archives until 1905, when they were discovered and brought to light.

One year after the signing of the Treaties of 1852, Tomas, the long-time Ipai native captain of Mesa Grande, was deposed, and Panto became captain of both the San Pasqual and Mesa Grande villages. The removal of Tomas followed a tradition established by the Indian Bureau and followed by Indian agents and superintendents, whereby they removed *alcaldes* that they found objectionable and replaced them with Indian captains more to their liking (Carrico 1987).

Captain Pablo Apis of Temecula (Pourade 1963) died in 1855, ending a long tenure as a participant in many of the important historical events of San Diego County. In 1862-1863 a smallpox epidemic swept through southern California, killing a vast number of native people, since they had no resistance to the diseases the intruders brought. The epidemic killed Captain Juan Antonio of the Mountain Cahuilla, along with many of his band. Even before symptoms of smallpox became apparent, it was highly contagious, eventually resulting in high fevers, convulsions, delirium, and a tortured death. California Registered Landmark No. 749 noted that the Cahuilla traditionally said that the US government provided the

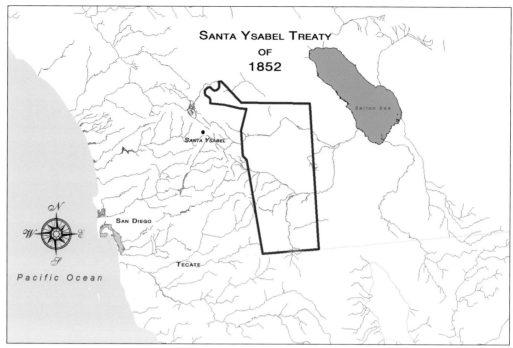

A large tract of land that would have included over a fifth of present day San Diego County was promised to the California Indians in the 1852 Treaty of Santa Ysabel, but the US Senate never ratified the treaties.

Indians with army blankets contaminated with smallpox. The disease reduced Juan Antonio and his Mountain Cahuilla people from a majority in the area to a minority.

In 1956 an archaeological expedition discovered Juan Antonio's burial site at San Timoteo Canyon. The archaeologists recognized him by the epaulets he was wearing, which Edward F. Beale, California's first superintendent of Indian Affairs from 1853-1856, had given him. Chief Juan Antonio, whose Cahuilla name was Cooswootna Yampoochie—meaning "He Gets Mad Quickly"—was later reburied with military honors. He lived from 1783-1863, and was born near Mount San Jacinto, serving as leader of his people from 1840-1863 (Pourade 1963 and Barrett and Markowitz 2005).

Also in 1856, Don Santiago Argüello gave a sworn statement to the US government, describing the day in 1835 that he witnessed the San Pasqual native people receiving the lands which were given to them by the Mexican government after secularization of the missions. Legitimate claims to native lands, including those at San Pasqual, which had been negotiated with the government of Mexico, had not been honored by the new American government after 1848. Argüello swore under oath on January 2, 1856, that San Pasqual was a regular pueblo, founded by order of the governor of Alta California. He said he was an official in the Mexican government at San Diego and witnessed the signing of

The fertile lands of San Pasqual Valley supported a number of Ipai settlements, including members of the Guachena, Nejo and La Chappa clans. *Drawing: Robert Freeman.*

the documents. Argüello's letter was forwarded to the Secretary of War, Jefferson Davis, along with a map of San Pasqual Valley, by Captain H. S. Burton of San Diego's Presidio.

Nonetheless, no action occurred to ensure or protect the claims of the San Pasqual Indians. The letter may have been forgotten, until it surfaced again in 1867 when it was sent to Washington by an Indian agent. The statement was in the papers collected by J. B. McIntosh, superintendent of Indian Affairs for California, and was forwarded to the commissioner of Indian Affairs, E. S. Parker, in 1869. The map could not be traced by the National Archives or the Indian Bureau. The papers are published as part of House Document No. 296, in a letter from the secretary of the Interior, in answer to the Resolution of the House of May 24, 1870, in relation to establishing an Indian reservation in San Diego County, California.

This is a copy of Don Argüello's letter, which was in the files of the Indian Bureau:

> The undersigned certifies upon his word of honor, that the Pueblo of San Pasquale in the County of San Diego was founded by order of the Governor of Alta California in consequence of the secularization of the Missions. For that reason, these lands called San Pasquale were given to several families of Indians belonging to the Mission of San Diego under a regulation of the Government of Alta California at that time and resulted in the founding of San Dieguito and Los Flores. The original documents of which should be found in the archives of the Government of Alta California. The signer of this

Frank Trask's Family Lineage

The Guachena, Nejo, La Chappa, and Trask family oral histories, passed down from generation to generation, recalled that Roswell Trask, an army veteran originally from Ohio, was living in the San Pasqual Valley with a full-blood Ipai woman when his first son, Frank Trask, was born in 1867. Family stories have suggested that Frank's mother may have died at the time of his birth or during his infancy, since records indicate that by the age of three Frank was living with Bridget Browne, a former school teacher from Ireland and probably Frank's godmother. While Roswell is shown in government reports as living in the San Pasqual Valley from 1867-1869, and as fathering a second son, evidence shows that by 1870 some non-Indians living in San Pasqual Valley in 1869 had gone to other areas, including Roswell Trask, who reportedly lived elsewhere (Almstedt 1983). Geneologist Lorraine Escobar reported that: "Roswell Trask left prior to the promulgation of the President's order declaring San Pasqual a reservation…" (Escobar 2011:Np). In addition, a June 16, 1870, *San Diego Union* newpaper report placed Roswell near Julian.

In this same year Roswell Trask was living with his third Ipai wife, Maria Catarina McIntire, whose mother was Angela Guachena, 4/4 Ipai at Mesa Grande, and whose father was white new-comer John L. McIntire, who surveyed much of the San Diego County region, including the town of Julian, along with serving as assessor for San Diego County, as supervisor for the County of San Diego, and as postmaster at Ballena.

Frank Trask continued to live for many years with the family of Bridget Browne, who was also godmother to two of his sisters; during this time his father Roswell Trask continued to live near Frank and his other children. Frank, described as "an industrious and progressive Indian," was designated as an Indian judge and police officer. He eventually married Leonora LaChappa in 1902 and in 1909 they moved to the new San Pasqual Indian Reservation in Valley Center, where they raised a family, made the land productive, and managed to hold on to the reservation lands in the face of encroachment and hostility from some non-Indian neighbors. Frank died from Spanish influenza in 1920.

Photo above: Frank Trask, whose father Roswell was living with an Ipai woman in the San Pasqual Valley when he was born in 1867. **Drawing left:** Roswell Trask arrived in the San Pasqual Valley in 1867.

document was witness to the issuing of these orders, being at that time in authority at San Diego and it was his jurisdiction to confirm these documents. In 1846 the land was asked as a grant by Dynofacio Lopez from the Mexican Government and the answer to the petition was that there was no vacant land as it belonged to the San Diego Indians of San Pasquale. For this reason it would be unjust to take away these lands from the Indians under any pretext. That they have no sufficient documents as these documents will be found in the Archives of the Government of Alta California in their proper places to which reference can be made in truth of this statement. Given at my Rancho of San Antonio January 2, 1856.

During the same time that Don Santiago Argüello offered his testimony, in January of 1856, Captain Panto met with US Army Captain H.S. Burton, who had been dispatched by the government to determine the conditions of the San Diego County native people. Panto and Burton met at the rancheria called San Bernardo, near present-day Rancho Bernardo. At the meeting Panto presented evidence to Burton that five or six white squatters had commandeered some of the best Indian lands in the San Pasqual Valley, which led Burton to decide that the Superintendent of Indian Affairs should get involved (Carrico 1987).

Captain Panto wrote a letter (NARA 1958) in 1856 complaining about the intruders' encroachment on his band's traditional tribal lands in the San Pasqual Valley. This letter was coupled with a letter written by Captain Burton, and sent to the Headquarters of the Pacific in Benecia, California. Burton's letter said: "The Indians of San Pasqual are friendly and anxious to remain so, but if their lands are taken from them without scruple, they must return to the mountains naturally discontented and ready to join in any depredation upon the whites." The adjutant general quickly sent a message to the Secretary of War, Jefferson Davis, after receiving the letters, and stated: "I think them of sufficient importance to claim your immediate attention in order that those Indians and other tribes may be kept quiet until the war in the North is brought to a close when I shall have troops sufficient at my disposal to give ample protection to the inhabitants of Southern California." (NARA 1958).

Burton also met with Manuel Cota, who was sanctioned by Cave Couts to take over the leadership of the northern Luiseños, including those from Pauma, Pala, Potrero, and Temecula. Cota expressed his distrust of most Indian agents, government agents, and military officials, noting that the US government seemed to be concerned only with the Indians of northern California. Burton could present no solutions for Cota. In June 1856 Burton met with Tomas, who had been deposed by Chief Panto at the Mesa Grande Indian Reservation, and learned of Tomas's sense of despair and hopelessness in connection with the deterioration he had witnessed in relation to the native people of San Diego County (Carrico 1987).

1865: First Multiband Meeting since 1852 Signing of Treaties

Luiseños, Cupeños, and other native people from surrounding territories joined with Indian agents Stanley and Lovett at Temecula in May 1865, so the Indian agents could learn more about the needs and grievances of the San Diego County native people. This was the first multi-band convening of Indians since the Treaties of Santa Ysabel had been crafted in January 1852. The agents also visited Pala and called on Manuel Cota, even reappointing him as leader of the Luiseños and Cupeños, because as Stanley said, "He has always been truly faithful to the government of the United States" (Hyer 2001:80) though Cota did not qualify as a Luiseño or Cupeño hereditary captain, since his father was a Mexican and his mother an Ipai. When Indian Agent Cave Couts had made him a leader over some of the Luiseño, Cupeño, and Cahuilla native people in 1853, many had not adopted him as their captain, and eventually forced his resignation, but Stanley and Lovett repeated the gesture of making him leader again, though they knew his past history.

San Pasqual and Pala Indian Reservations Created by Ulysses S. Grant

On the world front, John Wilkes Booth shot President Abraham Lincoln at Ford's Theatre on April 14, 1865. The president died at 11:00 a.m. April 15th and Vice President Andrew Johnson took over as the seventeenth President (Trefousse 1989). By January 1868 the US House of Representatives impeached Johnson for intentionally violating the Tenure of Office Act. Johnson pled innocent, claiming that the Act did not apply to him concerning his appointment of Ulysses S. Grant as the replacement of Secretary of War Stanton, since President Lincoln had appointed Grant's predecessor. The impeachment proceedings were successful in the House of Representatives, but failed three times in the Senate, falling one vote short of the two-thirds needed each time — the vote being 35 guilty and 19 not guilty (Stewart 2009).

Grant's past had included problems as well, though he was a graduate of West Point and a decorated lieutenant in the Mexican-American War (Smith 2001). Grant's father had predicted early-on that his son would never be successful in business, and had steered him toward the military (Longacre 2006). At the peak of the gold rush he was stationed in San Francisco, and had aided fellow infantrymen on the trip there, when a cholera epidemic broke out while the group was traveling overland through Panama. Grant also served at Fort Vancouver in the Pacific Northwest, and noted that the native people he encountered there were harmless. He said they lacked peace, being bothered by the whites in the area, and noted that the nearby Klickitat tribe had been powerful before their introduction to the white man's whiskey and smallpox (Simon 1967).

By 1854 he was stationed at Fort Humboldt in northern California, and his commanding officer had made him accountable for several instances of binge drinking. Grant agreed to sign a prepared resignation letter, rather than be court martialed, though he had been promoted to the rank of captain shortly before the situation had occurred.

By 1861 Grant had rejoined his wife and family in Galena, Illinois, and when 75,000 volunteers were needed to fight Confederate troops, the former army captain was the sole military professional in Galena. After Governor Richard Yates called on him to recruit and train volunteer units, he began working with Major John C. Fremont, who said he was a man of dogged persistence and iron will (Jones 2002). By March 1869, Ulysses S. Grant had been elected eighteenth president of the United States (Trefousse 1989), and the Union Army had defeated the Confederate military during the Civil War. By1870 President Grant would realize that it was time to set aside land for two California reservations, at the San Pasqual Valley and at Pala.

Ely S. Parker's Annual Report of the Commissioner of Indian Affairs for 1869 had helped illuminate the condition of those California Indians who would ultimately be most affected by these two reservations. His report stated that the Tule River reservation was in the southern part of the state, and that the Indians living there were brought about ten years before from the Tejon reservation, where they had surrendered the land to its owner. They then became known as the Tule and Owens River tribes. Parker went on to say:

> It may be expedient to remove these Indians to another reservation...the Indians readily engage in the various kinds of labor for their support and are quite successful, but they are averse to making improvements through an uncertainty as to their

---

Mission Indian Reserves

[In the Mission Tule Agency; twenty-two reserves; occupied by the Diegenes, Kawia, San Luis Rey, Serranos, and Temecula tribes; area, 282 square miles; established by Executive orders.]

DEPARTMENT OF THE INTERIOR, *January 27, 1870.*

To the PRESIDENT:

The accompanying papers are respectfully submitted to the President, with the request that the following lands in California be set apart as reservations for the Mission Indians, in the southern portion of that State, being the San Pasqual and Pala Valleys, and recommended by the Commissioner of Indian Affairs, viz: Townships 12 and 13 south, of ranges 1 east and 1 west, of the San Bernardino meridan, and township 9 south, of ranges 1 and 2 west, of the San Bernardino meridian.

With great respect, your obedient servant,

J. D. COX, *Secretary*
JANUARY 31, 1870

Let the lands designated in the foregoing letter of the Secretary of the Interior be set apart as reservations for Indian purposes, as therein recommended.

U. S. GRANT

Letter from President U. S. Grant creating the San Pasqual and Pala Reservations (see page 105).

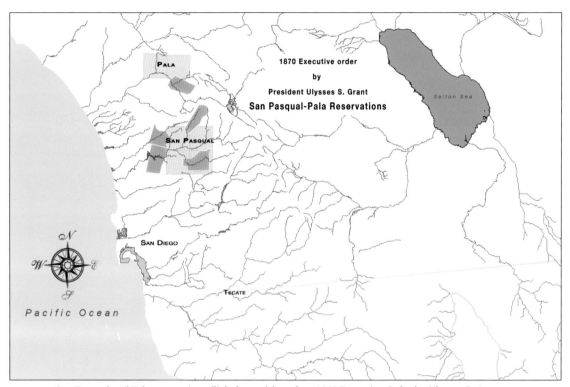

San Pasqual and Pala reservations (light brown) based on 1870 Executive Order by Ulysses S. Grant. Darker brown areas are Mexican land grants.

remaining in permanent possession of them. Only 300 remain on the farm, many having left and gone back to their old homes on Owen's River (Parker 1969:17).

In addition, Parker added that the Cahuillas had no reservation, and that nothing had been done to benefit their situation. Parker explained:

...General Mc Intosh was instructed during the past summer to visit them and see where a reservation could be located for their use...a reservation can be set apart for them upon land in and west of San Pasqual Valley, which would be sufficiently large for a home for all the Indians in the southern part of California, including those at Tule River farm" (Parker 1869:17).

Commissioner Parker then estimated that there were approximately 20,000 Indians in the entire state of California and suggested:

Congress should be very liberal toward this people, inasmuch as they are regarded as having no recognized rights in the country. They have of late years been peaceable, and it is no more than just, in view of their having quietly yielded to the whites a

DEPARTMENT OF THE INTERIOR
OFFICE OF INDIAN AFFAIRS
Washington, D. C., February 13, 1871

SIR: I have the honor to call your attention to a report from this office, dated January 15, 1870, in which was inclosed a letter from J. B.
McIntosh, Brevet Major-General U. S. Army, and superintendent of Indian
affairs for California, dated December 27, 1869, and report of Lieut. A.
P. Greene, U. S. Army, agent for Mission Indians in southern California,
dated Los Angeles, Cal., December 16, 1869, recommending that San Pasqual
and Pala Valleys in Southern California be set apart as reservations for
the Mission Indians in said State.

In my report above referred to I recommend that the following-described
lands should be set apart for said reservations, viz: Townships 12 and
13 south, of ranges 1 east and 1 west, and township 9 south, of ranges 1
and 2 west, of the San Bernardino meridian, California.

My recommendation meeting with the approval of the Secretary of the
Interior was forwarded to the President, who, on the 31st of January,
1870, ordered that the above-designated lands should be set apart as
reservations for Indian purposes.

It appears from the papers transmitted herewith that the citizens of
San Diego County protest against the order of the President setting apart
said lands for Indian reservations; that the Indians are unanimously
opposed to going on said reservations; that citizens have made valuable
improvements thereon, and that there are but few Indians on the lands set
apart as aforesaid; that recent gold discoveries have attracted a large
immigration thither, and the opinion of the press, together with other
evidence, would indicate that it would be for the best interests and welfare of the Indians, as well as others, that the order of the President
setting apart said lands for Indian purposes should be recinded.

In view of these facts, I would therefore respectfully recommend that
the order of the President be revoked, and that the aforesaid reservations be again restored to the public domain.

Very respectfully, your obedient servant

E. S. PARKER, Commissioner

Commissioner E.S. Parker recommends the revocation of the presidential order creating the San Pasqual and Pala Reservations.

country so wealthy in its varied resources, that our government should deal generously with them in providing a sufficiency of means for their relief and improvement (Parker 1869:17).

The letters illustrate the progress of the granting of lands for the San Pasqual and Pala reservations, which would be created for the Mission and Tule River Indians of southern California. (Kappler 1913)

According to Carrico (1987) the San Pasqual Reservation was within Townships 12 and 13 south and Ranges 1 east and 1 west of the San Bernardino Meridian. It was comprised

Hon. C. DELANO
Secretary of the Interior.

[First indorsement]
DEPARTMENT OF THE INTERIOR
Office of Indian Affairs, February 15, 1871

   Commissioner transmits papers in reference to San Pasqual and Pala Valley Reservations in southern California, and recommends that the order of the President setting apart the same be revoked and the lands restored to the public domain.

[Second indorsement]
DEPARTMENT OF THE INTERIOR, *February 17, 1871*

   The within recommendation of the Commissioner of Indian Affairs is respectfully submitted to the President, with the request that the order of the Executive for the restoration to the public domain of the lands referred to be given.
   The same afternoon as Delano's second endorsement, President Ulysses S. Grant responded by revoking the San Pasqual and Pala Reservations, as recorded below:

C. DELANO
Secretary of the Interior
Approved February 17, 1871

U. S. GRANT

Secretary of the Interior C. Delano endorses the recommendation to revoke the reservations.

of over 92,000 acres and included Ramona to the east, Mount Woodson to the south, Highland Valley on the west and Lake Wohlford to the north. The Pala Reserve was made up of Township 9 south, Ranges 1 and 2 west of the San Bernardian Meridian. Pala had about 46,000 acres, located between Palomar Mountain on the east, Pala Mountain on the south, Rice Canyon on the west and the second standard parallel on the north.

   Grant, then, following the recommendations of his advisors, including John B. McIntosh, who had written the commissioner of Indian Affairs about establishing a reservation at San Pasqual Valley and Pala, and Indian Agent Augustus P. Greene, who had made a trip there to examine the valley, created the two new reservations through an executive order on January 31, 1870.(See map on page 104.) The consensus was that there was enough land in the San Pasqual Valley for a reservation for the Ipai and possibly some of the Tule River Indians. Even with the government solidly behind the efforts to provide land for the Indians in their longtime native valley, those non-Indians who had squatted on the lands set aside for the reservation blatantly refused to remove to other locations, and even harassed and intimidated the native people in order to have the land for themselves (Shipek 2012:TS).

Michael Connolly Miskwish, a Tipai historian from Campo, described the attitudes of both the native people at San Pasqual and the whites who lived there during the time of the creation of the San Pasqual Indian Reservation:

> Many Indians objected to the proposed relocation to the reservation lands. They were suspicious of the reservation scheme, considering it a plan to dispossess them of their lands while keeping them close to labor for the ranches. Many whites also objected to the creation of the reservations because they opposed any restrictions on their ability to acquire any land they desired within the county (Miskwish 2007:93).

By February 17, 1871, Commissioner of Indian Affairs Ely S. Parker was writing the letter shown on page 105 to President Ulysses S. Grant.

As shown on the preceding page, the secretary of the Interior, Honorable C. Delano, presented his first endorsement of Parker's recommendation to revoke the San Pasqual and Pala Reservations on February 15, 1871 and his second endorsement on February 17, 1871.

The United States Congress passed the *Indian Appropriation Act* on March 3, 1871, revoking the sovereignty of Indian nations and making Native Americans wards of the American government. The act eliminated the United States having to negotiate treaties with the Indians, and instituted the policy that national tribal affairs could be managed without the consent of the Indians themselves. Reservations weren't permanently created until a new executive order in 1875 (Connolly Miskwish 2007:93).

Reservations of 1875 in San Diego County

In 1865 the Mission Indian Agency was created, holding jurisdiction over various bands of the Mission Indians of California. In 1875 the agency set aside federal lands for some of the southern California native people, after Luiseño native Olegario Calac of Pauma met with President Ulysses S. Grant in Washington DC. In 1875 President Grant made the decision to return 100,000 acres of land to 3,000-5,000 native people of southern California. Some government officials and private sector citizens thought that the granting of that large amount of land was too generous. Tanis Thorne said the generosity was deliberate:

> The 1875 executive reservations defined reservation boundaries based on township lines before sectionalizing land surveys had been done. Exempting large blocks of the public domain from filing by white homesteaders was prescriptive: the large blocks of protected reservation land, it was presumed, would embrace the existing village locations. Once the initial, hasty, and crude surveys were replaced by more systematic surveys, land not needed by Indians for self-support could be returned to the public domain (2012:41-43).

Thorne described the overly large reservations as a safety net, meant to protect homeless San Diego County native people, such as those who were being evicted from lands

The 1878 eviction of the Ipai from San Pasqual. *Drawing: Robert Freeman.*

originally designated for the ranchos. These new tracts included plenty of agricultural land and would be available for those native people who no longer had lands of their own. However, some of the lands included in the tracts granted by the executive orders of 1875-1876 through the new Mission Indian Agency were not the same, historic lands upon which the native people had traditionally lived. These newly dispensed lands did, however, give legal title to the bands, and also included the improvements, orchards, fields, and houses that had been created or used on these properties, which had become public domain lands once the native people had been evicted.

Thorne added:

A new era was inaugurated with the organization of the Rancherias into the Mission Indian Agency under federal protection. … [T]hese Rancherias now had a trust relationship with the federal government to counterbalance all the forces marshaled against them: virulent racism, extralegal violence, discriminatory state laws, and local economic interests bent on grasping all regional resources from agricultural lands, to transportation corridors, to mineral and water rights (2012:48).

During the 1870s and 1880s there was a certain double-mindedness concerning the land which had once belonged to the Indians of San Diego County. Thorne explained:

The Mission Indian Agency creation was a contradiction—the executive order reservations were created at the precise moment when Congress embarked decisively on the plan to dissolve the nation's reservations through individualization and privatization. There was no political will to fix or defend boundaries or to stabilize reservation communities in California. The political will was unfailingly directed toward the speedy dissolution of the reservations and the termination of federal responsibility. Federal ambivalence over the government's role in Southern California Indian affairs gave a distinct advantage to the settlers ... (2012:48).

Some technical and scientific problems concerning the new reservation lands were evident to Helen Hunt Jackson (Jackson 1883), who had been assigned as a special federal agent to investigate the living conditions of southern California Indians in the late 1800s. Jackson was convinced that the government had purposefully left the traditional native lands out of the new reservation boundaries, and had given the native people the worst of the lands in the region.

When discussing the surveying of Indian reservations after 1876, Jackson (1883:72-73) said that the survey lines had been "laid off by guess" on an imperfect county map by the San Diego surveyor. Jackson explained that if the plan was to avoid giving the Indians good lands, and to leave their villages outside the reservation boundaries, surveyors were successful. While the Capitan Grande Reservation was being surveyed, she noted, both the surveyor, Wheeler, and the Indian agent, who was a clergyman, were living in the home of Strong, the very man who first rented those lands and then stole the best part. If new reservation lines were to be surveyed, she suggested that Major Horatio N. Rust, whom both she and Abbott Kinney recommended, should supervise. Rust and Kinney were the only men in southern California that Jackson absolutely trusted.

Thorne (2012) elaborated on some of the reasons that the surveying of the reservation lands in San Diego County had been so inaccurate, and even detrimental, to the native people. The rough terrain coupled with the imprecision of early surveying methods accounted for some of the inaccuracies, but Thorne believed that the native people also were not given the lands which the federal government had allocated to them.

She outlined some of the negatives involved in the surveying of the new reservation lands, including the use of rods and chains for measuring; surveyors who neglected to adjust for magnetic north; bureaucratic complications; slip-shod work by inept surveyors; bureaucratic errors which sometimes occurred innocently, but other times were obviously and blatantly deliberate; records of transactions on Indian-owned sections that were "clouded"; and the confusion and time-consuming constraints which arose when resurveys had to be redone. The list went on to include congressmen and other public officials who refused to consider land surveys for native lands unless they were pressured by their constituents; confusion between the Department of Interior and the General Land Office over whose duty or obligation it was to do certain surveys; errors created by corruption and greed; and surveyors who took money from rancho owners to draw inaccurate boundaries—which also often left out large amounts of land, resources ,and water rights.

Add to those the bribing of federal officials, officials who assured whites or other non-Indians that they would receive the best lands; non-Indians who felt that Indians should not be allowed to hold lands or water rights of their own; lack of any concerted will on the part of federal, state, and local government officials to see that Indians' rights were taken into consideration and protected; and, Thorne concluded, the ethnocentrism and lack of knowledge about the Indian culture—all of which contributed to the inaccuracies which were rampant within the surveying procedures for the lands meant for the native people of San Diego County.

Though President Ulysses S. Grant established eight reservations in December 1875, including lands at Rincon, Pala, La Jolla, Agua Caliente, Santa Ysabel (including Mesa Grande), Sycuan, Capitan Grande, and Cosmit, none of the reservations were in the same locations as the native people had once lived, and no reservation lands were given to the Ipai of the San Pasqual Valley (Thorne 2012). Not one Ipai native person was listed as holding land within the San Pasqual Valley. Only William Perry Bevington was recorded on the tax rolls of 1878 as owning land there, with the amount shown as 160 acres (Carrico 2010).

In Temecula Valley, just north of Ipai territory, the sheriff of San Diego County filed an eviction notice in 1875 notifying the Luiseños there that they had eleven days to vacate their homes. They were forced to leave behind adobe houses, fruit trees, and irrigated fields. In time, a few of those Luiseños settled in Pechanga Canyon, almost within sight of their old homes (Carrico 1987).

On May 11, 1877, a grand jury report shown in the *San Diego Union* included remarks indicating that the Indians of San Pasqual had gone several years without an Indian agent assigned to them by the US government. One San Diego County attorney noted that they had no one to go to for advice or relief, and the grand jury concluded that "… On the part of the General Government in regard to the Indians in this County … we would recommend that the Secretary of the Interior be petitioned to have a Commissioner of Indian Affairs appointed to have charge of their interest in the County" (*San Diego Union* 11 May 1877). The recommendation preceded a petition from a variety of San Diego civic leaders, and several letters from Father Anthony D. Ubach of San Diego (Carrico 2010:TS), who pled for "my poor Indians." These communications were sent to the Secretary of the Interior in Washington DC.

By November 17, 1877, the San Pasqual Ipai were facing the same fate as their Temecula Valley neighbors to the north. Three men native to the San Pasqual Valley—Isadore, Ysidro and Pedro Juan—were targeted by white settler W. P. Bevington, who testified in San Diego County Court papers that since January 1876 he had "put the Indians on notice that they should leave the contested acreage, but they had failed to do so" (Carrico 2010:TS). This Ysidro appears to be Ysidro Nejo, the last captain of San Pasqual.

On December 14, 1877 A.B. Hotchkiss, the attorney for the Indian defendants, filed a statement asking that the case be thrown out on the grounds that the district court had no jurisdiction over the defendants; that the facts as stated by the plaintiff were not sufficiently stated to bring such a suit, and there was a defect in the parties named in the suit — implying that not all of the named defendants had standing in the case. On February 4, 1878, the district court judge ruled in favor of Bevington, and on the 12th instructed the County Sheriff Ward to remove and evict the Indians on the disputed parcel, and to collect court fees; the claim to $500.00 in damages incurred by Bevington was not upheld (Carrico 2010:TS).

The sheriff carried out his sworn duty to serve the papers of eviction to the three Indians, and learned at that time that the three had no personal property, no livestock, and no cash with which to pay the court costs, which totaled $28.80.

Carrico adds:

> To the east white settlers were also moving in the deep Pamo Valley and trying to establish farms and ranches. Settlers such as William Ingraham, Charles Lloyd, and Trow took up land, married local Ipai women, and set down roots. The Trows lived mostly in what is now Boden Canyon and María Alto Gaucheno, who was born at San Pasqual in 1835, married into this German family. ... Practically bursting with civic pride, in their March 1882 report on the community at San Pasqual, the San Diego Union found ... a most thriving settlement of about fifteen families. The valley being well watered by the river and many never-failing springs, the crops are a 'dead certainty' any year and the great acreage of alfalfa and corn which annually matures there, shows that there is no better location in he county" (Carrico 2010:TS).

Carrico pointed out that these actions represented a type of "non-Indian remedy" for gaining desirable lands that the invaders to the area wanted:

> For non-Indians the mechanism for adjusting to difficulties was to file land claims (Superior Court files 1878) ensuring that any lingering land issues were resolved in favor of the white settlers. The final crushing blow to the San Pasqual people came in 1878 when deputy County Sheriff Ward served a Writ of Eviction and forced the remaining villagers out of their ancient home. The Writ was issued in response to the filing of a claim by local rancher William P. Bevington for the last unclaimed 40 acres occupied by San Pasqual villagers (Carrico 2010:TS).

Carrico (2010) described the parcel of land commandeered by Bevington and offered the following comments:

> This parcel of land probably represents the last remnant of the Pueblo of San Pasqual and was located in the northeast quarter of the southwest quarter of Section 34 approximately 1,000 feet southeast of the San Pasqual Indian Cemetery and along the northern edge of the river...In the thirty-two years between their eviction in 1878 until establishment of the San Pasqual Reservation in 1910, the once prosperous

Leonora La Chappa's Family Lineage

Four generations of La Chappa/Trask women. (From left) Audrey Toler, Helen Trask Lawson, Leonora La Chappa Trask, and Feliciana Nejo La Chappa. *Photo: Trask-La Chappa family.*

Leonora La Chappa Trask was born in 1881 in the San Felipe Valley. Leonora's father and mother, Jose Antonio La Chappa and Feliciana Nejo La Chappa, were both full-blood Ipai and were born in 1859, Antonio at Mesa Grande and Feliciana in the region of Santa Ysabel. Their La Chappa, Guachena, and Nejo clans have been associated since ancient times with the part of Ipai territory that includes the San Pasqual Valley. One of Florence Shipek's typed notes at her archives at Sycuan included a notation that: "La Chappa, Pena and Guachena were all San Pasqual" (Shipek:TS). The Jacome Family Tree (Ancestry.com 2012) lends support to that information, showing Feliciana's mother, Maria Jesusa Nejo; Feliciana's half-brother, Jose Domingo Yanke; Feliciana's mother-in-law, Angela Guachena La Chappa; along with Feliciana Nejo La Chappa, as all born in the San Pasqual Valley, though the family's oral tradition has indicated that Angela was born at Mesa Grande, and Maria Jesusa, Feliciana, and Jose Domingo were born at Santa Ysabel.

The genealogical documentation of these clans go back to the times when Leonora's maternal great-grandfather, Jermain Anej [Herman Nejo] (Ancestry.com 2012), carried timbers from Cuyamaca to the San Diego Mission. E. H. Davis (1936) maintained that Leonora's paternal

Angela Guachena (La Chappa).
Photo: C. G. Dubois.

grandmother, Angela Guachena, had lived at the San Diego Mission as a child. Angela was born about 1819 (Census of Mesa Grande 1890), and her father was Cornelio Guachena, born in the region of Mesa Grande, according to family records. Antonio La Chappa's father, Jose Bastian La Chappa (Lambert/Briggs, Eortega, Devers, Jr. and Jacome Family Trees Ancestry.com 2014) and Jose Bastian's parents, Logario and Maria Jesusa La Chappa (1928 Indian Rolls), trace back to the late 1700s and early 1800s in the region of Mesa Grande. Jose Bastian La Chappa narrated a version of the Ipai creation story that was recorded by Edward Curtis (1907) and is presented in the first chapter of this book.

Leonora's mother, Feliciana Nejo, Leonora's maternal grandmother, Maria Jesusa Nejo, and her maternal great-grandparents trace back not only to Yaqui Well (as mentioned, Jermain Anej—Herman Nejo) but to the region of Santa Ysabel (Maria Louisa Guacheno—married to Jermain Anej) as well. Maria Louisa Guacheno was born either 1816 or 1826 (Census of Santa Ysabel 1910). Maria Louisa's parents were Jose La Luz and Mi-hap (N.d.) as shown on the 1928 Indian Rolls.

Leonora married Frank Trask in 1902 and had two daughters: Florence born in 1904 and Helen in 1905. In 1909 they were the first family to move to the San Pasqual Indian Reservation in Valley Center. For eight years following Frank Trask's death in 1920, Leonora remained a widow. Sometime after 1928, Leonora married Adolph Scholder, half Indian, and they lived on her allotment at the San Pasqual Indian Reservation. Leonora eventually separated from Scholder, and during the 1940s she married Barona Tribal Chairman Ramon Ames. Following their marriage, she moved with him to his reservation to live out her final days. She died September 8, 1953, and was buried in the Barona Cemetery.

Phillip Crosthwaite and Father Ubach are standing with an unknown man at the site of the San Pasqual Cemetery, circa 1882. Mr. Charles Hill was later the recipient of the cemetery and chapel, and passed the cemetery, the chapel, and the five acres on which they were built, to Father Ubach and the Catholic Church in 1897. *Photo: Richard Carrico.*

people of San Pasqual were essentially a tribe without a home. While families like the Bevingtons, Clevengers, Bandys, Rockwoods, and others moved into the Indian's adobes…the Mesa Grande Reservation was home to several important clans and large families directly related to the San Pasqual people. The ancient village of Tekemuk at Mesa Grande had been the summer and fall home to the people of Pa'mu and was well known to the San Pasqual people, some of whom had parents and grandparents from this village. Life on the reservation would at least not be amongst strangers or foreign clans (Carrico 2010:TS).

And so it was that in 1878, only four years after the death of their leader Panto, the lives of the Ipai of the San Pasqual Valley would change dramatically. As a result of the eviction, three groups of native people emerged. One group would go to live with relatives at other reservations, including nearby Mesa Grande and Santa Ysabel, where some of their relatives already lived. A second group would settle at the northeastern end of the San Pasqual Valley, going into the hills to live and later securing civil homesteads there. A third group would go to Escondido and more northerly regions, including Los Angeles, Ontario and Placentia, in search of new pieces of property on which to live, and in search of work (Farris 1997 and Lipps 1920 in Carrico 2010:TS).

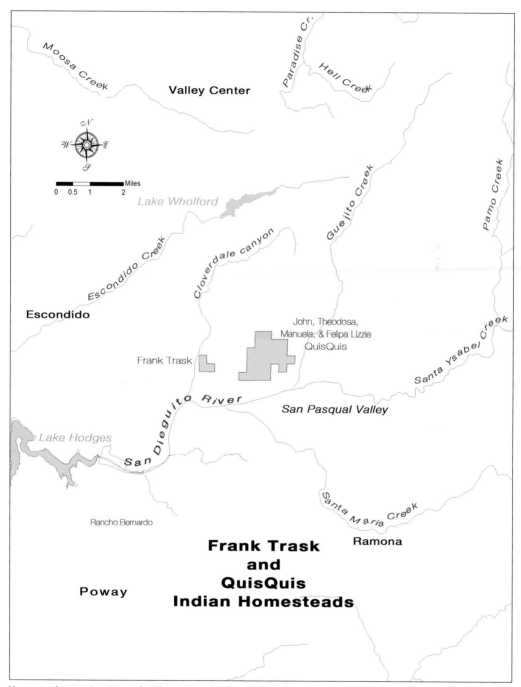

Homesteads near San Pasqual Valley, late 1800s (see page 116).

Ipai Trinidad Chrisano Ycheno sits in a doorway. The plight of Native Californians, living in poverty and often landless, had become a cause for reformers by the late nineteenth century. *Photo: E. H. Davis, San Diego History Center.*

Beck points out the strong connection between San Pasqual and Mesa Grande following the eviction of 1878: "The Indians gathered up their meager belongings and livestock. Many of them went to Mesa Grande where they were known and accepted and, where it is said, Panto had been their Captain as well" (Beck 2012: final paragraph).

1883–1887 Homesteads

Some of those people who were evicted from the San Pasqual Valley in 1878 used the Homestead Act (see below) to procure lands from the US government in the canyons to the northeast of their former homes, on public lands. Between 1883-1887, ten families, made up of about thirty Ipai, took up residence in the northeastern hills of the San Pasqual Valley, claiming land under civil authority (Lipps 1920 in Carrico 2010:TS). These homesteads were located above current-day Rockwood Canyon and had been acquired by gaining legal title to the public lands.

A half a century later, John P. Harrington made a trip through the San Pasqual Valley, accompanied by informant Ysidro Nejo, an Ipai who had lived both in the San Pasqual Valley and at Mesa Grande. They reportedly visited a canyon between the two Indian villages and took a photo of a place that Harrington described in his notes as the canyon to where some of the Ipai had moved after the evictions of 1878.

Father Ubach, of the Santa Ysabel Asistencia, reminisced in 1883 about what life had been like for the native people of the San Pasqual Valley before the arrival of the invaders who had stolen their traditional lands:

> San Pascual [sic] 17 years ago [that is in 1866] had a population of 300 [Indian] souls with more than 600 acres of very good agricultural lands; now occupied by more than 20 squatters that with the riffle [sic] in hand scare away the Indians, not leaving one. Whisky and brutal force; nothing but the cemetery and chapel [are] left. The few Indians that were left, two years ago [in 1881] had to go away and live among rocky mountains like wild beasts; there are no lands in this vicinity for the Indians (Carrico 2010:TS).

Indian Homestead Act — Dawes Act of 1887

During the 1870s and 1880s, a difference of opinion divided America (Canby 2004). One group saw the Indians as poverty-stricken, often homeless people, while the second group viewed the native people as being in the way of white settlers who wanted to take over the lands. Though the native people of all regions of the United States offered consistent, continuing, and effective resistance to the invaders, the two attitudes above seemed to be the prevailing ones among anglos. It was those attitudes that led to the General Allotment Act of 1887, also known as the Indian Homestead Act or the Dawes Act.

The Dawes Act included government legislation passed in 1887 that remained in effect until 1934. The act was meant to Americanize the native people, and history has shown that far from protecting the native people, the Dawes Act directly contributed to the fragmentation and gradual disintegration of many native tribes, bands and clans.

A second major effect of the Dawes Act was to increasingly open up native lands to settlement by those same invaders (and their descendants) who had stolen native lands across the continent. Under this act any native person who applied for an allotment could receive a parcel of private land, taken from lands previously held by tribes, which would then be held in trust for the next twenty-five years — at which time the deed would be turned over to the new owner. Depending on how the land would be used, the allotment might be 160, 80, or 40 acres, and people were allowed to choose their own allotments. Upon taking ownership of the land, the owner would also be entitled to full United States citizenship.

Indian allotments were given in the vicinity of San Pasqual Valley for those who applied and qualified. By 1894, Frank Trask and others from San Pasqual had been given Indian allotments in the area of the San Dieguito River.

With each head of family eligible to receive 160 acres, the native people could receive double that amount if they were going to graze animals. Additional members of the household could also receive 80 acres. During the twenty-five years that the title remained with the government, recipients of land would not have to pay taxes, since they would be learning land management techniques and how to manage as landholders. After the first

7/82   Morning Light   ROBERT FREEMAN

twenty-five years, however, many native people found themselves faced with excessive property taxes, which often meant they eventually lost their Dawes Act Allotment lands. During the Allotment Era, the native population reached its lowest point in history in terms of landholdings. In 1887 Native Americans held 138 million acres, but by 1934 they held only 48 million acres. 20 million of those 48 million acres were desert land (Canby 2004).

Thorne believed that the government positions created by the Homestead Policy, including the positions of Indian agents, were rampant with contradictions. Some government officials wanted the Ipai and other native people to apply for 160 acres of homestead land, toward the goal of eventually making them United States citizens. Others desired that the public domain lands intended for the Indians should be parceled out as quickly as possible. Quick dispersal of lands to the native people would mean that the lands left over could be parceled out to non-Indians. Some non-Indians had already settled on some of the best lands, even though those lands had been allocated for reservations. Much of the land allocated to the native people was of inferior quality, leading to them being unable to farm or live on it, with the result being that they would sell the property. Non-Indians who had been waiting in the wings could then avail themselves of the opportunity to acquire what had been a native allotment.

Some Native Americans were required to change their names to anglicized forms, supposedly to make the paperwork easier for government officials, but, perhaps, more as part of a deliberate effort to suppress the native culture. Though the government said that the Dawes Act was meant to promote land ownership among the native people, the end result was that the number of landless Indians increased, and the number of non-Indian settlers who took over Indian lands also increased. As native people lost their allotment lands across the continent, they sometimes also lost their eligibility to be recognized as Native Americans, along with the government benefits which may have resulted from that recognition. All of these impacts led to the destabilization of native society, meaning that the Dawes Act also added to the loss of Native American culture, traditions, and languages (Canby 2004).

Reformers Fight for Improved Conditions

Helen Hunt Jackson investigated the Indians' plight as a special federal agent in 1883. She recommended removal of all white settlers from the reservations, and suggested that lands be patented to Indian residents. No action occurred as a result of her investigations, except that the Federal Office of Indian Affairs was authorized to remove squatters from Indian reservations, using military aid.

Jackson and Abbott Kinney did help enlighten the US populace to the dismal living

Opposite page left: Government policies such as the Dawes Act led to an increase in the number of landless Indians, the destabilization of native society, and the loss of Native American culture, traditions, and languages. *Drawing: Robert Freeman.*

conditions of the once-prosperous Ipai in San Diego County. In July 1883 they wrote a report entitled: "*Report on the Condition and Needs of the Mission Indians of California,*" documenting the deplorable conditions of those living closest to the white settlements, rather than those living in the backcountry, who had continued their more traditional ways of agricultural pursuits and animal husbandry. The report revealed that native people were often forced to leave their adobe houses, fields, and animals, so that Americans and others could take them over.

The Jackson-Kinney report said:

> [T]hey have been driven out, year by year, by the white settlers ... robber whites who drove them out. The responsibility for this wrong rests, perhaps, equally divided between the United States Government, which permitted lands thus occupied by peaceful agricultural communities to be sold in market ... lands which had been fenced, irrigated, tilled and lived on by Indians for many generations. The Government cannot justify this neglect on the plea of ignorance. Repeatedly, in the course of the last 30 years, both Regular Agents in charge of the Mission Indians and Special Agents sent out to investigate their condition have made to the Indian Bureau full reports setting forth these facts (Jackson and Kinney 1884:TS).

Jackson also wrote the book *Ramona* in 1884 with the intention of sparking public interest in the plight of the Mission Indians of California, with her goal ultimately being to help the native people of southern California.

Jackson's final report numbered fifty-six pages and dealt mostly with the Mission Indians in the three southernmost counties of California. Well over half the report was documentary evidence, including the legal brief of Brunson and Wells, and letters and affidavits gathered during her three months in California. Jackson and Kinney (1883) detailed eleven specific recommendations summarized as follows.

1. Resurveying and marking existing reservations.

2. Removal of all white settlers from reservations.

3. The upholding and defending of Indian claims.

4. The patenting, with a twenty-five-year trust period, of both old and new reservations to Indian residents.

5. The establishment of more schools, one immediately at Rincon and a second at Santa Ysabel. Following an earlier recommendation by Jackson, it was suggested that only female teachers be employed in isolated villages. In addition, religious as well as industrial training should be included.

6. Proper supervision of the reservations was to include two inspections a year for each village or settlement.

7. Hire a law firm in Los Angeles to serve as special attorneys in cases relating to the Mission Indians.

8. A judicious distribution of farm equipment.

9. A fund for the purchase of food and clothing for the aged and the sick.

10. The purchase of two tracts of land, including the Pauma Ranch and the Santa Ysabel Ranch.

11. The San Carlos group in Monterey and other small bands north of the mission agency boundary should be included under its jurisdiction (Jackson and Kinney 1883).

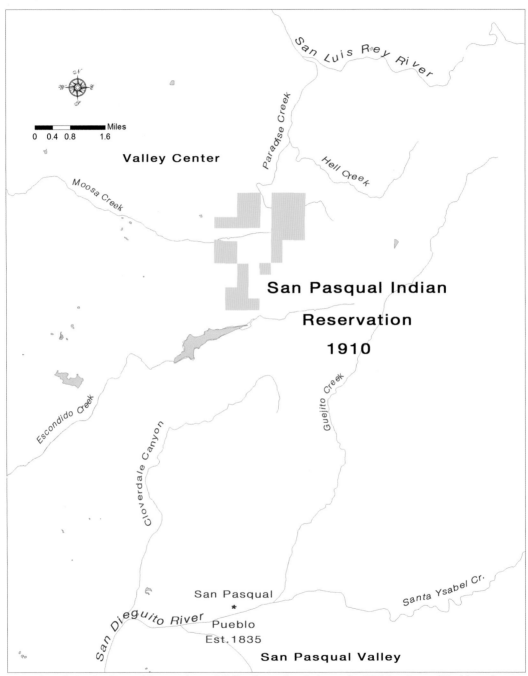

Location of 1910 San Pasqual Reservation and Valley Center in relation to the 1835 San Pasqual Pueblo and San Pasqual Valley.

5

A New San Pasqual Reservation

The last decade of the nineteenth century and the first two decades of the twentieth century marked the beginnings of today's San Pasqual Indian Reservation, though the Ipai had lived throughout the region for thousands of years before. This chapter will explore those beginnings.

Following the 1878 eviction of the Ipai from the San Pasqual Valley, the original native families were forced to relocate outside of their traditional homeland on neighboring reservations or wherever they could find refuge. In 1891, the Smiley Commission designated 2,000 acres of land for the San Pasqual Band, but the new reservation was placed in Valley Center in the midst of Luiseño territory, six miles north of the band's traditional lands. By 1907 no one from the San Pasqual Band had relocated to this new reservation, but white squatters had homesteaded some of the land, decreasing the original acres to 1,200. Although some Ipai wanted land only in San Pasqual Valley, United States government attempts to buy land there were not successful, so efforts shifted to the reservation in Valley Center, including buying out white squatter improvements on reservation lands or reaching legal settlements with white squatters who had encroached there.

In December 1909, Frank Trask, described in government documents as "an industrious and progressive Indian," along with his full-blood Ipai wife, Leonora La Chappa Trask, and their two daughters, Florence and Helen, moved onto the San Pasqual Reservation in Valley Center. In 1910 the reservation was trust-patented to the San Pasqual Band as a whole, although special agent to the Indians, Charles Kelsey, had recommended to the commissioner of Indian Affairs that the land be patented in the names of only those Indians actually living there.

Trask, an Indian judge and policeman, and his family kept the reservation lands intact and made them productive. Government lawsuits against white squatters, and one case of harassment against Trask by non-Indians who had trespassed on reservation lands, were documented.

Frank Trask died in 1920, leaving his wife, Leonora, age 39, and his two daughters, Florence, age 15, and Helen, age 14, to keep the reservation intact. The women lived there alone, with their families, until the arrival of others in the late 1950s.

The Establishment of the New Reservation

The land for the new reservation in Valley Center had been allocated in 1891, following the decision by an activist group named the Indian Rights Association to promote the well-being and acculturation of Native Americans. The group had been founded in 1882 in Philadelphia, and after forming a commission of inquiry, headed by Albert K. Smiley and other members of the Indian Rights Association, state and federal governments resolved to establish Indian lands for the sole use of dispossessed native people (Pancoast 1884).

On January 12, 1891, the US Congress authorized the following:

> Be it enacted by the Senate and House of Representatives of the United States of America in Congress assembled, that immediately after the passage of this act the Secretary of the Interior shall appoint three disinterested persons as commissioners to arrange a just and satisfactory settlement of the Mission Indians residing in the State of California, upon reservations which shall be secured to them as hereinafter provided (Pancoast 1884).

While the *"Act for the Relief of the Mission Indians in the State of California"* was created by the US Congress, the legislation was also supported by whites who hoped to gain lands for the Indians and by native people who hoped to see the return of some of their traditional lands within the state of California. On some rancherias, however, family groups and individuals were placed with unfamiliar people, and at times were placed on the same lands as their traditional enemies (Hyer 2001). Some Indian groups did move onto lands suggested by the Smiley Commission, and from 1892-1910, most of the lands pinpointed by the commission were put into trust for the Indians by the Federal Office of Indian Affairs.

On December 29, 1891, Albert Smiley issued a report referencing the Ipai who had settled in the canyons at the northeastern end of the San Pasqual Valley. Though he described them as being at Township 11 South, which was in Valley Center, it is clear from the details that his report actually referenced Township 12 South, in the San Pasqual Valley. Smiley wrote:

> On the San Pasqual Mountains, in T 11 S., R 1 W., S. B. M. are some 9 or 10 families of Indians, living on public lands. These were cruelly and wrongfully driven from the San Pasqual Valley a few years since; their land there, though granted to them by the Mexican Government, having been patented by the United States to white men. The difficulties attending an attempt to unsettle the lands thus held, are so great the Commission hesitates to recommend an effort to restore these people to their rights; a surveyor was therefore instructed to find on what descriptions of land they are living, and it accords both with the views of the Commissioners and the wishes of the Indians, that these should be entered as Homesteads, under the special provisions of the Homestead Law for Indians. The township has not been officially surveyed, but the survey made for the Commission by E. L. Dorn, a careful and competent surveyor, locates them…all in Township 11 South, R 1 West, San Bernardino Meridian.

Five unidentified Indian boys standing in front of a wagon and a house. Location is either Agua Caliente (now known as Warner Springs) or Warner Ranch. *Photo: Henry L. Davis, San Diego Historical Society.*

Was the government placement of the San Pasqual Band six miles north of their traditional valley an intentional effort to regroup them closer to other reservations, since their new reservation was near Rincon, Pala, Pauma Valley, and La Jolla, or were there other reasons for the group's relocation? The mis-location of the new reservation would occasion the exchange of a multitude of letters throughout the years, as government officials, Indian agents, native people, and white settlers sought to make sense of the presence of the San Pasqual Indian Reservation in Valley Center. It's hard to believe the government would make this kind of mistake.

Historian Richard Carrico noted the movement of the Ipai onto their reservation in Valley Center:

> As a result of the Act for the Relief of the California Mission Indians ... in 1910 some members of the band moved to the new reservation, but most families continued to live at Mesa Grande, Santa Ysabel and elsewhere. The first families at San Pasqual included Frank Trask, his wife, and his children (Carrico 2010:TS).

Meanwhile, on May 12, 1903, a southwestern Trail of Tears began for the Cupeño Indians of Agua Caliente (Hyer 2001). Cupeño is a Spanish derivation of the native place-name Kupa, with "eno" added, meaning a people or person who comes from Kupa (Dickason 1997). The native people called themselves Kuupangax-wichem, meaning "the people who slept here." Cupa was one of the smallest of the California tribes, never having more than a thousand people. They once lived at the headwaters of the San Luis Rey River in the valley of San Jose de Valle within a ten square-mile diameter. On May 12, 1903, they were forcibly evicted from their homes at Warner Springs and made to walk to the Pala Reservation, where the government relocated them on the same reservation as the Luiseños of Pala.

On September 5, 1903 (Hyer 2001), the San Felipe Ipai were also forcibly removed from their traditional lands, twelve miles south of Warner Springs, and were forced to walk to Pala, where they would live on one reservation with the Cupeños from Warner Springs and the Luiseños of Pala. Among the group of Ipai from San Felipe was Blun Nejo, whose father was Calistro Nejo and whose mother was Feliciana Nejo [La Chappa], mother of Leonora La Chappa Trask. Blun's paternal grandparents were Jose and Josefa Nejo. Jose Nejo had been captain (*Kwitutc*) at Mesa Grande, but was later shown at Pala (Gifford 1919-1920). Josefa's mother was Yecmai La Chappa, a surname meaning short. Yecmai means looking for a heart. Nejo was a Diegueño name from before Spanish times, with Nex being the correct Diegueño rendering of Nejo. The name meant "handing something (a gift) to someone" (Gifford 1919-1920:5-17).

In 1904 Mary Watkins, who had worked with novelist and anthropologist Constance DuBois (DuBois 1909) to help basketmakers at the Mesa Grande Indian Reservation sell their wares to Eastern buyers, was a neighbor of Frank Trask and Leonora La Chappa Trask. She wrote a letter attesting to Frank and Leonora's good character as they were working on moving into a residence of which she had knowledge. On July 26, 1904, the superintendent of the Indian School, Charles E. Shell, responded to Mrs. Watkins's letter and offered his pleasure in being able to assist Frank Trask, "an industrious and progressive Indian," in securing a home. The letter was addressed to Frank Trask's father-in-law, Antonio La Chappa, who served as captain and Indian judge at Mesa Grande. The superintendent not only commended Frank and Leonora in the letter, but added his admiration for Antonio as well:

> I have your letter written by Mrs. Watkins concerning your son-in-law, Frank Trask, who desires to occupy the place heretofore occupied by Beresford. In reply I have to say that I am always glad to assist an industrious progressive Indian to have a home, and Mrs. Watkins speaks well both of this man Trask and his wife. Before any change is made, I would like to know if this arrangement will [word illegible] anyone. I do not want to do anything that will make trouble as the change of Anita and Adolph did. ... Trask will plant trees and make a nice home. That's just what I want so others will see and do the same thing. That is the thing that I have admired most about yourself and I am glad to hear that you are trying to do the right thing in other ways. Write and let me know about this proposed change and I can then answer more intelligently about it. The Commissioner of Indian Affairs will be here the last of this week or the first of next and if any of your people want to see him you can come over. He is the head man of Indian Affairs at Washington.

Leonora La Chappa Trask.
Photo: *Trask-La Chappa family.*

Special agent to the Indians of California Charles E. Kelsey, who worked for ten to twelve years to gain lands for the native people in California, including the San Pasqual Band, stated:

> In September 1906 ... I was appointed Purchasing and Allotting Agent of Lands, Water Rights, etc. for the California Indians. ... In the previous fiscal year I had made an investigation of the conditions prevailing among Indians in California. I ... received my appointment in August 1905. I doubt if anyone in Congress or out had any idea of the difficulties of making such an investigation. ... The situation of the California Indians has no parallel in America. ... [I]t seems clear that at least 90 percent of the California Indians perished within the memory of men now living (Kelsey 1913).

On March 1, 1907, the Amended Homestead Land Act for Indians was passed by the US government (34 Stat., L., 1015-1022), authorizing the Secretary of the Interior to:

> Select, set apart, and cause to be patented to the Mission Indians in the State of California, such tracts as he may find on investigation to be in the occupancy and

127

possession of the several bands or villages of Indians which had not been selected previously for them by the Smiley Commission under the Act of January 12, 1891 [26 Stat., L., 712].

An August 12, 1907, letter from Charles Kelsey to the commissioner of the General Land Office requested: "The purchase of a trust for the San Pasqual Indians." That same year, the Sequoyah League — pro-Indian sympathizers — published a report on the living conditions of the displaced native people of California, where they talked about the San Pasqual Band: "Nothing yet has been accomplished for these Indians, but it is hoped that they may be cared for in the near future" [Bulletin 4 1907].

On August 25, 1907, Thomas M. Games, superintendent of the Volcan Indian School at Santa Ysabel, issued a report telling about the seven reservations, including San Pasqual, under his jurisdiction:

> These Indians are and always have been self-supporting ... engaged in farming and stock raising ... wheat, barley, corn, beans, hay and vegetables. Their stock consists chiefly of horses and cattle. ... [T]here are about 30 of the San Pasqual Indians, who are presumed to be under the jurisdiction of this agency.

By 1908 special agent to the Indians of California, R.S. Connell, was being dispatched by the commissioner of Indian Affairs to make an investigation of the San Pasqual Indians. A January 25, 1908, letter from white squatter Wilburn Reed, Valley Center, to the commissioner in Washington DC, revealed that Connell had already approached him about selling his "improvements" on the lands designated as the San Pasqual Indian Reservation:

> Agent Connell has shown me it is just a matter of time until I am dispossessed by the Indians, so the quicker it comes the better as if I am going to lose my farm here I wish to get land under some of the Reclamation Service projects before it is all gone. The value of my improvements on this place are easily worth $1500 ... the money to be paid by December first, upon which date I will vacate, leaving everything in good condition (Reed Letter to Commissioner of Indian Affairs 1908).

Government document L-80665-16 offered comments on Wilburn Reed's character:

> Wilburn Reed stands out as a conspicuous example; he has strong spirit and the other settlers have grouped around him, to resist the Indians being given the land that was set aside as a reservation. Reed, using thrift and industry, according to Kelsey, has increased the value of his 160 acres to a value of at least $5000 (Doc. L-80665-16 N.d.).

On January 29, 1908, Connell reported to the commissioner of Indian Affairs, Washington DC and began the letter by quoting the Commissioner's prior instructions to Connell:

> Referring to my instructions, '... Make an investigation of the San Pasqual Indians, who claim to have homesteads independent of the government ... you will ascertain if they have homesteads and are locally independent of the government or not'

Helen (left) and Florence Trask (second from right) attended Bear Valley Elementary School circa 1913. *Photo: Trask-La Chappa family.*

... there are 42 San Pasqual Indians, 20 of whom are scattered in among the surrounding tribes and reservations, 22 of whom are living in San Diego County. Of the last 22, four have used ordinary homestead rights. ... All of the San Pasqual speak the same as Mexicans. An official speaking through the average interpreter would believe that they desired to be independent of the Government and did not want anything to do with the Government, etc. but when one can question them further and can talk Spanish with them he learns their true feelings. They have no confidence in the government of the United States (Connell to Commissioner of Indian Affairs1908).

Also on January 29, 1908, Connell wrote a letter to Amos R. Frank, superintendent of the Indian School at Mesa Grande, that on the matter of purchasing land in the original San Pasqual Valley, which Mr. Frank had suggested and then thoroughly investigated, that it was, "... out of the question. ... [H]owever, if you know of any owners who wish to sell their holdings at a reasonable price ... procure their offers" (Connell to Amos Frank 1908).

Once white squatters on the reservation lands and some members of the Valley Center community realized that the San Pasqual Indian Reservation in Valley Center was going to be populated by the Ipai, their resistance and opposition to living near native people came to the forefront. Some of them hired attorneys in Washington DC, to plead their case for the reservation lands to be returned to the San Pasqual Valley, claiming that it was what the San Pasqual Indians really wanted. Others produced affidavits from those who said they had lived in the San Pasqual Valley before the eviction of 1878 and would take land nowhere but there. Some Valley Center community members, including several of the white squatters being challenged by the US government, mounted a concerted letter-writing effort, telling government officials that they were serious in their efforts to avoid living near Indians, or having their children go to school with them.

A February 17, 1908, letter from William P. Belshe, whom R. S. Connell had referenced in a January 29, 1908, letter because "his final patent was not issued and he got it held up, 120 acres being in the reservation," wrote to Frank Bond, chief clerk, US Land Office Agent, who referred the letter to Charles Kelsey. Mr. Belshe wrote:

> I am enclosing herewith a petition which I wish you to give your attention and consideration. The San Pasqual Indian Reservation was originally surveyed in Township 12 ... and was by some mistake placed in Township 11 ... around the patented lands and on lands on which Mr. Belshe, Mr. Woods, Mr. Reed, Mr. Dinwiddie, and Mr. Kiewiett have lived out their time with the intention of having said lands patented. The lands are not sufficient (I believe) to support the Indians and we pray that you will place the reservation where it belongs." The petition asked for the land to be given in Township 12, "Where the present homes of the Indians are (Belshe to Bond 1908).

Another letter written on February 17, 1908, from Kelsey to Amos Frank, mentioned a Main Report Kelsey had made on March 21, 1906, his Special Report of 1907, and his Final Report of 1913, the last before his retirement. All concerned the San Pasqual Indians. His letter notified Frank that buying out white squatter Wilburn Reed for $1,500, even before further funds were allocated, would be the course of action to take. He wrote:

> Only three of the San Pasqual Indians out of forty odd have homesteads from the public domain. One of these has been lost on a mortgage and the other two are almost worthless. This Wilburn Reed place is the chief one to be bought. All the others together should not amount to more than $500. Most of them have only one or two forties within the reservation with no improvements and their damage will be small (Kelsey to Amos Frank 1908).

Kelsey also offered to oversee the quitclaim process with Wilburn Reed, when Superintendent Frank was in that neighborhood in April. On February 29, 1908, Hugh J. Baldwin, superintendent of schools of San Diego County, wrote to Honorable S. C. Smith, House of Representatives, as he attempted to inform the congressman that the San Pasqual Indian Reservation had been placed in the wrong area: "With reference to a mistake that was made ... in an attempt to furnish an Indian Reservation near the San Pasqual River [actually Valley Center]. Unfortunately the township should be 12 instead of 11. The Indians wish to remain in township 12 near the San Pasqual Valley" (Baldwin to Smith 1908).

F. M. Conser, chief clerk of the Office of Indian Affairs, followed up on the above letter by assigning Charles Kelsey the following task: "You will ... report to this Office what lands should be reserved for the San Pasqual Indians ... and ... how the error which placed them in one township, when in fact they were living in another, occurred" (Conser to Kelsey 1908).

The acting commissioner of Indian Affairs in Washington D C, wrote to Charles Kelsey on March 5, 1908, and noted that on February 29, 1908:

> The Department granted authority for you to expend $1500 in the purchase of the improvements of Wilburn Reed, which he erroneously made on land belonging to the San Pasqual Indians; payment to be made on the execution of a quit-claim deed to the United States of all his right, title, and interest in and to the land occupied by Mr. Reed (Acting Commissioner to Kelsey 1908).

Hugh J. Baldwin, superintendent of schools, San Diego, wrote a letter on March 10, 1908, to US Congressman S. C. Smith:

> Please permit me to transmit to you, a communication with reference to a mistake that was made in a township in an attempt to furnish an Indian Reservation near the *San Pasqual River*. Unfortunately the township should be 12 instead of 11. The Indians wish to remain in township 12 near the San Pasqual Valley (Baldwin to Smith 1908).

By May 5, 1908, it was looking as though the US government was entertaining the idea of exchanging the reservation lands in Valley Center for lands in the San Pasqual Valley. White settlers and those who said they were native evictees from the valley had employed a letter-writing campaign which apprised government officials of their wishes for the exchange to become a reality. A May 5, 1908, letter from C. F. Larrabee, assistant commissioner of Indian Affairs, to Congressman S. C. Smith read:

> [T]he Office has called upon Special Agent C. E. Kelsey to report at the earliest possible time what lands should be reserved for these Indians, with the view to the restoration of either one or the other of the two tracts which have been set apart for their use, through an error in description (Larrabee to Smith 1908).

Another letter from white squatter William P. Belshe on May 15, 1908, to the Honorable S. C. Smith, of the House of Representatives, revealed how some of the whites in Valley Center felt: "We don't want to sell our homes and we don't like to be unjustly surrounded by Indians. Of all the land in the reservation on claim in our Township 11 there is not enough to do the Indians any good and will not be as satisfactory to them as their present homes" (Belshe to Smith 1908).

On May 28, 1908, Charles Kelsey sent a letter to the commissioner of Indian Affairs in Washington, D. C. informing him that: "R. S. Connell made a report Jan. 29, 1908, to the Indian Office recommending that … it would be better to buy out the squatters on the reservation actually set aside for the San Pasqual Indians [Valley Center]" (Kelsey to Commissioner 1908).

A September 7, 1908, letter from Kelsey to the commissioner told the story of what happened:

> I enclose you herewith a quitclaim deed executed by Wilburn Reed and his wife Sadie N. Reed to the [detailed land description follows] in San Diego Co., Calif. This land is within the limits of the San Pasqual Indian Reservation and has been occupied by Reed for some years as a squatter. On January 23, 1908 an agreement was made between Reed and his wife and Special Agent R. S. Connell, on behalf of the United States, by which Reed agreed to quitclaim to the United States whatever rights and improvements he possessed for the sum of $1500 (Kelsey to Commissioner 1908).

On November 29, 1908, five months after Connell visited white squatter T. H. Coomer and offered him $300 for his improvements, Coomer wrote to the Office of Indian Affairs, referencing his service in the Civil War and telling what he had done on the land: "Have cropped it [the land] two years and by virtue of over 3 years service in the War of '61 to '65 feel that it's hard for one to give it up for the pittance of $300 as appraised. Yet if this is just, I would."

On January 1, 1909, the territory of Thomas M. Games, superintendent of the Volcan Indian Agency, at Mesa Grande and Santa Ysabel, was divided, and Amos R. Frank was assigned as superintendent of the Indian School and special disbursing agent Mesa Grande. On January 7, 1909, Frank commented in a letter to the commissioner of Indian Affairs, "at San Pasqual the Indians are either scattered or dead." Mr. Frank would become instrumental during his tenure in locating San Pasqual Indians under his jurisdiction and attempting to find land allotments for them.

On January 26, 1909, though negotiations were still in progress concerning an exchange of reservation lands in Valley Center for lands in the San Pasqual Valley, all of the land in Township 12 S., R. 1 W — the land where the San Pasqual Indians had lived before their eviction — was included in the Cleveland National Forest by proclamation. Nevertheless, for years after, San Diego County locals — including Indian agents, native people, white settlers, and government officials — would continue to write a multitude of letters requesting either the purchase of land for the Ipai in the San Pasqual Valley, or the exchanging of lands at Township 11 in Valley Center for the original lands at Township 12 in the San Pasqual Valley.

Charles Kelsey and Amos Frank ultimately joined forces in their efforts to provide lands for the San Pasqual Band, exploring the possibilities of buying lands in the San Pasqual Valley while working to follow R. S. Connell's recommendations to buy out white squatters on the reservation lands in Valley Center. An April 10, 1909, letter from John Francis, Jr., acting chief of the Land Division, to Kelsey, illustrated that the two were making progress.

The letter read: "You are advised that under date of March 27, 1909 the First Assistant Secretary granted authority for the expenditure of $300 to purchase the improvements of T. H. Coomer, made on lands belonging to the San Pasqual Indians."

During this time some of the Ipai living at Mesa Grande had begun contacting the Indian agents, asking for allotments to ensure that the lands they were improving would not one day be taken over by white settlers, which frequently happened when native people migrated to their traditional seasonal locations in order to hunt, gather foods, or reunite with bands, clans and tribes from other areas. On May 8, 1909, Frank Trask and Julio Ortega, both of whom lived at the Mesa Grande Indian Reservation, submitted requests for allotments to Amos Frank. On that same day, Frank Trask also sent a request for an allotment to Francis E. Leupp, commissioner of Indian Affairs in Washington DC.

Frank Trask made a second request to Commissioner Leupp twelve days later, on May 20, 1909. On May 23, 1909 Commissioner Leupp told of the approval of Frank Trask's application for an allotment in a letter that read:

> On May 20, 1909 Frank Trask applied for an allotment of land on the Mesa Grande Reservation and said that his family consisted of himself, wife and two minor children. A copy of his application, which was approved by Amos Frank, Superintendent in Charge of the Mesa Grande Indians, is enclosed herewith.

On May 24, 1909, C. F. Hauke, chief clerk of the Office of Indian Affairs, responded to a letter that Amos Frank had written him, telling of the need for allotments:

> The Office is in receipt of your letter of May 8, 1909 transmitting a communication from Julio Ortega, requesting that allotments be made to the Indians of the Mesa Grande Reservation. The Office intends to allot all the Mission Indian Reserves in California at such time as the work can be taken up conveniently and an agent is available. (Hauke 1909 to Superintendent Frank).

On July 1, 1909, Amos Frank requested of the commissioner of Indian Affairs that three judge positions be established for his jurisdictional area, with a pay of $84 per year. A report from Harwood Hall, supervisor of Indian Schools, June 18, 1909, showed that there were four reservations within the Mesa Grande District, including San Pasqual, which had a population of thirty. Amos Frank was making progress in identifying San Pasqual Indians, and on July 8, 1909, he sent a letter to the commissioner of Indian Affairs, Washington DC: "Through the cooperation of our Mesa Grande Indian Judges we have found 64 San Pasqual Indians. ... I have asked that authority be given to establish an Indian Court to further cooperate with me in my investigation. Mr. Kelsey and other agents made quite an effort to obtain data."

On July 8, 1909, Amos Frank wrote to the commissioner of Indian Affairs:

> Through the cooperation of our Mesa Grande Indian Judges [this would include Antonio La Chappa and Ysidro Nejo] we have found 64 San Pasqual Indians. Through

eviction by the local courts they have been so intimidated that it was a long time that I could induce them to say anything for fear of being arrested. I have asked that authority be given to establish an Indian Court to further cooperate with me in my investigation. Mr. Kelsey and other agents made quite an effort to obtain data (Frank to Commissioner 1909).

Mr. Kelsey wrote the following letter to Mr. Frank on August 10, 1909:

I enclose herewith a letter from Wilburn Reed, which indicates that some of the low class whites on the Bear Valley mesa have been trying to work on the Indians and keep them out of their new lands for the benefit of the said white men. I think you'd better get in communication with Mr. Reed. ... [I]t is a valuable place and would sell for $5000 at least. You ought not to have any difficulty in getting two or three families of Indians to go there to live. It will probably not be wise to try to make the entire band, now or at any time go there.

A momentous occasion occurred at the San Pasqual Indian Reservation in Valley Center on August 30, 1909, when Amos Frank notified that same commissioner: "The survey has been made only a short time — the beginning of this summer, 1909. ... I found a regular mix-up as to lands claimed by the San Pasqual reserve. ... Homes for two or three families have been purchased by Mr. Kelsey, and he advised me to place several families on them ..."

A letter from Charles E. Kelsey on September 9, 1909, reaffirmed his instructions to Amos Frank when he informed him again that:

"There are one or two San Pasqual families at Mesa Grande I am told. Put them there [the San Pasqual Indian Reservation in Valley Center] if you can't get anyone else. I see no present prospect in getting anything in San Pasqual Valley. We have never had enough money to get enough land for one family there" (Indian Agent Charles Kelsey, 1909).

Also in October 1909 James M. Woods wrote a letter of grievance to the Office of Indian Affairs, containing the following partial statement: "Is this the white man's Government or an Indian Government that we have to live under. ... This Indian Reservation has been shoved onto us by mistake."

While Indian agents Kelsey and Frank were searching for one or two San Pasqual families from Mesa Grande to put at the San Pasqual Indian Reservation in Valley Center, the commissioner of Indian Affairs, R. G. Valentine, wrote to Amos Frank on October 11, 1909, informing him that: "The Office has received your letter of September 22, 1909 concerning an investigation by you of the situation in the San Pasqual Valley. ... Authority is hereby granted...for the purpose of obtaining data for the San Pasqual Indians to recover their homes [in Township 12, the San Pasqual Valley]."

Jose Burro and his wife Maria Waters. She was offered a place at the San Pasqual Reservation but was not interested in moving there. *Photo: E. H. Davis, San Diego History Center.*

During the month of October 1909 Amos Frank may have dispatched Frank and Leonora La Chappa Trask to Valley Center to see the Wilburn Reed improvements on the San Pasqual Indian Reservation, as evidenced by Wilburn Reed's October 26, 1909, letter to the superintendent and special disbursing agent: "How is our reservation coming along? There was an Indian and his wife here to look at the place. I wasn't at home so do not know what they thought of the place. I will be able to give possession on or before the first of December."

Government documents show that sometime before October 26, 1909, L.W. Green, special allotting agent, had offered the property at the San Pasqual Indian Reservation in Valley Center to Maria Antonia Waters of Mesa Grande, and she responded with the information that she was not interested in moving there. Green then wrote the following letter to Amos R. Frank:

> I have just had a final talk with Maria Antonia Waters and she says definitely that she will not accept the place which you offered her at San Pasqual, and that you may turn it over to anyone whom you please. I am sorry to have her throw away this chance on account of her grandsons, but I suppose that neither I nor Lonergan has power to compel her to go if she does not wish to do so.

Another government document, undated, signed by C. F. Hauke, the second assistant commissioner of Indian Affairs, noted of Maria Antonia Waters that, "Maria Antonia Waters was not at Warner's when land was removed to Pala [1903]. Has rights at San Pasqual Reservation, and Superintendent Frank offered her very desirable land there which she refused. Facts were submitted to Office for decision."

On October 27, 1909, Amos Frank wrote to the commissioner of Indian Affairs, after Mr. Frank had received a letter from Merrill E. Gates, secretary of the Board of Indian Commissioners, and Mr. Gates had expressed interest in getting lands for the San Pasqual Indians:

> Please find enclosed ... an original letter from said Indians asking for homes in the San Pasqual Valley. ... We have a San Pasqual Indian reserve, but it consists almost entirely of useless land and what is of use is patented by white settlers. I therefore recommend the following: (a) Purchase land for the San Pasqual Mission Indians at their original home in San Pasqual Valley ... and irrigate the same by a pumping plant.

On November 17, 1909, Wilburn Reed wrote again to Amos Frank: "I read your letter and was glad to hear from you. Am glad to hear you have someone to go on the place as we have to leave. I hope you can come over soon. We are moving as fast as we can."

Two references to securing lands for the Mesa Grande Indians occurred a few days apart when C. F. Hauke, chief clerk of the Office of Indian Affairs, wrote to Amos Frank:

> Your letter of December 15, 1909 reporting the names of owners from whom land can be obtained in the San Pasqual Valley for the Mesa Grande Indians, is received. This matter has been taken up with Special Agent for the California Indians [Kelsey], and at a later date you will be informed further.

By January 7th Hauke had notified Kelsey in a letter that, "Enclosed herewith a letter from Amos R. Frank ... giving the names of owners from whom land can be obtained in the San Pasqual Valley for use of the Mesa Grande Indians ... submit your report as to their purchase for the Mesa Grande Indians."

The First Family Moves onto the New San Pasqual Reservation

Government documents indicate that Frank Trask, Leonora La Chappa Trask, and their two daughters, Florence and Helen, moved onto the San Pasqual Indian Reservation in December 1909, on the land purchased for $1,500 from Wilburn Reed. Charles Kelsey's letter of December 28, 1909, was in response to a November 18, 1909, letter from the commissioner of Indian Affairs asking him to provide further information about white squatter James M. Woods. Mr. Kelsey maintained:

Mr. Woods is within the limits of the San Pasqual Indian Reservation as actually laid out and patented. As you have doubtless heard many times the Smiley Commission selected certain lands in T12 ... and through an error somewhere in the proceedings the corresponding descriptions in T11 ... were patented to the San Pasqual Indians. The matter remained in status quo until two years ago this coming spring, when Special Agent R. S. Connell investigated the matter and recommended that certain of the squatters be bought out. This has been done, and Superintendent Amos R. Frank, of Mesa Grande, who is in charge, has placed some of the San Pasqual Indians on the lands surrendered by the squatters. This is what Mr. Woods refers to in saying the Indians are coming onto the claims now. What Mr. Woods says about the quality of the land reserved for Indian use, is quite true. All the land of value in the mistaken reservation had been previously patented to private owners, excepting two or three tracts.

On one of the [white] squatter's tracts, that purchased from Wilburn Reed, the Indians [Trask family] sold $600 worth of fruit this season. The Indians are quiet, peaceable citizens, and are in no wise detrimental to the community. The presence of the Indians in that neighborhood does not in any way interfere with the sale of property, but it does interfere with the sale of claims of [white] squatters on the Indian lands. Where the shoe pinches with Mr. Woods is that he is occupying two or three forties of Indian lands, which he naturally is unable to sell.

There is a reason, however, why I am willing to buy out Mr. Woods. His claim, or part of it, lies between the Wilburn Reed place and the public highway. By buying him out we get access to the public road without a controversy. (Kelsey 1909)

A January 14, 1910, letter from the Office of Indian Affairs to James M. Woods informed the white squatter of his, "Erroneous Settlement on the San Pasqual Indian Reservation." The letter went on:

Replying further to your letter of October 25, 1909 regarding your lands being entirely surrounded by an Indian Reservation. ... [Y]ou have erected some improvements on land embraced on the reservation of the San Pasqual Indians. ... [N]o formal offer to sell the improvements erroneously erected by you on the San Pasqual Reservation has reached the Office.

Shortly after the government placed Frank Trask and his family on the reservation in Valley Center, the time to patent the San Pasqual Indian Reservation in Valley Center came — on the day of January 25, 1910, a letter from John Francis, Jr., acting chief clerk of the Land Division, to Amos Frank stated:

The Office wishes to have a patent issued to the San Pasqual band under the provisions of the Act of March 1, 1907 (34 Stat. L., 1015-1022). ... The report of

Supervisor of Indian Schools Harwood Hall, dated June 19, 1909, indicates that the present reservation of the San Pasqual Indians is worthless, rugged, rocky, mountainous land, and that it is not used by the Indians. ... This report of Supervisor Hall is not entirely correct, as ... T 11 S ... on which are located the improvements of Wilburn Reed and which were purchased for the San Pasqual Indians, are reported to be quite valuable, worth at least $5000.

Amos Frank wrote a letter February 19, 1910, to the commissioner, describing the original reservation in the San Pasqual Valley which had been established in 1870 by President Ulysses S. Grant, and which had been revoked by him in 1871:

> The land set aside was as follows: Townships 12 and 13 south, of ranges 1 east and 1 west, of the San Bernardino Meridian, California. ... [T]the old site of the Indian pueblo can be purchased for $75,000 ... about 600 acres and very fertile. The most of the San Pasqual Indians state that if they cannot have this, their own home, they do not want anything. ... One Indian family lives on the Reed tract and that will be about all it will support ... the white settlers have all the good land and the Indians the worthless lands. The way these Indians have been treated ... has been discouraging to all.

By March 4, 1910, John Francis, Jr., acting chief of the Land Division, wrote to Amos Frank: "Regarding your suggestion that additional land be purchased for the San Pasqual Indians, you are informed that if you should receive any offers from owners to sell their land at a reasonable figure, they may be taken up by you with Mr. Kelsey for his investigation and recommendation." On March 10, 1910, John Francis, Jr., wrote to Frank and told him that the office wished to patent lands to the San Pasqual Band under the provisions of the Act of March 1, 1907 (Amended Homestead Land Act for Indians).

Some people during this time had come to the conclusion that the Act was meant to take as much of the lands previously held by the native people as possible, and return those lands to the public domain for use by white settlers. The Amended Homestead Land Act for Indians, however, would eventually mean that the San Pasqual Band would have their lands at the San Pasqual Indian Reservation in Valley Center legally patented to them, and they would have a home for many years to come.

By March 19, 1910, Amos Frank notified John Francis, Jr., acting chief of the Land Division: "Special Agent Kelsey and I went over the lands omitted ... This will leave land sufficient for one Indian family." March 21, 1910, Amos Frank wrote to the commissioner of Indian Affairs and referenced a ditch running through "the entire length" of T. H. Coomer's improvements on the reservation land. He noted that:"This ditch belongs to the Escondido Mutual Water Company. ... Mr. Kelsey will look after said company so as to obtain water for the Indian family living on said reserve."

A March 22, 1910, letter from C. F. Hauke, chief clerk of the Office of Indian Affairs, to James M. Woods, informed him that:

The Office has received your letter of March 9, 1910, forwarding a protest against locating the San Pasqual Indians in Township 11 S. ... In response you are informed that ... the Office is not contemplating the extension of the San Pasqual Reservation beyond the boundary lines of the lands shown to be free from conflict with the claims of the San Pasqual Indians, and there is no intention of acquiring any land in the San Pasqual Valley for the purpose of enlarging the reservation.

On March 25, 1910, a report from Joe E. Norris, inspector, Department of the Interior, agreed with the white settlers about not providing lands for the San Pasqual Indians in Valley Center:

"The San Pasqual Indians are scattered through the surrounding country and at the neighboring towns ... there seems to be agitation as to the providing of additional lands for them. This, I believe, would not better their condition ... making them dependent wards of the government."

R.G. Valentine, commissioner of Indian Affairs, wrote to the Commissioner of the General Land Office on March 30, 1910, stating that: "The Office knows of no reason why all the tracts free from conflict and occupied by and in the possession of the Indians should not be patented to the band if they are surveyed." He then asked whether all the tracts reported to be free from conflict had been surveyed.

An April 7, 1910, letter from Charles Kelsey to the Office of Indian Affairs said:

The squatters upon the latter two tracts were bought out last year, and the land is now in possession of an Indian named Trask. I found him in the Wilburn Reed house. The house was as clean as most white houses, and the 2 little Indian children likewise. Trask had all the arable land outside the orchard planted in grain. The orchard was being ploughed, as is necessary in California. I thought everything in satisfactory shape. This valley has no water for irrigation and the ranchers raise cattle, grain, and some fruit without irrigation. It is rather a hard proposition to do so, however, as the rainfall is scanty, the elevation being about 1500 feet and not near the high mountains enough for heavy rainfall. Trask has about 10 acres under the ditch ... there is therefore no conflict of interest as to time of using the water and the ditch. The San Pasqual Indians as a band do not want to have the land charged to them, and it will probably be more satisfactory to all concerned if the patent does not issue to the band, but to individuals who have settled or may settle on the land.

S.V. Proudfit, assistant commissioner of the General Land Office, Washington DC, wrote to the Commissioner of Indian Affairs on April 19, 1910, assuring him that the lands for the new reservation had been surveyed: "In response to your letter of March 30, 1910 (Land 8521-1908, W. A. M) I have to advise you that the following described lands, said by you to be desired to be patented to the San Pasqual Indians, are shown to be surveyed by official plats of survey on file in this office." Kelsey would later remark that the matter of the land having been unsurveyed during the early days of the reservation would prove to be the reason why the white squatters would have such difficulty homesteading the reservation parcels of land (Kelsey 1913).

On April 22, 1910 Kelsey wrote to C. F. Hauke asserting:

> The one man living at the San Pasqual Reservation should receive his allotment, as the land occupied by him is in a high state of cultivation, and the man occupying it is able to keep it in good shape. There being room for only one family, the balance is to be used as timber, etc. By improvements, two families might find homes.

Hauke responded on April 27, 1910, to Mr. Kelsey's suggestion to patent the Valley Center land to Frank Trask as an individual: "The Office is of the opinion that the title of the band to these tracts should be fully protected by patenting them in the name of the tribe, notwithstanding the fact that the greater area thereof may be so mountainous as to be of little or no value for agricultural purposes."

On May 3, 1910, Kelsey recommended that Woods's right-of-way be bought: "If the right of way can be secured and Mr. Woods' feelings soothed at the same operation I think it will be wise to do it."

On the same day, Amos Frank sent a telegram to John Francis, Jr., acting chief of the Land Division: "James M. Woods is plowing land belonging to the San Pasqual Indian Reservation, California. He has been notified to stay off said reserve. Please advise." Mr. Francis' first return telegram must have gotten lost, because on May 6, 1910, he sent a telegram to Mr. Frank informing him that his previous telegram of May 4, 1910, had told Mr. Frank the following:

> If Woods has no color or title of right to occupy San Pasqual Reservation, Section six hundred twenty-six, Regulations Indian Office, nineteen four, authorizes you to remove him. Serve written notice to vacate and if not complied with remove him with your police force, if necessary. Proceed cautiously. Report fully by letter. As soon as any action shall have been taken in this case, you will report the facts to the Office in order that its files may be complete.

On May 10, 1910, Amos Frank took the advice that John Francis, Jr., acting chief of the Land Division, had given in his telegrams, and wrote a letter to Mr. James M. Woods and William H. H. Dinwiddie:

> By authority of the Federal Laws Sec. 2147-48, R.S. you are hereby notified to vacate any land or lands belonging to the San Pasqual Indian reservation, San Diego County, California. The penalty for violating said notice will make you liable to a fine of $1,000. If you have any color of right to occupy said lands, the Office will consider the same, but so far nothing can be shown that you have any right whatever.

On May 12, 1910, Amos Frank notified the commissioner of Indian Affairs that notice had been served on Woods and Dinwiddie:

Please find enclosed a copy of notice served on Mr. James M. Woods and Mr. Wm. H. H. Dinwiddie, Valley Center, California. ... [T]hey want about one week to put in their claims to the right to said lands, which will be forwarded to the Office as soon as received. Both have plowed the above lands and what could be sowed is in grain. They have been plowing these lands for years, and when they send in their statement as to their rights, it will then remain to see what is to be done. The trouble in the past is that they were unwilling or did not know what to do, except to abuse all that belonged to the Federal government, the superintendent [Amos Frank] getting his full share. I still hope that they will come through all right. When the notice was served, they then got busy at once. This matter has been tedious and difficult because ... the place [San Pasqual, was] seldom visited by any official.

The government was still making errors regarding the name of the San Pasqual Indian Reservation in Valley Center when on May 23, 1910, the commissioner of Indian Affairs recommended that the land in Valley Center, T 11, be patented to the San Pasqual Indian Mission.

Mr. Kelsey intervened for Frank Trask with the US government on May 23, 1910, when he sent a letter to the commissioner of Indian Affairs in Washington DC:

The Indian on the Wilburn Reed place, his name is Trask, wants the 40 for the limited amount of pasturage. It corners his other land and I think he should have the land. Trask has rather less than 10 acres of land below the ditch. In my former letter I mentioned the advisability of securing him and any other Indian who might want to come on this mesa, the right to bring summer water through the ditch of the Escondido Mutual Water Association, should the right to use the upper end of the said ditch be acquired by the government.

Richard Carrico commented in his book, *The San Pasqual Valley*, on the movement of the Ipai onto the reservation in Valley Center:

As a result of the Act for the Relief of the California Mission Indians ... in 1910 [1909], some members of the band moved to the new reservation but most families continued to live at Mesa Grande, Santa Ysabel and elsewhere. The first families at San Pasqual included Frank Trask and his children. The June 30, 1910 Census for San Pasqual Indians at Mesa Grande listed 86 Indians categorized as San Pasqual Mission Indians and the June 1913 Census listed 83 Indians. Family names included Alta, Alvarado, Castro, Contreras, Cota, Duro, Felix, Guachena, Larque, Lachusa, Martinez, Morales, Lopez, Orozco, Osuna, Ortega, Quisquis, Estrada, Soto, Revere, Stokes, Simona, Trask, and Weed. [2010:TS]

On May 26, 1910, patent No. 142190 was issued, and the land at the San Pasqual Indian Reservation in Valley Center became trust patented to the San Pasqual Band.

On July 18, 1910, Amos Frank wrote to the commissioner of Indian Affairs: "I respectfully request that the rights of the Escondido Mutual Water Company, Escondido, California be investigated. … I contend that the Indians living on said reservation have a right to the use of said water."

By August 6, 1910, Amos Frank was petitioning the commissioner of Indian Affairs, Washington DC:

> Is it the purpose of the Indian Office to purchase additional lands for the San Pasqual Indians? A man by the name of James M. Woods has bought a strip of land and as I see it means to shut in from the county road the one Indian family. I, therefore, respectfully recommend that a right of way at least be purchased for this Indian family. The cost should not exceed $200. But if he should continue to show the same spirit as he has heretofore the land will have to be condemned. That they are acting unbecoming is without question. Only one family living there and it remains to be seen whether we can get more to settle there.

C. F. Hauke wrote to Amos. R. Frank on September 2, 1910, in response to Mr. Frank's August 6, 1910, letter:

> [Y]ou are informed that the purchase of additional land for the San Pasqual Indians is not under consideration at present … these Indians are unwilling to settle on any land purchased for them unless it is located in the San Pasqual Valley, where they once made their homes. The high cost per acre of this land, and the large sum required to purchase a sufficient area, precludes any consideration of such a purchase … the one family, however, who has made their home on the Reed place should be furnished with a proper way for ingress and egress … the Office deems it proper to take up the matter with Mr. Kelsey.

A September 9, 1910, letter from C. F. Hauke, second assistant commissioner of the Office of Indian Affairs, to Amos Frank read:

> The Office has received your letter of August 6, 1910, wherein you … recommend that an expenditure of $200 be authorized to purchase a right of way for one Indian family now living on the Reed place. In response, you are informed … the one family … who has made their home on the Reed place should be furnished with a proper way for ingress and egress.

On September 26, 1910, the acting chief of the Land Division wrote to the commissioner of Indian Affairs and requested: "Please procure authority to expend $200.00 in purchasing a right of way from the San Pasqual Indian Reservation, to connect with the county road."

The authorization for payment of $200 for a right-of-way was granted by Frank Pierce, Assistant Secretary of the Interior, on October 8, 1910, as follows: "Authority is hereby granted you to expend $200.00 in the purchase of a right of way. … Payment, therefore, to be made from "Lands, Irrigation, etc., California Indians."

Removing Non-Indian Squatters: The Woods-Dinwiddie Lawsuit

James M. Woods had made an application for homestead for the land he was improving on the San Pasqual Indian Reservation, sometime before November 23, 1901, and he also owned land in his own name, but his application for the land within the reservation had been denied. An appeal was also denied, on November 23, 1901. On May 1, 1902, the General Land Office sent a letter to Mr. Woods stating that he could not acquire any rights in and to the lands in question. The case was considered closed. He was notified to vacate the premises. The letter also noted that: "The San Pasqual Indian Reservation was set aside by Executive Order on December 21, 1891, and embraces within it the lands occupied by James M. Woods and W. H. H. Dinwiddie." One of the main roads in Valley Center, Woods Valley Road, is today named after James M. Woods.

The lawsuit against Woods and Dinwiddie moved one step further when on July 11, 1910, J. A. Touele, acting attorney general, wrote to the US secretary of the Interior, bringing him up to date on where the lawsuit stood: "The Department is in receipt of your letter of July 6, 1910 (Land-Contracts 36632-1910, J G D), together with its enclosures, in which request is made that suit be instituted to eject one James M. Woods and one William H. H. Dinwiddie from certain lands within the San Pasqual Indian Reservation, California."

By January 31, 1911, John A. Francis, Jr., formerly acting chief of the Land Division, now had the title of attorney general. He wrote to the secretary of the Interior about the Woods-Dinwiddie lawsuit:

> Referring to your letter of July 6, 1910 … you are advised that suit was instituted November 28, 1910, by the United States Attorney for the Southern District of California … suit was also instituted against said Dinwiddie … the United States Attorney states that the defendants…stated that they neither occupy nor claim the lands mentioned in the suit.

On February 4, 1911, although the Frank Trask family had already lived on the San Pasqual Indian Reservation for two years and two months, Woods wrote to US Senator Frank Flint and enclosed a petition from other white settlers in Valley Center:

> The Indians do not wish to live on the land, for the simple reason that it will not support them. What they do want is the land in T 12. … The principal reason we settlers wish to have the matter straightened out is because the reservation practically surrounds our ranches. … We therefore trust that you will give the matter due and prompt attention, that the Indians may receive what they want and the settlers get what they are entitled to. … You will have the support of the Indians, the Indian Agents, and every other person in trying to get the reservation moved to T 12 South, where it belongs.

On February 20, 1911, C. F. Hauke wrote to Kelsey asking for more information about the Woods-Dinwiddie lawsuit and instructing Kelsey: "You will render the United States

Attorney such assistance in the preparation and trial of the case as may be necessary and required by him."

Excerpts from a letter written by Woods' and Dinwiddie's attorneys, Copp, Luckett & Pierce, dated March 4, 1911, informed the secretary of the Interior: We enclose herewith a petition from certain of the Indians corroborating our statement. ... that the San Pasqual Indians do not desire to be removed to Bear Valley in T 11 but desire to remain and have the land of their forefathers in San Pasqual T 12."

A report from Frank Pierce, first assistant secretary of the Interior, to attorneys Copp, Luckett & Pierce, in response to their March 4, 1911, petition, notified them that:

> On May 23, 1910 the Commissioner of Indian Affairs recommended ... that ...
> T11 [Valley Center] be patented to said San Pasqual Indian Mission. May 26, 1910
> the Department approved said recommendation, and patent No. 142190 was issued
> for the land above described, on July 1, 1910. It is noticed that the greater part of the
> lands in T12 [San Pasqual Valley] ... corresponding to the land reserved in T11 [Valley
> Center]...are shown to be vacant, by the tract book in the General Land Office.

Frank Pierce then presented an analysis of which lands were vacant, which had been homesteaded, and which had become a part of the Cleveland National Forest. He concluded:

> The Commissioner of Indian Affairs has been directed to make a report in this
> matter, and when the same is received, this Department will pass upon the necessity
> and propriety of recommending to the President that the land reserved for the said San
> Pasqual Band of Mission Indians be changed, as asked for by you. If it is determined
> that an error has been made in reserving and patenting lands for said band of Mission
> Indians, it will first be necessary for this Department to call upon the said band to
> reconvey the lands patented to them as above.

On March 15, 1911, C.F. Hauke wrote to Copp, Luckett & Pierce, saying: "You are informed that this Office does not contemplate taking any steps whatsoever to force the San Pasqual Indians to live on the land patented in their name. ... [O]ne or two families are now living on the land. In course of time it may be that others will seek a home there."

On March 30, 1911, C.F. Hauke wrote to the General Land Office: "It will be appreciated if you will inform this Office at an early date of the status of ... a small natural reservoir site ... to reserve it for the benefit of the San Pasqual Indians." An April 13, 1911, letter from C.F. Hauke, second assistant commissioner of the Office of Indian Affairs, to the secretary of the Interior read: "I have the honor to recommend that [reservoir] be reserved temporarily for the benefit of the San Pasqual Mission Indian Band pending an investigation into the advisability of recommending a permanent withdrawal of the tract by Executive Order."

On April 28, 1911, W. H. H. Dinwiddie wrote to Senator John D. Works, Washington, D.C.:

I take the liberty of writing to you in behalf of the residents of Bear Valley [Valley Center] to ask you to assist us in having a great wrong righted, a wrong committed upon the people of Township 11 S. of Range one West S. B. M. by placing the San Pasqual Indian reservation in Township 11 S. one West, when it should be in Township 12 S., one West, S. B. M., where the Indians live, and have lived for ages, and where they want to remain. It is a fraud, an imposition put upon us by the Indian Department, and they persist in trying to force the Indians upon us when they know that it is not right. We most respectfully ask you to communicate with Messrs. Copp, Luckett & Pierce, Attorneys in Washington D C. They have all of facts in the case. Hoping that you do us this favor.

On May 4, 1911, Kelsey submitted an Annual Report showing the following:

Upon the report of R. S. Connell, the U. S. bought out two squatters who had about all the good land on the reservation, and the land so acquired is held by Indians. ... Until the last two years no San Pasqual Indians have ever lived there and now there are but a couple of families. ... I saw Trask. ... He is an Indian, occupying the Wilburn Reed house, by virtue of his wife being a San Pasqual Indian.

In that same report, Kelsey offered an explanation for the placement of the San Pasqual Indian Reservation in Valley Center:

The [white] settlers in T 11 S., R. 1 W. S. B. M. [the San Pasqual Indian Reservation in Valley Center] now say the surveyor employed by the Smiley Commission [E. L. Dorn] was bribed by the [white] settlers in San Pasqual Valley to throw the reservation as far away from San Pasqual Valley as possible. The surveyor is said to have been drunk most of the time. ... Efforts have been made by various persons within the last 20 years to have this reservation set aside or cancelled. The Congressional delegations have made promises regularly every two years to try and have the reservation abolished, but without success.

Amos Frank responded on May 12, 1911, to a Kelsey letter of May 9, 1911, which read in part: "Is there anything new in the situation on the mesa, Bear Valley [San Pasqual Indian Reservation in Valley Center]?" Amos Frank's response read:

Dinwiddie and Woods still claim the land. Mr. Frank Trask, an Indian living there, attempted to get wood on the Dinwiddie tract and was at once notified by a band of men to leave it alone, subjecting himself to violence if he attempted to obtain the wood he went after. As the patent reads it is a part of the San Pasqual Indian Reservation, San Diego, California.

On May 14, 1911, Kelsey wrote to the commissioner of Indian affairs in reference to Frank Trask being chased off the reservation lands while attempting to cut wood:

Referring to the report upon the matter of alleged trespass upon the San Pasqual Indian Reservation, in California. ... I have held the report a few days in order to get a statement from Superintendent Frank. ... I can not say that I have been very much illuminated. It does not appear that W.C. Dinwiddie [William H.H. Dinwiddie's son] had anything to do with the band of white men that told Trask to keep away from the land, as Dinwiddie has been away from there some 18 months" [The original reference was most likely concerning William H.H. Dinwiddie, the subject of the government's lawsuit].

A May 15, 1911, letter from C.F. Hauke, second assistant commissioner of Indian affairs, to attorneys Copp, Luckett & Pierce, read:

Certain San Pasqual Indians in California ... do not want to be moved to land in Township 11. In response you are informed that this office does not contemplate taking any steps whatsoever to force the San Pasqual Indians to live on the land patented in their name. ... [R]eports from the Superintendent in Charge ... indicated that one or two families are now living on the land. ... [T]here is no money available to purchase lands for this band in the San Pasqual Valley, where they formerly made their homes.

A partial two-page letter of September 6, 1911, believed to be from the secretary of the Interior to John A. Francis, attorney general, Washington DC, read:

Regarding suit instituted to eject James M. Woods and William H.H. Dinwiddie from certain lands alleged to be within the San Pasqual Indian Reservation, California, I have the honor to transmit a copy of a complete report on this subject from Special Agent C. E. Kelsey, in which it is shown that Dinwiddie has not trespassed on any lands within the Indian Reservation since he was acquainted with the true location of the boundary. It is shown that although Woods at one time had a claim within the reservation limits he removed from the Indian land about 10 years ago but has on 2 or 3 occasions since put in crops when conditions were favorable, the last time being in 1909; that in 1908 and 1909 he allowed his cattle to run over the land but made no other use of it. He says that he wanted to ascertain if the Government really held the land and so plowed a part of the arable strip and put it in corn. After the Superintendent issued to him a formal notice to vacate the land, he claims he abandoned his crop and has not been on the land. Mr. Kelsey says he would doubtless be supported in this contention by his neighbors without exception and also believes that sufficient evidence would not be forthcoming to convince a jury that he is guilty of trespass. ... There appears to be but one Indian family living on the reservation and that family took up its abode within the last 3 or 4 years. Inasmuch as Dinwiddie and Woods are not now trespassing upon the reservation and it would apparently be difficult to prove a case against either of them, the land patented having been withdrawn for these Indians by Executive Order of December 29, 1891. (Fisher 1911)

On September 9, 1911, acting attorney general John Q. Thompson wrote to the secretary of the Interior explaining that the case had been dismissed:

> [T]he U. S. bought out two squatters who had about all the good land on the reservation, and the land so acquired is held by Indians. ... Until the last two years no San Pasqual Indians have ever lived there and now there are but a couple of families. ... I saw Trask. ... He is an Indian, occupying the Wilburn Reed house, by virtue of his wife being a San Pasqual Indian [1911 Annual Report by Kelsey].

Receipt is acknowledged of your letter of September 6, 1911 (Land — Contracts 8521-1908, 45329-1911, 67850-1911 RJH), in regard to the action pending in the Southern District of California to eject James M. Woods and William H. H. Dinwiddie from certain lands alleged to be within the San Pasqual Indian Reservation. Your recommendation, based upon the report of Special Agent Kelsey in the matter, that the case be dismissed without prejudice is noted, and the United States Attorney for the Southern District of California has today been instructed to carry out your wishes in regard to same.

On September 15, 1911 F. H. Abbott, assistant commissioner of Indian Affairs, wrote to the attorneys for Woods and Dinwiddie: "there appears to be no reasons why any consideration should be given the questions of discontinuing the present San Pasqual Reservation."

Frank Trask sent several letters to Thomas M. Games, superintendent of the Volcan Indian School at Santa Ysabel, regarding problems with the defective dam. His letter of March 11, 1912, read: "I wish to report that the dam that was built for me a couple of months past has partly washed out in the last rain. From the looks of the break there wasn't any concrete placed under the earth fill. It looks like a very poor piece of work and ought to be investigated."

On March 14, 1912, Games responded to Frank Trask in a lengthy letter:

Dear Friend, I have just received your letter of the 11th, reporting damage to the dam recently constructed for you, by the late rains, and I thank you very much for your promptness in reporting the matter. As we have had our heaviest rain here since the date of your letter, I fear the damage to the dam may be worse than first reported by you. On receipt of this letter kindly let me know if any further damage has resulted from the last rains. I am writing tonight to Charles R. Olberg, Superintendent of Irrigation, an account of the damage, as contained in your report, and asking him to meet me at your place as soon as practicable with a view to making an investigation of the matter. I could not accomplish anything by coming before hearing from him. It would seem that it must have been a rotten piece of work, as the rains have not been unusually heavy here. I do not think there is any doubt but that the damage will be repaired soon. If the work was defective in any way the burden rests on the Office of the Civil Engineer. Again thanking you for reporting the matter and wishing you abundant success, I remain, Very truly yours, Superintendent.

The Trask girls Helen and Florence dressed for Easter Sunday, 1916. *Photo: Trask-La Chappa family.*

Further documents concerning what happened from 1911-1913 regarding the procurement of lands for the San Pasqual Band are scarce, but the white squatters' attempts to move the reservation back to the San Pasqual Valley failed.

Mr. Kelsey confirmed in his final report before retiring, July 25, 1913, that the white squatters had now apparently abandoned their efforts to secure the reservation land:

> I saw Trask. ... [H]e is an Indian occupying the Wilburn Reed house. ... Trask told me that Woods was not now occupying any of the Indian land and that he had not done so for some months. ... [T]he affidavits attached to the correspondence were drawn by a newly employed lawyer, who was attempting ... to get the Indian land for Dinwiddie and Woods. ... [T]he statements are doubtless true. But like some other affidavits, they do not contain the entire truth. They do not show the abandonment by the parties of the land. These affidavits were gotten up on the theory that if the settlers could show that they were in possession of the land at the time the Executive Orders were issued reserving this land for an Indian reservation, that they would be legally entitled to hold the land. If they had made filings, this would probably be true. But there were no filings, as to the lands said to be under trespass, as the land was unsurveyed. The attorney apparently is attempting to make some claim of legal right, based upon prior occupancy. Such a claim can hardly be maintained.

Kelsey gave a lengthy recital as to why he felt the land on the west side of the valley would be forever worthless to anyone, but suggested holding the land on the east side, including the NW ¼ of Section 23, for a reservoir site. He added that:

> There is one band in Southern California, counted among those having reservations, for whom Congress should make provision. That is the San Pasqual band … the San Pasqual reservation was located in another township, in Luiseño territory, the San Pasqual being Diegueño. … There are now but one or two families on the reservation. The San Pasqual Indians almost unanimously refuse to consider the reservation as laid out for them and insist that the Government shall give them back their lands from which they were illegally ejected.

Settling In for the Long Run

By 1913 Washington politicians had moved away from efforts to secure more land for the California Indians, and, instead, were focusing on the broader view of the current living conditions of some of those same native people. John E. Raker, House of Representatives, Washington DC, Committee of Irrigation and Arid Lands, and member of congress from the Second California District, wrote to Cato Sells, Commissioner of Indian Affairs on September 22, 1913:

> Will you kindly have copy of report made by Honorable C. E. Kelsey, Indian Agent of California, made to your Department on March 21, 1906, on the Indians of California, their treaty regulations, the amount received by the Indians under the treaty relations and so forth, in Carlisle print, forwarded to me at your earliest convenience? Second, would also appreciate it if you would send me such copies of other reports made on the conditions of the Indians in California by other agents relative to the treaty stipulations with the Indians in California begun as early as 1852. Third, I am advised that the President forwarded a message to the Senate containing eighteen treaties made with the Indians in California. This was forwarded to the Senate in Extra Session January 19, 1905, and would most respectfully request from your Department, a statement as to what has been furnished to the various tribes of Indians in California under these various treaties. Such information as you may furnish is desired. Thanking you in advance …

Congressman John E. Raker also wrote a letter asking newly-retired Charles Kelsey for help in making sense of California Land Allotments as they related to the native people. Kelsey mentioned the Treaties of 1852 in a letter of response that he wrote on October 4, 1913, to the commissioner of Indian Affairs, explaining that the Supreme Court Case of 1903 that evicted the Agua Caliente Cupeño Indians from their native lands at Warner Springs revealed certain facts about the Indians' rights. These rights were directly connected to the rights given to the native people by the Mexican government. Kelsey noted:

> The decision turned upon the point that the Act of Congress required the Mexican Grant Commissioners to report upon Indians upon Mexican Land Grants. In no case

did they mention the Indians. The Supreme Court held that the Commissioners would be presumed to have done their duty, in absence of evidence to the contrary. As this question had not been raised in any other court and had not been litigated at all, there was no testimony in the record which the court considered as proving failure to make report upon the Indians … about 2000 Indians have still no land.

Those invaders who had commandeered all they could from the people native to these lands, and had given nothing in return, were well-known by Charles E. Kelsey. An October 4, 1913, letter from Kelsey to the commissioner of Indian Affairs, Washington DC, expressed Kelsey's thoughts and feelings, as he contemplated the 1905 retrieval of the eighteen Indian treaties of 1852 that the government had made with California Indians. These treaties had been hidden away for fifty-three years within the secret Senate archives, and after they were discovered, Kelsey stated that, "The government took everything ceded in the treaties and more i.e. the reservations, and paid nothing."

By the time the Trask family had lived on the San Pasqual Indian Reservation for seven years, working hard to make the land productive, T. F. McCormick, superintendent of the Pala Indian School, requested information from the commissioner of Indian Affairs at Washington DC, regarding the reservation and Frank Trask. He received a response from E. B. Merritt, assistant commissioner of Indian Affairs, on January 5, 1917:

> Receipt is acknowledged of your letter of December 7, 1916, in which you say that there are four families of San Pasqual Indians who desire to remove to the San Pasqual Reservation and establish homes there and ask the status of one Frank Trask who is said to be using nearly all the good land on the reservation. In answer you are advised that from the records of the Office it appears that under date of May 20, 1909 Frank Trask applied for an allotment of land on the Mesa Grande reservation and said that his family consisted of himself, wife and two minor children. A copy of his application, which was approved by Amos R. Frank, Superintendent in Charge of the Mesa Grande Indians, is enclosed herewith. The Office has no further knowledge of when or upon what authority Frank Trask removed to the San Pasqual reserve, but it is presumed he was allowed so to do as he is an Indian and has a San Pasqual wife by whom he has reared a family. It appears further that the lands were, under the Acts of January 12, 1891 (26 Stat., L. 712) and March 1, 1907 (24 Stat., L. 1022) patented to the San Pasqual band and are now held in trust by the Government therefore. As the lands of this reservation are held in common by the band, there would seem to be no objection to permitting other homeless families of San Pasqual Indians to remove thereto and establish homes thereon.

The man who had reported to E. B. Merritt that four families had an interest in the San Pasqual Reservation may have been the same man who conducted the 1917 Annual Report for the San Pasqual Indian Reservation, since T. F. McCormick conducted the annual report for 1920. The Pala Indian School was shown as reporting statistics for the San Pasqual Indian Reservation in Valley Center for the year 1917. Section III showed one male and three females as the population, with a total of four. One family lived on the San Pasqual Indian Reservation, with one head of family, no families living in tents, tepees, or other temporary structures, and number of houses one, with wooden floors. No births occurred in 1917. One Roman Catholic missionary was working in that jurisdiction. The number of Indians who were church members or had been baptized or attended church services, included all four members of the Trask family.

The Pala Indian School reported statistics for the San Pasqual Indian Reservation in Valley Center for the year 1920. Section V showed that Frank Trask was the name of the Indian farming the San Pasqual Indian Reservation site. The report showed Trask as half Indian, age 53, farming 11 acres of beans, corn, fruit and grain, and earning an income of $815; 149 acres were shown as grazing lands, 160 acres of agricultural land leased. Total grazing lands were 160 acres.

Those listed as the population of the reservation were one adult female (18 and over), and two female minors (to 17, inclusive). The total was three. Those same females were said to be mentally sound and were from the Mission Tribe. The adult female was a citizen of the United States [note at bottom of page says, "Some question as to citizenship of California Indians"], all spoke English, all could read and write the English language, and all wore modern attire. The 1,200 acres, belonging to the tribe as a whole, was valued at $3.50 per acre for a total of $4,300. The estimated values of the Trasks' belongings included:

Home, barn, corrals, etc.: $700

Furniture: $30

Tools, Agricultural Implements, etc.: $60

Wagons, vehicles, etc.: $70

Livestock, poultry, etc.: $375

Value of other property: $25

Total Value: $1,150

The house had six rooms or more and there was one barn and one well. In 1920 there were apricots, prunes, pears, and almonds planted, but in 1919 there had been also been peaches, plums, and figs.

Rainfall for the site being itemized included:

January, 3 inches; February, 3 inches; March, 2 and ½ inches; April, 1 inch; May, 2.4 inches; June, 0 inches; July, 0; August, 0; September, 0; October, 2.4; November, 1 inch; December 2.5 inches. Total: 14 inches.

There were three people under the supervision of the preparer of the report, from the Pala Indian School.

During the years 1919 through 1921, representatives of the United States Indian Service considered granting allotments of San Pasqual Reservation lands to the Trask family "as a preliminary to granting patents in fee and closing out the affairs of the government there" (Hoffman 1919:2). Paul T. Hoffman, superintendent of the Pala Indian Agency, explained

The Mission Indian Federation

In the Fall of 1919 Julio Norte, a well-known Indian leader from Morongo, presided as chairman or grand president of the first Mission Indian Federation Conference (Johnson 1966), where two vice-presidents, a secretary-treasurer, and a chief-of-police were also appointed. Seventy-five California Indian leaders representing 2,000 of their fellow Indians got together for the first time that day in the East Prospect Avenue home of Jonathan Tibbet at Riverside, California. From the beginning, the Federation looked for the inclusion of whites, such as Jonathan Tibbet, a pioneer-turned-activist who helped the Indians of California find their voices, and at whose home meetings were held in April and October each year in Riverside, from 1919-1930. The group felt that Tibbet and other non-Indians could help them take the message of tribal sovereignty and justice to Federal Government Officials. The two main issues of water supply for Indian lands and various encroachments upon treaty rights stood at the forefront of the group's concerns, along with boundary disputes on reservations, better education for Indian children — nearer to their homes than the Sherman Indian Boarding School in Riverside — and self-determination for native people. Younger tribal members, who were more interested in the topic of citizenship than their elders, formed their own activist group, called The Progressive League of Mission Indians, headed by Ignacio Costa, after they had presented their ideas to Mission Indian Federation members and had been asked to leave the meeting.

At some of the Mission Indian Federation meetings, expressions of ill-will or hostility toward the federal government were put forth. At one point in 1921, Tibbet and several other Federation members were arrested and charged with "alienating the confidence" of Mission Indians of Southern California in the federal government. It took two years before the charges were dropped. Tibbet died in 1930 at the age of 74, but meetings were held at his home until worsening economic conditions during the time of the Great Depression resulted in reduced participation.

to the commissioner of Indian Affairs that "an Indian family consisting of Frank Trask, his wife and two children" had been located on the reservation around 1910 or shortly before and had made the land productive, but since other San Pasqual Indians continued to refuse to accept allotments on the reservation, he and other government officials were exploring the possibility of resurveying the lands for purposes of allotment and liquidation of reservation lands (Hoffman 1919:2).

After Frank Trask's death in 1920, Hoffman recommended "allotting Mrs. Trask and her two daughters who are San Pasqual Indians" (Hoffman 1920:1). In spite of this recommendation, funds to carry out the new survey were not available and the plan for allotment and dissolution of the reservation did not proceed. Trask family descendants are thankful that the reservation remained intact, and that their ancestors were able to hold on to the land for future generations.

The first month of 1920, Frank Trask, who had farmed his family's allotment at Valley Center for eleven years, contracted the Spanish influenza. Family members report that he

Helen Trask at the San Pasqual reservation, circa 1918. *Photo: Trask-La Chappa family.*

retreated to one of the outbuildings at the back of the property, which had been purchased for his family by the government from Wilburn Reed, and spent the last week of his life working to avoid passing on the contagious disease to his wife and two daughters. On January 31, 1920, Frank Trask, age 53, died, leaving Leonora, age 39, Florence, 15, and Helen, 14, to maintain the lands at the San Pasqual Indian Reservation in Valley Center on their own.

Genealogist Lorraine Escobar (2011) noted of Frank Trask the year he died that: "the 1920 Annual Statistics Report agrees with the notion that he was half Indian, which would have entitled him to a land allotment in 1909."

Carrico pointed out that:

Between 1920 and the 1950s the San Pasqual Reservation was apparently irregularly and sparsely populated, with many families staying at Mesa Grande, many living in Escondido and Valley Center, and several families moving to the Anaheim and Placentia areas in search of work. The federally approved roll of San Pasqual Indians of 1933, based on a census of May 18, 1928, indicates that few families had made the permanent move to the reservation [Carrico 2010:TS].

La Chappa women and girls traveling. (From left) Petra La Chappa Cota, unidentified girl, Hazel Campagnoli, Leonora La Chappa Trask, Nelda Campagnoli, Feliciana Nejo La Chappa. *Photo: Trask-La Chappa family.*

The Nejo/La Chappa/Trask Family, circa 1918. Left to right, beginning with standing adults: man in hat and girl in front of him (unknown), Petra La Chappa Cota, Feliciana Nejo La Chappa; Leonora La Chappa Trask; Sylvester La Chappa; Bruno La Chappa; Helen Trask and Pete La Chappa. In the front row are Nelda Campagnoli Taylor and her sisters Zelma and Hazel. *Photo: Trask-La Chappa family.*

Oscar H. Lipps, supervisor of the U. S. Indian Service, reported that in 1920 Rev. John O'Brien, a priest who worked in Escondido, listed the population of San Pasqual Indians as:

> 49 adults, 27 children, comprising 12 families—most probably not living on the reservation, but rather living in Escondido and Valley Center. In 1920 the only family that can definitely be documented as living on the new reservation consisted of one male, one female over the age of eighteen and two minor females living in a single dwelling with a well. The adult female, probably Leonora Trask aged thirty-nine is listed as full blood and the two young women, probably her daughters Florence and Ella, as 'more than one-half blood' [Lipps in Carrico 2010:TS].

As the years passed, most of those who asserted that they were descendants of native people who had at one time lived in the San Pasqual Valley still refused to move to the San Pasqual Indian Reservation in Valley Center. They were adamant about wanting land in the San Pasqual Valley. Eventually, censuses for the San Pasqual Reservation reflected their reticence to go to Valley Center. Annual censuses taken from 1923 through 1926 all reiterated that "The San Pasqual Indians refused to occupy reservation set aside for them—through an error the reservation was located in the wrong township—and withdrew. For years they have been living around Escondido, and have lost their identity as Indians." The 1923 Census reported "This family [Leonora La Chappa Trask, Florence and Helen] formerly lived at Mesa Grande, but removed to San Pasqual in 1908 [1909] at solicitation of Amos Frank, then Superintendent."

6

The Growth of the Reservation:
A New Tribal Roll and Constitution
for San Pasqual

United States policies toward native people routinely fluctuated, due largely to US Supreme Court cases, congressional rulings, and public sentiment. These policies affected every Native American tribe and the individuals that comprised them. Federal policies influenced state and local laws, regulations, and actions, as the case of San Pasqual illustrates. Social movements (for example, organizations that advocated for Native American rights), events, and the particular personalities of native and non-native leaders, agents, bureaucrats, and intermediaries have left both positive and negative impacts that now form part of the history of San Pasqual. This chapter will explore some of the policies and personalities that interacted to create both problems and solutions for the San Pasqual band.

Seven major periods in Native American history have been identified. They are the British Colonial Period, Early United States Era, Removal Period, Allotment Era, Reorganization Era, Termination Era, and the current Period of Self-Determination (Canby 2004). The seven periods and the impacts they had on native people are highlighted here:

British Colonial: The Indian Intercourse Acts were passed in 1780 and endured until 1834. These acts attempted to regulate relations between Indians and non-Indians living on Indian land.

Early United States Era: After the Louisiana Purchase in 1803, the US government and white settlers took Indian lands as their own. The case of *Johnson v. McIntosh* allowed American seizure of Indian land, based on the belief that European occupation of Indian land gave the invaders the right to take the land. Readers can see Steve Newcomb's *Pagans in the Promised Land* for expanded information on this topic.

Opposite page: Jose Trinidad Christiano Huacheño singing a song. *Photo: C.G. Dubois.*

Removal Era: The policy of "ethnic cleansing" became apparent during the early 1800s and led to the Indian Removal Act, when Congress gave approval for President Andrew Jackson to take land away from the native people and to remove them to the western portion of the country. In 1821 Jackson set into existence the Trail of Tears, resulting in the demoralization and death of so many natives. San Diego County's own Trail of Tears occurred in 1903 when the Cupeños and Diegueños were forcibly removed from their Indian lands at Warner Springs and San Felipe and placed at Pala with the Luiseños who were already there.

Allotment Era: During the 1870s and 1880s a difference of opinion divided the country. One group saw the Indians as poverty-stricken and homeless, while the second group viewed them as merely in the way of white settlers wanting to take over the land. Native people in all regions of the United States offered continued resistance to these invaders. By 1887 the General Allotment Act, also called the Indian Homestead Act or Dawes Act, was put into effect. Each head of household could receive 160 acres, and the amounts were doubled if grazing was to occur. Eighty acres would be given to additional members of the household. Title was to remain with the government for twenty-five years, meaning allottees would not have to pay taxes as they learned land management and landholder techniques.

When the twenty-five years had passed, many native people found themselves faced with excessive property taxes, which meant they eventually lost their Dawes Act Allotment lands. In 1887 the native people had held 138 million acres, but by 1934 that number dropped to 48 million acres. Of those, 20 million acres were desert.

Reorganization Era: On June 2, 1924, Native Americans became citizens of the United States, and retained tribal citizenship as well, resulting in dual citizenship for America's native people. It would be 1948 before all states allowed Native Americans to vote. In 1928 the Meriam Report was released, documenting that the Dawes Act and Allotment policies had been utter failures. Passage of the Indian Reorganization Act of 1934 officially marked a new era by cancelling the allotment policy, and instituted new efforts to provide the legal frameworks that would allow native self-governance. Tribes began creating their own constitutions and laws, which tribal members would vote to ratify. (Haas 1957)

Termination Era 1953-1964: In 1953 the passage of House Current Resolution 108 attempted to change the status of native people so they would share the same responsibilities and entitlements as other citizens of the United States. With no land, native people would lose their sovereignty, be subject to taxes, and lose their status as wards of the state. Over twelve years, 109 tribes were terminated, causing dire consequences in terms of their receiving education or healthcare benefits, and destabilizing any financial stability they might have. Presidents Lyndon B. Johnson and Richard Nixon can be credited with the legislation which would move the country away from termination and toward native self-governance.

Self-Determination Era: By the late 1960s, termination was being replaced by native self-governance. In 1968 the Indian Civil Rights Act was passed, ensuring that the Bill of Rights extended to native people, and delineating federal, state, and tribal jurisdictions in such cases as adoption and child custody. By 1978 the Indian Child Welfare Act would make sure that Indian adoption and custody cases would be determined by the tribe (Canby 2004).

1928 Indian Rolls

On May 18, 1928, the US Congress authorized the attorney general of California to bring a lawsuit in the US Court of Claims (45 Stat. 602) on behalf of the Indians of California, for benefits they would have received under the eighteen treaties negotiated with the US government in 1852.

(Readers can find more detailed information on this Act of Congress by researching the following: SEVENTIETH CONGRESS. SESS. I. CH. 624. 1928. May 18, 1928. CHAP. 624 — An Act Authorizing the attorney general of the State of California to bring suit in the Court of Claims on behalf of the Indians of California.)

These treaties had been submitted to the US Senate for ratification on June 1, 1852, but were never ratified. Section 6 of the Act stipulated that no part of any judgment should be paid out in cash on a per capita basis. Rather, a trust fund should be established, with appropriations made by Congress for educational, health, industrial, and other purposes benefitting the California Indians.

The act authorized the secretary of the Interior to create two census rolls. Roll 1 was the roll of California Indians residing in California on May 18, 1928. For purposes of the act, the Indians of California were defined as those living in the state on June 1, 1852, and their descendants living in the state on May 18, 1928. Roll 2, authorized by section 7 of the act, was the roll of non-California Indians residing in California on May 18, 1928. No limit on the degree of Indian blood was fixed, and no requirements regarding tribal recognition or the maintenance of tribal relations were established for either roll.

Five-page forms comprised the applications, containing information about the applicants themselves and minor children, followed by an affidavit signed by two witnesses. The application showed the name of each person, position in family, age, sex, birth date, and degree of Indian blood. There was also information concerning residence, marital status, land allotments, and ancestry. Those on Roll 1 would share as beneficiaries in any favorable judgment recovered in the US Court of Claims. Roll 2 was for informative purposes only (Act of Congress: 45 Stat. 602).

Applications for enrollment were to be accepted for two years from the date of the act, and the secretary of the Interior was allowed an additional year to alter or revise the rolls. On approval by the secretary, an Amending Act of April 29, 1930, extended the time for filing applications to May 18, 1932, and the time for the final closing of the rolls to May 18, 1933 (Amending act of Congress: 46 Stat. 259).

More than 23,000 applicants filed for inclusion on the rolls, on a total of 11,253 applications. Of these, 10,719 applications were approved; 534 were rejected, and 216 involved appeals. Applicants who were rejected had sixty days from their date of rejection to appeal. Some appeals ended in reversal, with the applicant being enrolled. A total of 23,542 were accepted to Roll 1, with 1,245 accepted to Roll 2 and 1,135 rejected.

As mentioned, the Indian Reorganization Act (48 stat. 984) of 1934 officially marked a new era, becoming a reality in May 1935. By 1944, the 1928 Act to recover compensation for the lands taken by the government following the rejection of the 1852 treaties had culminated with the native people of California being awarded $17,500,000 for the 7.5 million acres stolen from them. The government, however, deducted the lawyers' fees and all monies the government had spent on the Indians of California during the last half of the nineteenth century from the award, which amounted to costs of $12 million—leaving barely $150 per person for the 36,000 native people in the state of California (Sutton 1994).

Under the Indian Claims Act of 1946, California Indians brought a second claim for reimbursement against the federal government, requesting compensation for lands not affected by the 1944 settlement. These lands included those not taken as a result of the 1852 treaties, Mexican land grants, and reservations originally not included. The total of these lands was about 65 million acres. In 1964 the native people were awarded $46 million, which meant that the United States government bought California for 47 cents an acre (Sutton 1994).

US Government Termination Policies

Starting in 1945 the topic of federal termination of Indian reservations came up among government bureaucrats in Washington DC, as another way to get native people to become part of mainstream American society (Orfield 1964). Other motives included the ideas that if the government could terminate Indian reservations, they could negate the native peoples' tribal sovereignty, dismiss any promises they had made to them throughout the previous hundred or more years, collect federal taxes from those previously exempt, and distribute reservation lands to whomever they chose. Each state would then take over the responsibilities, which the federal government abdicated, though some states legislatures were resistant to these changes because it meant increased costs for them as they assumed criminal and civil jurisdiction over native people.

While some native people were eager to discontinue their relationship with the federal government and were even willing to pay taxes, others resisted the states having control over their affairs without their consent, and worked to retain their tribal sovereignty. After Arthur Watkins was elected to the US Senate in 1946, the idea of turning the jurisdiction of federal Indian reservations over to the states began to mushroom.

In 1953 the Senate and House of Representatives passed Resolution 108 which read as follows:

Whereas it is the policy of Congress, as rapidly as possible, to make the Indians within the territorial limits of the United States subject to the same laws and entitled to the same privileges and responsibilities as are applicable to other citizens of the United States, to end their status as wards of the United States, and to grant them all of the rights and prerogatives pertaining to American citizenship (Haas 1957).

In 1954 the state of California held hearings at various Indian reservations, to hear from the native people what their ideas about termination were. On November 16 and 17 of that year hearings were held at Palm Springs for native people living in San Diego County. Testimony reflected whether native people or their spokespersons were for or against termination, and the numbers of people and amounts of acreage on each reservation. The most compelling evidence, however, came when native people testified as to their living conditions, their past history of dealings with the state and federal governments, their disappointments in past policies of dealing with California bureaucracy since 1848, and their hopes for the future. These hearings would reflect that for any native person to be eligible for the benefits that would result from termination of Indian lands, they would need to be enrolled members at one of the California tribes or bands, and their group would need to have a tribal constitution.

The chairman of the hearings of the Senate Interim Committee on California Indian Affairs was John Bohn. He stated the following on November 17, 1954, the second day of the hearings for San Diego County:

We are holding hearings all over the state to study the impact of proposed Federal legislation to terminate supervision over the Indians of California. This committee was created by the Senate of California and has no power to determine whether Federal Supervision over the Indians of California will be terminated. This decision can only be made by the Congress of the United States. However, by the passage of House Resolution No. 108, Congress has already indicated its intent to terminate, and it therefore becomes the obligation of the State of California to require that any such legislation made adequate provision to avoid undue financial hardship on the State and its political subdivisions. It is also the obligation of the State of California to protect the interests of the Indian citizens and to make certain that any terminal legislation passed by the United States Congress does not ignore the rights of the Indians, but, on the contrary, makes adequate provision for their protection. It is therefore the purpose of this committee to study the problems of the Indians of California and to make appropriate recommendation to accomplish these results. That is the obligation of this committee.

Though Bohn contended that the Senate of California had no authority to determine whether termination would take place or not, he did reinforce that the quest for termination was in the works. Testimony was taken from representatives of the following tribes, including Inaja, La Posta, Barona, El Capitan, Pauma/Yuima, Rincon, Santa Ysabel, Mesa Grande, San Pasqual, Campo, Cuyapaipe, Manzanita, Pala, and Los Coyotes. The committee also gathered figures on the number of families on each reservation and acreage totals, and testimony revealed that several reservations had an old and a new reservation (Old Campo, New Campo, Old Pala, New Pala, Old San Pasqual, New San Pasqual), and some of the reservations had only one family or a few people living on reservation lands, including Cuyapaipe, Manzanita, and San Pasqual.

Speakers at the hearings included Frederick George Collett (Senate Hearings 1954), a Methodist minister who had founded the Indian Board of Cooperation, a nonprofit corporation. The group aimed to help native people maneuver through the US Court of Claims and gain passage of the bill meant to provide reparations for stolen land; the board was said to have been created to provide guidance in ways that would ultimately help better the lives of native people. Early costs incurred to fight the government in legal battles came from the native people themselves, since they paid four to six dollars each to belong to the Indian Board of Cooperation.

During his speech Mr. Collette mentioned that the question had arisen concerning what an Indian was, but he had no definition, though he felt there should be one. He pointed out that the definition of what constituted an Indian for the purpose of settlement claims was those Indians residing in the state of California in 1852 and their descendants now living. He conceded that there was no description of what an Indian was for the purpose of reservations or for tribal purposes. Collette espoused the idea that those who wanted to be free should be allowed to adopt the privilege of doing so, along with being able to assume the responsibilities that go along with such a proposal.

Mr. Purl Willis, who described himself as a counselor and advisor to the Mission Indian Federation, also appeared at the hearings and proposed the idea that the group was serving as the voice of the Mission Indians, along with defending their rights. He credited his group with being the sponsors of Public Law 280, a method whereby states would assume jurisdiction over reservation Indians at the time of termination. Willis explained that the Mission Indian Federation caused the suit to be brought against San Diego County to enforce state welfare laws. Though Willis asserted that the Mission Indian Federation represented most of the Mission Indians, other speakers and tribal representatives proved that there was a diversity of opinion about the question of termination.

Problems common to all the reservations in San Diego County became clear during testimony from spokespeople and tribal representatives. Those problems included dubious reservation boundary lines; enrollment problems; who belonged where; old bands versus new bands; those wanting government's involvement in their lives versus those who didn't; claims of fraud in elections; some tribes having no tribal council, no tribal rolls and no constitution; poor economic status; little or no opportunity for employment on reservation lands; lack of education among middle-aged and older people; poor quality land (rocky, brush-covered, mountainous, remote, worthless); poorly built or nearly non-existent roads; poor sanitation facilities (open sewers, contaminated water, bursting pipes, etc.); no hospitals or healthcare on reservations; and unresponsive or unreceptive county health facilities that were unreliable, far away, and for indigents. Also mentioned as problems on the reservations were extravagant levying of liens by the government, and problems with inheritance of lands. Some tribes already had constitutions and tribal rolls, while others had one or the other, and some tribes had neither.

Creating a tribal constitution and enrollment list was not always an easy proposition, as was clear from the fact that even the federal government refused to touch the subject of tribal enrollment lists during the time of the 1954 California Senate Interim Hearings. A final report from the hearings stated that before December 31, 1956, the Department of the Interior must finally and officially establish ownership lists—rolls—for each of the affected Indian properties in California. A special panel of judges would be appointed, preferably by the Judicial Council of California, with power to recommend changes to the Secretary of the Interior prior to actual creation of the lists. Adequate provision for appeal in individual cases was also suggested, most likely through the same panel of judges.

The Senate Interim Committee also avoided using the term tribal "roll" to avoid confusion because since 1928 federal authorities had compiled a so-called Roll or Enrollment of California Indians, in connection with the claims asserted by the Indians of California against the United States as a result of the Indian Claims Act, and upon which judgment had been rendered. Closer to the time the committee was reporting, that enrollment had been extended for the purpose of claims that at the time were being prosecuted before the Indian Claims Commission.

Because of the nature of those claims, eligibility of enrollment was based upon the ability of any person to trace his ancestry to an Indian who was resident in California in 1852 or upon other designated dates. It was believed that those existing rolls had no necessary relationship to the problem of determining the identity of persons entitled to share in the distribution of specific trust properties, for the reason that those distributive rights arose out of entirely different circumstances.

The committee noted that groups or bands of persons living on the trust properties during the Senate Interim Hearings, or most directly claiming an interest in those trust properties, were not always members of the same tribe. More often than not, these persons represented composites of many tribes, with a considerable number of non-Indians living there as well. The committee chose to deal with the issue on the basis of persons, rather than either tribal affiliation or percentage of Indian blood. They recognized that, historically, certain lands were acquired for, or were the property of, certain tribes or certain named bands.

The committee came to the conclusion that the problems of each of the parcels of trust properties must be considered separately, since the properties were so varied that no exact pattern could be established on a statewide basis. It was because of these wide variations in properties that the committee chose to avoid generalities by not using the term tribal rolls, and by not defining the percentage of Indian blood required for participation.

Following the Senate Interim Termination Hearings in 1954, a group asserting that they were descendants of those evicted from the San Pasqual Valley in 1878 began a concerted effort to be allowed to move onto reservation lands on the San Pasqual Indian Reservation in Valley Center. These would be descendants of those who had refused to accept those same lands years before, when the lands were first designated by the Smiley Commission in 1891, again when the lands became part of the Amended Homestead Act of March 1, 1907, and later when they had been trust-patented to the San Pasqual Band on July 1, 1910.

During the years 1909-1954, Frank Trask, Leonora La Chappa Trask, Florence Trask, Helen Trask, and their descendants had been the only Ipai to live on the lands of the San Pasqual Indian Reservation in Valley Center. In 1954, with federal termination of Indian reservations a distinct possibility, those who said they were descendants of San Pasqual Indians but had refused to accept the reservation in Valley Center, may have realized that if they were to share in the benefits that might be distributed after terminaton became a reality, they would need to be listed on a tribal roll and have a tribal constitution.

The resources of reservation lands would be given only to those members of the band who were listed on tribal rolls as tribal members, and as part of a tribal group with a constitution. More detailed information about specific occurrences at the Senate Interim Termination Hearings of 1954 as they affected the San Pasqual Band can be found in chapter seven. Florence Trask appeared at the hearings at the side of her stepfather, Ramon Ames, tribal chairman of Barona, who explained how the Trask family had been placed at the reservation in Valley Center. Others spoke concerning the removal of the reservation to Valley Center in 1891 and the placement of the Trask family there in 1909.

The following section provides a description of what was going on with the Trask family and others at the San Pasqual Indian Reservation in Valley Center during the years 1956-1966, when the tribal rolls were created and certified by the Department of the Interior, and from 1966-1971, when the San Pasqual Band's constitution would be certified.

Questions have arisen as to why descendants of the two groups who were evicted from the San Pasqual Valley in 1878 waited so long to seek reservation lands on the San Pasqual Indian Reservation in Valley Center. Those who had secured homesteads from the federal government on public lands northeast of their former homes in San Pasqual Valley, and those who had gone elsewhere to seek new homes and work, were now wanting to claim lands which previously they had strenuously rejected. Several censuses had even noted that they had lost their identity as Indians (San Pasqual Censuses 1923-1926). Speculations about why they were returning centered upon several issues. Some theories included the ideas that the people may have finally given up on their efforts to get back tribal lands in the San Pasqual Valley; that the economy may have worsened and the reservation offered a safe haven and free land, and that the possibility of termination of all Indian reservations in California may have entered into considerations.

The New San Pasqual Enrollment Committee

In 1958, Thelma Terry and Sosten Alto approached anthropologist Florence Shipek on behalf of the newly-constituted San Pasqual Enrollment Committee. Shipek stated in a 1994 affidavit: "The Bureau of Indian Affairs informed them they would have to prove they were the descendants of the original people. The elders asked me to help supply that proof" (Shipek 1994).

A handwritten note from the anthropologist's archival materials at the Kumeyaay Community College at Sycuan further explained her participation in the enrollment process for the San Pasqual Band:

> [A] committee of San Pasqual Indians approached me for aid in proving who were the descendants of the original band of San Pasqual Indians. The Bureau of Indian Affairs was trying to organize the present descendants into a band and had issued a notice to all those who might possibly have an interest in San Pasqual to attend a meeting. A committee was appointed to determine what the qualifications for membership should be (Shipek 2012:MS).

Extensive notes and letters from that era reveal the questions that prevailed as the enrollment committee attempted to create a list of who belonged on the San Pasqual Indian Reservation in Valley Center and who didn't. Participants at meetings included members and descendants of the Trask family, descendants of the families who had secured homesteads in the northeastern part of the San Pasqual Valley after the 1878 eviction, and descendants of those who had gone to other areas to find new homes and jobs. From 1956 to 1962 the enrollment committee also worked with John L. Pappan, program officer, Riverside area BIA field office.

The process of enrollment was long and involved, and is described later in this chapter in detail, but in brief, by 1958 the baselines for enrollment were determined and the term "blood of the Band" came into existence, as a term meaning that Indian lineage suitable to meeting the requirements for enrollment must trace to the San Pasqual Indian Census of 1910.

At the suggestion of Audrey Lawson Toler, daughter of Helen Trask Lawson Ward and granddaughter of Frank Trask and Leonora La Chappa Trask, a blood quantum of one-eighth degree was decided upon. Though the tribal enrollment process began in 1956, it would take until 1966 for the Membership Roll to be certified by the Department of the Interior, and the San Pasqual Band's Constitution would be certified in 1971. By this time, it had become evident that termination of the reservations in southern California was not going to happen. The Bureau of Indian Affairs Sacramento Area Office certified the new tribal roll as follows:

> I hereby certify that to the best of my knowledge and belief the attached Membership Roll for the San Pasqual Band of Mission Indians, naming 229 members, contains only those persons living as of January 1, 1959, whose enrollment applications have

Florence Trask Wolfe. *Photo: Trask-La Chappa family.*

been approved in accordance with membership provisions, published by the Secretary of the Interior on March 2, 1960, (25 CFR Part 48), which designated the June 30, 1910 Census for the San Pasqual Mission Indians as the applicable Census Roll for determining the Band's membership. I further certify that the degree of San Pasqual Indian blood, as shown on the attached roll, has been computed in accordance with a Secretarial decision interpreting "blood of the Band" to be total Indian blood of a person named on the Basic Census Membership Roll dated June 30, 1910." — Leonard M. Hill, Area Director July 1, 1966

As mentioned, the creation of Native American tribal constitutions had begun following passage of the Indian Reorganization Act of 1934 (Canby 2004). The San Pasqual Band was organized as an Indian Reorganization Act (IRA) tribe, and has an IRA constitution. Codes of Federal Regulations dictate federal policies on enrollment for the tribe. For a native person to qualify for membership in the San Pasqual Band, the burden of proof is with the person claiming to be Indian — the person who is seeking tribal membership. As the enrollment process proceeded, controversies persisted as to whom was eligible to attend meetings, who was qualified to vote, and who possessed enough "blood of the Band" to be enrolled as a San Pasqual tribal member.

Though Florence Trask Wolfe had served as spokesperson for the San Pasqual Indian Reservation since the 1930s, following the death of her father, minutes from the November 24, 1957, enrollment committee meeting showed the following comments from Orlando Garcia, field representative of the BIA Riverside Area Field Office, who told those assembled:

[A]t the present time the BIA does not recognize any group or individual with authority to act on reservation matters. ... Mrs. Mary Matteson and Mrs. Florence Wolfe are without authority to act in any official capacity on reservation matters and they have been notified to that effect by the BIA. At the present time it appears that most of the reservation problems can be attributed to a lack of tribal organization and membership rolls.

One purpose of the meeting was to elect an enrollment regulations committee, but participants were concerned about who to elect, since some believed that not all of those listed on the 1910 Census rolls were truly San Pasqual Indians. Mary Matteson asserted: "There are people on the census rolls who are not members" (Garcia 1957:3). Mr. Garcia stated: "You can nominate anybody who thinks he has an interest in the San Pasqual Reservation, regardless of whether he is here or not" (1957:3).

The following people were nominated, the nominations were seconded, and the number of votes were recorded: Sosten Alto (32); Thelma Terry (27); Felix Quisquis (21); Audrey Toler (21); Florence Wolfe (20); George Martinez (18); Mary Mae Perez (16), and Mary Matteson (11). It was agreed that the person with the most votes would become chairman of the committee. The following were voted in as the enrollment regulations committee: Sosten Alto (chairman), Thelma Terry, Felix Quisquis, Audrey Toler and Florence Wolfe. The newly elected group agreed to hold their first meeting on December 8, 1957.

A March 12, 1958, letter from Orlando Garcia to Sosten Alto included the following comments:

We have been asked by several people to clarify the authority of the San Pasqual Enrollment Regulations Committee. ... Apparently some of the people have reason to suspect the committee of acting as a tribal governing body. It is our understanding that the committee was elected for the sole purpose of drafting enrollment regulations. Of course, members of the committee must investigate all available sources of information on which to base those regulations. Some people might have a misunderstanding in this respect. Since the San Pasqual Band is unorganized and are without a Tribal Business Committee this office has sent information material to the chairman of the regulations committee. ... [W]e have also requested that such information be turned over to the Tribal Business Committee if and when one is elected.

A September 15, 1958, letter from Shipek to Dick Thomas, American Friends Service Committee, revealed that Shipek recognized that to carry out a complete genealogical history of the San Pasqual group would be difficult and would require funding, travel, and time to interview each one; she also reflected the desire of some she was representing to use the 1909 San Pasqual Census rather than the Census of 1910. Referring to a San Pasqual Regulations Committee meeting, she noted:

Mr. Papan wouldn't accept their word about the 1909 roll because he hadn't seen it and the 1910 roll is not so very good. ... I also noticed their use of kinship terms and I believe that a complete study of the group would reveal without the aid of any papers who belonged and who didn't. Ezell tells me that such a study has been used elsewhere to prove prehistoric ownership and occupation and tribal organization. This would take some expense money for I would have to do a lot of driving to visit and have extended talks with each one. How many of the reservations are in this sort of a mess of trying to get their enrollment straightened out? Mr. Garcia said that only three in Southern California actually had approved rolls as yet.

On September 23, 1958, Shipek again wrote to Dick Thomas saying:

> Here is a summary of my observations concerning the September 14th meeting. . .
> Without anyone presenting any proof of belonging to the Band, the people present voted on what should constitute eligibility for membership and enrollment in the band. . . . All those who felt they had a right to vote were asked to sign a tally sheet but voting slips were passed out and collected independently of signing the tally sheet . . . [M]y husband saw several at the rear who had signed the sheet walk out and say, 'what is the use of voting they are going to control it anyway' . . . The exact meaning of 1/4 and 1/8 degree of blood was not explained. The woman sitting next to me, neither knew the meaning nor how to write either symbol . . . I firmly believe that working with the records I am finding and with a proper anthropological study such as Dr. Ezell described, a proper determination could be made and proof supplied as to the actual members of the band, and their descendants.

The anthropologist's handwritten notes showed the following: "The Bureau has a census made on June 30, 1910 supposedly of Indians living on the reservation; this census lists Trask and every individual in his family, several families whom the Indians claim are Mexican and some of the San Pasqual people" (Shipek MS:2-4).

Several months after the meeting of 1958, where blood quantum and other requirements for enrollment were made specific, the enrollment committee sent the regulations and enrollment list to the secretary of the Interior, for his acceptance and for submission of the document to the Federal Register. Before acceptance of the regulations and enrollment list could occur, however, and before submission of the document to the Federal Register, a protest letter from some of those seeking to be on the enrollment list was sent to the secretary, outlining grievances about some procedural elements that had occurred as part of the process to get to that point. Questions of who had been allowed to vote, of who had registered on voting lists, and of the use or nonuse of voting slips arose as issues. Later, changes interjected into the document by the secretary of the Interior would emerge as issues as well.

Enrollment applications and instructions on how to complete them were sent out in the spring of 1960. The enrollment committee spent the summer of 1960 meeting together, examining all applications, and either approving or denying the applicants. As certain committee member applications were being considered, the committee member who was being examined would withdraw from the process, and an alternate would take over.

At the conclusion of these considerations, recommendations for approval were given to 202 applicants, while 113 applicants were denied. The Office of Indian Affairs later approved 197 of those 202, denied 85, and gave 32 over to the commissioner of Indian Affairs for his decision. The enrollment committee noted later that the main area of disagreement concerning the 32 people given over to the commissioner of Indian Affairs was as to whether they possessed blood of the Band. All bureau officials later offered their acceptance of those 32, verifying that they did possess blood of the Band.

One of the families submitted to bureau officials for final acceptance or denial was the Trask family and their descendants. Those enrollment committee members objecting to the family's acceptance did so because they claimed that the Trasks had never been "adopted" into the San Pasqual Band. From that time on, Florence and Helen Trask and their descendants would become the focus of an unfounded yet prolonged scrutinization that would continue for more than half a century, to current times. A genealogical study of the Trask family at that time included information that has since been corrected to reflect a more accurate blood degree. The extent of information available on family history in the mid-1950s was much more limited than it is today in the twenty-first century, with much greater access to correspondence and communications, the advent of the Internet, cell phones, and many other technologies that have contributed to vastly improved resources for researching genealogical records. With increased motivation for many families to learn about their family history, and the sharing of this information, the available resources also expand, enabling researchers to learn in much greater detail about family kinship and lineages.

"Who are your people?" has always been a topic of conversation among the Ipai of San Diego County, and continues to be to this day, since it is estimated that more than 600 generations of native people have lived within the Ipai territory over the past 12,000 years. Envisioning those ancestors takes a person back to the time before the Egyptian pyramids were constructed.

Documenting their relationships with one another and their blood quantum becomes a daunting task, especially since the documentation of native history has been primarily through oral tradition. Going back and writing down what those relationships and personal interactions actually were, involves vast amounts of time and effort. Calculations of the Trask family's genealogy in the mid-1950s differed from those in existence today, as has been considered by the Bureau of Indian Affairs, with input from the Band's enrollment committee or designated committees. The bureau has always been supportive in examining and analyzing new information that has come forth, and in correcting the records to show those changes, which have always reflected current, more up-to-date information.

Misinformation, Controversy, and Eligibility

Controversy beginning in the late 1950s has lingered on the San Pasqual Indian Reservation, stemming from the actions of anthropologist Florence Shipek who was negatively influenced by certain people for whom she was working to create the tribal roll.

Shipek categorized Frank Trask as a "white caretaker" and said he was hired by the federal government to take care of the San Pasqual Indian Reservation lands in Valley Center, adding that Leonora La Chappa Trask was an Indian from another tribe. Shipek asserted that the couple's two daughters had no rights at the San Pasqual Indian Reservation in Valley Center (California Indian Legal Services Letter 1969). Shipek began to circulate this blatant misinformation reflecting her clients' bias toward Frank Trask, Leonora La Chappa Trask, and Florence and Helen Trask, in stark contrast to the preponderance of documented information.

A June 10, 1965, report to the enrollment committee from Felie [Felix] Quisquis with the subject, "Enrollment Problems of the San Pasqual Band of Mission Indians," used the same language found in Florence Shipek's handwritten and typed manuscripts from her archives at Sycuan. The report outlined a history of the San Pasqual group of people from 1824 on, and included the notion that there were people currently being scrutinized who were considered "undoubted members" of the Band.

Mr. Quisquis's letter claimed that the anthropologist plus the old "undoubted members," after examining all the evidence and the Bureau Rolls, felt that the 1909 San Pasqual Census Roll was the only accurate one to use. They thought that the 1890 Roll was difficult to use because of the phonetic spelling of names and that the 1910 Roll contained the names of husbands or wives who were not San Pasqual Indians, in addition to some persons in other categories that were not members of the Band. The report stated that after several meetings and some letters being exchanged between the enrollment committee and bureau personnel, the bureau insisted it could not find the 1909 Roll, which Shipek said she had found (Shipek 2012:MS).

The enrollment committee, finally, to get the process going, agreed to base the enrollment on the 1910 Census. They inserted the words "blood of the Band" in all the clauses relating to membership, feeling that this wording would protect them from the non-San Pasqual people whom they felt were on the 1910 Census roll.

Quisquis's report stated that there were some people living at that time [1965] on the San Pasqual Reservation who had been disapproved, and the BIA was asked to have them move off. The bureau, however, responded, "... until the final roll is approved by the Secretary, no one is approved or disapproved. We feel that all those who are disapproved should be made to leave and should also pay back rent; particularly those who have moved on since 1950, who do not belong."

A bulletin with a reference date of 1966 that circulated among those living on the San Pasqual Indian Reservation presented self-contradictory evidence against Florence and Helen Trask:

> The applicants' father was non-Indian; he was a white employee of the Mesa Grande
> Agency of the Office of Indian Affairs. He had been employed as caretaker for the
> San Pasqual lands and the houses which were on the land when it was purchased in

1909 for the San Pasqual Band of Mission Indians. As evidence, we quote a letter dated April 7, 1910 from the Chief of the Education Division (Dortch 1910), Office of Indian Affairs, to Amos Frank, Superintendent of Mesa Grande (Ref. SC-4 0987):

> [T]hree positions of Judge at $84 a year were established on July 1, 1909 for San Pasqual, to be effective October 1, 1909 … on February 1, 1901 you appointed Frank Trask to one of the positions.

This "evidence" is odd indeed, since Trask's appointment as an Indian judge is actually further evidence of his Indian heritage. Frank Trask's father-in-law, Antonio La Chappa, was serving as judge during this same time at the Mesa Grande Indian Reservation. Two other government documents show that Frank Trask was also appointed as policeman for the San Pasqual Indian Reservation in 1910. A letter from First Assistant Secretary Frank Pierce to the commissioner of Indian Affairs on April 5, 1910, stated: "Authorization is hereby granted you for the establishment of one position of police private at $20.00 a month at the Mesa Grande Agency, California, effective April 1, 1910, payable from the appropriation, 'Pay of Indian Police 1910,' under the Act approved March 3, 1909" (36 Stat. L., 786). At the bottom of the page was noted RES-29, 8919, Frank Trask. A second Memorandum for Appointments (Mesa Grande) dated April 6, 1910, read: Please establish the position of police private for the San Pasqual Indian Reservation, under Mesa Grande Superintendent, salary $20.00 per month, effective April 1, 1910, and appoint Mr. Frank Trask, recommended by the superintendent and special agent Kelsey (RES-26, 8870). Frank Trask's brother-in-law, Sylvester La Chappa, was serving during this same time as policeman for the Mesa Grande Reservation.

In 1987 Shipek published a book that included her claim against the Trask family:

> In 1910 the Bureau hired a non-Indian caretaker to protect the purchased improvements, which included a small house. This caretaker had a part-Indian wife who was a member of the Santa Ysabel Band, and their children, two daughters, continued to live on the reservation long after he and his wife were deceased. The bureau, while originally recognizing their Santa Ysabel origin, began to list this family as residents of the San Pasqual Reservation in 1910 and neglected to write in the employee status of the father, a non-Indian" (Shipek 1987:93).

Shipek does not offer actual documentation of her claims about Frank Trask being a non-Indian white caretaker hired by the Bureau of Indian Affairs, but rather it appears to have been based on her acceptance of certain clients' assertions. Clearly, the thorough review of the numerous government documents presented in previous chapters consistently show Trask as half Indian, and as having received the first allotment on the San Pasqual Indian Reserve in Valley Center in 1909 with his native wife, Leonora La Chappa Trask.

When those attempting to create a new tribal roll reached an impasse in 1969, and business was at a standstill for over a year, the California Indian Legal Services became involved, resulting in the following material being circulated. An April 18, 1969, letter from

California Indian Legal Services to Mr. Jess Town, area field representative of the Bureau of Indian Affairs at Riverside, contained information similar to that circulated by Florence Shipek and the enrollment committee and read in part:

> As you know, this office has been working for some time with various members of the San Pasqual Band of Mission Indians, including the Acting Spokesman, Mrs. Mary Matteson. ... The San Pasqual Band has not met officially for over a year because of an incident which took place during the Band's last meeting. A serious confrontation involving the threat of physical violence was narrowly averted. ... [I]t appears certain that the Band will remain completely unable to function unless and until the long-standing enrollment dispute is finally settled. ... All the evidence clearly indicates that the Trask family resided on the San Pasqual Reservation in 1910 only because Frank Trask, a non-Indian, had been hired as the Reservation's caretaker (California Indian Legal Services Letter 1969:1-7).

The erroneous information in the letter begins with the misleading representation of Matteson as "Acting Spokesman" and continues with the false claims against the Trask family. As mentioned previously, Mr. Garcia's letter of November 1957 had expressly stated that the BIA was not recognizing any group or individual as having authority to act on reservation matters, and had added that Mary Matteson and Florence Wolfe were notified that they had no authority to act in any official capacity.

In an August 2014 conversation between David Toler and Robert Pelcyger, who was a young attorney working for California Indian Legal Services at the time of the 1969 letter, Toler asked why he had referred to Frank Trask as a "white caretaker." Pelcyger responded that Mary Matteson had said that. (Pelcyger has gone on to become an influential and well-respected attorney that has worked with Indian organizations, including the San Luis Rey Indian Water Authority.)

The consequences which followed the anthropologist's and others' erroneous remarks prompted some newcomers to the San Pasqual Reservation in the late 1950s to adopt the mantra: "You don't belong here. Go back to Mesa Grande" (Lawson, Toler and Herrera interviews 2010). Some people at the San Pasqual Indian Reservation today still believe Shipek's mistaken claims, which circulated widely and are still being circulated today via the Internet, planted newspaper articles and television stories, bulletins sent out to San Pasqual tribal members, and protests conducted by some descendants of tribal members. They choose to ignore the factual evidence showing that Frank Trask was born in 1867 when his father was documented to be living in the San Pasqual Valley, and that Leonora La Chappa Trask was descended from the Ipai clans of La Chappa, Guachena, Nejo, and other clans that traditionally inhabited the San Pasqual Valley of San Diego County.

On February 16, 1994, long after the enrollment process had been concluded, Shipek submitted an affidavit that further explained the procedures she had used to come up with her version of who should be part of the tribal rolls and who shouldn't:

I also interviewed all the San Pasqual band elders and some related Mesa Grande Band elders whose parents had been accepted at Mesa Grande as refugees from San Pasqual in 1876. Specifically Porfidia Duro (age about 95) whose father was Ysidro Nejo, first assistant to Captain Panto Duro, the leader of San Pasqual from before Kearney entered in 1846. ... I also interviewed Laura (Lorenza) Spoletti, Porfidia's sister. ... From each elder, those of San Pasqual and the Mesa Grande elders, I also inquired about their knowledge of other families as well as their own. The people with whom I spent the most time were those past 80 years of age in 1958-59 and then those past 70 years. ... I sat with the Enrollment Committee and worked with them at all their meetings. I also sat with them at all band meetings and the band and committee meetings called by the Office of Indian Affairs. At all meetings I was assisting the Enrollment Committee and making notes of the events at each meeting. (Shipek 1994)

Shipek noted that she interviewed Porfidia Duro and Lorenza Spoletti, two sisters whose father was Ysidro Nejo; she said that the two women's parents had been accepted at Mesa Grande as refugees from San Pasqual after the eviction of 1878. Trask family descendants have wondered how Shipek so easily accepted Porfidia and Lorenza's parents as having relocated to Mesa Grande, but never interviewed Florence or Helen Trask to learn from where their clans had derived, though their maternal great-grandmother was Feliciana Nejo La Chappa, identified by Gifford in 1919 as the cousin sister (i.e., first cousin) of Ysidro Nejo, the father of Porfidia and Lorenza. Florence and Helen's paternal great-grand-mother, Angela Guachena La Chappa, had been mentioned by historian Edward Davis (1936) as living at the San Diego Mission as a child. Unfortunately, Shipek clearly accepted her favored clients' claims at face value and neglected to conduct the archival and ethno-graphic research that would have shown the ancestral connections of Leonora LaChappa and Frank Trask to the San Pasqual Valley.

After the enrollment committee had spent the summer of 1960 examining all the appli-cations, accepting some and rejecting others, they had given thirty-two names to the commissioner of Indian Affairs for his decision. As mentioned, BIA officials ultimately offered their acceptance of those thirty-two people, including the Trask family, and verified that they possessed blood of the Band. The decision involved correspondences among a number of participants, including the commissioner of Indian Affairs, the associate solici-tor of Indian Affairs, the area director of the Office of Indian Affairs in Sacramento, and the San Pasqual Enrollment Committee.

It was during this time that someone from the San Pasqual Enrollment Committee used a pencil to cross out a 4/4 degree blood for Leonora La Chappa Trask on an indi-vidual history card and wrote in 7/8, a notation which would take the Trask family descendants years to correct (Toler 2014). It is important to alert readers to the problems that can result from someone mishandling enrollment papers, or papers showing a native person's blood quantum, when one degree of blood quantum is arbitrarily changed to another. Blood degrees need to be substantiated with documents or other means of official verification.

The alleged reason for Leonora being described as 7/8 (rather than full blooded) was the claim that Leonora's father Antonio only had 3/4 blood when he married Feliciana Nejo, who herself was 4/4. This claim presumed that Antonio's mother Angela Guachena La Chappa (see photo) was half Indian and half white, leading to the erroneous conclusion that Leonora's blood was only 7/8 and not the true 4/4. Antonio's father (Leonora's grandfather) was Jose Bastiano La Chappa, the narrator of one of the Ipai origin stories at the beginning of this book. The BIA, based on the preponderance of evidence, eventually corrected this error.

A July 1965 letter from H. E. Hyden, the associate solicitor of Indian Affairs, to the area director of the Bureau of Indian Affairs in Sacramento, presented further information about the eligibility of Trask family members and their descendants to be enrolled on the San Pasqual Band of Diegueño Mission Indians of California Tribal Rolls. The commissioner of Indian Affairs had presented to the associate solicitor of Indian Affairs the job of making a final determination as to whether members of the Trask family possessed "blood of the Band," and were eligible for enrollment in the San Pasqual Band.

The associate solicitor of Indian Affairs concluded:

> The record shows that the names of both Mrs. Ward and Mrs. Wolfe appear on the June 30, 1910 Census roll of the San Pasqual Band of Mission Indians, which has been designated as the basic roll for determining membership in the Band. Moreover, there is conclusive evidence that not only have these two been considered as members of the Band since they took up residence on the San Pasqual Reservation in 1909, but for the major part of the ensuing years, members of the Trask family have been the only residents of the San Pasqual Reservation. In view of the foregoing, we believe both these individuals to be clearly eligible for enrollment under Part 48.5 (a), Title 23, Code of Federal Regulations. ... [P]ersons of Indian blood who were recognized as Band members when the basic roll of June 30, 1910 was compiled, may be considered to be of the blood of the San Pasqual Band. ... [T]he children of Mrs. Ward and Mrs. Wolfe could qualify for enrollment, provided the Indian blood they derive from their respective mothers totals at least 1/8 degree. ... Pursuant to the authority delegated to the Solicitor by the Secretary of the Interior (210 DM 2.2A (4) (b), 24 F. R. 1348), and redelegated to the Associate Solicitor by the Solicitor (Solicitor's Regulation 19, 29 F.R. 6449), the applications submitted for final determination for the persons referred to herein are approved for enrollment as members of the Band. You are instructed to place the names of Helen Trask Ward, Hugh Lawson, Jr., Earl F. Lawson, Eleanor L. Rey, Audrey Mae L. Toler, Allen E. Lawson, Florence Trask Wolfe and Robert Lee Stewart on the membership roll of the San Pasqual Band of Mission Indians. At the earliest possible date, you should notify each of the individuals, as well as the Enrollment Committee, of the action taken by this office (Hyden 1965).

Leonora La Chappa Trask's paternal grandmother, Ipai Angela Guachena La Chappa. *Photo: E. H. Davis, San Diego History Center.*

Setting the Record Straight

In July 1991 members of the Trask-La Chappa family wrote a letter to the Office of Indian Affairs, tracing their Ipai history in the region, noting that their ancestors lived in what is now San Diego and Imperial Counties and Northern Baja, settling near *Tukumak*, now known as Mesa Grande, *Setmumumin*, now known as Santa Ysabel, and *Mititekwanak*, now known as the San Felipe Creek region. Before the appearance of the United States government in these areas, the ancestors of the Trask-La Chappa family moved throughout their traditional band and clan territory with the seasons, as most of the native people did. Normal migratory routes included following the watershed to the *Ahmukatlkatl* (San Pasqual) and *Sinyau-Pichkara* (Rancho Bernardo). The southern route to *Paulpo* (San Diego) was also used along the eastern migration route. These migratory movements were a part of the family's true Indian heritage, with bands spending time at different parts of their ancestral clan territories at different times throughout the year.

All the creek tributaries of Mesa Grande, Santa Ysabel, and other Ipai sites east of San Pasqual that flow west toward the Pacific Ocean merge to become the San Dieguito River. Numerous ancient native sites have been recorded along the San Dieguito River, as well as along the entire Pacific coast of southern California and beyond, including the territories of the *Chumash* (around modern day Santa Barbara), *Tongva* (Gabrieleño),

175

Trask family descendants in 1956 at the San Pasqual Reservation: (From left) Allen Lawson, (boy below unknown), Joe Herrera, Dave Toler Jr., Cheryl Calac (Lawson), Dennis Toler, Elenor Herrera (Little El), Ann (Herrera) Rodriguez, Douglas Toler, Freddy Herrera, Darla Toler, (baby) Darrow Toler, and the matriarch Helen Trask Lawson Ward.

Acjachemen (Juaneño), *Payómkawichum* (Luiseño), Ipai, and Tipai territory extending into Baja California. (The author recognizes that each native group may have their own name or names for their tribe, and the present interpretation is not meant to be insensitive to those preferences.)

The Kumeyaay-Ipai of these areas did not marry into their own clans. Rather, young girls would go through the puberty ceremonies and rites, preparing to have a relationship with someone from a differing clan. Each girl would then leave the village and move with her new husband to the region of the husband's clan. Subsequent gatherings and get-togethers among clans would provide opportunities for reuniting and creating memories among the groups. Since each clan was comprised of close-knit families, the regrouping of clans connected by intermarriage would most likely be close-knit too. Such groupings of people meant that relationships among families were well known by all those involved in the groups. With celebrations and get-togethers occasioning movement of people, and with seasonal migrations a normal occurrence, those who lived within the area of discussion would, naturally, come into close contact with each other from time to time.

In a conversation between the author and San Pasqual tribal member Victoria Diaz about subjects related to Ipai culture, Diaz commented that her great-grandmother Manuela Quis Quis was born in or around one of the Ipai villages near San Dieguito, mentioning how common it was for *shimul* members to move around for marriage and social contact, and how proud her family is of their native heritage. This clan is another prime example of cultural interaction throughout Ipai territory.

Members from the Trask-La Chappa family noted in the 1991 letter to the Bureau of Indian Affairs that time and mixed-marriages may have changed the original bloodlines of the family, but nevertheless, Trask-La Chappa family members always remained in the same region as their ancestors, and worked to carry on old, traditional ways, as the grandparents of the clan taught them. Those writing the letter acknowledged that during the times of the ancestors, people often did not claim their entire blood degrees, because being identified as Indian might lead to discrimination and animosity from other ethnic groups, along with other repercussions. Such instances of claiming only a portion of one's blood degree was often evidenced by a transitioning of old traditional ways passing into new progressive ways, especially as the dawn of the Industrial Era took place in the United States.

Those Trask-La Chappa family members who wrote the 1991 letter expressed their desire to maintain traditional cultural ways, with the goal being to share with family members their cultural heritage. They noted that being a tribal member was necessary if one was to achieve those goals.

Therefore, descendants of Frank Trask, Leonora La Chappa Trask, and of Leonora's parents, Antonio La Chappa and Feliciana Nejo La Chappa, asked that the records within the National Archives, showing Antonio La Chappa and Feliciana Nejo La Chappa as full-blooded Indians, be reflected in current San Pasqual Band of Mission Indians enrollment records. A description of those persons who were direct descendants of Frank Trask, Leonora La Chappa Trask, Antonio La Chappa, and Feliciana Nejo La Chappa was attached with the letter. By November of 1993 the legitimacy of their corrected bloodline would be acknowledged by the Bureau of Indian Affairs, which corrected Leonora LaChappa's blood degree from 7/8 to 4/4.

> *Our family is proud that Frank and Leonora, with their daughters, Florence and Helen, came to the reservation in 1909 and by June of 1910 San Pasqual Reservation was not only patented, but came into a trust status, which preserved the lands that were set aside in 1891, and allowed the land to become a home for those who reside there today.*

On November 2, 1993, the superintendent of the Department of the Interior wrote a letter to the chairperson of the San Pasqual Band, referring to the issue of appeals of certain persons' membership status, which had been dismissed, and that in accordance with the 25 CFR (Code of Federal Regulations), 62.10, the decision was final for the Department of the Interior. Those listed as being accepted for membership within the San Pasqual Band were all descendants of the Trask-La Chappa family. Sent with the letter were the original enrollment applications and attachments, and the notice that any questions could be directed to the superintendent, at the Tribal Operations Branch.

In August of 2002 another San Pasqual tribal member wrote a letter to the same superintendent mentioned as having written the November 2, 1993, letter above, bringing up

April 21, 2014
To whom it may concern:

For clarification of the status of certain families on the San Pasqual Reservation:

There is much information that has been circulated—some correct, some incorrect. Opinions have been made on this information. There have been legitimate questions on the status of the Trask family. This family is of native blood, and, over the years—as many families of native blood—has become mixed.

When it comes to Frank Trask being described as being hired as a "white caretaker" with the San Pasqual Reservation in 1910, this phrase or term was coined by a hired anthropologist and a few others who were in the process of organizing the San Pasqual Band in the late 1950s, early 1960s. Our research has shown that it was said during those meetings of just a few people that he was hired as a "white caretaker."

Our family knew this was not the case, and has researched the Federal Archives and have the document that those above referenced. It was this document that shows that in actuality he was appointed an Indian Judge for the San Pasqual Reservation. To be an Indian Judge you had to be Indian.

Those who at that time referenced Frank Trask as a "white caretaker," had in their possession the document showing Frank Trask as an Indian Judge, and yet used their discretion to interpret that document incorrectly, and to write a book called "Pushed Into the Rocks," which subsequently has been referenced by others. This has grown out of perspective and is used to slander our family today. It just goes to show how one can be influenced by what they read, even when it is incorrect.

Everything that my Grandmother, Helen Trask Lawson, told me as a young man has been correct—that her father was Indian (half Kumeyaay). He married Leonora La Chappa, full-blood Kumeyaay. I realize that some documents showed Leonora as other blood degree. There are many other documents that show her as 4/4. The multitude of documents show through the preponderance of evidence that she was full-blood.

Also during this time that the tribe was being organized, there was discussion of what constituted "blood of the band." That was a legitimate question, and was discussed openly by all of those participating in this process—the question being that Frank and Leonora were at Mesa Grande, and that is correct. This was, and is, very common with native people of this region. Our clans of the La Chappas, Guachenas (Wachenas, Huachenas), Nejos (Anejs) have been recorded in the San Pasqual Valley from as far back as history has been recorded, and, we are sure, beyond recorded time.

So when the people that were in the organization process, which included the United States Department of Interior's Bureau of Indian Affairs; these officials, and the people, participated together in the question of "blood of the band," it was not just in reference to the Trask family. There were other families (clans) that were also subject to "blood of the band" discussion. Through the organization process, language was constructed that included the interpretation of "blood of the band." The Certification of the Base Rolls of 1966 clearly defined the term.

Through this process the 1910 Census was accepted as the document that determined who was qualified to be San Pasqual Band members, stating that the membership roll contained only:

> Those persons living as of January 1, 1959, whose Enrollment applications have been approved in accordance with membership provisions, published by the Secretary of the Interior on March 2, 1960 (25 CFR Part 48), which designated the June 30, 1910 Census for the San Pasqual Mission Indians as the applicable Census Roll for determining the Band's membership. I further certify that the degree of San Pasqual Indian blood, as shown on the attached roll, has been computed in accordance with a Secretarial decision interpreting "blood of the Band" to be total Indian blood of a person named on the basic membership Census Roll dated June 30, 1910.
>
> There is also language in the Federal Code of Regulations that has provisions that if erroneous information is submitted for enrollment, there is a process for disenrollment.
>
> When the language of this process was presented for a vote, it was overwhelmingly approved, but, of course, not all agreed. The irony of what has taken place today, is that the few that questioned the interpretation of "blood of the band" then, do not seem to oppose it now. It appears that some of those who were in question as to whether they were "blood of the band" then, are now opposing the interpretation.
>
> This process used to organize San Pasqual was similar to other tribes that were organized earlier, using Census records to establish rolls. We do not claim to be experts on other tribes' processes. We know there are many other factors involved in their organizing."

In conclusion, our family does not advocate pursuing others for disenrollment. We do believe in and respect the laws. Our family is proud that Frank and Leonora, with their daughters, Florence and Helen, came to the reservation in 1909 and by June of 1910 San Pasqual Reservation was not only patented, but came into a trust status, which preserved the lands that were set aside in 1891, and allowed the land to become a home for those who reside there today.

Respectfully,
David L. Toler, Jr.
San Pasqual Enrollment No. 365

cc: Robert Eben, Superintendent Indian Affairs, Riverside
San Pasqual Enrollment Committee
San Pasqual Tribal Council

Joe Herrera, Hugh Lawson, Jr., Helen (Sis) Lawson, Florence Trask Wolfe, Bob Stewart, and Mary Alice Stewart.

the issue again that some San Pasqual Band members felt that there were people who had been put onto the San Pasqual Rolls by deceit, people who did not possess one-eighth degree of Indian blood.

A month later, in September of 2002, the superintendent's representative, the acting superintendent of Indian Affairs for California, responded to the August 2002 letter. The acting superintendent referenced written requests and telephone requests from the author of the August 2002 letter, and reminded the writer that because tribal enrollment is an internal issue, it must be handled at that level. The issues and concerns of the August 2002 letter-writer were referred to the enrollment committee of the San Pasqual Band for resolution. The acting superintendent then forwarded the correspondence to the San Pasqual Enrollment Committee.

As recently as April 24, 2014, Trask family descendants made available correspondence that described who they are and the unjust controversies they have faced throughout the years. The letter on preceding page went to the enrollment committee of the San Pasqual Band, to the San Pasqual Tribal Council, and to officials of the Bureau of Indian Affairs:

Many positive events have occurred on the San Pasqual Indian Reservation in Valley Center since the formation of the tribal roll and tribal constitution. During the 1950s

(Carrico 2010), some local Indian tribes, including the San Pasqual Band, retained legal counsel to get back the water rights that the federal government had taken illegally during the 1880s, in conjunction with local water agencies, who had put a dam in the San Luis Rey River, upstream from the Ipai in Valley Center. Non-Indian farmers and ranchers benefitted from the water diversion, while the native people suffered from the reduced water flow that ensued after the dam was placed. In 1951 several of the tribes involved brought a lawsuit and the San Pasqual Band joined the effort to regain their lost water supply in 1971. In 1985 a settlement was made, bringing payments of money and increased water supplies to the tribes who had for so long been affected.

Today, most members of the San Pasqual Band work together to create a lifestyle conducive to the best interests of all. About 750 people reside on the San Pasqual Indian Reservation in Valley Center, with 120 of the 200 enrolled tribal members included in that number. About half of the residents are non-Indians who rent homes there and work for the casino or in tribal government. The remaining residents are descendants of tribal members—called lineals. Though the reservation was made up of 1,378 acres when it was patented on July 1, 1910, the tribe bought an additional 533 acres of land in Valley Center in 2001, bringing the total to 1,912 acres. That total is far less than the 92,000 acres patented to the band in 1870 when their reservation was created in the San Pasqual Valley, and even less than the 4,000 acres actually designated within the San Pasqual Valley for them at that time.

7

Family Histories, Testimonies, and Headlines

This chapter outlines the stories of the La Chappa, Guachena, Nejo, and other clans from San Diego County who were the ancestors of Florence and Helen Trask and their descendants, and who can be seen to have inhabited all areas of the San Diego County region. Documentation of the web of intermarriages and interactions among the native Ipai people that exists in San Diego County goes back to the times of the creation of the San Diego Mission in the late 1700s.

Regarding the establishment of the reservation, we can be critical or we can give credit to the United States government — with one crucial question being, why government officials didn't make more of an effort to locate the new San Pasqual Indian Reservation nearer the Band's traditional lands in the San Pasqual Valley? In some of the letters exchanged among government officials and California Indian agents, it could be seen that cost was a factor, given the higher land values in the San Pasqual Valley. We can also speculate that convenience was a factor, since Valley Center was nearer to other native communities, including Rincon, La Jolla, Pauma, Pala, and also Mesa Grande, Santa Ysabel, Los Coyotes, and Pechanga. The research and results presented in this book help to elucidate the actions and outcomes of the government's intentions and the Trask-La Chappa family's participation in these historical processes. Land was set aside for the People — the Ipai — and our family went through the process and came to this location. By doing so, the San Pasqual Reserve became a trust patented Indian Reservation July 1, 1910. The Trasks were of native blood and were qualified, as were others. They established a home here in 1909 and, fortunately, others have come.

Oral Tradition: Memories of Early Days on the Reservation

With questions answered as to how Frank Trask, Leonora La Chappa Trask, and their daughters, Florence and Helen, came to be where the San Pasqual Reserve was located in 1909 — at Valley Center, California, in ancestral Luiseño territory — other questions naturally arise. How did the family adjust to living in the home that the federal government

Opposite page: Cinon Duro. *Photo: E. H. Davis, San Diego History Center.*

Clarence Wolfe, Ernie Lawson, Sr., Lenora Trask Ames, Ramon Ames (with Black Hat),
Ernie Lawson, Jr., Cheryl Calac, Lena Lawson, Audrey Toler, Florence Wolfe.
Photograph taken on San Pasqual Indian Reservation, about 1947.

Leonora and Ramon Ames visit the San Pasqual Reservation, circa 1947. Clarence Wolfe (left), Ernie Lawson,
Sr. (sitting on car), Leonora Trask Ames (on car), Ramon Ames (with black hat), Ernie Lawson Jr. (child),
Cheryl Calac (child), Lena Lawson (second from right), Audrey Toler (face), Florence Wolfe (right).
Photo: Trask-La Chappa family.

had bought out from white squatter Wilburn Reed? How did Leonora La Chappa Trask,
age 39 at the time of Frank Trask's death in 1920, and her two daughters, Florence, 15,
and Helen, 14, manage to keep the reservation going, and to what extent were they able
to retain their traditional Ipai ways and pass them on to their descendants? This chapter
addresses the challenges that Leonora, Florence, and Helen Trask faced in keeping the
San Pasqual Indian Reservation in Valley Center operational for all the years between
the time of Frank's death in 1920 and Leonora's death in 1953, and the roles that Trask
family descendants have played in keeping the reservation intact to current times. What
was life like for the two teenage girls as they lived with their widowed mother, tending
their father's fruit trees and planting, irrigating, and harvesting the crops that not only
provided their food, but when sold served as their means of income? Personal interviews
reveal added dimensions, shedding light on the remembrances and recollections of Trask
family descendants and other native people, many of whom knew Leonora, Florence, and
Helen personally.

Since Leonora La Chappa Trask lived until 1953 and her mother, Feliciana Nejo La Chappa,
lived until 1942, Trask family elders were able to share a multitude of remembrances of the

two women, along with memories of Florence Trask, who lived to 1990, and Helen Trask, who lived until 1972. Their descriptions and comments provide intriguing glimpses into what these women were like, and offer a window on Ipai cultural ways, rituals, and native celebrations, which have played such a large part in the lives of Trask family descendants.

Florence and Helen Trask's children, all of whom still live on the San Pasqual Indian Reservation in Valley Center and who are now in their late 80s, recall growing up in their mothers' care, offering views of the two women that go far beyond what any government records or reports can provide. Florence and Helen Trask's grandchildren and great-grandchildren also add their perceptions of who their ancestors were, along with their knowledge of how their ancestors' lives changed throughout the decades.

Many of the Trask family descendants commented on the changes that have occurred on the reservation in Valley Center since they were children, and especially since others began arriving to claim lands at the reservation in the late 1950s. Trask family descendants comment on how they have handled the verbal and written assaults against them that have persisted from the late 1950s to the present day, and outline steps that the family has taken to dispel the patently false misinformation that anthropologist Florence Shipek and others put forth (see previous chapter).

One government record in particular (Superintendent San Pasqual Jurisdiction 1920) offered Trask family descendants baseline information with which to compare later reports, since it was taken the same year that Frank Trask died. Throughout the years they were at the San Pasqual Indian Reservation in Valley Center, Leonora, Florence and Helen were regularly monitored by the Office of Indian Affairs and later the Bureau of Indian Affairs, by California Bureau of Indian Affairs personnel, by superintendents of the Volcan, Mesa Grande, San Pasqual and Pala jurisdictions, by California Indian agents, by census takers, and by representatives of the Escondido Mutual Water District.

These reports not only chronicled the family's agricultural pursuits, income, amount of acreage used, products sold, and livestock and poultry raised, but they also revealed the family's ability to read and write English, their religious preferences, citizenship status, type of housing, accumulation of furniture and personal belongings, and the type of clothing they wore.

Frank Trask appeared on the 1920 Annual Report (Report of the Superintendent of the San Pasqual Jurisdiction 1920), as half Indian, age 53, farming 11 acres of beans, corn, fruit and grain, and earning an income of $815; 149 acres were shown as grazing lands, with 160 acres of agricultural land leased. Total grazing lands were 160 acres. Only details on the three females were itemized, including that they were mentally sound, and were from the Mission Tribe. The adult female was a citizen of the United States, and added that all three females spoke English, could read and write the English language, and wore modern attire.

Helen Trask Lawson often recalled for her children and grandchildren how Ipai friends from Mesa Grande had traveled to the San Pasqual Indian Reservation in Valley Center

Helen Trask, circa 1917. *Photo: Trask-La Chappa family.*

by buckboard in 1920, to retrieve her father's body and return him to the Mesa Grande Cemetery for burial. Helen recalled that the men had covered her father's eyes with coins and a bandana before taking him away. Another family member pondered Frank Trask's dilemma, as he must have realized that he had the dreaded Spanish influenza. He reportedly moved out of the main house and into an outbuilding during his final week of life, apparently attempting to spare his wife and two daughters from the contagious disease.

The worldwide pandemic had begun in 1918 (Dauer 2012), and of the 105 million people living in the United States that year, an estimated 675,000 to 850,000 had died of the influenza, with 368 people dying in San Diego County. The pandemic continued throughout 1919 and into 1920 and proved to be one of the most severe influenza outbreaks ever to occur in the United States. Healthy life expectancy during that time was age 53 for men and age 54 for women. Frank Trask was 53 years old in 1920.

Helen Trask Lawson's younger daughter, Audrey Lawson Toler, told in her interview what had happened after her grandfather had died: "They had to work, my mom and Aunt Florence, to help their father, and later in order to survive. They went to Bear Valley Elementary School on Guejito Road. It was a one-room schoolhouse and they were picked up by horse and buggy. It was about four miles from where they lived." She noted that after her grandfather's death, "When they did the Censuses for San Pasqual, only Leonora, my Mom and Aunt Florence were on them."

Fortunately for Leonora, Florence, and Helen, by 1920 Charles E. Kelsey and Amos R. Frank had taken care of the issues of securing a right-of-way across reservation lands to the nearest accessible public road, had secured a dam for the family — though it proved to be a leaky one — and had run interference with white settlers who had squatted on San Pasqual Indian Reservation lands, and who had subsequently objected to the Ipai from the San Pasqual Valley being placed anywhere but in their original homeland territory, six miles south of Valley Center.

The canal of the Escondido Mutual Water Company (Dady 1935) ran through the San Pasqual Indian Reservation, and Eleanor Herrera, the older daughter of Helen Trask Lawson, recalled at age 86 how she and her sister and brothers had played as children near the canal:

My grandpa, Frank Trask, died when Mom was about 15. … [I]t must have been hard. My mother was a serious woman. Helen didn't speak Kumeyaay. Our grandfather said they were to learn English first. They never learned the other languages. My mother was good. She'd help us out when we needed it. She grew up with us kids. My mother could be very lenient, and she could also be very strict. My mother made us toe the line. I was born on the San Pasqual Indian Reservation in 1925. I will turn 87 in May of 2012. We lived over where our cousin Bob lived later. We played around the ditch line, or in it. It was just the five of us kids (Ernie, Eleanor, Earl, Audrey and Huey) and our two cousins — Bob, and his brother, Dougie, who made seven. There wasn't much to do except play. We all had to get along or we wouldn't have had anyone to play with. Other people started moving here in the early 1970s (Herrera 2011).

Shortly after Helen lost her father to the Spanish influenza, Hugh Lawson, born in 1899 and from a pioneer family in the Poway area, was traveling with a friend to the San Pasqual Indian Reservation in Valley Center and discovered Florence and Helen Trask out watering crops on their land. Audrey Lawson Toler explained:

My dad met my mother when there was a big dance in Escondido. He and a friend traveled by horse and buggy to get up here. There wasn't a road to drive, I don't imagine. He said a guy said, 'There are a couple of good-looking Indian gals. Let's go ask them to the dance.' When they got to the little ranch my dad said, 'My God, we can't ask them to the dance!' Mom and Aunt Florence were out in the field, working with a hoe, in the mud, bare-foot. They had to keep that homestead going. Evidently there were fruit trees, apricots, pears, and they planted a garden to grow vegetables to eat (Toler 2011).

Hugh Lawson did invite Helen to the dance in Escondido that day. She accepted his invitation, and that was the beginning of a lifelong friendship which led to their marriage, though they later divorced and Helen married Fred Ward. Hugh Lawson, Jr., son of Helen

Helen and Florence working in the fields on the
San Pasqual Indian Reservation, circa 1920.
Photo: Trask-La Chappa family.

Hugh Lawson, born in Poway in 1899,
at the San Pasqual Indian Reservation.
Photo: Trask-La Chappa family.

and Hugh, Sr., noted about his father: "On my dad's side, we know that he and his thirteen siblings were all born in Poway. My grandmother on my dad's side, Rose Meeks Lawson, was born in Oregon and came to California as a baby. My grandfather, Tom Lawson, was born in Harlan County, Kentucky" (Lawson 2011). More information on the history of the Lawson family can be found in the final chapter of *Blood of the Band*.

Florence Trask Stewart Wolfe's younger son, Bob Stewart, was born in 1927 and lived his entire life on the San Pasqual Indian Reservation. He gave an interview before his death in 2012 at age 85, offering insights about his mother, Florence, and his Aunt Helen.

He also confirmed that both Florence and Helen attended Escondido High School after they finished at Bear Valley, and that his mother and aunt were the only two Indian students at both sites. Stewart noted:

> My mother told me that when the family came down to Valley Center, the house was there, but the people — their name was Reed — still lived in it. Frank and Leonora had a tent, and they and the two girls lived out in back. That wasn't for very long. The stories I heard were, nobody would come here anyway. What could you do here? There was no water, no anything. Frank Trask was a farmer and a rancher, and he worked this place. He worked all around, anywhere there was work. Everybody in those days knew how to ride. I heard that he was a good man. He was half Indian — distinctively Indian. From what I was told, nobody would live here, and this reservation would have gone back to the federal government. Frank took charge of it here.
>
> The house was built by Wilburn Reed, back in the 1800s. The small ranch house first, made of redwood, with wooden floors, a big living room with a brick fireplace, two or three bedrooms, and a long back porch, then the cabin, which was built in the 1930s. No electricity. No water. An outhouse. In the 1930s there was a barn out in back, and fruit trees, apricots, and peaches. Across the creek there were some plums. There were some walnut and almond trees, pear trees, all fruit trees. The family brought in electricity in the early 1950s. The house didn't have any water, but there was a well down on the other side of the creek that we had dug by hand, about 25 feet deep, and we used more or less surface water, but when the creeks ran, ha-ha, the well came up" (Stewart 2011).

Allen E. Lawson, Jr., is the oldest grandson of Helen Agnes Trask Lawson. He was also fortunate enough to have known his great-grandmother, Leonora La Chappa, and to stay with her and her husband, Chairman Ramon Ames, on the Barona Indian Reservation in the late 1940s and early 1950s. He had a good relationship with all of his elders and has fond memories of those early years. His experience of reservation life during his formative years had a profound impact on his future commitment to tribal economic development and service to his own tribe and to Indian Country.

Allen is an enrolled member of the San Pasqual Band of Indians and was elected chairman of the Band in 1996. Since then he has been re-elected to ten consecutive terms, winning his latest election in 2015. Chairman Lawson's long tenure has been instrumental in bringing governmental continuity and political stability on the San Pasqual Band. His success in securing a tribal-state gaming compact for the band in 1999-2000 attracted significant human and financial capital to the San Pasqual Reservation. He has devoted much of his adult life to his band; his efforts to bring economic development have resulted in significant jobs for tribal members as well as improved quality of life on the reservation.

In addition to his work for his own band, Chairman Lawson has represented the band at numerous regional and state-level organizations and been a speaker at many high-profile events. For many years, he served as the vice chairman for the California Nations Indian Gaming Association (CNIGA). He currently serves as the band's representative to the Southern California Tribal Chairman's Association (SCTCA) and is the tribal representative for all San Diego tribes on the board of the San Diego Association of Governments (SANDAG). All these commitments have shared the same goal: to ensure that the San Pasqual Band is recognized as an outstanding member of the community. Through his hard work and dedication to the position of chairman, he has played a role in strengthening the sovereignty and political position of the San Pasqual Band while at the same time advancing tribal sovereignty for all tribes.

David Toler III, great-grandson of Helen Trask Lawson and grandson of Aubrey Lawson Toler, also participated in an interview and noted:

> In 1871 the valley reservation was rescinded and in 1878 the native people were evicted. Most of them said, "If you don't give us land here, we won't go anywhere." Those people were adamant about not wanting land anywhere else. If they would have worked along with Charles Kelsey and Amos Frank, the Indian agents would have purchased more land for this reservation. They would have purchased other ranches out from the settlers. This reservation would be a lot bigger and nicer than it is now. The Indian agents were willing to work with the people.
>
> What I'm seeing is, in 1909 Amos Frank became the Indian agent, and they're calling him the school teacher, but he's actually the agent disbursing the land, and there's a letter from the Indian Office saying, "Okay, go ahead and situate the families on the San Pasqual reserve, set aside as Township 11." That's when Frank and Leonora went down there. But it sounded like the agents couldn't get anybody else to go. Yeah. Amos Frank was excited, because he was a new superintendent of the Indian School and was the special disbursing agent. He said, "I'll situate families there immediately." Amos Frank was doing the censusing—we're on the 1910 Census. But historically, our family being from the Guachenas, the Nejos, and the La Chappas, I'm thinking of the historic ties we had with San Pasqual, because it's all the same people. That's why we went to Mesa Grande, because we had ties. My great, great, great grandfather, Antonio La Chappa, was the captain and the judge at Mesa Grande. He was Leonora's father. Leonora's twin, Sylvester, was the policeman at Mesa Grande. That's why we went there. We had ties (Toler III 2011).

Helen Trask Lawson, a happy, outgoing person. *Photo: Trask-La Chappa family.*

Bob Stewart provided further glimpses of his mom, Florence, and his Aunt Helen:

Florence was a very good woman. Very helpful and always good to people. I thought she was intelligent. Anybody who came to the house, they sat at the table with us. No matter what we had to eat, we sat down and ate. My Grandmother Leonora was exactly the same way, but she was more strict, more precise. About Helen and Florence—Helen was more outgoing, much more. She was friends with everybody, no matter what color they were—black, white or green—it didn't make any difference. A very happy, outgoing person. My Grandmother Leonora had diabetes. ... It just keeps going—I have it too. Leonora was born in 1881 and died in 1953. Helen died in her sleep in 1972 of congestive heart failure. My mom had diabetes and died in 1990—she had been born in 1905. Helen had five kids: Ernie, Eleanor, Earl, Audrey and Huey (Stewart 2011).

Audrey Lawson Toler added of her mother Helen and Aunt Florence that:

My mother was very pretty. I have a picture of her at about age 33 with my great-grandmother, Feliciana, and my grandmother Leonora. My mother and Aunt Florence liked to talk, but my mother never talked about her background. My Aunt Florence only had the two boys—there were five of us. And we had Doug and Bob half the time. We only had two cousins. My mother was social and outgoing. She liked to go to the funerals and all the fiestas, and she knew a lot of Indian people from different reservations, but Florence didn't. My mother never drove. We had the best parents.

191

Florence Trask Wolfe, photographed by David L. Toler, Jr., at her home on the San Pasqual Reservation circa 1969.

Audrey Lawson Toler (bottom row, second from left), Lena Montes Lawson (top row, middle), and Amelia Basquez of Pechanga (bottom row, middle) while attending the Sherman Indian School. Audrey was born in the San Pasqual Valley in 1927 and has lived on the San Pasqual Indian Reservation in Valley Center most of her life.
Photo: Trask-La Chappa family.

We got along with our mother and dad, and our stepfather, Fred Ward—they were just like playmates. Helen would make a cake or pie just to take one bite. She and Aunt Florence were both about five feet tall.

We got along with our parents wonderfully. My sister Eleanor and I were in charge of doing the dishes. My mother would dirty up every dish; she was a wonderful cook, then she would tell us and Bob Stewart and his brother Doug, "Alright, forget about those dishes. We're going to town for the movies." She loved the movies. She loved the city life. She loved to travel. She'd say that once or twice a week, "Forget those dishes. Let's go to town" (Toler 2011).

Lawson Toler also told in her personal interview how all of Helen Trask Lawson's children had attended the structured and disciplined Sherman Institute in Riverside during the 1930s:

When I was about 12 years old, all of us kids went to the Sherman Indian School. My mother hadn't been married to her second husband, Fred Ward, very long. Money was hard to come by. My brothers Ernie and Earl, and my sister Eleanor, were already there. I went in 1939, from the seventh grade until halfway through the ninth. When I left school, Huey went. Sherman was free, was very well supervised, and I guess my mother felt it was an opportunity for us all to have schooling (Toler 2011).

Hugh Lawson, Jr., also detailed his stay at the Sherman Institute:

Oh, for me, it reminded me of a Japanese prison camp. My brother, Earl, loved it, because he played sports. ... We got up at about 5:30 and made up our beds and washed up and went outside and they put you in units. We went to breakfast, came back, grabbed this big old broom and swept the whole street. Then we went to school. In the afternoon we went to work, in the garden for seventh graders, and the following year you could learn to be a welder—it was like a trade school. I was there two and a half years. The way they treated you, it was cruelty. Today they'd throw them in jail. They had a belt line and you had to run through it. You took off your belt and wacked a poor guy. That was discipline, I guess. If you messed around you had to mop the floors, stuff like that. I was fifteen when I left Sherman. That's why when I joined the Army in 1946 it was no problem. ... Then in the 1960s I moved back up here ... then I moved up here again in 1970, and I've been here ever since (Lawson 2011).

Eleanor Lawson Herrera also contributed information about her stay at Sherman:

At the Sherman Indian School we made friends that we've kept to this day. I remember standing in line, and behind me was a girl named June Bond. I didn't know until years later that her oldest son would marry my daughter, Ann. I had a friend named Martha in Old Town, and years later my oldest son would marry her daughter (Herrera 2011).

Martha's daughter Sharon Herrera died in June of 2014. In his interview, Bob Stewart spoke about his older brother, Douglas.

Douglas Stewart (far left) and Bobby Stewart (far right)
on the San Pasqual Reservation circa 1937.
Photo: Trask-La Chappa family.

Pete La Chappa, son of Sylvester and
Modesta La Chappa, born 1910.
*Photo taken by David L. Toler, Jr. on
the San Pasqual Reservation in 1969.*

194

My brother Douglas was born in 1924 and was killed during World War II, in the crash of a B17. His plane was shot down over the Baltic Sea. When my brother and I were young, we just played around here. We went to the white school in Valley Center. There were just two Indians from San Pasqual at Valley Center, my brother and me. There were lots of Indians from Rincon, Pala, and Pauma around the area. There was no other way. You were an Indian, and you were an Indian. In a way, there was some racism, with kids up to a certain age. The whites fought the Indians. We did see that. In those days, being an Indian was no prize. My Grandmother Leonora spoke Kumeyaay/Diegueño. She also spoke Spanish. She was very particular about everything. My grandfather, after Frank, was Adolph Scholder. No nicknames. I was Robert. My grandfather was Adolph. I didn't know Frank Trask, since he died before I was born. (Stewart 2011)

Not only did Florence Trask Stewart Wolfe's older son, Doug Stewart, serve and perish in an air crash during World War II, but Florence and Helen's cousin, Pete La Chappa, son of Leonora's twin brother, Sylvester, also served in the Armed Forces during the Second World War, landing in Italy. Audrey Lawson Toler sang Pete's praises, telling how he had been captured by the enemy, managed to escape, but then had to live with the traumatic memories, often resorting to alcohol to dull them, but, finally, returning to his family on the reservation in the 1960s:

I'll tell you a good story about Pete La Chappa. He was my mother's cousin. He was a linguist, so he enlisted in the Army in World War II. Did you know that in World War II every reservation had somebody enlisted in the service? He could do everything. He talked every kind of language, and he knew so much. He was teaching Bob Stewart's wife, Mary, some Indian words because he knew the language. ... He finally ended up back on the reservation! I have family members and ancestors from every reservation in San Diego County. That just amazes me (Lawson 2011).

Audrey Lawson Toler shared remembrances of her grandmother, Leonora La Chappa Trask, who had been born in the San Felipe Valley, and her great-grandmother, Feliciana Nejo La Chappa, born at Santa Ysabel:

We always knew we were Indian. We went to see Grandma Leonora and Great Grandma Feliciana. It was just something we knew. Leonora could speak Kumeyaay, English, and Spanish. She was married to Ramon Ames. They called him Chief Ramon Ames. My grandma dyed his hair black and her hair black. They say he would lead the parade in El Cajon. We'd only go up to see my grandmother with my mother and my Aunt Florence. I stayed with my grandmother for a while when she was in Barona, and she had that acorn stuff [schawii]. I tried it with milk and sugar. Yuck! I don't care how I tried it, it was no good. A traditional dish, that acorn stuff. I can't stand it myself. That dish is horrible. People say, 'Oh, I had that all the time.' Uh-uh. People didn't have that all the time. It was just a traditional dish. And that was hard to do, collect acorns. My grandma wasn't somebody I would visit all the time with my kids. Leonora was full blood.

My great-grandmother, Feliciana, died when I was 15. We would go up and see her. I was scared, because she didn't speak English. She spoke Indian and Mexican. She'd go "Hooka, hooka, hooka. Hello." I don't know how that's spelled. We never had a written language, you know, until the Japanese decided to make us an alphabet.

I will tell about my great-grandmother's funeral — they don't have that kind of funeral anymore. Everybody brought food and cooked it. I can remember — it was a very vivid memory — I can remember her home. She lived in an old, wooden, weather-beaten house. It couldn't have been more than a living room and kitchen, with an outdoor bathroom. My mother went up there quite often. This was when she died. I was 15 when I went up, and I stayed in the car most of the time, sleeping, because I was pregnant with my oldest son, Dave Toler. They had my great-grandmother in a casket, setting on a couple of saw horses. And there was a group of people around her, how many people I don't know. But there was a group around her, all singing Indian songs, and there were two or three women — at least a couple women in the kitchen, cooking — and one or two would get up, would go in there and eat and cook. I can tell you exactly what they were serving. When one woman would leave the kitchen another would come in, and they continued chanting, and they did that all night long. Potato salad and stew. About every funeral I went to, potato salad, stew, beans, tortillas, and maybe cake. That was the standard thing. Now, the last one I went to, they had the beans, stew, rice, I think they even had spaghetti. The last one I went to, no singing. We just went to the cemetery. That's a lost art, nowadays.

They kept that up all night, all night long, the whole night. They would just get up, two at a time, to help with the food in the kitchen, and eat. Sitting around the casket in old, straight-back chairs, and singing. I couldn't begin to tell you what they were singing, and the women sang too. Great-grandmother's husband, Antonio La Chappa, was captain and Indian judge of the Mesa Grande Reservation. He had died a long time before, in 1929.

Leonora La Chappa Trask Scholder Ames
Born January 8, 1880 — died September 8, 1953
Married:
Frank Trask (b. 1867, d.1920)
Adolph Scholder (b. 1874, d. 1941)
Ramon Ames (b. 1871, d. 1956)

I've got pictures of Angela La Chappa, whose father was Cornelio Wachena. Angela was born in the Mesa Grande area, in the San Dieguito watershed, in 1833 and lived until 1907. Edward Davis said that she had lived at the San Diego Mission as a child. Angela married Jose Bastian La Chappa, Leonora's grandfather. Thinking back, we always knew we had Indian in us, it was something we grew up with. It wasn't something we found out when we were 20 years old. We always knew it, because we lived on the reservation. I can always remember Feliciana in a long dress, and she

San Pasqual Reservation, late 1940s. (From left) Florence Trask Wolfe, Helen Trask Flores, Concepcion, Henry Trask (Frank's half brother), Clarence Wolfe. *Photo: Trask-La Chappa family.*

seemed like she was 100 years old. But you know, looking at pictures, they couldn't have been that dog-gone old. Anyway, looking at a picture of when I was about four years old, and my mother had to be in her 20s, and my grandmother in her 50s, and my great-grandmother in her 70s, my great-grandmother looked like she had to be 100 years old. It must have been a hard life. I remember momma went to see her, things like that (Lawson 2011).

Leonora La Chappa Trask remained a widow for eight years following Frank Trask's death in 1920. According to records (1928 Indian Roll Application and Censuses of San Pasqual 1932, 1933,1934, 1936) sometime after 1928 Leonora La Chappa Trask married Adolph Scholder, half Indian (Census of Ballena 1880), and they lived on her allotment at the San Pasqual Indian Reservation in Valley Center. It is unknown when Leonora separated from Scholder, who died May 5, 1941 (Death Records of San Diego County 1941), but on December 16 of an unknown year during the 1940s she married Barona Tribal Chairman Ramon Ames. After their marriage she moved with him to his reservation to live out her final days. She died September 8, 1953, and was buried in the Barona Cemetery. Ramon Ames lived from April 14, 1877, to January 24, 1956 (San Diego County Death Index 1956).

David L. Toler III, son of Dave Toler and great great-grandson of Leonora La Chappa Trask, recalled visiting Barona in October of 2012 to see if he could find Leonora's final resting place. He came upon an elder at the Barona Cemetery who shared a story about how he had once visited the Ramon Ames household and observed Leonora resting in her livingroom. Toler said: "She was comfortably curled up in a chair watching TV — faraway from the screen — covered in a blanket to keep her warm. The time would have been some-time before her death in 1953" (Toler III 2011).

Mr. Bo Mazzetti, tribal chairman of the Rincon Band of Luiseño Mission Indians, recalled his long association with the Trasks and their descendants in an interview:

> We used to take the flume, the canal, to Valley Center. We'd get on at Rincon and ride it all the way to Mrs. Wolfe's house. We'd get off there. I've known the Stewarts and the Tolers all my life. We used to ride down the flume with them. We'd ride on a board. Florence Wolfe was strong-willed and determined. She ran the reservation. All these people knew each other from Sherman Indian School. My father, Max Mazzetti, went to Sherman. It's definitely important to know who your family's people are. We grew up with our families. We know who is who. Always have.
>
> That's the best thing about gaming. We can fight back now. We can get the best attorneys, and we can put money into the restoration of the culture. We can pay out to people who know it — to retain it, and to train others. Many of these guys went to Sherman Indian School. It was a continuation after World War II, getting back together. All the major Indian leaders from the 1950s, 1960s, they all knew each other from Sherman. That's always been there, the mingling of clans. That's how tribes got to know each other. ... I think tribes are beginning to realize what the BIA did when it started initiating blood degrees. You go by descendants. That's the only way to keep tribes alive. Indigenous peoples are all assimilated to a point. What you need to do is not forget where you come from, to remember who your people are. You need to remember your customs, traditions and heritage. You can do both, assimilate and maintain heritage (Mazzetti 2011).

Frankie Orosco, a San Pasqual tribal member who served as vice spokesperson 1970-1972, told of his father's interactions with Florence Trask Wolfe, and acknowledged his family's history on the San Pasqual Indian Reservation:

> The thing with our family, the reason we didn't come up in 1910, it was the wrong area, it was not old San Pasqual. My dad was born in 1898. My first uncle, who was the oldest, was born in 1892. In my description he was Indian. He was Ipai. Everybody in my dad's family are, on this side. My grandfather died in 1847. After the eviction, a lot went to Santa Ysabel, Mesa Grande, and a lot came to town. My grandfather actually went to Corona, California. He became a lawman. My father was Augustine Orosco. ... We never used the word Kumeyaay. We used the word Diegueño. The only reason we didn't want to come out here was it was like signing a paper, giving up old San Pasqual. Ever since I was young, all that was driven in my mind was go to school, get educated, and learn how to get that land back. My father finally said, "We are going to make a move to the reservation. We're not going to get San Pasqual back." My father went to talk to Florence Trask Wolfe. He wanted to make it so assignments were passed on from generation to generation (Orosco 2011).

George Brown, Jim Martinez, J.J. Martinez, George Martinez; Irene Martinez, behind them, around 1925 in San Pasqual Valley. *Photo: Martinez family.*

In the mid-1970s Diana Martinez and her family moved onto the San Pasqual Indian Reservation in Valley Center, and Diana recalled in an interview how her mother had known Florence Trask Wolfe for years. It was then that Diana had her first interactions with the person who served as tribal spokesman for the reservation:

In 1973 when we came up, and later, Mrs. Wolfe was always nice to us. I think the attempts to organize and move onto the reservation were just so we could become formalized again, so people could move onto the reservation. It was a different generation that didn't care to move onto the reservation. They heard of or had friends who were on the reservation and weren't treated so well. When the tribe was evicted, they went to Escondido, right over the hill. They weren't educated, to know about homesteads. Later, my mom would tell my dad, "There's Indian land up there. We could have it for free." When my mom investigated more, she met Mrs. Wolfe. She must have known Mrs. Wolfe before, because they were trying to get organized. When my parents wanted to move up to the reservation, they didn't know how. They didn't know what process to go through, other than to move onto the land. So they didn't do it. When we moved up here it was really rough. It wasn't until the tribe was reorganized and there was a land assignment ordinance that they could get up here. That was the mechanism for people to apply for land assignments. Florence Wolfe had a real gruff voice and real big eyes, and she was very hospitable. She tried to do what she could to help people with the maps, but she really couldn't go out there and visit the site because she was so

Left photo: Thomas Martinez, Ms. Dar Martinez, Ms. E. Martinez around early 1910.
Right photo: Tillie Martinez with Tony's son around 1919. *Photo: Martinez family.*

elderly. Her house was kind of basic. I remember the living room, it was nice and orderly. She had a table where you could look at the maps. She had people who lived around her. She had a well there too, and renters. She was the unofficial spokesperson. Even when our families weren't formally organized they knew each other and who their families were. I don't remember Helen, I just remember Mrs. Wolfe. I've always been good friends with Audrey Toler and her family, and with Mrs. Wolfe. The Trask family—their lineage goes back to Indian lineage. God blessed us with this land. Sure, we would love to have the land back from the old San Pasqual Valley (Martinez 2011).

James Baker, a tribal member who lives on the San Pasqual Indian Reservation in Valley Center, offered the following statements in his interview:

My grandmother lived in the old San Pasqual village, in the ancestral village, and she was evicted—Rose Lieres. Her mother, Clara Juana Quisquis, was married by Indian custom. We took DNA tests and blood tests. I'm really white. My mother was from Sweden. But if you look at my dad, we had several tribal members who were trying to say I was adopted. We put a nip in that right quick. We took paternity tests. We also did the DNA tests. My father is Calaway Baker and my mother is Bona Anderson.

My DNA test came out 16 percent. I had Asian blood and I also had European blood. I think that Asian blood is part of the Indian blood as well. My grandmother was baptized on the old Mesa Grande Indian Reservation in 1899, and we have the original baptismal certificate from St. Joseph Cathedral in San Diego signed by Reverend Eubeck.

David Toler's grandmother, Leonora La Chappa Trask, was the sponsor of my grandmother. There was Pedro La Chappa and there was Reynaldo La Chusa and Bernard La Chusa. I have the baptismal certifications of my grandmother's siblings as well. I think there were four children. They were baptized in the brand new little adobe chapel at Mesa Grande in 1899. It's still there, though it's in disrepair and is not being used.

John Quisquis was Cahuilla and came from Agua Caliente, married by Indian tradition; certificate of baptismal, St. Joseph Cathedral, San Diego California. Jose Maria Lieres, child of Jacinto Lieres and Juana Quisquis, born on San Pasqual on the fourth day of August, 1899. Bernardo La Chusa and Leonora La Chap. Grandmother Rose Lieres, child of Jacinto Lieres and Juana Quisquis born in San Pasqual on the nineteenth day of December, 1898. I think because they established a homestead, that's the reason we stayed there longer. Ed Wachena was my grandmother's nephew; his mother, Lena Wachena, and my grandmother were half sisters. They had the same mother but different fathers. My father said they tried to drive out there by the Wild Animal Park [now called San Diego Zoo Safari Park] to find the old homestead, but couldn't find it. My dad grew up in Ramona. His DNA was 51 percent European/49 percent Native American. You should see some of the photographs I have. The native people are holding baskets.

The war record, 1917 draft registration card, showed Raymond Lieres, brother of Jose Lieres, with his residence as Mesa Grande, 1896. Place of birth San Pasqual, California. That was the cause of the dissension. They didn't go by the original list that the school teacher had, because a lot of the children who had moved from San Pasqual when they were evicted went to school in Mesa Grande. They had a list of the children who were Indian and those who weren't. Somehow the list disappeared, but later reappeared. I guess you have to get it through the Bureau of Indian Affairs in Riverside. So the enrollment committee went by the 1910 Census—anybody living in the San Pasqual Valley, it didn't matter what race they were, they were included in the census. My grandmother, Rose Lieres Baker, was a cook for John D. Spreckles in Coronado, the tycoon who owned the Hotel Del Coronado. My grandfather was white, from Kentucky. He bought the ranch in 1925. When they were evicted they were dispersed to different areas. People picked up their lives, found a place, so you know there was not that great a chance of going to the reservation, when they've already established roots somewhere else.

In the case of my grandmother, she married my grandfather and they bought a ranch in Ramona. There was no need for them to go to the new reservation, although we did, when it was offered to us in 1974. I've lived here almost forty years. We originally lived over by the canal, but it was so treacherous. There was no electricity, no water. It was so bad that we moved off. That was the first time, in 1973. Then my father's brother had a land assignment on Woods Valley Road, so they traded. We were able to get water from the Valley Center Water District. My dad's brother never moved up here. My dad was a fireman and became disabled with severe arthritis. I remember times he couldn't get out of bed. It was rough. We lived here many years without electricity. We had water. A neighbor, fortunately, ran a cord from his home to supply us with electricity. Our property adjoined private property. Of course we had water. But no, it was pretty rough. I was five or six when we moved up here. Gee, there were only less than ten people prior to the 1970s.

We're all related. You didn't want to marry your relatives. The records don't go back that far. They didn't have birth certificates. They had baptismal certificates. My dad's dead-set on DNA. If you don't have that, you're not Indian. You're either Indian or you're not. You don't know that until you take a DNA test. I agree with him. You are what you are. We weren't required to take them. We wanted to know for ourselves. We're proud of our Indian heritage. I don't know how it was that everybody all of a sudden moved up to the reservation in the '70s. ... My uncle, Felix Quisquis, moved on in 1970, sometime around there. I knew Florence Wolfe — she'd talk in a real low, deep voice. She had a little dog name Boo Boo. She had cats too. There was always the scent of animals. I can remember the smell because I'm allergic to most animals. I recall her sitting in a wing-back chair. There was a foot stool. She had a pond around the house and a shed in back. My dad always spoke well of Florence.

Maybe it was termination. Maybe if they didn't move on the land the government would seize it. It was too valuable to just have nobody live there. None of us speak Indian or live Indian. San Pasqual doesn't have any Indian culture. We're descendants of Indian people that practiced their traditions. As a child I went with my parents to the events held in Santa Ysabel. The Indians at these fiestas are just not friendly, unless they really, really, really know you. Cahuilla, Agua Caliente is very strict. You need to prove lineage. You have to have been married on the reservation. You can't blame them. They want to preserve their heritage.

My dad, he says his mother wouldn't teach him how to speak Indian. She spoke fluent Spanish as well. They wanted him to speak English. Our traditions died two generations ago. The blood's running out, and that's what the people are worried about. And it is. If you go back, it takes two full blooded Indians to make a child that is full blood. That hasn't happened since the 1800s. Each generation you lose half. You go full blood to half, a half to a quarter, from a quarter to an eighth. That's four generations right there. We're down to that fourth generation. I've been a tribal member since 1986. I have been here forty years, longer that most of the others. I'm one of the younger people who have been here my whole life. I guess Audrey and Eleanor were here, and their kids (Baker 2011).

Clara Juana Quisquis (center)
holding Calaway Baker.
Photo: James Baker.

Nibs, also known as Whiskers. *Drawing: Robert Freeman.*

James Baker remembers his father Calaway Baker narrating many stories that provide further details of their family's history:

> Our great grandmother was Clara Juana Quisquis, who married Jacinto Lieres from Soboba Indian Reservation. They were married by Indian custom on the San Pasqual Reservation. Their leader was Ponto Duro ...
>
> Clara and Jacinto had four children: Jose Maria Lieres, Barbara Lieres, Raymod Lieres, and Rosa Lieres. They were all born in San Pasqual and spoke fluent Indian. When the family was evicted from San Pasqual Valley they moved to Mesa Grande. The children were later baptized by Father Ubeck of St. Joseph's Cathedral in the chapel on the Mesa Grande Indian Reservation in 1899, which was an extension of the missions of California. We have the original baptismal certificates of all four children. We have found documentation on ancestry.com that Raymond Lieres served in the military in World War 1. It states he was born in San Pasqual and later had moved to Mesa Grande.
>
> As for Jose Maria and Barbara Lieres we are still searching for information. Rosa Lieres later moved from Mesa Grande to Coronado, California; she was the personal housekeeper for the Speckles family. She lived there at the Speckles mansion. Rosa later moved to Star Park in Coronado where she married our grandfather Hobart Baker from Kentucky. Rosa had a child from a previous marriage, her name was Mary Lieres. They then moved to Ramona, California where they raised a family of five children: Mary Lieres Baker, Lenine Baker, Virginia Baker, Hilda Baker and Calaway Baker. However before the children were born they established the new San Pasqual Reservation in 1910. Rosa never returned to the San Pasqual Reservation.
>
> My grandmother Rose attended Indian School at the St. Boniface Indian School in Banning, California from 1909-1912. There she learned how to read and write in English. This was a Catholic school and was conducted by mother superior. It was a very strict institution and demanded continuous efficiency. Later, the school

Flora Pena holding Calaway Baker. Flora was a Lloyd and then married Sylvester La Chappa, Leonora's twin; Flora later married Felix Pena.
Photo: James Baker.

was destroyed by fire and what remains today is a foundation and a road named Indian School Road in Banning, California.

My Grandparents' home in Ramona California was a gathering place for Indians; they would come from Mesa Grande, San Ysabel and the other reservations. They would all sit at a round oak table in the dining room and the entire conversation would be in Indian language. We can only imagine today what those conversations were about.

The Indians would come down from the hills and my grandfather would buy liquor for them. At that time Indians could not buy liquor. One Indian fellow would ride down by horseback. His name was Nibs. My father's family called him Whiskers. He would load his bottles into a leather satchel and would return to Mesa Grande on horseback.

My grandmother Rose was a traditional Indian, in keeping with tradition she cooked many types of Indian meals. She would make tortillas by hand and then warm them on a wood stove. She peeled acorns and mashed them; my dad says it was real bitter. She also canned all kinds of fruits and vegetables. She always had a pot of beans and corn bread. My Grandparents' home was decorated with many Indian artifacts, Indian dolls, paintings and different types of native artwork.

My father Calaway Baker was born in the home in 1934. He remembered one time his family went to an Indian fiesta on the San Ysabel Reservation in 1938. My father was lost and crying until an Indian fellow found him and returned him safely to his family. My father went to Ramona Elementary School; he was the only Indian student along with one Mexican and the rest were all white. They all got along with each other and they all remain friends to this day. My dad graduated from Ramona high school and later joined the military. He never attended Indian School, however his sister Mary attended St. Boniface Indian School just like her mother did.

My father married my mother Bona Belle Anderson. Her family was from Great Britain and Sweden. My mother was the great great grand niece of the writer Jane Austen and is a distant cousin of Kate Middleton. This information can be verified through ancestry.com. Calaway Baker and Bona Belle Anderson would have two children: my sister Lisa Ann Baker and myself James Edward Baker. We all returned to the reservation in 1973. My father applied for a five acre land assignment located on Canal Road. Living there was quite rural; you had to cross wood planks over a canal that ran through the reservation, there was no safety. I can remember being mortified that we might end up in the canal. However at this time there were only four residents that lived on Canal Road.

The first residence belonged to Mary Matteson, the second resident was Bob Stewart, and then you came to our assignment. Further back was Linda Panchetti and then Florence Wolfe. Since we had no electricity and no sewer, we ran a pipe from the canal for water; it was almost like camping, but under extreme conditions. We lived in a Mobile home and we were all quite happy.

My sister and I, we attended Indian School at the tribal hall. Our teacher was Ann Rodriguez; she always had a smile and was very nice to everyone. The classroom had different groups; one was for learning how to speak native language. We would use the stereo cards that would say a word in English and then in Indian; it was really quite informative. I remember to this day some of the native words that we had learned. Station two dealt with doing homework that was left over from Valley Center Elementary School, it was quite helpful. Station three taught us how to make Indian jewelry and other Indian artwork. My sister Lisa did beadwork and I worked on a loom. We made Indian eyes and beaded chokers. We had a real good time, everyone was very nice and friendly. We would always end with a nice movie and a little treat afterwards. Our bus driver was Georgia Caylor. I would always sit behind her. I can remember to this day she would always be smoking cigarettes and her cigarette smoke would blow in my face. I think that's the reason why I don't smoke to this day.

As children my sister and I attended all tribal council meetings with our father. Our Chairman at the time was Bob Stewart and Secretary Mary Matteson. The tribe had very little money yet moving in the right direction. Bob Stewart was a very nice person. I have known him most of my life. Everybody liked him he did a lot of good work for the tribe. Mary was a true Indian she fought for the rights of Indian people. She stood her ground. Mary was a tough lady; you may not like what she had to say but she was very truthful when saying it. Mary had many relatives from all different tribes — she knew who was and wasn't related. In 1986 my father became Vice Chairman of the tribe. Our Chairman was Diana Martinez; Our Secretary was Mr. Alfonzo Orosco. The two delegates were Daniel Orosco and Francis Jones. They were all volunteers. The Business Committee had very little money in its account. Most of the agenda was sent out by donations from the Business Committee. I remember going to Diana Martinez's home. She would be on the floor with the typewriter writing out the agenda. Everything at this time was done by hand as we didn't have computers or cell phones and all the modern technology that we have today. This board has received very little recognition in all the work that they did over the years. It is quite unfortunate. My father's ideal was to propose gambling on the reservation. He invited many investors that were interested. In this ideal it would bring revenue to the tribe and put a lot of people to work. The first thing we had to do was to bring it before the General Council and have a vote on it; we won by two votes. However it wouldn't be till much later that the casino would become a reality (James Baker, personal communication 2015).

Native Julie Holder offered her perspectives on the encroachment of San Diego County native lands in a 2011 interview:

There was displacement of the ancestral villages, not simply from evictions, that was later; it was displacement primarily from invasion. As the foreigners came in they invaded the lands, forcing Indians to move into the hills.

The definitive dates were the first wave of migrations of Spanish priests along with Spanish, mestizo and indigenous soldiers in 1769, Sierra, Portola then Anza. Those years were the colonization of new lands. Then jump to 1846 when the American flag was raised over Old Town, San Diego suggesting a new wave of foreign invaders, then again in 1849 when gold was discovered and the old world begins to assault our shores and overpowers the mountains ... those were the events that most affected the California Indians. At that time, Indians had no rights, no protections by law; we would not become citizens of the United States until 1924.

I believe another perspective never understood by the invaders, is that Indian people are connected to their lands, not simply by opportunity, but out of love and understanding for what the lands provide. Land is a complement to our life, she is a mother to our existence, and she helps us exist, she provides and nurtures us with her waters, and offers us food, shelter and healing. Everything we care for and respect comes from her, and we have been taught to never take more than we need of her generosity. She is our benefactor, blessing us with her wealth, we do not own her secrets nor do we wish to steal them, we believe if you take only what you need and let her rest, if you are fortunate, she will continue to offer you more. In addition, the bones of our people are nestled in her rocks and protected in her creases; we honor those places by protecting them and letting them rest undisturbed.

As the land travelers, we knew there was plenty of land so we could pick up villages and keep going, believing there would always be these places to come back to. Since everything we used was provided by the land, we could take our homes and goods and just walk away, finding other clans who are related and continue to live as always, hunting and gathering and tending to the lands that harbored our homes, isolated from the invasion of outsiders, on what we believe is still plenty.

With this understanding of abundance, Southern California Indian villages tended to be distant from each other. Each clan could recite their own family and village history, but I believe they did not have a clear sense of the immensity of the entire population. Separated by the mountains, rocks and deserts, Indian people have many languages, but have never written books on the story of how the invasion affected their lives. Because these languages were not written, it is somehow thought that our oral history was not valid, and there is little study of our story from the Indian perspective or validated by the Indian perception that makes a suitable truth to the outside world. California Indian history has been interpreted by outsiders, non-Indian people for so long and is so convoluted that in essence, you'll be rewriting American history if you tell our story.

Among Indian people, we know each other by our connections to our lands, places and our people. The tribes are small communities who came together in annual gatherings, it's there we would find wives and husbands and band together with other villages. You always have a grandmother, uncle, aunt or cousin connected by family. When foreign cultures began the invasion of Indian lands, the Indian people kept moving away, not only because they believed the lands were abundant; they also believed the invaders would eventually go away.

But after the first wave of colonization, the invasion would become a greater concern for tribes. There were no roads, only the well-worn trails named by the invaders; the Kings Highway was a pass the Soldiers forged by foot. The natural coves on the bays brought invaders by ship, up from Mexico or down from the North. Inland they would skirt the deserts, the Rocky Mountains were natural boundaries and protection, slowing down a larger invasion, and forcing the last wave to go around and migrate down from Oregon or from the coast. As these roads were worn into the lands, the sickness and cultures were introduced to whoever came into contact with this invasion. Leaders like Panto recognized the signs, not simply by population increase, but by the sickness and disease being introduced into their world. In 1849 when the gold rush fever spread, the invasion began in earnest.

When you talk about a tribal village, you're talking about a family here, the Nejos living over there; the Duro's living on the other side, the Guachenos over the hill in the valley. You're talking about family communities connected by traditions of family who married into a wealth of communities outside their own clans.

When the acorns were ripe they went and harvested the acorns, when it was hot, they walked over the mountain to the sea. That was their migration. When the deer were bountiful and birthing, they went and found the deer. That's what they ate, what they wore as they walked all over. Indian people walked just as much and they migrated just as much then, as we do now. They would go to the ocean when the grunion were running and harvest the grunion. After a few days of drying, they walked back inland because it got cold at the ocean, all along the way they met and traded with other human beings and made their tribes stronger and their connections wider. Their wife would be from another village, she would bring her knowledge and skills to her husband's family. Indian people would meet at a harvest of acorn or pine nuts, a fiesta, funeral or eventually a Saints day. They would bring home acorn and a new wife, introducing her traditions and cultures to their home ensuring a strong and more durable clan.

At first, I believe many of our people lived at the coast, but these were the first villages to be invaded. As more of the foreigners came, the more inland our people went. We are a logical, practical, enterprising, gracious people, who live and know our lands and her secrets. We have lived on these lands far longer than anyone knows and we know her hills and valleys intimately. When somebody came and bothered you, you left. Our people kept moving further away, trying to avoid sickness, going back into the hills, into the cracks, places we always used, but had not chosen to live, simply because there were better lands and places to live on or near. We went to our inland families, to the lands of the grass people and the rivers of the water people. Our valleys became the names of the Saints and our villages became the names of the landmarks they protected. Warner Springs was Cupa and a stopping place for many travelers, San Pasqual was a meeting place for Saint's Days and fiestas, Pala was on the way to the sea and was a well-worn path to our burial grounds.

There are many stories of a family going off to gather and hunt, when they come back all their household goods were scattered outside and their home was occupied by a white person, since there was no protection by law, no rights and they would be threatened by death for trying to protect what was rightfully theirs, they could fight or be killed, simple as that. The Indian people know there is more land, they know where the food lives so they forge on, moving to the next place. Eventually as there becomes more competition for water and food, they kept going farther and farther away, but farther can simply be a day or two of traveling a well worn path with a rest at the first place that has water and comfort or simply going to visit relatives in less populated areas.

There is no mass communication; all the story is by word of mouth, Indian news. The people would hear horror stories. It was like gossip, bits and pieces of information. There was a bounty on Indians, 25 cents for women and children, scalps, and breasts. There are untold horror stories of bloody battles all over California. There is genocide ... and I believe as a people we have suffered post-traumatic stress syndrome from 1769 to current times.

Casino money has offered a great opportunity to American Indians but it's also created a competition among our own people. At one point in our history, Indian people had to choose how they would survive; some families moved into towns and would work to help their people back on the tribal lands. The people who were left on the reservations continued to survive in much the same way they had for centuries. Fast forward to now, when those who left, after years of living among the outsiders, had few ties to the tribal lands, but continued to have grandmothers, aunts, uncles and cousins living on the reservation, and casinos start to pop up, then the race back to the reservations becomes the opportunity.

Those who returned had suffered displacement, loss of traditions, language and the loss of community. The family who remain on the reservations also suffered loss of opportunity, lack of education, poor health and poverty. No bands of American Indians have beat genocide and while casinos finally offer the Indian people a portal to "the American dream" of riches and wealth, the Indian identity continues to be overshadowed by the last two hundred and forty six years of post-traumatic stress syndrome suffered by all Indian people.

Now the issue has become, "who is really Indian"? The reservation Indians resent the Urban Indians returning only to take advantage of the current opportunity of abundance. So now you must prove you are Indian. Genocide is the deconstruction of cultures. The American government has forged this deconstruction onto the American Indian people since 1846. Not only were Indians not citizens until 1924, but our history, births, deaths and responsibility was in the Department of War until the termination act. This left Indian people without historic documented and validated identity; we were the original enemy combatants and have been historically treated as such. Outside of the Jewish people in Nazi Germany, the Indian people are the only race required to prove their degree of Indian blood. How much pure blood one carries can be equated to the genocide of the Jews with Hitler's need to prove, "how much Jewish blood was carried by each individual Jew." The product of this demand was Hitler's excuse and his foundation for genocide.

I believe this is where the modern Indian has failed our own future and money has not helped "heal" our past. As Indian Nations we have not *insisted*, no, we have not *demanded* this genocide of our people be acknowledged and amends be paid to all our past people and our future children. And, while Casinos have given us a place at the table, we know there is a large population of people who believe that Indian people deserve what they have, and wish them well. Then on the other hand, there are many people who believe we should be punished for finding a way to take advantage of this previously unattainable American dream.

As we grow in our Native nations with this benefit of money, many opportunities unfold before us. The first thing I see our people doing is to form a search party to find and buy back our history. A history confiscated from our lands and homes as the spoils of invasion. Long forgotten baskets, images, artifacts and trinkets of information living in the archives of governments, churches, education centers and museums. Each tribe finds a way to weave this commandeered legacy of their history, language and traditions back together piece by piece. This buy back of our history, helps in our understanding of who we are, as we piece back our words and our traditions one by one.

As Native Nations our responsibility to our future is to build and continue to tell our own story and help our children know the truth of our ancestor's stories. We now have the opportunity to do this with the only currency this invading society has ever valued — the dollar bill. This time and place in history has allowed the Indian people a chance to finally own our version of the American dream. Oddly, the irony continues to be that the "American dream" was always built on the backs of our Indian people, on the lands of our ancestors, in the homes and burial places we have never abandoned nor forsaken. (Holder, personal communication 2015).

Anna Morales, Helen Mendez, and Frank Mendez were also interviewed and offered their perspectives on how the San Pasqual Indian Reservation in Valley Center was settled throughout the years. Anna said:

We didn't become familiar with the name Trask until later years. When I was going to those meetings with my mother and grandmother, I don't recall hearing the names Florence and Helen Trask. I couldn't say much about it. We were going to meetings in 1949, 1950, my mother, my grandmother and me, up in Valley Center. (Morales 2011)

Helen Mendez, age 94 at the time of the interview, added: "I was born in Escondido in 1917. My father was Alex Alvarado and my mother was Tomasa Alto Alvarado. My dad was Spanish, my mother was Diegueño, San Pasqual. He used to work at the Fenton Ranch in San Pasqual." (Mendez 2011)

Anna explained of her mother:

She married Frank Mendez. My father used to drive the horses and buggies. First we were living in Poway. We had horses, goats, cows, and pigs. It was a big ranch. My dad used to mow hay. We had workers — nine men. We moved to Escondido from Poway in 1928. My father was not a follower, he was a leader. He signed his name with an 'X.' (Mendez 2011)

Frank Mendez interjected: "Henry Fenton owned 90 percent of the valley. There was only one place he didn't have — Charlie Judson's ranch. Henry Fenton had "Old Timers" Day' once a year. He allowed the workers to homestead in San Pasqual." (Mendez 2011)

Anna added:

My father was Mexican from Mexico. He came up here when he was 15 years old, in 1925 — Avio near Michoacan, Mexico, on the Pacific Coast. He devoted his life to agriculture. He was a foreman for the groves around here—avocados, lemons, and oranges. Then he retired. He never went back to Mexico. He became a U. S. citizen. He passed on eight years ago. I remember staying in San Pasqual with Grandma and Grandpa in 1938, down by the monument. I was born in Escondido. None of us had an interest in living up on the reservation. We thought it was too primitive and it would take a lot of money to get established. My dad had his work here. He would travel to different groves. After I got married it was the same thing. My husband had his work. (Mendez 2011)

Anna's mother added: "He was thinking of growing avocados up there, but it was too much work." She noted that: "As they got older, they didn't want to be too far from town. It was kind of isolated on the reservation." (Mendez 2011)

Anna then commented on the efforts to create an enrollment list and constitution, and linked the topic to the Federal efforts to terminate Indian reservations across the United States, including those in California. She explained:

> We did hear about termination. I don't think it was that, though, a fear of termination. People saw opportunity. We weren't so much interested in the land, but we wanted to make sure our descendants knew where they came from. I'm still working with my granddaughter, Jennifer Morales. She's 15 years old. It was a boom, like with the Gold Rush. My mother, she doesn't realize what's been going on. We're down here in the first place. Lineage keeps getting less and less, because blood gets mixed. My granddaughter may want to know, one day, "Where do we stem from?" Her descendants may ask, "Where do we come from?" I wish they would have done this when my mother was younger. It was live and let live." (Mendez 2011)

Frank Mendez added: "People thought they could organize and get land and that it would develop into something. Other than that … in the 60s I knew about it, but I didn't want to get involved. If you can trace your heritage, that's better than going by a census" (Mendez 2011).

Termination Policy Leads to Changes at San Pasqual

The year after Leonora La Chappa Trask died at Barona in 1953, a new chapter would begin for Florence and Helen Trask at the San Pasqual Indian Reservation in Valley Center. By 1954 the United States government was threatening to terminate all Indian reservations in the United States, and in order for native people to receive any benefits at the conclusion of that process, they would need to be listed on official tribal rolls, and their band would need to have a written tribal constitution.

Though the Trask family and their descendants were verifiably the only Ipai residents of the San Pasqual Indian Reservation in Valley Center from 1909 to the mid-1950s, they would be confronted with challenges from some of the newcomers arriving at the reservation in Valley Center, who questioned why Trask family members and their descendants were living on San Pasqual Indian Reservation lands.

In November 1954 the state of California had convened Senate Interim Termination Hearings for San Diego County in Palm Springs, seeking input from tribal representatives of all San Diego County Indian reservations. On November 17, 1954, fourteen months after the death of his wife, Leonora, Ramon Ames, tribal chairman of the Barona Indian Reservation, stepped up to give his testimony at the hearings. Standing next to him was his stepdaughter, Florence Trask Wolfe, who had served as spokesperson for the San Pasqual Indian Reservation since 1920 when her father, Frank Trask, had died. Mr. Ames stated:

> If we people would get together and ask for it, we would get what we should have, but we are fighting one another. That's all I have to say, except this is Florence May from San Pasqual—not the new Pasqual but the old Pasqual. This land was set aside for the San Pasqual people, but they didn't want to accept them; they sent Frank Trask over there about thirty or forty years ago and they enrolled all the Indians (Senate Interim Termination Hearings Transcripts, Palm Springs, California, November 17, 1954).

Documents accessed for *Blood of the Band* (Johnson and Toler 2012), conclusively indicate that Mary Matteson worked closely with Florence Shipek and other members of the San Pasqual enrollment committee in the late 1950s, strongly influencing them to promote the notion that Frank Trask was hired as a white caretaker and that his wife was from a location other than San Pasqual.

Following Ramon Ames's and Florence Trask Wolfe's appearances at the Senate Interim Termination Hearings on November 17, 1954, at Palm Springs, Mary Matteson offered her version of the history of the San Pasqual Band and how the Trask family had come to reside at the reservation in Valley Center in 1909. Matteson began her statement by saying she had lived on the San Pasqual Reservation for three years prior to the 1954 hearings, then added:

> It seems like a lady in there who calls herself the spokesman [Florence Trask Wolfe], she lets others come in, and other people she doesn't let them come in there, she holds them out, and all of them are anxious to come in and build their homes, and she won't let them, and she has the idea it is all for her family, herself and her sister and their children and their grandchildren. They are going in there and getting everything. The land isn't any good. It is grazing land, but they are getting the flat land there and the San Pasqual Band don't like that one bit, and I went into Riverside, into the office. ... She said for me to go ahead and talk to the rest of the people. ...

There is no information that Florence Trask Wolfe ever denied access to anybody who was entititled to have an assignment on the San Pasqual Reservation lands. During the tribal reorganization process, certain requirments needed to be met before individuals could officially receive assignments.

> Now, they want proof from the rest of the San Pasqual people. We have to get proof that we are from that band, and they don't have any proof that they are from that band of Indians, they are just living there. I have to get my mother's birth certificate

and my birth certificate to show we belong there. There is another family living there and she had to do the same thing. We belong to that tribe. I think that one of you gentlemen said that if we could prove that we were a descendant of that tribe we would be entitled to the land (Transcript of Senate Interim Termination Hearings for San Pasqual 1954).

The questioner for the committee, John Bohn, responded: "No, I don't think it went that far. The gentleman you are referring to was discussing rights under the judgment and rights by reason of being a member of a particular tribe or reservation."

Matteson continued:

All right. We have been trying to get her out as spokesman but she said the Indian Bureau had put her in as spokesman, and the Bureau says that she just sends her name in, she is not elected by the people, so I don't think it is fair for her to do that, because her nephews and nieces can come in and build houses without proving they belong there; well, why can't our people do that? They are the original San Pasquals. This is a new Pasqual. Before that they didn't know whether they could get in there or not, and they told her, I believe Commissioner Myars told them they had no rights in there. Still, she won't let our people in, so that is our problem.

I feel, and the rest of our San Pasqual people feel we should be set free. My father paid taxes and he was without education and if he, being without education could, I guess the rest can do it. I am ashamed of my people today they can't pay taxes. We paid plenty of taxes. We pay taxes on gasoline and sales tax. If we can drive new automobiles we can pay taxes on the gasoline they use. Why can't they pay taxes like anybody else, like me? I am independent. I can pay my own taxes. Gosh, they can work. They have two hands. They talk about the Indian Bureau not doing anything for them but they still want them in. Well, they have been in there for a number of years. What have they done for them, nothing. Do you think they are going to start now? They didn't do it before. They won't do it after, so I really am ashamed of my people who say, 'I can't do this.' They down the Bureau but still want to stay under it. Sometimes I get disgusted with my own people. They just don't want to help themselves. They could and I want this settled about this reservation too. I was advised at the Office to send in my mother's certificate and get the San Pasqual people to sign it, and that is what I am goin' to do, because there has to be something done about it.

I forgot to say that I belong to the Mission Indian Federation. My father and my mother belonged to it. I am secretary-treasurer of it, and I believe the federation has done a lot of good work. It is the oldest organization. It is about three years old and has done much for the people, but they still want to buck us. Why? There are the ones who still say the Bureau doesn't do anything for us. They knock the Bureau down and still want to stay under it. I don't think they know their own minds. That is about all I can say (Matteson 1954).

Mr. Bohn then asked for the name of the spokesman of San Pasqual and whether there was a tribal council. Mrs. Matteson responded that the spokesman was Florence Wolfe, and, no, there was not a tribal council. The questioning of this witness continued, as Mr. Bohn attempted to understand Matteson's position. A partial record of the testimony follows:

Q. What is the total population of this particular band, do you know?

A. You mean the old band or the new ones on the reservation?

Q. The San Pasqual Band. Is there an enrolled list or tribal roll?

A. I don't believe so.

Q. There are apparently two bands involved, the old and new bands, is that it?

A. Yes.

Q. How many are in the old band, roughly?

A. Well, I should judge three or four or five hundred, including children.

Q. Are those people living on the reservation?

A. They can't get on — I was lucky to.

Q. Had they moved off the reservation?

A. On the old reservation they were; they kicked them out and then the government moved these people.

Q. In other words, there was a different San Pasqual reservation once from the present?

A. Yes, the one now they call it San Pasqual, California. The white people have the best land and they moved us off into the mountains.

Q. In other words, the old San Pasqual was moved off some land in the past and then there was a new San Pasqual reservation set up?

A. Yes.

Q. Now, the people who moved onto this present San Pasqual Reservation are a different band from the ones who were moved into the mountains?

A. Yes, that is right, they come from Mesa Grande.

Q. What happened to the group that was moved from the other lands, have they just dispersed?

A. Yes, some went to Mesa Grande.

Q. Now, the new band at this time on San Pasqual, do they have any tribal council?

A. Well, they have a spokesman and it is just a family affair.

Q. And the spokesman you refer to in that new band is Mrs. Wolfe?

A. Yes.

Q. And to the best of your knowledge she elected — she was elected by the new San Pasqual Band?

A. I don't know. At the office they say she just sends her name in.

Q. And how many are there in the new group?

A. Twelve or thirteen, that is with the children. I would say about six adults.

Q. How long or how large is this reservation?

A. I believe about 1,300 acres.

Q. And out of that 1,300 acres how much of it is farming land?

A. Well, I would say about—they class it as grazing land.

Q. All grazing land?

A. Yes.

Q. And your problem is that you think some of the old San Pasqual Band should be entitled to move back onto this new San Pasqual Reservation?

A. We have asked for it and we have tried to settle people back there on their land but they won't let them. Quite a while back they had some kind of trouble there where they jumped a claim from Felix Quisquis, who proved he belonged to that band of Indians. He was away a month and this woman's niece built a home there; and he has a right there more than she.

Q. Was this land from which they moved the old Pasquals, was that sold?

A. I think so.

Q. Do you know whether there is any such fund or whether the money was used to purchase the new reservation?

A. No, I don't.

Q. You don't know whether there is any such fund or whether the money was used to purchase the new reservation?

A. I am not too familiar about that; I suppose so—when they took the old Pasqual away (Matteson, Mary 1954).

Mr. Leonard Hill, Sacramento area director of the Office of Indian Affairs, then offered his explanation of the history of the San Pasqual Indian Reservation:

I would like to clear up a point or two in connection with this reservation. Our records show there are about 1,343 acres in the reservation. The reservation was acquired and set aside by executive order out of the public domain for the San Pasqual Band of Indians and trust patents issued to the San Pasqual Band. This area is up in the mountain tops; it doesn't have more than a few acres of flat land in any one place that I know of. It is practically useless, as far as any productive agriculture is concerned, but it has now become valuable for homesites. It is in the higher elevations and is very desirable. It is on a highway.

There was no San Pasqual Reservation land sold for the benefit of the Indians. The San Pasqual Indians formerly claimed the valley area where they made their homes, and they were subjected to the same treatment as other Indians in California. They were driven off the land and the land acquired by non-Indians; the present reservation wasn't purchased; it was established by setting it apart from the public domain. The San Pasqual Indians were a rather independent lot. They said, 'This land is useless,' and they refused to move onto the place for many years, and have refused until very recently.

Meanwhile Mrs. Wolfe and her ancestors—I think her father and mother formerly were enrolled members of the Mesa Grande moved onto the reservation. An Indian Bureau school teacher, as I understand the history, permitted the young couple who needed a place on which to live, to move to the San Pasqual Reservation. There was a house there and someone had dug a well. Later the federal government bought out the squatters' interest and this made living quarters for this family so that the Wolfe family were moved onto the San Pasqual Reservation at the suggestion of an Indian Service schoolteacher. That is the way I get the story. Mrs. Wolfe and her family, father, and mother, have lived on the reservation, I suspect for forty years, unmolested, and they were recognized by the Office of Indian Affairs as having a right to occupy it.

There was no demand from anyone else to occupy the property, but it is true, nevertheless, that the trust patent has been issued to the San Pasqual Band of Indians. I don't believe Mrs. Wolfe is a member of that band; so here you have a problem where a group having a trust patent to the land, not having occupied it for thirty or forty years, and someone comes in and is allowed to stay there, and that right is recognized, since the movement was sponsored by the Bureau in the first place. The result is that you now have an argument between the San Pasqual tribe and the people who have occupied the property for the past forty years.

Without attempting to choose sides, I just wanted to reiterate what the witness said, that this is the situation and it does create a very difficult problem. I don't see how — a layman's opinion, the San Pasqual Band can be deprived of land patented to them by the federal government. Unfortunately, the San Pasqual Band would have nothing to do with the Bureau for the past half century, so we have no census roll or list of the band. It is going to be difficult to obtain a roll of those people and make a determination of what equities they have in this land. It is a very difficult problem. That is all I have on San Pasqual (Hill, Leonard 1954).

Mary Matteson had noted at the hearings in 1954 that she was secretary-treasurer of the Mission Indian Federation, and that both her parents had belonged to the Federation, a group favoring termination of all Indian reservations. Although the federation's intent was to protect the assets of native peoples, history has shown that such a policy would have eliminated the reservation system and the opportunities that it has provided for all those living on reservations today and in the future. At the hearings in November 1954, tribal leaders from San Diego County expressed their confidence in or opposition to the Mission Indian Federation, clearly delineating whether they were for or against the termination of their reservations, and expressing their feelings about how they desired their futures to be. Katharine Luomala commented that:

Native, aggressive perseverance and independence were again demonstrated in the 1930s when the Mission Indian Federation, formed for self-government with captains, judges armed, and policemen, challenged federal authority. The federation and a counter organization called Southern Mission Indians have divided people as bitterly as probably the Franciscan missions originally did. As then, factionalism has contrarily fostered tribalism. ... Equally spirited has been reaction to mid-twentieth-century changes in federal and state Indian policy (Luomala 1963:91-98).

One thing was clear — should termination become a reality, native tribes would need to be organized and have tribal rolls and constitutions in place in order to receive lands and other benefits from the government. It was in that climate that those who had formerly objected to the San Pasqual Indian Reservation being placed in Valley Center appeared at the reservation in the mid-to-late-1950s, desiring to create a tribal roll and constitution for the Band. Thus also began their efforts to research not only their own genealogical histories, but those of the Trask family and their descendants as well. With technology at a very different level in the 1950s than it is now, native tribal family histories were usually passed down by word of mouth. Sometimes family members' histories would not be consistent, even in the cases of siblings or twins. Some native people would avoid claiming their native blood degree, perhaps preferring to join in the more mainstream society. Securing government records, letters, baptismal certificates, marriage records, and other means of officially documenting a family's genealogy could prove to be a difficult and time-consuming matter.

As noted in chapter six, when Thelma Terry and Sosten Alto approached Florence Shipek, PhD, in 1958 (Shipek 1994), it was with the intention of searching relevant censuses, government documents, records and genealogies, to learn who would ultimately meet the enrollment requirements and who wouldn't. Also noted was that from 1956 to 1962 the enrollment committee also worked with Mr. Pappan, of the Bureau of Indian Affairs, to create the list of tribal members and the Band's constitution.

The following information surfaced in 2012 at Shipek's archives at the Kumeyaay College in Sycuan, where a Trask family member accessed notes showing that Shipek was aware of a great deal of information concerning the placement of the Trask family at the San Pasqual Indian Reservation in Valley Center. Shipek commented on what she had learned "… in 1957, while working on the San Pasqual membership genealogies …" and indicated that she was aware of the government's insistence that there was only enough land at the San Pasqual Indian Reservation in Valley Center for one or two families. She added:

> The Reservation, which was finally patented to the San Pasqual Indians, did not contain sufficient water for a dry farming subsistence for more than one family. Without the development of an irrigation system no other families could feasibly reside there. For the San Pasqual Band to have maintained even a portion of its community pattern on that reservation, irrigation water as well as domestic water was necessary (TS Shipek Archives 2012:25).

Shipek also mentioned Charles E. Kelsey's insistence that San Pasqual Indians should not be, in her words, "told to reside at the Reservation." She noted: "He suggested, instead, putting one or two families at most upon the Reservation, as that was all the Reservation could support" (TS Shipek 2012:30).

Amos R. Frank, superintendent of the Indian School and special disbursing agent Mesa Grande, agreed with the government's contention that the San Pasqual Indian Reservation in Valley Center would support only one or two families, as shown in an April 22, 1910, letter to C. F. Hauke, the chief clerk of the Office of Indian Affairs, when he referenced Frank Trask:

The one man living at the San Pasqual Reservation should receive his allotment, as the land occupied by him is in a high state of cultivation, and the man occupying it is able to keep it in good shape. There being room for only one family, the balance is to be used as timber, etc. (Amos R. Frank, 1910 Letter to C. F. Hauke, Chief Clerk of the Office of Indian Affairs).

Shipek noted that before Frank Trask died, the Irrigation Service had reported that at San Pasqual: "Farming will never pay. ... [P]oultry, bees, and cattle would support two ... families" (Irrigation Report 1919 in Shipek Archives 2012).

A letter from Charles E. Kelsey to the Office of Indian Affairs referenced the crops that Frank Trask was cultivating, even though water on the reservation was scarce:

Trask had all the arable land outside the orchard planted in grain. The orchard was being ploughed, as is necessary in California. I thought everything in satisfactory shape. This valley has no water for irrigation and the ranchers raise cattle, grain, and some fruit without irrigation. It is rather a hard proposition to do so, however, as the rainfall is scanty, the elevation being about 1,500 feet and not near the high mountains enough for heavy rainfall. Frank Trask has about 10 acres under the ditch. ... [T]here is therefore no conflict of interest as to time of using the water and the ditch. The San Pasqual Indians as a band do not want to have the land charged to them, and it will probably be more satisfactory to all concerned if the patent does not issue to the band, but to individuals who have settled or may settle on the land (Letter from Kelsey to Office of Indian Affairs 1910).

A final report from Indian agent Charles E. Kelsey later outlined the situation: "There are now but one or two families on the reservation. The San Pasqual Indians almost unanimously refuse to consider the reservation as laid out for them and insist that the government shall give them back their lands from which they were illegally ejected" (Kelsey 1913).

Shipek also made mention of what was happening with the San Pasqual Band before their 1878 eviction and after:

The 1870 Federal Census of the San Pasqual and Pala Districts showed none of the individuals classified there as Indian. There were first and last names (as compared with the 1860 Census, which showed first names only except for Jose Panto). All in this 1870 Census were classified as white, even Jose Panto. His wife was shown as Dolores. An additional 1870 Federal Census was taken of the San Pasqual Valley Reservation, and all were identified as white. A few were Mexicans who are known from later records to have had children with San Pasqual Indian women (US Census Records 1870 in Shipek 2012 MS:2-4).

A second handwritten note showed: "Bureau Census telling of need for Reservation for San Pasqual Indians, which has some Mexicans listed on it also" (Shipek 2012:MS:24). She also noted: "The Bureau has a census made on June 30, 1910 supposedly of Indians living on the reservation; this census lists Trask and every individual in his family, several families whom the Indians claim are Mexican and some of the San Pasqual people" (Shipek MS 2012:234).

Other of Shipek's archival notes revealed that she had access to further information about the Trask family and their tenure at the San Pasqual Indian Reservation in Valley Center:

> The caretakers placed on the reservation maintained a small farm. A small stream crossing the northeastern end of the Reservation was occasionally diverted to irrigate his crops. The point of diversion was outside of the Reservation and near the diversion point was a rock fall which almost formed a natural dam to the small stream. By Executive Order dated April 15, 1911, the quarter section on which this natural dam existed was reserved as a part of the San Pasqual Reservation (Southwest ¼ of section 14). In 1912 the Irrigation Service cleared the brush from the rock fall and attempted to fill all openings. The dam face was covered with clay and earth to prevent passage of water. An outlet gate was also provided. As the reservoir filled with water, pressure behind the rock and earth dam caused seepage through the barrier. Between 1912 and 1918, some efforts were made and money expended to render the dam watertight but without success. Following the failure of this effort, the Department of Interior made no more efforts to provide irrigation water from any supplies on the Reservation. At no time did the Department of Interior attempt to supplement the water supply available to the Reservation through attempts to tap underground water sources (Shipek 2012 TS:31).

Shipek stated:

> During the period in which the caretaker occupied the reservation, he did conduct some agricultural activities. He generally planted one or two acres of corn and beans; an acre of garden crops, and he maintained a small peach orchard and a mixed fruit orchard existing of approximately 900 trees (Shipek 2012 TS:32).

Nine hundred trees! To this day, Trask family descendants marvel at how Leonora, Florence, and Helen Trask kept the lands at the reservation intact and operational after Frank's death in 1920. Shipek's archival notes (Reports of the Superintendent of San Pasqual Jurisdiction 1917 and 1924) stated that the number of trees on the Trask family allotment from 1917 to 1924 declined from 900 to 735 in 1917 and to 40 in 1924, and attributed the decline to a lack of water. She further maintained that Frank Trask died six years after his actual date of passing, saying in her notes: "Trask, the caretaker, died in 1926 and his wife and two daughters were trying to maintain a ten acre orchard (Letter to District Superintendent 1926) according to the Bureau Farmer. They were attempting to restore the formerly cultivated fields but there was no water; only dry farming was possible" (Shipek TS). In actuality, Frank Trask had died in January 1920, a clear reason for the three women to be struggling as they alone maintained the fruit trees and reservation lands.

Shipek was, once again, presenting mistakes (the year of Trask's death) and misinformation in calling Frank Trask a "caretaker," as evidenced by the government appointments designating him as an Indian judge, a police private—with his wages appropriated from the "Pay of Indian Police, 1910" (Pierce 1910) — along with dozens of other government reports, records, and letters showing him to be half Indian or referring to his Indian blood. One typed note in Shipek's archives stated: "This place [Wilburn Reed's improvements purchased for $1,500] is now occupied by one Rincon Indian named Frank Trask and his family. These are the only inhabitants of the Reservation" (Shipek TS: N.p.). Again, Shipek's information is inconsistent as here she herself correctly identifies Trask as Indian but now she claims that he is from a Luiseño reservation.

United States Indian censuses would eventually show that the groups that had "scattered" or who had settled in the canyons to the northeast of the San Pasqual Valley, all of whom had resisted accepting the reservation lands in Valley Center after the Smiley Commission designation of 1891, after the Amended Homestead Act of March 1, 1907, and after the trust-patenting on July 1, 1910, had not become a part of the San Pasqual Indian Reservation during the 1920s.

Other censuses of the San Pasqual Indians at Volcan or Mesa Grande confirmed the contention that after the group's eviction from the San Pasqual Valley in 1878, some had relocated to Mesa Grande, Santa Ysabel, or other nearby reservations. Carrico (2010) showed that in 1890 there were 132 people listed on the census of the San Pasqual Indians at Mesa Grande, including 65 males and 67 females. Shown were those with the last names of La Chappa, Wachena, Nejo, and others.

The 1907 Census of the San Pasqual Indians of the Volcan Indian Agency listed the following:

(Name, Age)
67. Frank Trask 39
68. Leonora Trask 26
69. Florence Trask 3
70. Ella Trask 1
92. Antonio La Chappa 48
93. Felician La Chappa 47
94. Sylvestre La Chappa 26 (twin to Leonora)
95. Bruno La Chappa 25
96. Savelita 9

(1907 Census of the Mesa Grande [Santa Ysabel Nos. 1 & 2] Indians of Mesa Grande, June 30, 1907).

Here are items from the 1913 Census of the San Pasqual Indians of the Volcan Indian Agency, listed with their item number, family role, year of birth, and sex, and dated June 30, 1913:

• Frank Trask Husband 1869 Male
• Leonora Trask Wife 1881 Female
• Florence Trask Daughter 1905 Female
• Ella Trask Daughter 1907 Female

(1913 Census of the San Pasqual Indians of Volcan Indian Agency, June 30, 1913).

Shipek noted that the Trask family and their descendants and spouses were encouraged to farm through the 1930 period. The anthropologist listed the acreage and crops grown, and the amounts of money the family made, as well as the livestock they possessed through the years until 1944. Shipek noted that Florence had taken over as spokeswoman for the reservation and had continued to seek help with getting water from the Office of Indian Affairs, the precursor of the Bureau of Indian Affairs. Her notes showed: "On May 16, 1939 Mrs. Florence T. [Trask] Stewart, Spokeswoman of the San Pasqual Reservation, wrote to John W. Dady, superintendent for the Office of Indian Affairs in Southern California, to ask if it was possible for the reservation to get water from the Escondido Mutual Water Company for irrigation purposes" (Shipek 2012 TS:N.p.)

Shipek's notes showed that Florence received the following reply from the Escondido Mutual Water Company: "We are sorry to report that the water belonging to the Escondido Mutual Water Company is confined to usage within a very restricted district. ... [T]he attitude of the stockholders is very much at present against any water usage outside of the District's present boundaries" (Dady Letter 1935).

When the third-oldest of Helen Trask's grandchildren, the author of this book, arranged a meeting in 1990 with Shipek at her home in Point Loma, he told her that his family knew that Frank Trask was half Kumeyaay and believed to have been born in the San Pasqual Valley in 1867. Toler added that Leonora was full-blood Indian, from the La Chappa, Guachena, Nejo, and other San Diego County clans, with ancestors and descendants who connected with all regions of San Diego County, including San Pasqual. Shipek replied: "I put a disclaimer in the book!" (Toler 1990). Shipek's denial of responsibility for only presenting the biased views of some of her clients and the recognition that she did not have access to complete information can be found in the preface to *Pushed into the Rocks*: "Any errors are strictly my own, but the longer I work under the constantly changing external conditions and legal situations, the more new information comes to light to improve my understanding of past events" (Shipek 1987:xviii).

Unfortunately Shipek's misinformation has continued to circulate throughout the decades, and does so today.

At the time of the San Pasqual tribe's efforts to reorganize, including forming a list of tribally enrolled members and a constitution (enrollment documents of 1966), it was determined that Mary Matteson's blood line traced to Mesa Grande and other locations, as did that of others involved in the reorganization process. While working to determine the genealogy of some of those of the San Pasqual Band, Shipek made a note about a conversation she had with Porfidia Duro, the daughter of Ysidro Nejo [E. W. Gifford said Feliciana Nejo was cousin-sister to Ysidro Nejo], at Mesa Grande, regarding Mary Matteson:

I will quote my conversation with Porfidia Duro:

"Will you tell me about Mary Matteson's mother's family?" The informant answered:

"Why does she want to be enrolled on San Pasqual? She belongs on Mesa Grande. Her mother belonged to Santa Ysabel. What does Mary want to change for?"

Augstina La Chusa (left),
Mary Lieres (right) and
Mary Ortega Matteson (center).
Photo: James Baker.

Shipek: "Who was Mary's grandfather?"

Informant: "Her grandfather was Francisco La Chusa—belonged to Mesa Grande. This is where Mary belongs."

Shipek: "Who was Francisco La Chusa's mother?"

Informant: "I don't know her name. I remember Maria Augustina used to always call my mother-in-law Grandma. And one time I asked her, 'Why does she call you Grandma? You're not her Grandma.'"

Person answering: "Her grandmother was my sister; that's why she calls me Grandma."

Shipek: "Who was your mother-in-law?"

Informant: "Trinidad La Chapa, she married *illegible* Duro."

Shipek: "Where was your mother-in-law from?"

Informant: "She belonged to San Pasqual."

Shipek: "Did she have any other sisters and brothers?"

Informant: "Maria Antonio, and there were two or three more, but I don't know their names now." (Shipek TS 2012:N.p.).

In the Headlines

Several newspaper articles in the 1980s addressed issues involving the San Pasqual Band, generally focusing on problems related to enrollment. In 1984, against a backdrop of severe unemployment, the tribe was dealing with an influx of residents that had increased from just a few families in the 1950s to about fifty households. By 1988, newspaper articles describe an increasing number of people seeking to establish tribal membership as $2.5 million from the settlement of a legal case that was about to be dispursed to enrolled tribal members, and some of the effects this would have on the community.

One headline in a 1984 edition of the *Escondido Times Advocate* read "Local Indian Reservations Struggle to Become Self Sufficient" (Schleuss 1984). Reporter Heinz Schleuss explained that Mary Matteson described herself as "one of the last true San Pasqual Indians left." The article stated that only two Indian families lived on the San Pasqual Indian Reservation in Valley Center when she said Matteson moved there in 1951. By 1984 there were fifty households on the reservation, and Robert Stewart, younger son of former spokeswoman Florence Trask Stewart Wolfe, was chairman of the Band. Stewart noted that the unemployment rate on the San Pasqual Indian Reservation in Valley Center in 1984 was sixty percent (Schleuss 1984).

A July 3, 1988, *Los Angeles Times* article, entitled "Bad Blood: Money Seekers Claiming San Pasqual Indian Ancestry Reopen Rift," reported this of the San Pasqual Band in Valley Center: "There is infighting among already enrolled Indians about whether other, long-time reservation residents possess true San Pasqual Indian bloodlines" (Gorman, 1988:1).

The article stated that with per capita monthly monetary amounts of $2,000 anticipated in 1988 for enrolled tribal members, and disbursal of a large monetary award from the US Claims Court Case which had been settled in 1983, the Band was interviewing people connected with the San Pasqual Reservation regarding tribal enrollment, in anticipation of parceling out $2.5 million, which had been accruing in a bank account since the court case concluded. The Claims Court settlement was for a canal put across the reservation decades before, without Indian approval, to transport water from Lake Henshaw to Escondido and Vista. The result of news of the monetary award becoming public was that many of those claiming to be of the San Pasqual Band, but who had never settled on the reservation, were now checking their blood quantum to see if they qualified for enrollment.

Reporter Tom Gorman wrote:

> The payoff has also rekindled a history of bickering among some San Pasqual Indians over one another's rightful claim to the band, and has refocused attention on bureaucratic sloppiness by the Bureau of Indian Affairs at the turn of the century, when the first official roll of the band was established.
> The last official census of the San Pasqual Indians, conducted by the Bureau of Indian Affairs in 1959 and approved in 1966, listed 229 official San Pasqual Indians (Gorman 1988:1).

The article quotes Chairwoman Diana Martinez as remarking: "Some have San Pasqual lineage but it's too thin. I figure that 200 at most of the 475 will qualify. There are lots of rumors that people affiliated with other tribes are trying to enroll in ours" (Gorman 1988:1).

The L. A. *Times* article continues:

> A few people share a lingering bitterness that members of the band's two or three most prominent families are enrolled as San Pasqual Indians and have been since 1910 — even though, they allege, they have little or no true San Pasqual blood.
>
> That controversy goes to a 1910 BIA Census of the San Pasqual Indians, when people were included within the band simply because they lived in the San Pasqual Valley. Apparently little or no effort was made to determine whether those counted by the BIA agents were indeed San Pasqual Indians and to what blood degree.
>
> Should some of those families who were counted in the 1910 enrollment be disqualified as San Pasqual Indians, the membership rolls of the San Pasqual Indian band would be cut in half or more — effectively doubling the individual money shares to the remaining members.
>
> The likelihood of such widespread disqualifications is considered slim or none, the BIA says, but it hasn't stopped people like Mary Matteson from raising a ruckus.
>
> Matteson and several others, admittedly making up a minority viewpoint, complain that the 1910 BIA Census included people of Mexican descent who had no blood ties to the Mission Indians who settled the San Pasqual Valley (Gorman 1988:1-2).

Gorman stated that formal membership to the band includes the right to five acres of reservation property, free and clear, and noted that Matteson also said, "We want them to prove they are San Pasqual Indians. Back in 1910, the BIA didn't know beans from hash" (Gorman 1988:2). However the outspoken Matteson's viewpoint is contested by many tribal leaders:

> Other Indian leaders at San Pasqual agree with Matteson that the BIA may have botched the original enrollment in 1910, but they say it is a wrong that now cannot be corrected and has to be accepted. "If you were red, white, black or yellow, you still got your name on the original roll just because you lived in San Pasqual Valley," said Jim Quisquis, Chairman of the reservation's enrollment committee. "Back in those days, bloodline wasn't an issue. The programs that we have today that talk in terms of bloodline didn't exist then."
>
> Frances Muncy, acting tribal operations officer in Riverside for the Southern California agency of the bureau, agrees also that the government would be hard pressed to rectify any errors — and that the burden of proof that someone was not an Indian would rest with those making a complaint.
>
> "The burden of proof rests with those making the allegations. I don't think there's any way you can get people to stop complaining [about the 1910 enrollment]. It's coming to a head now because of the money. But I've told Mary [Matteson] she can

blame the Bureau from now till Doomsday, but nothing much will be done about it unless the tribal enrollment committee makes its own recommendation to disqualify certain people."

Many other members of the community felt that the squabbles over census-taking methods of the past should be put aside in order to help the community move forward.

> "We can't go back to 1910, and now it's like beating a dead horse," [Jim] Quisquis added. (Gorman 1988:2).
> Eighty-one year old Felix Quisquis, another member of the enrollment committee, said he could recall the carelessness of BIA agents in taking a census on the reservation, even in later years. The Quisquises are distant relatives. "The Indian agent would point over to another hill and ask me who lived there. I'd tell him who I thought lived there, and he wouldn't even check it out. It was a lot of word of mouth. And that's why our rolls are all screwed up."
> Paul Contreras, vice chairman of the tribe, said he resents people like Matteson bringing up the ancestry issue once again. "If they'd stop worrying about the past and start looking to the future, maybe some things would get done around here."
> The enrollment process is not expected to be completed for several months, and it is then open to appeal to the BIA by people who feel they were unfairly left off, or by others who say they can prove someone who was included should not have been. Meanwhile, reservation leaders are looking to the day the money will be in hand, especially because there is no locally generated tribal income.
> Martinez said the money might go for a water-filtration system, a church, a youth club, a cemetery or a store. "We've got the $2.5 million in accounts all over the country," Martinez said, "And we've got so many dreams. This is our moment" (Gorman 1988).

Reporter Eric Eyre wrote in a 1989 *Times-Advocate* article with the headline, "For Mary Matteson, Indian Problems Mean Personal Investigation" that Mary Matteson, born in 1912 in Placentia, near Los Angeles, was raised there and went to the San Pasqual Indian Reservation in Valley Center in1951. Land was tax-free there, and Matteson said, "It was a pretty place then."

According to Eyre: "'She's tough, she speaks her mind, you don't want to get on the wrong side of her, and she spews out opinions like machine gun pellets,' are all descriptions other people have used to describe her. She described herself as 'always in hot water'" (Eyre 1989).

8

Genealogy:
Who Are Your People?

Trask family members and descendants have interacted extensively with relatives and friends in San Diego County throughout their years within Ipai territory. This chapter reveals the results of extensive genealogical research and adds evidence to support the idea that not only was there a complex interactive network that existed among the clans of the native people of San Diego County, connected to the watersheds in which the Ipai lived, but those relationships continue today and can be identified and valued. The following pages provide detailed genealogical information on a number of people who have been important to our family's and our region's history, presented roughly in order of birthdate.

This chapter contains numerous entries from the journals of ethnographer John P. Harrington, whose largest compilation of field notes was carried out between August and September 1925, and in December 1927, with the Mesa Grande and Santa Ysabel areas serving as his focus (Harrington 1913-1933; 1925). Many of Harrington's notes, photos, and other materials are housed at the Smithsonian Institution and some of his California materials are currently being studied at the University of California at Davis and the Pechanga Band of Luiseño Indians.

Note that in the nineteenth century, as government officials required Indians to use surnames, many Kumeyaay adopted their clan names for this purpose. However, since clan names were originally passed on through oral tradition rather than in writing, the new written forms of the names varied greatly. For example, the ancient clan name "Letcapa" appears in government and church documents, researcher's notes, and other documentation in a variety of ways, including Lachapa, La Chapa, LaChapa and La Chappa. Nonetheless, all of these forms refer to the same lineage of the Letcapa family.

Jermain Anej and Maria Louisa Guacheno

Jermain Anej's genealogical information (Ancestry.com 2012) included a note that he carried timbers from the Cuyamaca Mountains to the San Diego Mission to help construct buildings there. Born at Yaqui Well (Ancestry.com 2012), he lived until 1888. He married

Opposite page: Narciso La Chappa. *Photo: E. H. Davis, San Diego History Center.*

The house of Jose La Luz at the edge of Warner's Ranch, 1931. *Photo: E. H. Davis, San Diego History Center.*

Maria Louisa Guacheno, who was born at Santa Ysabel in either 1816 or 1826 and was shown on two different 1910 censuses as either 84 or 94 years of age.

Maria Louisa's parents (California Indian Rolls 1928) were Mi-hap and Jose La Luz at San Pasqual, with a further discussion of a Jose La Luz who lived near Santa Ysabel included later in this chapter. Jermain and Maria Louisa had at least ten children, three of whom were listed: Maria Jesusa Nejo, born in 1840 at Santa Ysabel and died there in 1906; Maria Dominga, born 1863, and Maria Louisa, born 1865 and died 1941.

Records have been found showing the younger Maria Louisa Nejo as married to a Luciano La Chappa, born 1865 (Ancestry.com 2012). Harrington's information for the 1906 Census for Volcan showed: Luciano La Chappa, husband, age 41; Maria Louisa (Nejo), wife, age 39; Juan, son, age 21; Alejandro, son, age 20; Inocencio, son age 17; Ysedro, son age 15; Victoria, daughter, age 9; Luisa, daughter age 6; Esperanza, daughter age 5; Francisco, son age 4; Marguerita, daughter age 6 months, and Maria Nejo [believed to be Maria Louisa Guacheno Nejo, mother of Maria Jesusa, Maria Dominga and Maria Louisa]. She was listed as mother, age 80.

Maria Louisa Guacheno Nejo also appears on the 1910 Census, along with her daughter, Maria Louisa, shown as married to Luciano La Chappa born, 1865, with their children: Juan born 1885; Alejandro born 1886; Inocencio born 1889; Ysedro born 1891; Victoria born 1897; Louisa born 1898; Esperanza born 1901; Francisco born 1902; Marguerita born 1906, and an infant born 1907.

Maria Louisa Guacheno's mother has been identified as Mi-Hap and her father as Jose La Luz (California Indian Rolls 1928), both 4/4 at Santa Ysabel. One Jose La Luz, living near Santa Ysabel and other regions, was the subject of many of Harrington's notes as he traveled Ipai territory from 1913-1933:

> Santa Ysabel; Jose Luz house; painted rock, 36 paces to highway; old road.
>
> Cueva de las Pulgas – referring to the people of San Pasqual; Jose La Luz, an old man who cooked here recently … says he was Descanso, Baja or San Diego County; married to Juliana; lived at old adobe near Warner's. Capitan Grande called that because a big Indian chief lived there. Kamijaj: Arroyo Del Agua—at San Pasqual; Kawakipaj: those at San Pasqual who are at the coast. Ysidro Nejo is the best informant.
>
> 6_18 Jose la Luz interview, August 9, 1925 at Davis's place. An old man whose beard the cook here recently cut. Has lived at San Diego, Los Angeles and other places. Says he was born at Descanso, but cannot answer whether that is in Baja California or in San Diego County. Mr. Davis says there may be more than one Descanso. He is married to a woman named Juliana, now sickly and old. They live at the adobe where the road to Santa Ysabel joins the road to the Henshaw Dam and the road to Warner Springs. He say Juliana was born at Tu'w'I (Monkey Hill); at the end of the interview I took his picture, front and side views. Nelmen, Descanso, where informant was born.
>
> 6_19 Jose La Luz interview, August 9, 1925: qakusijaj: Agua Hechicera, over by Volcan or somewhere. Qajaj: Rosario, down by Descanso; kwitjamak, Capitan Grande—name means shoulderblade. It is called in Spanish Capitan Grande, because there was a big Indian chief there. "I asked about the tribe Inkipa, which Davis says is a tribe of the Indians near Campo. Informant says the form is njikipa, a tribe of Indians south of here. They live at Wikipaip. Kwikapa: Cocopa; aqakwaaqwat: Rio Colorado. Akwat: informant says this tribe lives down in Mexico. The word means skin. They speak a different dialect.
>
> 6_22 Harington and Davis interviewed Jose La Luz at where the highway from Santa Ysabel meets the highway from Henshaw Dam, called Susana Canyon—born at Descanso, but uncertain if in California or Mexico. His wife, Juliana, born at Monkey Hill Rancheria and she is called in Spanish a San Josean. A long list of place names followed. Some of them were: Kwilyamak: Capitan Grande; Kwikapa: Cocopa; Mohave name "Yakawa'avira," literally "tough mouth." In informant's language, he says it would be aka'awir, tough mouth, but doesn't know it to be a tribe.
>
> 11_4 Profile of a w i l y k w a n f u r looking at Painted Rock. Then, after Painted Rock, passes Jose La Luz's old adobe. It is nameless. Then started up the Santa Ysabel road, up grade. After coming one mile from the old adobe, passed on our right a g t a a s a, identified by a meadow on right side of mouth of canyon. Angel says this meadow is next and to be a house of adobe, up the canyon where the big oaks are seen was a spring around the corner of the hill from that house. This place is called El Carrizo in Spanish and the locality is called La Puerta del Carricito. At the left of the mouth of the

next much larger canyon beyond this canyon is the two-story Santa Ysabel ranch house with upstairs veranda.

11_6 Map: Nameless spring and cienega on hillside; ranch of Juanito of Santa Ysabel on hillside. They ran him out of Santa Ysabel; nameless spring and water trough; upper veranda ranch house; big canyon; big highway; Jose de la Luz's adobe.

11_26 Elrino, a brother of Jose La Luz was passing by the first Santa Maria ranch house site and drank water. He was carrying a pound of wool to San Diego and down the road an Indian ___ [illegible] crazy. Silvestrio Portilla (brother of Pablo Portillo, had the San Jose Ranch) had been living 5 or 6 years. Chin was hauling a load of wool from San Jose Ranch to San Diego with 2 yokes of oxen. He drank the water and got crazy and left the oxen beyond the hill, southwest of the spring and went on foot, crawling and staggering to San Pasqual on foot.

12_8 Angel says that he was in q a w i t once and Luis, a son of Julian (Jose La Luz's wife) and Juan Yacqui were there. Juan Yacqui made a drink by boiling the dates. It was thick, color of coffee and sweet. I understand that Juliana was there too. Juan Yacqui used to take dates from Palm Canyon to Julian and sell them for $10.00.

Yaqui Well, Anej's birthplace, is marked today by a sign on State Route 78 at the turnoff to the Borrego area. The well has been curbed and preserved by authorities from the Anza-Borrego Desert State Park, and though there is nothing at the site to note its historical significance, Yaqui Well was an important stop for the mule-skinners who traveled to the Arizona Territory and helped early native and non-native settlers and Army personnel of the region survive (Mac Mullen 1963).

W. H. Ball created his own freight company in 1857, using mules to pull his wagon trains, some as long as one mile, and supplying food, household items, tools, and other necessities for those within the Phoenix, Prescott, Wickenburg areas. Though the railroad had connected the East Coast to the West Coast, it ran to the north of this region and was cut off by the Grand Canyon. Ball Freighters delivered supplies to the settlers and Army posts until 1884 when the railroad became available in Arizona. Then Ball Freighters operated in Death Valley, carrying Borax.

It was W. H. Ball who discovered water at the site today known as Yaqui Well. Needing a water supply for the thirty to forty rifle-carrying mule skinners who drove each mile-long train, often accompanied by new settlers who joined them for protection from the Apaches, Ball discovered water at the foot of Grapevine Canyon. Jerry Mac Mullen explained that: "Ball had three routes. The northern road took him across the Colorado at Needles. By the southern route, Ball followed the stage road as far as Warner's, then on up to Montezuma Valley and down the Grape Vine. And here, in the wash, Ball found water" (Mac Mullen 1963).

Elmer Ball, grandson of W. H. Ball, tells the story of how his grandfather found water at Yaqui Well when he says: "The Old Man found the water at the foot of the Grape Vine, but it wasn't much good—muddy and hard to get out. So he left two Yaquis there. He told 'em how to fix the well. He said he'd pick em up on his next trip. Indians respected the

Old Man. He always did what he said he would. On his next trip down from San Berdoo he found the well just as he had told 'em to fix it, a wooden curb four-foot square, and the well deepened so the water was sufficient. They drew it up in buckets ..." (Mac Mullen 1963:N. p.).

Mule skinners working for Ball were then able to stop at Yaqui Well to water their hundred or more horses and fill the barrels that were hung on the sides of the wagons, as they completed their three- to four-month-long trips. Their mules were never replaced during those trips, but, instead, started and finished the entire journey with the mule-skinners, whose bullwhips could be heard for great distances, cracking like pistol shots as the men urged their animals onward.

Maria Angela Guachena

Maria Angela Guachena, the mother of Jose Antonio La Chappa, has been shown as born in either 1819 (Census of Mesa Grande 1890), 1823 or 1833 at Mesa Grande (Census of 1894). Her father was Cornelio Guachena, birth date not known (California Indian Rolls 1928). Angela married three times, and can be found with the last names of Chivo, McIntier and La Chappa. She married her third husband, Jose Bastian La Chappa, sometime before 1859 (California Indian Rolls 1928) and he lived until 1889, while she lived until 1907.

Angela was described in a 1936 San Diego newspaper article by historian and photographer E. H. Davis, who noted that Angela lived at the San Diego Mission as a child, and said that she served her people at the Mesa Grande chapel as their spiritual advisor. Gifford added that after Angela's death in 1907, Angela's daughter, Petra La Chappa Cota, served as the "High Priestess" for Mesa Grande church services until her death in 1936 (chronicled later in this chapter).

Censuses and genealogical records (Census 1893 and Ancestry.com 2012) show that before 1850 Maria Angela Guachena married Jose Chivo. Before 1857 she married John L. McIntier, and before 1859 she married Jose Bastian La Chappa.

Maria Angela Guachena (Ancestry.com 2012) married Jose Chivo sometime before 1850 when their daughter, Teresa, was born in Julian. Teresa lived until October 16, 1888, and Angela is shown on the 1893 and 1894 censuses with two of her daughters, Natalia and Petra. Teresa Chivo first

Angela Guachena (La Chappa).
Photo: C. G. DuBois.

married Manuel Banegas and later married Luis Lopez. Teresa Chivo Lopez and Luis Lopez had the following children: Maria Concepcion Lopez, born 1870, who married Francisco Cota in 1886 and had a child, Feliciana Cota, born 1894. The child, Feliciana, died in 1896 of gastroenteritis. Later, Maria Concepcion Lopez, granddaughter of Maria Angela Guachena, married Henry Trask, born 1869, who was half-brother to Frank Trask and the son of Roswell Trask. Maria Concepcion died in 1955.

Teresa Chivo Lopez and Luis Lopez (Ancestry.com 2012) had a second child, Natalia Lopez, born 1871; Natalia married Vincent Nielovich in 1899 and they had one child, Mary E. Nielovich, born 1899; Natalia died June 23, 1902 at age 31. Teresa Chivo Lopez and Luis Lopez had a third child, Petra Lopez, born 1883. Teresa Chivo Lopez's daughters (Census of Mesa Grande 1893), Natalia Lopez, age 22, and Petra Lopez, age 10, were living with Angela La Chappa, their maternal grandmother, shown as age 60 and a widow on the 1893 Census. Petra La Chappa Cota, age 29, Angela's daughter, was also listed, as was Francisco La Chappa, son, 1, and Jose LaChappa, age 50, nephew.

Maria Angela Guachena's second marriage, to John L. McIntier, who was born in Pennsylvania in 1826, occurred sometime before 1857, which is when their daughter, Mary Catherine [Maria Catarina] was born in Poway (1860 Census, Agua Caliente Township). This marriage illustrates the increasingly common occurrence in the 1800s of the native people marrying outside their native culture, after the arrival of newcomers to the area. John McIntier came to the San Diego area in 1850 as a government surveyor and did most of the early surveys of San Diego, as far north as Los Angeles. In 1852 (Census of 1852 Santa Ysabel) he was shown to be living at the Santa Ysabel Ranch and in 1856 he moved to Ballena (Census of 1856 Ballena), where he located on government land. Though no evidence has been found to tell the story of how he and Maria Angela Guachena met and married, it is known that they had three children, Maria Catarina, Pancho, and Antonio [Anthony or Tony]. Maria Catarina has also been called Mary Catherine (Dave Toler 2014).

The 1860 Census showed a change of spelling for John L. McIntier's name, along with the following information: John L. McIntire, born 1826 & Family #617, Farmer, Age 34, from Pennsylvania (U. S. Federal Census 1860 Agua Caliente Township).

An 1866 Report of the California State Agricultural Society showed John L. McIntire as the assessor for San Diego County and included a report he had made on his district:

> The lands of this county will produce as fine grapes, figs, olives, and oranges, as any county in the State. Wheat grows remarkably well, the grain being decided by wheat growers to be the largest and finest in the State. In the mountainous districts, immense fields of barley are raised, which by the way, is sold to emigrants, mostly coming into our state by the northern route. ... I have the honor to submit for your consideration.
>
> John L. McIntire, County Assessor,
> San Diego County (McIntire 1866).

Angela Guachena La Chappa,
Leonora's paternal grandmother,
holding a basket she presented to
Constance Goddard Dubois.
Photo: C.G. DuBois.

An October 1867 letter to the surveyor general from Assessor McIntire read: "Sir: In compliance with the law, I herewith beg leave to transmit to your office my annual report of statistics, etc. of San Diego County; boundaries north by Los Angeles and San Bernardino Counties, east by the State line and Mexican boundary, south by Lower California, and west by the Pacific Ocean."

McIntire was elected supervisor of the County of San Diego in 1867 and served three terms in that office. By 1870 he had surveyed and laid out the town of Julian for D.D. Bailey (Official Register of the United States 1891). In 1891 McIntire served as postmaster at Ballena at the compensation of $219.88 per year. In 1860 (Census of 1860 Agua Caliente Township) McIntire would have been 34, so when he began his tenure as postmaster of Ballena, he would have been 65 years old. In 1892 and 1893 he served as the assessor of San Diego County (McIntire Letter to Houghton 1866), and he was also the judge of the Ballena Judicial District for ten years (City Directory for Los Angeles).

Unknown is when or why Maria Angela Guachena and John L. McIntire split up, but it is known that she married Jose Bastian La Chappa of Mesa Grande before 1859 when Jose

Antonio La Chappa was born. They had at least three other children: Petra La Chappa, born sometime between 1864-1866, who lived until 1942; Juan Diego La Chappa, born about 1865 or 1866; and Ignaciana Incarnaciona La Chappa, born about 1877 and lived until 1908 (Ancestry.com 2012 and US Indian Census 1890).

A Mesa Grande Census of 1893 shows Angela Guachena La Chappa listed with two of her granddaughters, Natalia, age 22, and Petra, age 10, daughters of Angela's first-born daughter, Teresa Chivo Lopez, whom she had given birth to while married to Jose Chivo. In 1893 Angela was age 60 and a widow, since her third husband, Jose Bastian La Chappa, had died in 1889. Angela's second daughter, Petra (born sometime between 1864-1866 and lived until 1942), and her husband, Juan Maria Cota (born December 23, 1866) were also shown on that census, along with Angela's nephew, Jose La Chappa.

The Mesa Grande (Volcan) Indian Census of 1893 also showed other members of Angela Guachena's family, including her great-grandchildren, Fidelio La Chappa #80; Maria Lavina La Chappa #82, and Filberto #84, all listed above her, and all grandchildren of Angela's older son, Pancho McIntyre, and his wife, Concepcion. Parents of the children were listed as Baptisto La Chappa and the younger Concepcion McIntyre, daughter of Pancho and Concepcion.

Maria Jesusa Nejo

Maria Jesusa Nejo was the mother of Feliciana Nejo La Chappa, born in 1859, and to Jose Domingo Yanke, born in 1857. Maria Jesusa had two sisters, Maria Dominga and Maria Louisa, and censuses indicate that Maria Louisa married Luciano La Chappa and they resided at Mesa Grande (Ancestry.com 2012).

Maria Jesusa Nejo married Fred Coleman, the first miner to discover gold in 1869 in San Diego County at Julian, and together they had twelve children (Ancestry.com 2012). Born in 1832 in Kentucky, Fred Coleman's parents were Frederick W. Coleman and Ida Stephens. Counting Maria Jesusa Nejo's twelve children from Fred Coleman, and her children Feliciana Nejo La Chappa and Jose Domingo Yanke (Yaqui), Maria Jesusa had a total of fourteen children (*A History of the Coleman Family* accessed 2012). Fred Coleman lived until 1904 and Maria Jesusa Nejo Coleman lived until 1906.

The Coleman children included: Susie, who married William Henry Williams in 1900; Mary, born 1861 and died 1952; Laura, born 1866, who married Sam Martinez; Nancy, born 1872, who married John Henry Bunton; William Francisco, born 1876, who married Kate Thing and died 1951; Henry, born 1878, who married Daisy Good; Charles B., born 1879, who married Mary Chapuli; Bob Crawford, born 1884, who married Susie Charlie; Bill Coleman, no information; Theodore La Chappa-Coleman, who married Mary La Cruiz (Coleman Family Tree 2012). There is a William Francisco Coleman, born January 1876, shown in *A History of the Coleman Family*, which leads Trask family descendants to believe that he may be the same William Coleman who appears in the records of John Peabody Harrington.

Jose Trinidad Christiano Huacheno,
uncle of Angela La Chappa.
Photo: C. G. DuBois.

Members of the Trask family who were recorded as being informants for John Peabody Harrington included Antonio La Chappa, Ysidro Nejo, Jose La Luz, and Maria Jesusa Nejo Coleman's son, William Coleman, as shown below:

Coleman was born at Santa Ysabel, San Diego County. Was raised at Inyaxaa (Inaja), Laguna, etc. Born January 15, 1877 on Saturday at 9:45 a.m. Has been employed at Campo 24 years variously as former interpreter, and now is policeman and rationer. No Indian name (Harrington 1913-1933:26_3). Coleman: "There are 2 different places to go to get Gypsum" (Harrington 1913-1933:27_5). Coleman: xitpak: Squaw Root; they use seeds for pinole, roots for indigestion; cook the roots. Harrington said, "The more you drink, the quicker you get well" (Harrington 1913-1933:27_12).

Fred Coleman was living with Maria Jesusa Nejo and their children near the base of Volcan Mountain at Santa Ysabel in 1869. While herding cattle in the Spencer Valley area, he stopped to water his horse in a small creek, and looked down to see bright flecks shining there. A February 17, 1870, *San Diego Union* article described Coleman as a former

235

worker in the gold fields of Northern California and noted that he recognized that the bright glitter he was seeing was gold. He went to his pack, pulled out a skillet he carried, and began to use the placer method to pan for gold. A second method, called hard-rock mining, was used only after miners figured out where the gold vein had originated. The same article reported that:

> No rich strikes yet. A district was organized 60 miles from San Diego City near the Santa Ysabel Ranch, called the Coleman District. 75 prospectors present putting sluices to test placers. An old placer miner informs that these are surface diggings. There is no indication of any considerable deposit. Another resident of section says gold placers present for a long time, attracting little attention because past prospecting would pay no more than $1.50 to $2 a day"

The seventy-five prospectors working the surface diggings of the Coleman Mining District created a tent city and called it Emily City. Fred Coleman formed the district and was elected camp recorder. He also built a toll road from El Cajon to make it easier for others to reach the new mining district. Gold mining in Julian continued for several decades. The mines in Julian were credited with producing more than $3 million in ore between 1870 and 1893. On February 22, 1870, gold was found at the Washington Mine in Banner, where the population grew to 1,000, with three stores, four saloons and a hotel.

Other mines included the Golden Chariot, which yielded more than $1 million in three years, the Ready Relief, the Hubbard, the Oroblanco, and the Ranchita (McGrew 1922). Connolly Miskwish (2007) noted that the discovery of gold meant that more whites, Mexicans, Californios, and Sonorans appeared within the Ipai territories, either on their way through to other places, or to take up residence, often settling on traditional Ipai lands within San Diego County.

Roswell Trask

Roswell Trask was born in 1835 in Strongsville, Cuyahoga County, Ohio. As a young man, he followed his adventurous spirit, setting out for the furthest reaches of the United States and reaching California in 1860, where he joined the United States Army on September 21, 1861. With only about 600 military troops in California after 1847, the state of California was often a difficult place to live. The California Gold Rush of 1849 had created an explosion of people, buildings, towns and roads, with the population numbers, which didn't include native people and Californios—mushrooming to over 100,000. These people sent great amounts of gold to the East, perhaps influencing federal legislators to allow California to enter the Union as a free state, by-passing the usual preliminary territorial status that other states went through. By 1860, involvement of those in the western US in the Civil War meant sending gold east, recruiting or funding a limited number of combat troops, and perpetuating military fortifications. By 1862 Congress had authorized the Central Pacific Railroad, and the first rails were laid in 1863, connecting with rails from the east by 1869 (Matthews 2012). This was the climate which Roswell Trask entered as he came to the state of California in 1860.

Roswell served in the US Army from 1861-1866, settling during that time in San Diego County. It is well-documented that in the late 1860s he lived in the San Pasqual Valley, and Trask family descendants' oral traditions relate that he was living there with Frank's mother, a full-blooded Ipai woman, when Frank Trask, who always identified himself as half Indian, was born in 1867. Roswell's three marriages, all to Ipai women, produced a total of eight children.

Roswell Trask's father was Roswell, Sr., who was a physician in Strongsville, Cuyahoga County, Ohio. He served both as an assessor and a trustee for Cuyahoga County. Born on May 4, 1798, in Heath, Franklin, Massachussetts. Roswell's mother was Harriett Stacy, who was born in 1799 in New York, and their genealogical history can be traced as far back as Eleanor Deane, born in 1586 in Chard, Somerset, England, with other ancestors hailing from Ireland, Wales, and Massachusetts. Eleanor died in June 1613, in Taunton, Bristol, Massachusetts. Such names as Galley, Herrick, Elliott, Brown, Hathorne, Hoskins, Caswell, and Wilbore are found in Roswell's genealogy. Roswell Trask and Harriett Stacy had seven children, of whom the younger Roswell was the fourth born.

The younger Roswell Trask's paternal grandfather was William Trask, born 1761 and died 1821. William Trask's father was Benjamin Trask, born 1716 and died 1776, and William's mother was Mary Elliott, born 1722 and died 1774. These would be the younger Roswell's great-grandparents. Roswell's paternal grandfather, William, married Bathsheba Haskins, born 1761 and died 1846. Bathsheba's father was William Haskins, born 1717 and died 1798. Bathsheba's mother was Eliza Coal, born 1724.

Roswell Trask's paternal great-grandfather was Benjamin Trask (father of William) born 1716 and died 1776. His paternal great-grandmother was Mary Elliott, born 1722 and died 1774. Their children were: William, Benjamin, Hannah, Abel Haskins, Bathsheba, Minerva, Roswell, Erasmus, Loammi, and Lowell. These would be the younger Roswell's great aunts and uncles.

Roswell Trask was at Yankee Junction, Placer, California, in 1860 (Wade 2011), and after joining the Army became a part of G Company, the fourth regiment of infantry, where he served until his discharge on March 14, 1866, at Fort Yuma, California. The Fourth Regiment of Infantry was a regiment organized at Sacramento, Placerville, and Auburn, from September 21, 1861, to February 1, 1862. Company G was organized October 26, 1861, at Camp Sigel, near Auburn, California.

The first commander was Colonel Henry M. Judah, who served until November 1861. Colonel Ferris Forman was next in line, serving until August 20, 1863. Colonel James F. Curtis commanded the Fourth Regiment next, until it was disbanded because of consolidation November 30, 1865. The Fourth Regiment headquarters were originally at Auburn, Placer County, California. Company G was stationed at Camp Sigel, near Auburn until January 1862. Company G then went to Camp Union near Sacramento, until June 1862,

Roswell Trask US Army in Ipai territory 1865. *Drawing: Robert Freeman.*

and following that were stationed at Camp Latham until September 1862. Company G's next stop was at Camp Barracks until November 1862, then at San Diego until August 1865 and at La Paz, Arizona, during the month of September 1865. September 1865 to March 1866 are not recorded for Company G, and the muster rolls and monthly returns do not give accounts or remarks for their service.

Roswell Trask was at San Diego from November 1862 to August 1865. He re-enlisted as a Veteran Volunteer March 24, 1864, at New San Diego, California, and was discharged at Fort Yuma, California, March 14, 1866, with his company. His service record follows:

1860: Roswell Trask was at Yankee Junction, at Placer, California.

1861: Roswell was CW enlisted, at Auburn, California, October 14, 1861. Private G Company; 4th Infantry Regiment; Mustered out at Fort Yuma, California (1880 note).

October 26, 1861: Company G was organized October 26, 1861 at Camp Sigel, near Auburn, California.

March 24, 1864: Roswell re-enlisted as a Veteran Volunteer at New San Diego, California.

March 14, 1866: Roswell Trask was discharged at Fort Yuma, California with his company, Private, G Company, 4TH Infantry Regiment.

Roswell Trask was living in the San Pasqual Valley when his oldest son, Frank Trask, half-Indian, was born in 1867. Two government reports — B. C. Whiting's Annual Report of 1869, covering 1867-1869, and J. B. McIntosh's August 25, 1869, letter from the Superintendent of Indian Affairs in California to the US Congress — showed Roswell living in the San Pasqual Valley (Whiting 1869 and Almstedt 1983).

By 1869 Roswell was living with a different woman, Matiana Warner in the San Pasqual Valley, when his second son, Henry Lloyd, was born on January 1, 1869. Martiana Warner (Contreras) was born in 1847 (Ancestry.com 2013) and died in 1922 at Ontario, San Bernardino, California. Matiana's father was Thomas T. Warner, born 1807 in England, and died in 1871 at Rancho La Grulla, Baja California Norte, Mexico. Henry Lloyd Trask lived until January 18, 1962 (San Diego Tribune 1962).

On January 30, 1869, Roswell's whereabouts were described in the *Sacramento Daily Union*, which reported:

> On the afternoon of January 23rd an affray occurred at Laguna Station in this county, between Roswell Trask and John King, both of whom were in the employ of George McConnihe, proprietor of the station. Trask being temporarily in charge during McConnihe's absence, and King as teamster, which resulted in Trask shooting and instantly killing King, week before last (Sacramento Daily Union 1869).

Another newspaper account, on February 2, 1869, in the *San Francisco Bulletin* stated:

> A correspondent at the *Bulletin* reports that a gentleman just in from the Fort Yuma Road claimed that several attempts had been made by a gang of villains to rob several of the stage stations on the road. At the 'Laguna' the attempted robbery was unsuccessful and the scamp was shot by Trask and killed" (San Francisco Bulletin 1869).

The Laguna Grande Station was located ten miles southeast of the Temescal Station, which was between Temecula and Murrietta.

By 1870, however, Roswell had left Matiana, his second child, Henry, and the San Pasqual Valley. The Census of 1870 for San Pasqual showed Henry living in the valley with his mother, Matiana, and his stepfather, Calvin Washburne. That census also listed Captain Jose Panto and his wife, Dolores, indicating that all of the individuals listed that year were white.

The June 16, 1870, edition of *The San Diego Union* included mention of Roswell Trask when it reported: "We have had two shooting scrapes this past week. ... [T]he second shooting involved Roswell Trask, who reportedly came upon a Chinese man who was trying to ride a bucking horse." The report placed Roswell near Julian in 1870.

Three years after they began living together, Roswell Trask married Maria Catarina McIntire, on April 6, 1873. She had been born April 7, 1857, in Poway and lived in Ramona until her death in 1938. Roswell was said to have called his wife Molly (Deposition 1884), while some called her Maria Catarina and others called her Mary Catherine.

Marriage records of San Diego County entitled, "Application and Consents of Parents for Marriage, 1868-1890" showed the following: Groom's Name: Trask, Roswell; Bride's Name: McIntyre [McIntire], Mary; Signator: Thompson, W. H.; Date of Application: March 18, 1873 (1860 Census Agua Caliente and Application and Consents of Parents for Marriage, 1868-1890).

Roswell and Maria Catarina had six children together:

1. Charlie (Carlos) L. born March 4, 1872 or 1874.
2. Rosa Ellen, born February 1876.
3. Annie or Ana Minerva (Roswell's sister's name), born May 13, 1877 or 1878.
4. Adela (Della) born November 3, 1879; her godmother was Bridget Spelman (Brawner) Browne, with whom Frank Trask lived.
5. Josephine or Josefina born February 9,1882, and died October 28, 1925. Married Clarence Alexander King born February 17,1879 CA, and died March 6, 1940, Los Angeles, CA. Clarence's father was George Valentine King, born August 18,1845, in Brooklyn, New York and died February 28, 1895 in Los Angeles, California.
6. Bertha May, last child, born May 6 or 9, 1883, who married Albert Muehlig November 29, 1905.

There may have been a child between Della and Josie, and Charlie may have died in infancy.

On October 1, 1877, two San Diego County Land Records were recorded in Roswell Trask's name and on August 2, 1881, a third was recorded (Document 548/CACAA087465). In 1879 and 1883 Bridget Browne became godmother to two more of Roswell Trask's children, daughters from his marriage to Maria Catarina—Adela and Bertha May.

The Census of 1880 showed Roswell and his family living near Frank Trask and Bridget Browne, now a widow, in Ballena [Ramona]. October 23, 1884, found Roswell and Maria Catarina (Deposition 1884) near a valley with springs and good grazing land. It was that day that Roswell was shot in the back by his wife's brother, Pancho McIntyre, who was drunk and on horseback, with the bullet going into Roswell's lungs. His family moved Roswell into their house and placed him on a mattress on the floor, where he stayed for the next two days. The family sought help from a local doctor and also sent a messenger to San Diego, trying to find a second doctor, in an attempt to save Roswell's life. When Maria Catarina moved her husband, she found the bullet in his sock.

In the deposition, Maria Catarina made mention of the fact that Roswell's son, Frank, and her younger brother, Antonio, were at the house the day that her husband was shot. She answered a query about whether she showed a trunk belonging to Pancho or Antonio to a Mr. Russell after the shooting by saying: "I don't know, the boy Frank was there and Antonio; I don't know that anybody came" (Deposition 1884 N. p.). Roswell died October 25, 1884, shortly after 1:00 p.m. The deposition held by the County of San Diego spelled out as many details as were forthcoming at the time. The timeline of events connected with the deposition and court case were as follows:

October 23, 1884: Roswell was shot in the back by Pancho McIntyre.

October 25, 1884: Roswell Trask died at home from wounds, after the bullet went through his back and lungs. Samuel Warnock and other neighbors made Roswell's casket. Tom Woods, a preacher who had just arrived in Ballena from Scotland the day before, preached the funeral. Roswell was buried under an oak tree, which is now part of the Golden Eagle Farm in Ramona.

December 24, 1884: Pancho McIntyre pled guilty to murder in the second degree.

December 29, 1884: Pancho McIntyre was taken to San Quentin State Prison to serve a 20 year sentence.

James Booth, A. O. Tucker, W. C. Littlepage, and F. R. Sawday further certify after diligent search and inquiry, I am unable to find J. L. McIntire (Taken from records in the San Diego Courthouse, April 29, 1975).

Maria Catarina's youngest brother, Anthony, was mentioned by Harrington in one of his notes: "Antonio McIntire (Shocleh mestizo) lives on the road to left — we look to Kodiva's, he lives on the hill where the charo is on other side of Mataguay" (Harrington 1913-1933:5_28).

Pancho McIntyre's infant daughter, Concepcion, had stayed with her mother, also named Concepcion, and her father at Roswell and Maria Catarina's home the night before the shooting (Deposition 1884). Sentenced in 1884, Pancho's release may have occurred about 1904. Recently discovered genealogical records show that his daughter, Concepcion, went on to marry and have children. The California Indian Rolls of 1928 showed Pancho's daughter, Concepcion McIntyre, as married to Jose Pablo Guacheno. The documents indicated that they had a daughter, Rosalie Soto, in 1899. Jose Pablo Guacheno's mother was unknown, and his father was Pedro Juan Guacheno. The 1928 affidavit showing Rosalie Soto was signed by witnesses Roscindo Couro and Javiel Subis. The records showed Rosalie Soto as #4630 and listed her children as well.

Other Ancestry.com records accessed in 2012 showed that Concepcion McIntyre and Jean Baptiste La Chappa, born 1879, had a son, Fidelio, born 1901; a son, Vidal, born 1903; a daughter, Filiberta, born 1903 or 1904; a daughter, Mary Lavina, born 1905; a son, Loriano, born 1907; and Maria Francis, born 1910. These would all be Pancho McIntyre's grandchildren and Angela Guachena's great-grandchildren. Jean Baptiste La Chappa's parents were shown as Valentino and Trinidad La Chappa. Harrington (1913-1933) showed a Juan Baptiste La Chappa at Laguna, near the Cuyamaca Mountains (Harrington 30_2): 30_2 Juan Baptiste La Chappa at Laguna, 1905.

Tom Lucas, Kwaaymii of Laguna Ranch, offered a lengthy explanation concerning a Juan Baptiste La Chappa and his brother, Captain Valentine La Chappa, during a 1975 interview with Richard Carrico at Laguna Ranch. He noted that the village at Laguna Meadows was called *Sh'quah* by the native people, meaning the mountain itself or anything that bristled with timber. He also had this to say when asked about Valentine La Chappa's tenure as captain at Laguna:

Chief Valentine was the last. After he was gone Juan Baptise—that was his brother that was left ... he declined to take it ... but he said, 'I'll help [with] what I can.' Strangely enough, after he made his comment on all that, his brother died—all of them just died off one by one—and left only a very few of his relatives. They moved over to Santa Ysabel and they merged with those people over there. ... [T]hat was the end of that. This Juan Baptiste, he lived there until 1918—he and his wife. His wife was a Nejo Indian and I had a picture showing. The Nejo comes from the San Felipe. The San Felipe like Banner Grade. There was a whole Indian tribe in there and she came from that country. She was one of the last. So, strangely enough, the two of them died 2 days apart. So that finished that off.

Jose Bastian La Chappa

Jose Bastian La Chappa was the father of Jose Antonio La Chappa. Born in 1839 at Mesa Grande, he lived until 1889. His parents were Logario and Maria Jesusa La Chappa (California Indian Rolls 1928). In addition to being mentioned by historian/photographer Edward S. Curtis (1907) as the narrator of a popular creation story, which is included in an earlier chapter, Jose Bastian[o] La Chappa, who married Angela Guachena, was found on a variety of US censuses and family trees (Ancestry.com) in San Diego County:

Devers, Jr. Family Tree (Ancestry.com 2013)

Born 1839 CA, USA 1920 residence: El Cajon

Spouse: Angelia

Child: Jose Antonio La Chappa born about 1859 [died 1929]

Eortega Family Tree (Ancestry.com 2013)

Jose Bastian La Chappa born abou 1839 CA, USA

Child: Jose Antonio La Chappa born about 1859

Lambert Briggs Family Tree (Ancestry.com 2013)

Jose Bastian La Chappa born about 1839

Spouse: Maria Angela Guachena born about 1827 [1823 or 1833] Died about 1911 [1907]

Jacome Family Tree (Ancestry.com 2013)

Jose Bastian La Chappa born about 1839 CA, USA

Child: Antonio Jose La Chappa born about 1859

Mesa Grande Indian Reservation

Spouse: Feliciana 1859-1942

Children: Ignaciana Incarnaciona 1877-1908; Sylvester 1879 [actually 1881]; Leonora 1880; [twins, born 1881]; Bruno 1882; Agnes 1894; Savalita 1898; Natalia Lopez granddaughter 1871; age 23.

The US Indian censuses of 1895 and 1896 show these same people, census numbers, names, and dates of birth, all one year older on each census.

Jose Maria A-co-pal Luchapa, Jose Agua, Joe Water, Jose Burro: A Man of Many Names

One record (Cuyamaca Village National Register Form 2013) shows Jose Maria A-co-pal Luchapa as living at Cuyamaca, in the village of Yguai, and as being captain of that group. Trask family descendants believe that there may be a blood relationship between Jose Maria Acopal Luchapa and their La Chappa, Guachena, Nejo, and other ancestors. Luchapa serves as an example of how some of the native people lived in a variety of regions in San Diego County and also took on a wide assortment of names throughout their lifetimes.

In 1912 E.H. Davis (Cuyamaca Village National Register Form 2013) interviewed Jose Maria A-co-pal Luchapa and throughout the years took a multitude of photographs identifying him by the names of Jose Maria A-co-pal Luchapa, Jose Agua, Joe Water, Joe Agua, Jose Burro, Joe Burro and Jose Burro Aguae. In one

Jose Burro, a man of many names.
Photo: E. H. Davis, San Diego History Center.

photo Luchapa aka Waters is standing at Mesa Grande in 1910 with Narciso Lachappa, also spelled Narcisco/Narcisso La Chapa/LaChapa/La Chappa. Another 1910 photo in San Diego County shows Joe Burro Waters standing with Andres Lachapa, believed to be the son of Juan Diego La Chappa, Antonio La Chappa's brother, and a group of men, while a third photo shows Luchapa/Waters standing in front of his home at Pechanga, made of mud-bricks with a shingle roof (San Diego History Center 2014).

Ethnologist John P. Harrington took note several times of Jose Maria A-co-pal Luchapa aka Joe Waters, Agua, Burro as the historian was traveling through San Diego County in the early 1900s (Harrington 1913-1933) and wrote: "Francisco Til told Angel this morning that Joe Waters, also called Jose Burro, who is at Pala and is very old ... lived at Mesa Grande years ago. Knows the places around Escondido Twin Oaks well and the battleground with D. on one side and K. on the other and also a hill that is bare on top there" (Monday, 14, 1925: Note 9_18).

Note 27_5: "... Ed Davis went with Joe Waters to top of a mountain where there was a hole in the ground. Davis found the hole. No man will go to this place."

Harrington's Note 28_2: "Joe Waters at Mesa Grande; wiikayay = grayback; the Placer mines northeast of Hodges" [this is near the San Dieguito River Valley].

Harrington (Census of Mesa Grande 1906) records Jose Waters as Census #75, husband, age 64, and his wife, Maria, as #76, age 56. Jose Waters's birth date, then, would have been about 1842 and his wife's birth date about 1850. Other censuses (Censuses of Mesa Grande for 1900, 1902, 1905, 1907 and 1908) also show Jose Waters as married to Maria Waters, born about 1850. Jose Waters appears on the Mesa Grande censuses of 1897-1899 as born in 1846 but from 1900-1908 is shown as born in 1842, and from 1910-1927, the last census in which he is listed, he is shown as born 1841. US Indian censuses (Censuses: Harrington, John P. 1906, 1907, 1908 and Ancestry.com 1900, 1902, 1905, 1907, 1908) for the early 1900s show Jose and his wife Maria as living at Mesa Grande.

On some censuses Jose Waters (Census taken by Estudillo, Francisco 1897 and Wright, L. A. 1898, 1899) appears directly above Antonio La Chappa and his wife Feliciana's brother, Jose Domingo Yanke, with each of the three men listed as husband, but no wives shown. In others (Censuses of Mesa Grande 1901, 1902) Jose Waters is shown directly below Antonio La Chappa and his wife and children. From 1911, when Jose Waters is first shown as a widower, to August 14, 1927 when Jose Waters's death is recorded, he is shown directly above Jose Domingo Yanke and his wife Lorentia (Loretta La Chusa Yanke), with censuses (Censuses of Mesa Grande) from 1912-1914 and 1922-1925, showing Felicidad Guachena Yanke, Jose Domingo's stepdaughter, in the grouping of four. In 1926 Jose Waters is directly above only Lorentia, and Jose Dominga and Felicidad are not shown.

Just as Jose Luchapa Waters was shown in several different locations (Yguai, Mesa Grande, Pechanga) and was called by many names, Jose Domingo Yanke's history from 1901-1937 reveals a similar story, with a multitude of names recorded.

Earlier censuses (Censuses of Mesa Grande 1893, 1894) show a Jose La Chappa, ages 50 and 51, as nephew to Angela Guachena La Chappa, Leonora La Chappa Trask's paternal grandmother. Angela's nephew's birthdate is calculated to 1843, and Angela's third husband was also Jose La Chappa, and her son, Leonora's father, was Jose Antonio La Chappa.

Jose Maria Acopal Luchapa aka Waters's wife, Maria, is a person of interest because in 1909 the Special Allotting Agent offered a Maria Antonia Waters the first Indian allotment at the San Pasqual Reservation in Valley Center.

Another document, undated, was signed by C.F. Hauke, the second assistant commissioner of Indian Affairs and read: "Maria Antonia Waters was not at Warner's when land was removed to Pala. Has rights at San Pasqual Reservation, and Superintendent Frank offered her very desirable land there which she refused. Facts were submitted to Office for decision." Following Maria Antonia Waters's refusal to accept the lands offered to her in Valley Center, Amos R. Frank, superintendent of the Indian School and special disbursing agent Mesa Grande, heeded the directions of California Indian agent Charles E. Kelsey to resettle one of the San Pasqual families at Mesa Grande to the reserve in Valley Center, and gave the first San Pasqual Indian allotment to the Frank Trask family in December 1909.

Years of births play an integral part in research, and on one census (Census of 1902 Mesa Grande) Jose Waters is shown directly below the Antonio La Chappa family, and is followed by his wife, Maria Waters, born 1850. Listed next is a Jose La Santo Waters, born 1865, and a Maria Antonia Waters, born 1860. A Jose Santos Waters appears from 1905-1909 (Censuses of Pala, Agua Caliente, and San Felipe) as born about 1862, with his wife, Maria Antonia Waters, born from 1847-1865, leading to the question of whether there were two sets of Jose and Maria Waters or only one. In 1908 Census (Census of Pala, Agua Caliente, and San Felipe), Jose Santos Waters is shown as born about 1848 and his wife is shown as born about 1849. Maria's two grandsons, Ervano Wainwright, born 1898, and Aparicio Wachenio, born 1891, are also listed in 1908.

In connection with the search to learn if there was only one Jose Waters and one Maria Waters, three censuses (Harrington, John P. Census of Pala, Agua Caliente, San Felipe 1905, 1907, 1908) showed the Mesa Grande native people as counted by the Pala Agency, listing those at Mesa Grande and Santa Ysabel as part of the Pala, Agua Caliente and San Felipe Mission Tribes. US Indian censuses (US Indian censuses of Mesa Grande 1905, 1906, 1911) also showed them at Mesa Grande and counted by the Pala Agency. Amos R. Frank (Census of Mesa Grande 1911) showed their tribe as Santa Ysabel Nos. 1 & 2 Mesa Grande Reserve, under the jurisdiction of the Mesa Grande School Agency. By 1914 and 1915 (US Indian censuses of Mesa Grande 1914-1915) the Mesa Grande tribe was shown to be under the jurisdiction of the Soboba Agency. From 1922-1926 (US Indian censuses of 1922-1926) the Mesa Grande tribe was identified as part of the Mission Indian Agency of the state of California.

Jose Domingo Yanke

Jose Domingo Yanke was Feliciana Nejo La Chappa's half brother, as previously mentioned. As #2841 on the 1928 California Indian Rolls, he was shown as born in San Felipe, and was age 72 in October 1929, living at the Mesa Grande Indian Reservation. His son was shown as Juan Antonio Yanke (Woods), born 1886 in Julian, age 42 in 1928, and identified as ¾ Indian, living at the Santa Ysabel Indian Reservation. Signing Jose Domingo Yanke's 1928 Indian application were Maria Angela Guachena's daughter, Petra La Chappa Cota, and Mauricia Campagnoli, second wife of Nelda Campagnoli Taylor's father, Frank Campagnoli.

Some Trask family descendants believe that Jose Domingo Yanke's real name may have been Yaqui, since his maternal grandfather, Jermain Anej, was born at Yaqui Well. Sam Ward, Cahuilla, said that the Cahuilla native people often went to Yaqui Well to get relief from the heat (Personal Communication 2014), and Trask family descendants speculate that perhaps they have other lineal ancestors from that region, in addition to Jermain Anej. Jose Domingo's maternal great-grandfather, Jose La Luz, may provide further evidence, since one of Harrington's notes shows a son of a Jose La Luz's wife at a place called "qawit" with a Juan Yaqui (Harrington 1913-1933:12_8). Trask family descendants continue to search for more clues, though they already have a wealth of information about Jose Domingo Yanke and the many names representing him in San Diego County records.

Genealogical and public records (Ancestry.com and Censuses of San Diego County) illustrate the many renderings of names among native people during the early years of record keeping in San Diego County. Jose Domingo Yanke and his two wives serve as prime examples of how differing government records reflected differing spellings of names and dates of occurrences. Jose Domingo's first wife, Carlotta, who died, appeared once as a 4/4 Indian from Soboba. Listings for 1901-1937 provide clear evidence that Jose Domingo, his second wife, Loretta, and her daughter Felicidad lived on the Mesa Grande Indian Reservation during those years. Jose Domingo is shown as follows on the censuses: 1901 Jose Domingo Yank, born 1857; 1902 Jose Domingo Yank, 1857; 1905 Jose Domingo Yank, 1857, wife Loentia; 1906 Jose Domingo Yank, 1857; 1907 Jose Domingo Yank, 1857; 1908 Jose Domingo Yank, 1857; 1910 Jose Domingo Yanco [Jose Domingo Yanes] [Jose Doming Yanes], age 55; wife Rorencia Yanco, age 45; stepdaughter, Felicidad Guachene, age 17; 1912 Indian Census, Jose Domingo Yanko, 1855; 1913 Indian Census, Jose Domingo Yanko, 1855; 1914 Jose Domingo Yanke, 1855; 1915 Jose Domingo Yanke, 1855; 1917 Jose Domingo Yanke, 1855; 1918 Jose Domingo Yanke, 1855; 1919 Jose Domingo Yanke, 1855; 1920 U. S. Federal Census: 1860; residence Ramona in 1920; 1921 Jos D. Yanko; 1922 Jos D. Yanko. 1855; 1923 Jos D. Yanko, 1855; 1924 Jose Domingo Yanke, 1855; 1925 Jose Domingo Yanks, 1855; 1926 Jose Domingo Yanke, 1855; Indian Census: Jose Domingo Yanks, 1855; 1927 Jose Domingo Yanke, 1855; 1928 Jose Domingo Yanks, 1855 (Voter Registration); 1929 Jose Domingo Yanke, 1855; 1930 Jose Dom Yanke, 1855; 1931 Jose Dom Yanke, 1855; 1932 Jose Dom Yanke, 1855; 1933 Jose Dom Yanke, 1855 (U. S. Indian Censuses & San Diego City Directory); 1934 widowed; 1936 Jose Domingo Yanke, 1855, widowed; 1937 Domingo Jose Yanke, 1856 (San Diego Directory says Jose D. Yanke).

He is listed variously as Jose Domingo Yanke; Jose Domingo Yank; Jose Domingo Yanks; Jos D. Yanko; Jose Domingo Yanco; Jose D. Yoncho; Jose D. Yencho; Jose Dom Yanke; Domingo Jose Yanke; Jose Domingo Yanes; Jose Doming Yanes, and his place of residence is always Mesa Grande or Ramona.

Jose Domingo's second wife, Loretta La Chusa Yanke, was #2489 on the same 1928 rolls, born in 1861 at Mesa Grande, and 4/4 Indian. She had a twin, Juan La Chusa. Her father was Ramon LaChusa, 4/4 Mesa Grande (To-co-mac), who died in 1916. Her mother was Maria Jesusa Quilp, 4/4 Mesa Grande (To-co-mac), who died in 1894. Ramon LaChusa's father was Jacinto LaChusa and his mother was Loviga LaChusa, both 4/4 Mesa Grande.

Maria Jesusa Quilp's father was Ses-jua-lo and her mother was Maria Juana. Loretta La Chusa Yanke's first husband was Santiago Guachene, born 1859 in the San Pasqual Valley. She had a daughter, Felicidad, born about 1895, with Santiago. The 1910 Census showed Loretta as Rorencia, born 1865, age 45. In 1912 she is shown as born about 1866. In 1915 she was Lorentia Yanke, and in 1926 she was shown as Loretta Ycheno Yanke [Guachene], born 1886, age 40, Mesa Grande, and her daughter was listed as Felicidad Yanks, born 1893. In 1927 she was Loretta Ycheno Yanke, age 41, Mesa Grande.

According to Harrington (Harrington 1913-1933 and Harrington with Ysidro Nejo 1925) Loretta's twin, Juan, born 1861, married Dolores Renteriz #2491, born 1867 at Mesa Grande, who had five husbands: Jose Antonio La Chappa [not Leonora La Chappa's father] born 1847, 4/4 Mesa Grande; Jose Cuevas, born 1857, 4/4 Matajual; Salvador Duro, born 1842, 4/4 Can-ma-hal (Mesa Grande); Aristirez Stokes, born 1859, white, had son, David, with Dolores, born 1895, ½ Indian ½ white; Juan La Chusa, Loretta's twin, born 1861, 4/4 Mesa Grande. Dolores's maternal grandfather was Miguel Quisquis, 4/4 San Pasqual. No other ancestors were shown on the 1928 California Indian Rolls. Affidavit witnesses: Roscindo Couro, acquainted with Dolores 45 years; Jose Domingo Yanke, acquainted with Dolores 40 years.

Jose Antonio La Chappa

Leonora La Chappa's father, Jose Antonio La Chappa, was born at Mesa Grande in 1859. Genealogical histories for (Jose) Antonio's La Chappa, Guachena and other ancestors have been documented nearly as far back as the time of the arrival of the Spanish. Antonio's maternal grandfather Cornelio Wachena and his paternal grandparents, Logario and Maria Jesusa La Chappa, are believed to have been born in the early 1800s or before, since Antonio's mother, Angela Guachena, was born in either 1819 (Census of Mesa Grande 1890), 1823 or 1833 (Census of at Mesa Grande 1894).

Harrington mentioned Antonio La Chappa as the ethnographer traversed Ipai territory in the early 1900s: "Antonio La Chapa lives in the first house south of the American schoolhouse [in Mesa Grande], to the right of the road. He is a good informant" (Harrington 1925:4_2). Ethnographer E. W. Gifford (1919-1920) noted that Antonio La Chappa and his family lived in House #11 at Mesa Grande, and that his wife, Feliciana Nejo La Chappa, was cousin sister to informant Ysidro Nejo, at one time Captain Panto's First Assistant (Shipek 1994).

Native leaders Captain Antonio La Chappa and General Cinon Duro, the last hereditary leader of the Mesa Grande Band (whose Creation Story can be found in chapter one) attended the 1892 Celebration of the 350th anniversary of the arrival to San Diego by Cabrillo (Smythe 1908). The leaders brought some of their people to the celebration, to showcase their clothing and lifestyle for those in attendance. A newspaper reporter covering the event noted:

> One of the most interesting features was the presence of a number of Luiseño
> and Diegueño Indians, both men and women, garbed and decorated in a manner
> which was practically historically correct. These people came from their homes ...
> at the personal request of Father Ubach, and were by him drilled for their part in the
> ceremonies. ... [T]he Luiseños were under the command of Chief Jose Pachito and

Jose Antonio La Chappa tends a
barbecue at Mesa Grande before 1929.
Photo: E. H. Davis,
San Diego History Center.

General Pedro Pablo, and the Diegueños under Chief La Chappa and General Cenon
Duro. The latter was the last Chief of the Mesa Grande Indians, and died in October
1906 (Smythe 1908:458).

An assortment of government letters mention Antonio as captain, including a letter
of November 18, 1908, where he was issuing a complaint against a policeman at Mesa
Grande [not his son Sylvester]. A December 2, 1908, letter from Mary Watkins narrates
how Antonio prevented the same policeman from having a fiesta with alcohol, and, for
brevity, the closing of a February 15, 1909, letter from Antonio will serve to show his position as captain at Mesa Grande: "... So here I'll close. Hoping to hear soon again from you.
Respectfully, Captain Antonio La Chappa."

Along with serving as captain of the band at Mesa Grande, Antonio La Chappa also
served as an Indian judge there at the same time as Ysidro Nejo (Records of Regular Court
of Indian Offenses 1912) and Rosindo Couro (Frank 1912). Amos Frank, who had been
instrumental in identifying San Pasqual people at Mesa Grande in his efforts to allot the
new San Pasqual Indian Reservation lands in Valley Center, was retiring from his position
as superintendent of the Indian School and special disbursing agent at Mesa Grande when
he wrote a letter on August 8, 1912, representing the Department of the Interior, United

States Indian Service, from Grand Portage, Minnesota, to Thomas M. Games, superintendent of the Volcan Agency, at Santa Ysabel stating:

> Dear Mr. Games:
>
> The appointments of Antonio La Chappa and Rosindo Couro as Judges of Indian Court of Offenses have been approved or else no payment would have been made. I have just received information from Auditor for Interior Department that my business for Mesa Grande, California has been closed and found correct.

During that same time, Antonio's son, Sylvester (Leonora's twin brother), was serving as chief of police at Mesa Grande and Antonio's son-in-law, Frank Trask, was serving as judge and police private at the San Pasqual Indian Reservation in Valley Center.

On August 10, 1912, Thomas M. Games responded to a telegram he had received from the US Commissioner of Indian Affairs, and negated allegations from humanitarian and author Constance DuBois concerning eight "destitute" Indians under his jurisdiction. He mentioned Antonio La Chappa's position at Mesa Grande as judge in his response:

> The above named [destitute] Indians are all personally known to me, and in addition to my own knowledge of them I talked regarding them with the following named Mesa Grande Indians from whom I obtained the above information — which is borne out by the records of this office: Antonio La Chappa, Judge; Ysidro Nejo, Judge; Fiesta Committee — Rosendo Couro, Julio Ortega, Leandro Soto; Sylvester La Chappa, Chief of Police.

Jose Antonio La Chappa lived at Mesa Grande until his death on July 2, 1929 (Death Certificate of San Diego County 1929), while his wife, Feliciana Nejo La Chappa, lived until 1942.

Feliciana Nejo

Leonora La Chappa's mother, Feliciana Nejo La Chappa, was born in 1859 in the region of Santa Ysabel and lived until 1942. She was alive for thirty-three of the forty-four years that Leonora lived with her children and grandchildren on the San Pasqual Indian Reservation in Valley Center. Feliciana Nejo's mother was Maria Jesusa Nejo, born in 1840 at Santa Ysabel. Maria Jesusa Nejo's father was Jermain Anej of Yaqui Well, whose birthdate is unknown, but he lived until 1888. Maria Jesusa's mother was Maria Louisa Guacheno, born at Santa Ysabel in either 1816 or 1826 (Ancestry.com 2012). Maria Louisa Guacheno's father was Jose La Luz and her mother was shown by her Ipai name of Mi-Hap (California Indian Rolls 1928).

Gifford noted that Feliciana Nejo La Chappa was the mother of Blun Nejo, son of Calistro Nejo and grandson of Jose and Josefa Nejo. Jose Nejo was identified as captain at Mesa Grande, but was shown at the time of Gifford's notations as living at Pala. Blun's paternal grandmother, Josefa, was shown to be the daughter of Yecmai La Chappa, with Yecmai meaning "looking for a heart," and La Chappa meaning "short." Gifford identified the name Nejo as being a Diegueño name from before Spanish times, with Nex being the correct Diegueño rendering of Nejo. Nejo meant handing something (a gift) to someone (Gifford 1919-1920:5-17). In addition, Gifford noted (House 7), that the name Watcheno [Guacheno] was the same as KwiLp [Quilp], meaning something swinging back and forth.

Gifford also pointed out: "At House #11 at Mesa Grande … Blun Nejo, Feliciana's son by Calistro Nejo … Calistro was son of Kwitutc (Jose Nejo) now of Pala. Leonora Letcapa, daughter of Jose Antonio and Feliciana, twin sister of Sylvester Letcapa (house #10). Jose Antonio [La Chappa] was born at Atarap, just below Mesa Grande store" (Gifford 1919-1920: House #11 and Note 5-17).

When the authors of *Blood of the Band* discovered that on the 1860 Census of San Pasqual there was a Maria de Jesus living in the household of Captain Panto, called by some Panto La Chappa (Peet 1973 and Ryan 1980), they expanded their searches to learn if this was their Maria Jesusa, who gave birth to her first child, Jose Domingo Yanke, in 1857 and her daughter Feliciana in 1859.

Aware that the Jacome Family Tree on Ancestry.com had noted that Feliciana, her mother, brother, and mother-in-law, Angela Guachena, were born in the San Pasqual Valley (though family members have always believed that Feliciana, her mother and brother were born in the Santa Ysabel area, and that Angela Guachena was born in the Mesa Grande region), authors of this book have continued to research historical records to see if they can learn more about the true relationship of those listed on the 1860 Census. That census listed the members of Panto's household, in addition to himself, as Maria, age 50, Juan, 30, and Maria de Jesus, 28. Historian Glenn Farris said of the three persons who are listed in addition to Panto that, "Whether these latter three are actually related to Panto is uncertain" (Farris 1997:149-161). Since at the time of the 1878 eviction from the San Pasqual Valley, many Ipai had gone to live with relatives at Mesa Grande, Trask family descendants continue to explore possible connections of Maria Jesusa and other family members with Panto [La Chappa], who was captain of both the San Pasqual and Mesa Grande regions.

Ysidro Nejo, relative of Feliciana Nejo La Chappa. *Photo: E. H. Davis, San Diego History Center.*

Harrington noted in his diaries as he traveled through the San Pasqual Valley that: "The Indians were run out of San Pasqual. .... But Ysidro Nejo went to Mesa Grande" (Harrington 1925:24_16). Feliciana Nejo La Chappa was said to be cousin sister (first cousin) to Ysidro Nejo (Gifford 1919-1920).

Jefferson Davis Swycaffer

Sometime after October 25, 1884 Maria Catarina McIntire Trask married Jefferson Davis Swycaffer of Ballena. J.D. Swycaffer (Lepper, Ruth 2005) was born in 1861 in Old Town San Diego, and had been the third reported birth in San Diego County, and the first white child to be born in Old Town. Together he and Mary Catherine raised five children: Claud, Alonzo, Loyd, Jesse, and Mamie.

The 1900 Census showed Mary Catherine Swycaffer, age 45 years old, and Jefferson D. Swycaffer, 40 years old. The 1910 Census showed Mary Catherine Swycaffer, age 50 (born 1856 or 1857); Jefferson D. Swycaffer, age 48; Della

Jefferson Davis Swycaffer.
Photo: E. H. Davis, San Diego History Center.

Trask, 29; Claude R. Swycaffer, 19; Mary L. Swycaffer, 17; Jessie R. Swycaffer, 16; Alonzo Swycaffer, 14; LLoyd B. Swycaffer, 9, and James Owens 65. The Swycaffer household was obviously a blended one, since Della was Mary Catherine's child from Roswell Trask, the other children belonged to Mary Catherine and J.D. Swycaffer, and the relationship of James Owens was unknown.

Jefferson Davis Swycaffer's family had a long history of military and public service (Beck 2004). J.D.'s great-grandfather, Anthony Swycaffer, had served in the Revolutionary War; his grandfather, John B. Swycaffer, had served in the War of 1812; his father, Joseph Swycaffer, who was born in 1820 and lived until 1908, had enlisted in the Army during the Mexican-American War, and while in the service of the United States, sailed around the Horn, arriving in San Francisco August 19, 1850. Eighty-six of those onboard, almost half the crew, died of sickness and scurvy, but Joseph survived to go on to San Diego, where he fulfilled his military obligations until he was released in 1853. He first saw Ballena Valley, between Santa Ysabel and Ramona, in 1851 while engaged in service at Warner Springs and still stationed with the Army in San Diego.

After his enlistment date was up, he and Samuel Warnock, another formerly enlisted man, contracted with the government to operate the military mail. From 1855 to 1857 Joseph Swycaffer was a US government Express Rider, and rode a mule between San Diego and Yuma, a one-month trip. The San Diego Guards formed in 1856 and Joseph served as a fourth sergeant, with the group disbanding during the Civil War in 1861. He homesteaded 160 acres at Ballena, and married Martha Ward, who had been born in Texas, in 1857. Swycaffer's cattle ranching operations were so extensive that he grazed his herds from the mountains to the coast in San Diego County. From 1868-1869 he was a San Diego public administrator and was also appointed prairie judge. He served as Chief deputy sheriff in San Diego County and was elected to the County Board of Supervisors for three terms.

Jefferson Davis Swycaffer was one of Joseph and Martha's twelve children, and he preferred to be called J.D. Joseph, Martha, and their children homesteaded 160 acres in Ballena, between Ramona and Santa Ysabel, in 1851, running a cattle ranch there. Joseph Swycaffer also served as chief deputy sheriff in San Diego County and served on the San Diego County Board of Supervisors. J.D. Swycaffer worked on his family's ranch as he was growing up, and during the 1870s, with drought conditions prevailing in San Diego County, he drove most of the cattle to Yuma, Arizona, and sold them there. He stayed in Arizona for several years, operating a freight line between Yuma and Tucson. After he returned to Ballena, his father moved from Ballena to La Jolla, where the elder Swycaffer died in 1908 at age 88.

J.D. married Mary McIntire Trask, widow of Roswell Trask, who already had six children (Census of 1880 Ballena Township), including Charlie (Carlos), Rosa Ellen, Ana Minerva, Adela, Josephine, and Bertha May, and the couple then had five children together, including Mamie, Jessie, Claude, Lloyd, and Alonzo. The family eventually moved to Julian, and J.D. was reportedly a busy man in the early days of that town. He was a cattle rancher; owned the Washington Hotel in Julian and the Stonewall Hotel in Cuyamaca; drove a mail stage from Julian to Foster, which was near Lakeside; mined for copper, and ran a butcher shop. Joe Swycaffer, son of J.D.'s son, Alonzo, reportedly ran a saloon and a restaurant in Julian, and helped operate riding stables at Cuyamaca and Warner Springs. In 1912 J.D. and Mary Catherine and their children moved back to Ballena to the ranch, where he continued to raise cattle. Family members pursued ranching throughout the years, with Claude engaging in horse racing and Alonzo and Loyd riding and roping, showcasing their skills in several Hollywood B-rated movies.

Petra La Chappa Cota. *Photo: E. H. Davis, San Diego History Center*

Jefferson Davis Swycaffer died in the early 1950s. Mary Catherine had died March 6, 1938 (Death Records of San Diego County: Ancestry.com). He was interviewed for an article in the *San Diego*

Union in 1951, shortly before his 90th birthday. When asked if he continued to work cattle, J.D, said: "I still get into the saddle a little, but in my day I never played second fiddle to any cowhand when it came to ropin' or brandin' a steer. I never saw the steer I couldn't rope or the horse I couldn't gentle" (Lepper, Ruth 2005).

Petra La Chappa Cota

Three 1936 newspaper articles from the San Diego Historical Society showed the same photograph of E.H. Davis and Petra La Chappa Cota, daughter of Angela Guachena and Jose Bastian La Chappa, and reported upon Petra's death that year, with the notation that Davis had called Petra the "High Priestess" of Mesa Grande, for her work there with her native people. The photographer that day commented that most of the native people at Mesa Grande objected to being photographed, wary that part of their spirit might be captured by the camera. After Davis urged Petra to pose with him in front of the camera, however, she agreed. The caption also noted that Petra had preached happiness, and that her fellow native people were mourning her death.

Petra was laid to rest near the Mesa Grande Chapel, where each Sunday she had taught others lessons from the Bible. Petra had taken over for her mother, Angela Guachena La Chappa, as spiritual advisor for their people at the time of Angela's death in 1907. Davis believed that Angela had been raised at the old Mission de Alcala as a child. The Rev. Dennis Barry, of El Cajon, officiated at Petra's funeral service, in the same chapel where she had taught for many years. Petra La Chappa Cota was buried in the Campo Santo Cemetery next to the grave of her husband, Juan Maria Cota, and not far from the home in which she had lived for seventy years. Indians and white friends from every part of San Diego County attended the simple rites.

Davis offered his opinion that her self-sacrificing spirit had resulted in her death, since he believed that her tending to her ill sister-in-law, Feliciana Nejo La Chappa, had resulted in her death, due to exhaustion, her age, her delicate health, and her frail body.

Petra, sister of Antonio La Chappa, was born sometime between 1864-1866. Not only did she marry Juan Maria Cota, who was born December 23, 1866 (Ancestry.com 2012) but they took in and raised three of his nieces after his sister died. Petra La Chappa was #2476 on the California Indian Rolls of 1928. She was shown as born in 1865 or 1866, was 4/4 Mesa Grande, and was shown to be age 63 in 1928 at the time of her California Indian Roll Application. In 1929 Petra worked as a housekeeper (Census of Mesa Grande 1929). One of the witnesses to Petra's affidavit on the 1928 Indian application was Jose Domingo Yanke, brother of her sister-in-law, Feliciana Nejo La Chappa, and the other was Mauricia Campagnoli, second wife of Frank Campagnoli, father of Nelda Campagnoli Taylor and her two sisters, the three little girls that Nelda and Juan Maria took into their home.

Nelda Campagnoli, born in 1912, and two of her three sisters, Zelma and Hazel, grew up with their Cota, La Chappa, and Trask relatives in Mesa Grande, following the death of Nelda's mother. In 1928 Nelda met Banning Taylor at a Mesa Grande fiesta when she was 16, and shortly after meeting, the couple traveled to Escondido in a buckboard and married. As was the custom, the bride later lived at her husband's home at the Los Coyotes Indian Reservation, where Banning Taylor served fifty-three years as Tribal Chairman. Debbie Moretti, one of Nelda and Banning's granddaughters (and seventh great grand-daughter of Antonio Garra), has been researching her family's ancestry to learn more about their famous ancestor and other family members. Conversations with Nelda at age 101 revealed that Nelda's blood ancestry traced back to Angela Guachena (Chivo, McIntire, La Chappa) through the Guachena/Chivo line.

Nelda's genealogy traces back to Angela Guachena Chivo's daughter with Jose Chivo, Teresa Chivo, who was born in 1850 in Julian and died October 16, 1888. Teresa and Luis Lopez had their daughter, Maria Concepcion Lopez, who married Maria Concepcion Lopez, born 1870, married Francisco Cota in 1886 and had a first child, Feliciana Cota, who was born in 1894 and died in 1896 of Gastroenteritis (Ancestry.com 2012). Later Maria Concepcion Lopez married Frank Trask's half brother, Henry. Two other of Concepcion and Francisco's children, Sarah and Juan Maria Cota, help provide important clues as to how the network of marriages and raising children occurred within the Ipai clans of San Diego County. Sarah married a man of Italian descent, Frank Campagnoli, and had four daughters and one son in five years, with the son dying shortly after birth and Sarah dying of tuberculosis shortly after that.

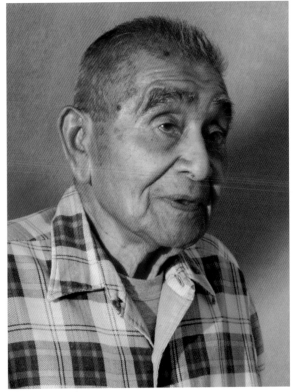

As noted, Juan Maria Cota married Petra La Chappa—the daughter of Maria Angela Guachena and her third husband, Jose La Chappa—and after the death of his sister Sarah's baby boy, and of Sarah herself, he and Petra adoped three of the four remaining daughters. Nelda Campagnoli Taylor was 100 years old when she provided this information in 2013.

Sam Ward, a Desert *Cahuilla-Luseño from the Torres Martinez reservation.*

Juan Diego La Chappa

Angela Guachena La Chappa and Jose Bastian La Chappa had a second son, in addition to Jose Antonio La Chappa—Juan Diego La Chappa, born about 1865 at Mesa Grande. The 1913 Mesa Grande Census showed him as #113, birthdate 1866, living until 1922. Juan Diego married Dolores Pico, born 1865, who died in 1918. They had a son, Andres, shown on the Devers, Jr., Family Tree (Ancestry.com), as born about 1891 in Santa Ysabel. The 1913 Mesa Grande Census, however, shows an Andreas S., son, born 1889, #117. The 1906 Mesa Grande Census shows that Juan Diego and Dolores had a second son, Jose La Chappa, born February 3, 1901. The 1906 Census showed the four family members, Juan Diego, Dolores, Andres, and Jose as ages 41, 41, 15 and 5. Dolores Pico's father was Tomas Pico and her mother was Florencia Pico.

Frank Trask

Frank Trask was born in 1867 while his father, Roswell Trask, was living in the San Pasqual Valley. Government records show Frank as half Indian, and Trask family descendants believe that his mother was San Pasqual Ipai, but that she may have died during his infancy, since by 1870 he was living with an Irish former schoolteacher, Bridget Browne, in the Warner's district (Census 1870). Bridget Browne was shown as born in Ireland in 1830 and age 40 at the time of the census. Her husband, Peter Browne, age 50, was born in Tennessee in 1820, and Charles Thompson was also listed, age 6. The group was living at Dwelling 78, Family 79, and nearby was Mrs. Sarah Warner, godmother to Frank's half brother Carlos, son of Roswell and Maria Catarina. In the same community were Mary Ann Dyer, godmother to two of Roswell and Maria Catarina's daughters, Ana Minerva and Josefina. Also living at Warner's in 1870 was Joseph Swycaffer, who later married Maria Catarina after Roswell Trask died.

The 1880 Census showed Frank at Ballena (Ramona), still living with Bridget Browne as a boarder, at Dwelling 19, with Frank's mother shown as born in California and his father born in Ohio. Throughout the years Frank and Bridget would routinely live near Roswell and his third wife, Maria Catarina Trask (Census 1880), daughter of Angela Guachena and John McIntire. On October 23, 1884 Frank Trask was 17 years old (Census of Ballena 1884) and was still living with Bridget Browne, now a widow. That day would offer profound changes for Frank Trask, since it would be the day that his father died.

By August 14, 1889, Frank was in the San Pasqual Valley, marrying Lucrezia Rios of El Cajon. All his witnesses were residents of the San Pasqual Valley. Mr. Henry (W. H.) Thompson (the same person who had served as witness at Roswell and Maria Catarina Trask's Application for Marriage in 1873), Perferio Osuna, and Henry Trask's half sister, Carrie (Carolina) Washburne, served as witnesses (Marriage Certificate 1889). Frank's marriage eventually dissolved, and sometime around 1902 he married Leonora La Chappa. Their two daughters, Florence and Helen, were born in 1904 and 1905. On July 8, 1909, a letter from Amos R. Frank, superintendent of the Indian School and special

Frank Trask. *Photo: Trask-La Chappa family.*

disbursing agent to Mesa Grande, to the commissioner of Indian Affairs read: "Through the cooperation of our Mesa Grande Indian Judges we have found 64 San Pasqual Indians. ... I have asked that authority be given to establish an Indian Court to further cooperate with me in my investigation. Mr. Kelsey and other agents made quite an effort to obtain data."

Frank Trask would be appointed as a judge February 1, 1910, for the San Pasqual Indian Reservation, and as a police private there the same year (Pierce 1910). Thorne (2012) pointed out that native Ipai served as judges and mayors for their villages during the time of the missions, and that the Franciscan friars relied upon them as translators, intermediaries and disciplinarians. Haas (1947) noted that at the time of the Indian Reorganization Act (1934) that Indian judges were conscientious and able in dispensing justice. ... Low wages ($84 per year in the case of Frank Trask in 1910) were often slow in coming and their training in law and legal procedures was often slight.

On February 28, 1910, Frank Trask used Department of Interior stationery and wrote to Superintendent Amos Frank as follows: "Called on Water Co. Directors. ... I showed them your letter. If you come down here bring the res. law book with you" (Shipek MS). Frank Trask died of the Spanish influenza on January 31, 1920.

Ignaciana Incarnacion La Chappa

Genealogical discoveries in 2013 (Gifford 1919-1920 and Ancestry.com) revealed that Jose Antonio La Chappa and Feliciana Nejo La Chappa had at least two daughters, Leonora La Chappa Trask and Ignaciana Incarnacion La Chappa, Leonora's younger sister. Another Ancestry Family Tree (Jacome 2013) listed a third daughter, Savalita, born 1898.

The Devers (Devers Family Tree on Ancestry.com) showed Leonora's older sister as born 1877 at the Mesa Grande Indian Reservation and dying in 1908 at the age of 31. Their mother, Feliciana, lived until 1942 and their father, Antonio lived until 1929. Gifford mentioned Encarnacion Letcapa, born at Takumak and living at Mesa Grande: "Trincolino Moro, brother of Domingo Moro of Pala, from Warner's Hot Springs (Kupa); daughters; 3 sons; all children at Sherman School and in Pala. Wife is dead. Encarnacion Letcapa, born at Takumak. (There are no Indians living now at Mesa Chiquita, Kama'xas. All are at Mesa Grande Reservation)" (Gifford, 1919-1920: House #8).

Incarnacion (Gifford 1919-1920) lived in the home of Trincolino Moro and was shown (Ancestry.com Devers Jr. Family Tree 2013) as married to Tranquelino Simivuat, born 1848 and died 1949. The couple's children were shown as Sarah Moro, 1895-1958 who married Claude Devers 1895-1964. Sarah and Claude's children included Claude, Jr. 1922-1983 at Pauma; Robert 1923-1961; Leatrice Juanita 1927-1995; Vivian N. 1929-1999 at Pala. Juanita Moro, 1898-1955, married Andrew Calestro Majel 1891-1937 and their children included Ruby 1921-1975; Lorena 1922-2011 who married Gene Edwin Dixon 1927-2010 at Pauma; Andrew Jr. 1924-1955, and Leland 1929-1970 who married Narcissus Ann Magee 1935-1970; her father was Fred Magee 1912-1992. Their children Patricio Moro, 1899-1982; Gavino Moro, born 1908, and Oceano Moro, born 1905 show little other information.

Leonora La Chappa Trask

Leonora was born in 1881 in the San Felipe Valley (Toler 2011), twelve miles south of Warner Springs in San Diego County. Harrington (Note 5 1913-1933) said the Diegueño name for the San Felipe Valley was *Mickwatnak*.

Leonora was one of the many California Indians who went from her isolated home in the backcountry of southern California to the Phoenix Indian School in Arizona (Games, Thomas 1902), providing many opportunities which she may not have been afforded otherwise. Leonora attended the school as a live-in student from 1900-1902, and her final report pointed out her "Sobriety, morality and industry," and indicated that she adapted well to the school's regimen. Thomas Games submitted the following progress report about Leonora La Chappa:

Phoenix Indian School

RECORD OF PUPIL AFTER LEAVING SCHOOL
[This data shows Leonora born in 1884, but she was born in 1881; her father is shown as Domingo La Chappa, but that is Leonora's uncle, brother to her father, Jose Antonio La Chappa.]

Name Leonora La Chappa Phoenix Indian School

Age at time of leaving school 18 Grade

Total Number of Years in school and where, giving number of years at each school: Phoenix: *September 1900 – September 1902*

Tribe Mission Degree of Indian **Blood** Full

Present Address Valley Center **State** California **County** San Diego

Land owned 30 acres possibly more

Allotment 30 acres possibly more

Inheritance None

Purchase None

How improved? Give description of house and number of rooms; tell how furnished and cared for; general statement regarding home life: *Frame; 4 rooms; very good; Home*

life all that could be desired—seems contented and happy with her husband and two pretty, bright little girls.

Description and value of personal property Good—horses, cattle and vehicle—farming and garden vehicles.

How much land is being cultivated? By owner: *30 acres*; By others: none

Approximate annual income from land cared for by owner *$600*

Annual Income from rentals None

If not engaged in agricultural pursuits, what is present business, and what is approximate annual income therefrom? None

Standing in the community Good

Give definite, specific reasons for grading *Sobriety, morality and industry.*

What special line or lines of training received while at school have apparently been of the most practical value? Don't Know

[Submitted by] Thomas M. Games

Sylvester La Chappa

Sylvester La Chappa was the twin brother of Leonora La Chappa Trask, born in 1881 in the San Felipe Valley. Sylvester's oldest son, Pete La Chappa (Pedro on Census of 1913), has been shown to have the same name as the Pedro La Chappa who aided the American soldiers after the Battle of San Pasqual. Pete's mother, Sylvester's first wife, was named Modesta, and was 4/4 from the La Jolla Indian Reservation (Census of San Diego County 1910). Sylvester's son, Pete, is shown on the censuses of Mesa Grande for 1910, 1911, 1912, 1913, 1920 and 1929 as born in 1910 and living at Mesa Grande, while the 1913 Census listed him as Pedro La Chapa, born June 29, 1910, and living with his mother, Modesta, at the La Jolla Indian Reservation. The 1913 Census for Mesa Grande showed Sylvester as a widower, listed with his son Pete and a second son, Pablo Domingo La Chappa, born 1912, along with other family members. Family history records that Pete lived with Sylvester's mother and father, Feliciana and Antonio La Chappa during some of his growing-up years, as was so common in native communities.

Sylvester was noted by E. W. Gifford in the early1900s, as the historian detailed individuals and families who were living at Mesa Grande and the San Felipe Valley, along with mentioning their interpersonal relationships. In House #10 at Mesa Grande was Sylvester La Chappa (shown as Silvacio Letcapa) (Gifford 1919-1920). Charliloit (in actuality this name refers to Charley Loyd) Letcapa was shown as Sylvester's wife, along with the information that her father was a Mexican and her mother Diegueño. Gifford recorded that three or four sons and no daughters lived there as well. In reality, Charliloit (Charley Loyd) was the father of Sylvester's second wife, Flora Lloyd, born in the San Pasqual Valley in 1895 (US Indian Census Mesa Grande 1929), whose father was Mexican and whose mother was 4/4 Ipai. Flora's mother, Dolores Quisquis, was born in the San Pasqual Valley.

All of Sylvester and Flora's nine children were also born in the San Pasqual Valley (California Indian Rolls 1928), and their names were shown as: Eugene, Henry, Agnes, Ernest, Elizabeth, Gilbert (Urbano), Philip (Candido) (Charles), and Serafina Grace. After Sylvester's death in about 1932, and sometime before 1940, Flora married Francisco Pena. The 1940 Census showed Flora Lloyd married to Felix Pena, born 1895, and living with their son Felix, 3, and four other children: Eugene, 26, shown as Felix's grandson; Elizabeth, 23, granddaughter; Ernest, 20, stepson, and Phillip, 13, stepson. The family was living in Ramona in 1940 (Census 1940).

As mentioned, Sylvester served as police chief for the Mesa Grande Reservation. An April 1, 1912, document from Thomas Games, superintendent of the Volcan Agency, Mesa Grande, evaluated Sylvester as he completed his tasks as police chief, showing: "Is doing good work and is worthy of favorable mention. He has been willing and faithful in carrying out my instructions" (Games 1912:1).

On June 17, 1912, Superintendent Games instructed Sylvester La Chappa: "As a duly authorized officer of the United States you are hereby invested with authority to arrest one _____ [name] of Los Coyotes Indian Reservation and bring him to the Office of the Superintendent of the Volcan Indian School on the 17th day of June 1912" (Games 2012).

Hugh Lawson, Sr.

The young man who notice Helen Trask working out in the fields on the San Pasqual Indian Reservation circa 1920 was Hugh Lawson, Sr., a native of Poway. His father was Thomas Shelton Lawson, a Civil War veteran from Elizabethtown, Kentucky, and his mother was Rose Meeks Lawson from Oregon, who came to California at the age of 16 months with her father who was a photographer. Hugh Lawson's parents were early pioneers in the Poway region [*Pauwai* in Ipai]. His mother eventually came into touch with her mother again after she had married Thomas. By then both of Rose's parents had remarried and had other children.

Thomas Lawson was working a dairy near the coast when he met Rose, who was working at the Escondido Hotel, where Pomerado Hospital is now. Hugh's sister, Bessie Lawson Hickey, wrote in her memoirs at age 86 in 1992. "Papa delivered dairy products to her kitchen where Mama was a waitress. The rest is history" (Hickey Memoirs 1992).

Thomas Lawson had come to California with a brother. In 1886 when Thomas and Rose settled in Poway Valley, they already had five children. Eventually the family grew to fourteen children, including Bessie, who was born in 1906. The other family members were Leona, Mabel, Newell, Robert, Hugh, Pearl, Jessie, Albert, Hanford, (Bessie), Clarence, Seton, Susan, and Davey. Bessie recalled that her brother Robert was either a judge or justice of the peace. "They called him the Judge," she said.

"We had around 600 or 700 acres on both sides of Pomerado Road, called Escondido Avenue in the early days," Bessie reminisced in a 1962 memoir and in personal notes:

The Poway Valley. *Photo: Escondido Historical Society.*

Our neighbors were the W. K. Lawsons (family cousins), the Kirkhams, Eberts,
John Franks and Friedrichs. We raised hay and grain mostly, also had a small dairy,
orchard and vineyard and the usual farm animals such as cows, pigs, chickens, pigeons
and horses.

The family lived in the area of Poway known as Merton, in a two-bedroom house
with two outside rooms and a big barn. Some of the older children had already left by
the time the younger ones were born. Leona had married and had a baby, which meant
that her own baby and her baby sister were just a year apart.

Papa had built a bunk bed in the big bedroom. ... [W]e really had 'em stacked up.
In the hot summers, the children used to sleep outside on haystacks. We had the usual
iron stove, no running water. A water pump was just outside the kitchen. Always a
big garden. ... [W]e had a big grove of Eucalyptus trees and had campers come and
stay. Drove what was called Tally-Ho's, usually gay colors and pretty high-stepping
horses. I heard Papa tell them that we lost a little girl. I wondered why they didn't try
to find her. ... Papa would get the groceries in San Diego by the 100-pound bag, such
as beans, rice, macaroni that was in a wood box lined with blue paper. Sugar and flour
came in hundred pound sacks and lots of them. The only cookies I knew were Ginger
Snaps and soda crackers, or maybe graham crackers. He also got coffee beans (Hickey
Memoirs 1992)

Bessie told how neighbors would trade produce and her mother would make soap.
Bessie said she and her brothers and sisters "roamed all over the hills, and rode if we could

catch a horse. I remember when the road was paved. Took several weeks for it to set. It had to be watered every day."

About half a mile south of the Lawson Ranch was the Merton School, where in 1912 eight of the fifteen students were Lawsons, and two school board members were also from the Lawson family. Bessie wrote about completing the eighth grade at the Merton School in 1921, and noted, "I was the graduating class!" The school closed after that, due to dwindling enrollment. Bessie recalled that her teacher was Hannah Ebert, who signed her name H. M. C. Ebert and lived next door to the school, where she grew watermelons. Bessie's brothers would trade mushrooms for melons, though Bessie speculated that the watermelon growers didn't eat the mushrooms, since her mother would put a silver 50-cent piece in with the mushrooms and if they turned black she would get rid of them. "It's a miracle she raised us all. She was a wonderful person," Bessie concluded.

Pete La Chappa (and Pedro La Chappa)

Harrington (1925) noted that informant Ysidro Nejo had mentioned a Pedro La Chappa, who lived in the San Pasqual Valley during the 1846 Battle of San Pasqual. La Chappa had helped the American forces by cooking animals for them after their defeat at the battle, before the troops moved north. Ysidro Nejo pointed out Pedro La Chappa's house as he walked with Harrington through the San Pasqual Valley, and noted that the residence was in the northeast section of the valley. Trask Family members, researching possible connections that might exist between the older and younger Pete La Chappas, noted that the younger Pete La Chappa was raised by his grandmother, Feliciana Nejo La Chappa, said to be cousin sister of Ysidro Nejo (Gifford 1919-1920), who provided the location of the older Pete La Chappa's house for Harrington.

On January 3, 2013, Nelda Campagnoli Taylor at the age of 101 spotted the younger Pete La Chappa in a family photo that included three generations of La Chappas, Nejos and Trasks, along with Nelda and her two younger sisters. In the photo, Nelda was sitting in front of the woman she identified as her "Musa" or aunt—Petra La Chappa Cota, who was married to Nelda's maternal uncle Juan Maria Cota. Petra and Juan had adopted the three little girls, Nelda, Zelma, and Hazel Campagnoli, after their mother died of tuberculosis following the birth of five children in five years and the death of the youngest child, an infant son.

Petra stood in the photo next to her brother Antonio La Chappa's wife, Feliciana Nejo La Chappa. Next to Feliciana were her daughter, Leonora La Chappa Trask, and Feliciana's two sons, and Sylvester. Helen Trask stood next to her two uncles and her cousin, Pete La Chappa, who was born in 1910. At age 101 Nelda identified each person in the photo by name, then began relating how during her years at Mesa Grande she and Pete would play in the countryside together. Pete was being raised by his grandmother, Feliciana. Nelda exclaimed: "Pete would make makeshift cars and we would slide down the hills near our homes!" she added, "Oh, I loved that Pete La Chappa!" (Johnson 2013). Pete died in 1983, while Nelda Taylor had just celebrated her 102nd birthday in September 2014.

The Trask family's younger Pete La Chappa can be traced throughout multiple regions in San Diego County. His father was Sylvester La Chappa, twin brother to Leonora La Chappa Trask, and both were born in the San Felipe Valley in 1881 (Censuses of Mesa Grande 1881-1935). Pedro's mother was Sylvester's first wife, Modesta La Chappa (Census of San Diego County 1910). Modesta was shown at both the Mesa Grande and La Jolla Indian Reservations (1910 and 1913) and Pete was shown at both locations as well (Censuses of Mesa Grande 1910, 1911, 1912, 1913, 1920 and 1929 and US Federal Census La Jolla 1913). The 1913 Census for the La Jolla Indian Reservation listed him as Pedro La Chappa, born June 29, 1910 and living with his mother there. The 1913 Census for Mesa Grande shows Pete's father as a widower, with his two sons, Pete, and Pablo Domingo La Chappa, born 1912, along with other family members. Sylvester later married Flora Lloyd (Indian Census of Mesa Grande June 30, 1929) and together they had nine children.

Pedro or Pete La Chappa's stepmother, Flora Lloyd, was born in the San Pasqual Valley in 1895 (Indian Census of Mesa Grande 1929), and his maternal stepgrandmother, Dolores Quisquis, was also born in the San Pasqual Valley (Indian Census of Mesa Grande 1929). Flora's father was Charley Lloyd, of Mexican descent. Each of Pete La Chappa's nine stepsiblings, children of Sylvester and Flora, was born in the San Pasqual Valley, including Eugene La Chappa, Henry La Chappa, Agnes La Chappa, Ernest La Chappa, Elizabeth La Chappa, Gilbert (Urbano) La Chappa, Philip (Candido) (Charles) La Chappa, and Serafina Grace La Chappa (1928 Indian Roll Applications).

After Sylvester's death, which occurred sometime in the early 1930s, Flora Lloyd married Felix Pena (Ipai), born 1893, and the Census of 1940 showed them living with their son Felix, 3, and four of Flora's children by Sylvester: Eugene, 26, Elizabeth, 23, Ernest, 20, and Phillip, 13. Death records for San Diego County confirm that the younger Pete La Chappa lived until August 3, 1983.

Family records, interviews, and photographs have shown the close connections between Pete La Chappa and his mother at La Jolla Indian Reservation, his La Chappa relatives at Mesa Grande, his stepmother, step-grandparents, and nine stepsiblings at the San Pasqual Valley, his connections to the Campagnoli and Cota families in Mesa Grande and Los Coyotes, and the strong bonds he shared with his Trask-Lawson cousins at the San Pasqual Indian Reservation in Valley Center. Further examinations, outlined below, reveal even more family and tribal connections, providing a glimpse of the network of relationships that existed among the native people of San Diego County. Native people interacted with, intermarried, and adopted into their families native people from a variety of bands, clans and families. Pete La Chappa lived with his paternal grandparents, Feliciana Nejo La Chappa and Antonio La Chappa, throughout some of his growing up years, experiencing even more connections with more people.

In addition to San Felipe (birthplace of Pete's father and Aunt Leonora), La Jolla (his mother Modesta) and Mesa Grande (his paternal grandmother Feliciana), Pete was connected to Santa Ysabel (his paternal grandfather Antonio; Antonio's parents Jose Bastian

La Chappa and Angela Guachena; Jose Bastian La Chappa's parents Logario and Maria Jesusa La Chappa, and Angela's father Cornelia Guachena). Also from Santa Ysabel were Pete's grandmother Feliciana's mother, Maria Jesusa Nejo, Maria Jesusa's mother, Maria Louisa Guachena, and Maria Jesusa's two sisters, Maria Dominga and Maria Louisa. Maria Jesusa Nejo's father was Jermain Anej, from Yaqui Well.

Pete's relationship to his paternal great great-grandmother, Maria Louisa Guacheno, gave him connections to her father, Jose La Luz, believed to be from the Santa Ysabel region. John P. Harrington made notes concerning a Jose La Luz several times in his 1913-1933 travels in San Diego County. He stated that Jose La Luz was born at Descanso, and had lived at Warner Springs, Volcan, San Diego, Susana Canyon, and, in 1925, lived near where the road to Santa Ysabel joins the road to the Lake Henshaw Dam (Harrington 1925:6-15).

Pete's grandmother, Feliciana, also provided connections to Julian, through her stepfather, A.E. or Fred Coleman, since Coleman was the first non-Indian to discover gold in San Diego County, at Julian, in 1869. Pete also had a connection to the San Pasqual Valley through his Aunt Leonora's husband, Frank Trask, whose father, Roswell, was living there in 1867 when Frank was born. Roswell's second son, Henry, was shown as living at San Pasqual on the 1880 Census. Pete's Uncle Frank Trask also gave him a connection with Agua Caliente (Warner Springs), where Frank lived before moving to Ramona. Pete shared a connection with Poway through his paternal great-grandmother, Angela Guachena La Chappa, whose daughter, Maria Catalina, was born there in 1857, and where his cousin, Helen Trask Lawson's husband, Hugh, was born in 1899.

Trask family descendants also believe that the younger Pete La Chappa had ties to the Cuyamaca Mountains through Jose Maria Acopal La Chappa, born about 1842 and captain at the Cuyamaca village of Yagui, who also lived at Mesa Grande (Censuses of 1897-1899, 1900, 1902 and 1905-1908) and Pechanga (San Diego Historical Society 2014). The family is currently researching records to learn if a blood connection exists through the Jose Bastian La Chappa and Angela Guachena line, since the 1893 Census of Mesa Grande showed Angela's nephew, Jose La Chappa, age 50 (born 1843), as living in her household. In addition, Pete La Chappa had connections to Pauma Valley and Pala (Gifford 1919-1920), since relatives of his father moved there or were relocated there by the government. A number of La Chappas, Guachenas, Guachenos, and Nejos live today at Pala, following the 1903 removal of the San Felipe Ipai in 1903.

Epilogue

To see and experience a way of life through the words, writings, and images of our ancestors and others who lived in a different generation has given me the opportunity to think beyond today's often-shortsighted views. Especially when we take into consideration that these historical personalities from our past were raised by parents and grandparents whose knowledge and experience was inherited from many previous generations. This can take us back to a time before non-Indians colonized this land, and in many cases, deep into prehistory.

I often try to imagine what the Ipai world was like before the arrival of the Spanish and other non-Indians, at a time when the land was being managed in ways that helped to provide for all, including humans, wildlife, and every part of Mother Nature. A world in which bands of people understood the needs and wants of others, and knew the importance of protecting the People, while also sharing the natural bounty of Mother Earth. Over the millennia, our Ipai ancestors evolved into a complex society that understood that life is more than just a physical reality. They created and transmitted stories of origins and mythologies that reflected the depth of their well-developed religious beliefs. They have left us a rich legacy of songs that even today reinforce our ancient connections to our surroundings, and to our way of understanding the universe. Songs which continue to echo in this land as they are sung around fires under skies full of brilliant stars; songs that identify, name and relate to the movements of the heavens and of the days and seasons of our lives. A musical tradition that has been strong enough to survive in spite of dramatic, often tragic changes, and yet continues as a vibrant gift to future generations.

This leads us to the question of how much was conveyed, and how much was lost. We all know that something may be lost and something may be gained through transitions and transformations. Given that so much knowledge has been passed on through oral tradition, we recognize that there have been many outside influences during the recent transitional period since non-Indians arrived on our shores. Undoubtedly there have been impacts

Opposite page: Juncus basketry, an ancient Kumeyaay tradition that has continued into the present. *Photo: Photo Darkroom.*

from the many changes that were necessary for the People's survival. Considering the many challenges faced by Ipai people who managed to survive through tumultuous times, much credit should be given to those who carried on the traditions and customs and those who to this day, continue carrying the ways that they were taught.

Leroy Elliot, longtime tribal chairman of the Manzanita Band of Kumeyaay Indians, has been a living example of those who have worked hard to preserve native cultural heritage and transmit that knowledge to the upcoming generations. (Sadly, Mr. Elliot passed away during the writing of this book.)

You have to have the education about who you are and where you come from. That makes you a full person. I feel that the creator has left me here on this earth to help people, and that's what I do (KPBS 2012). — Leroy Elliot

Another great guardian of our Kumeyaay traditions was Tony Pinto, longtime tribal chairman of Ewiiaapaayp Band of Kumeyaay Indians. Mr. Pinto inspired many, and thanks to his teachings and the example he set by living a traditional life, many of these ways are still being carried forward today.

Years ago, in conversation with the author, Mr. Pinto commented about his travels as well as the relationships made with native people when he stayed in downtown San Diego, where he developed a friendship with Pete LaChappa. It is reassuring to know that our Ipai and Tipai peoples have continued to move and adjust to the changes in our world, even in the core of San Diego's inner city. Both Old Town and the Horton Plaza areas were remembered by native elders as places where many native people gathered socially to keep their native identity strong.

At one time or another, we ask ourselves, how did we come to be living where we live today? In many cases it's because of our roots, because our parents, our great-grandparents, and a long line of ancient ancestors were born in this region. These ancestors' lives were linked to the wider region by clan membership, by marriage, and by seasonal movements throughout the land. While there might have been some core families that may have stayed year round in one site (weather permitting), most moved with the conditions. Geographic movement and customs requiring marriage outside of the clan led to the maintenance of a diversified gene pool and extensive social networks between bands. How better to keep this vital balance, ensure access to a variety of natural resources, and maintain a healthy society, than to anchor one's identity in an entire region, rather than just one site.

Today when one has conversations with those with native blood, they will share with you that their families were not only from their reservation, but also from other places. So many changes have taken place since the Spanish missionaries arrived and tried to radically change our way of life, bringing devastating diseases and forcing us into permanent settlements. Later, when New Spain became Mexico, officials, and colonists continued to take our lands, granting huge tracts as ranches, including mission lands that were supposed to be ours. Again we moved to where we could survive, often working as cowboys, cooks, and ranchhands for the newcomers. When we became part of the United States in 1848, government policies sought to move us away from lands that were desirable to the new influx of miners, farmers, and ranchers, eventually creating lines and boundaries to define reservations that suited their needs, often outside of our traditional territory. Even an international border came to separate northern and southern Kumeyaay people.

At this point in our history, the United States government has established a trust responsibility with tribes, with tribal sovereignty and government-to-government relations. There are differing opinions as to whether this is best for all, however each tribe does have the opportunity to form their own government under the laws of this country. The southern California tribes are unique in many ways; after thousands of years of moving throughout a wide territory and having relations throughout an even wider region, we have been separated and placed on the reservations, in some cases near each other and in others, with many miles in between. In some respects this has lead to a certain degree of independence. And yet there is still the need to honor our ancient relationships with other bands, since we are all related through blood, marriage, culture and history.

The traditional gatherings that take place on many of the southern California and Arizona reservations, as well as in Baja California, are vital for helping to keep intact the ways we inherited from our ancestors. How this will materialize in another hundred or two hundred years and beyond is unknown. But if the perseverance that has persisted among those who participate in our cultural life is any indication, the future is bright. The spirit is amongst us.

There is much more that has not been conveyed because of the fast decline of the populations that existed until the time of the European expansion and America's manifest destiny philosophy. This makes it all that much more important today that we in this region continue to strengthen our connections with all of our neighboring tribes and in the bigger picture, all of the tribes across this wonderful land of ours.

I will finish by thanking all the people that have been open-minded and sincere, and have shared with me their most valuable asset: respect. I am truly humbled. I hope that this work will inspire more people from the communities referenced here to also trace their heritage to the ancient clans that continue to exist in our homeland. This includes future generations, since it will be today's young people and those that are yet to be born who will carry the ways onward in years to come.

David L. Toler, Jr. 2015

Bibliography

Act for the Relief of the Mission Indians. 1891. Smiley
 Commission. (26 Stat. L. 712).

Act of January 12, 1891, 26 Stat., L. 712, patented
 to the San Pasqual band; held in trust by the
 U. S. Government.

Act of March 1, 1907, 24 Stat., L. 1022, patented
 to the San Pasqual band; held in trust by the
 U. S. Government.

Act of Congress of May 18, 1928. 45 Stat. 602.

A History of the Coleman Family. 2012.
 Personal Communication.

Almstedt, Ruth Farrell.

1977 *Diegueño Curing Practices*. San Diego, California:
 San Diego Museum of Man,

Alta California. 13 November, 1851.

Alta California. 3 December, 1851.

Alta California. 11-14 December, 1851.

Alta California. 2 January, 1852.

Alta California. 8 January, 1852.

Alta California. 15 January, 1852.

Amending Act of April 29, 1930 (46 Stat. 259).

Amended Homestead Land Act of March 1, 1907.
 (34 Stat. L. 1015-1018).

Ames, Ramon. (Chairman of the Barona Band of Mission
 Indians) 1954. *Senate Interim Termination Hearings*.
 Palm Springs.

Ancestry.com Census Mesa Grande. 1900. Waters,
 Jose and Maria.

Ancestry.com Census Mesa Grande. 1902. Waters,
 Jose and Maria.

Ancestry.com Census Mesa Grande. 1905. Waters,
 Jose and Maria.

Ancestry.com Census Mesa Grande. 1907. Waters,
 Jose and Maria.

Ancestry.com Census Mesa Grande. 1908. Waters,
 Jose and Maria.

Ancestry.com 2012.

Ancestry.com 2013.

Ancestry.com, 2012. *Coleman Family Tree*.

Ancestry.com. 2014. *Devers, Jr. Family Tree*.

Ancestry.com. 2014. *Jacome Family Tree*.

Ancestry.com. 2014. *Lambert Briggs Family Tree*.

Annual Report for San Pasqual Indian Reservation.
 1917. Pala Indian School.

Annual Report for San Pasqual Indian Reservation.
 1920. Pala Indian School.

Application and Consents of Parents for Marriage.
 1873 in 1868-1890. Roswell Trask and
 Mary Catherine McIntyre.

Aschmann, Homer. 1959. "The Evolution of a
 Wild Landscape and its Persistence in Southern
 California." *Annals of the Association of American
 Geographers* 49.

Atkins, John D. C. 1886. *U. S. Census of the San Pasqual
 Valley*. Washington, D. C.: Office of Indian Affairs.

Baker, James. Interview, San Pasqual Reservation
 May 2011.

Bancroft, Hubert Howe. 1884. *History of California*
 Vol. 5. Berkeley: University of California.

Bancroft, Hubert Howe. 1885. *The Works of Hubert Howe
 Bancroft Vol. xix* 1801-1824. San Francisco:
 A. L. Bancroft Company.

Bancroft, Hubert Howe. 1886. *History of California
 1542-1890 Vol. 3*. San Francisco: The History Company.

Bancroft, Hubert Howe. 1890. *History of California
 1542-1890*. The History Company, San Francisco:
 The History Company.

Barnett, Mrs. 1966. Interview of December 20-22.
 Pablo Apis granted Rancho.

Barrett, Carole A. and Markowitz. 2005. Harvey
 Editors. *American Indian Biographies Revised Edition*.
 Pasadena: Salem Press.

Bartlett, John Russell. 1854. *Bartlett's Narrative*.
 New York: G. S. McManus Company.

Bean, Lowell John. 1972. *Mukat's People*. Berkeley: University of California Press.

Bean, Lowell John. 1978. *Handbook of North American Indians*. General editor W. C. Sturtevant Vol. 8. Washington: Smithsonian Institution.

Beauchamp. 1998. Personal Communication with Richard Carrico: San Diego.

Beck, Darrell. 2012. *The Saga of the San Pasqual Indian Pueblo, 1835-1878* IN the *Ramona Home ~ Julian Journal*.

Beck, Charles Darrell. 2004. *On Memory's Back Trail: A Story History of RAMONA and the Backcountry of San Diego County*. Ramona: Backcountry Press.

Bibb, Leland. Moss, James Ed. 1976. "William Marshall: The Wickedest Man in America A Reappraisal." *Journal of San Diego History*. San Diego Historical Society Quarterly Vol. 22 No. 1.

Bonekemper III, Edward H. 2004. *A Victor Not a Butcher: Ulysses S. Grant's Overlooked Military Genius*. Washington D.C.: Regnery.

Brauner, Bridget household. SD 4. ED 71. Dwelling 19. Family 19.

Brigandi, Phil. 2010. *A Short History of Temecula, California*. Temecula Valley Historical Society.

Brinton, D. G. 1866. Artificial Shell Deposits of the United States. Washington: Smithsonian Institution.

Bull, Charles. 1977. *Archaeology and Linguistics, Coastal Southern California*. Master's Thesis. San Diego State University Evidence for San Diego Prehistory. San Diego: Society for California Archeology.

Bull, Charles. 1983. *Shaking the Foundations: The Evidence for San Diego Prehistory*. RECON. San Diego. IN *Society for California Archeology*. 1983. San Diego.

Bulletin. 1966. *Frank Trask Appointed Indian Judge February 1, 1910*.

Burrus. 1776. *Diario del Capitan* vol. 1.

Canby, Jr., Willim C. 2004. *American Indian Law*. St. Paul: West.

Carrico, Richard. 2nd ed. 2008. *Strangers in a Stolen Land: Indians of San Diego County from Prehistory to the New Deal*. San Diego: Sunbelt Pulications.

Carrico, Richard L. 1997. "Sociopolitical Aspects of the 1775 Revolt at Mission San Diego de Alcala." *The Journal of San Diego History: San Diego Historical Society Quarterly* Volume 43 Number 3.

Carrico, Richard. 2010. *The San Pasqual Valley*.

Carrico, Richard L., Cooley, Theodore, and Joyce Clevenger. 1991. *Final Archaeological Investigations at the Harris Site Complex*, San Diego: South Coastal Information Center.

Castillo, Edward D. 1998. *Short Overview of California Indian History*. California National American Heritage Commission. www.ceres.ca.gov-/nahe/default.html.

Caughey, John Walton. 1952. *The Indians of Southern California in 1852: The B. D. Wilson Report and a Selection of Contemporary Comment*. San Marino: Huntington Library.

Census Agua Caliente Township. 1860. National Archives Catalog 2353568.

Census Ballena. 1856.

Census Ballena Township.1880. San Diego County. Brauner, Bridget household. SD 4. ED 71. Dwelling 19. Family 19.

Census Ballena. 1884.

Census Ballena. 1940.

Census La Jolla Indian Reservation. 1910.

Census La Jolla Indian Reservation. 1913.

Census Mesa Grande [Indian]. 1881-1935.

Census Mesa Grande [Indian]. 1890. Indians of Mission Agency by Rust, Horatio N.

Census Mesa Grande [Indian]. 1893.

Census Mesa Grande [Indian]. 1894.

Census Mesa Grande [Indian]. 1897. By Estudillo, Francisco.

Census Mesa Grande [Indian].1898. By Wright, L. A.

Census Mesa Grande [Indian].1899. By Wright, L. A.

Census Mesa Grande [Indian]. 1900.

Census Mesa Grande [Indian]. 1901.

Census Mesa Grande [Indian]. 1902. By Wright, L. A.

Census Mesa Grande [Indian]. 1903.

Census Mesa Grande [Indian]. 1904.

Census Mesa Grande [Indian]. 1905.

Census Mesa Grande [Indian]. 1906.

Census Mesa Grande. 1906. Harrington Papers 1913-1933.

Censuses for Mesa Grande & Santa Ysabel #2 in the John P. Harrington files. 1906. By Charles E. Shell.

Census of the Mesa Grande Indians of Santa Ysabel Dist. No. 2. 1907. Taken by Thomas M. Games.

Census Mesa Grande. 1907. Harrington Papers 1913-1933.

Census Mesa Grande [Indian]. 1907.

Census Mesa Grande. 1908. Harrington Papers 1913-1933.

Census Mesa Grande [Indian]. 1908.

Census Mesa Grande [Indian]. 1909.

Census Mesa Grande [Indian]. 1910.

Census Mesa Grande. 1910. Trask, Frank household. 1910 US Indian Population Census. San Diego County. Mesa Grande Reservation. SD 8. ED 136. Dwelling 22. Family 22.

Census Mesa Grande [Indian]. 1911.

Census Mesa Grande [Indian]. 1912.

Census Mesa Grande [Indian]. 1912.

Census Mesa Grande [Indian]. 1913.

Census Mesa Grande [Indian]. 1913.

Census Mesa Grande [Indian]. 1914.

Census Mesa Grande [Indian]. 1914.
Census Mesa Grande [Indian]. 1915.
Census Mesa Grande [Indian]. 1916.
Census Mesa Grande [Indian]. 1917.
Census Mesa Grande [Indian]. 1918.
Census Mesa Grande [Indian]. 1919.
Census Mesa Grande [Indian]. 1920.
Census Mesa Grande [Indian]. 1921.
Census Mesa Grande [Indian]. 1922.
Census Mesa Grande [Indian]. 1923.
Census Mesa Grande [Indian]. 1924.
Census Mesa Grande [Indian]. 1925.
Census Mesa Grande [Indian]. 1926.
Census Mesa Grande [Indian]. 1927.
Census Mesa Grande [Indian]. 1928.
Census Mesa Grande [Indian]. 1929.
Census Mesa Grande [Indian]. 1930.
Census Mesa Grande [Indian]. 1931.
Census Mesa Grande [Indian]. 1932.
Census Mesa Grande [Indian]. 1933.
Census Mesa Grande [Indian]. 1934.
Census Mesa Grande [Indian]. 1936.
Census Mesa Grande [Indian]. 1937.
Census Pala, Agua Caliente, San Felipe. 1905.
Census Pala, Agua Caliente, San Felipe. 1906.
Census Pala, Agua Caliente, San Felipe. 1907.
Census Pala, Agua Caliente, San Felipe. 1908.
Census Pala, Agua Caliente, San Felipe. 1909.
Census San Diego County. 1860. IN Farris, Glenn. 1997.
    *Captain Jose Panto and the San Pascual Indian Pueblo
    in San Diego County 1835-1878.* Footnote 40.
Census San Diego Township. 1860. Microfilm on file.
    California Room, California State Library. Sacramento.
Census San Diego County. 1870. Browne, Peter household.
    Warner's Rancho District. San Diego Post Office [page
    number stamped 530]. Dwelling 78. Family 79.
Census San Diego County. 1870. Sacramento: Records on
    File at the California State Library.
Census San Diego County. 1872. Warner Rancho District.
    Carlos Trask. Baptism entry 24 June 1872.
Censuses of San Diego 1880-1920.
Census San Diego County. 1900.
Census San Diego County . 1910.
Census San Diego County . 1940.
Census San Pasqual Valley. 1852.
Census San Pasqual Valley. 1860. Greenwood, Alfred B.
    Director US Office of Indian Affairs.
Census San Pasqual Valley. 1870.
Census San Pasqual. 1880. Washburne, Calvin family
    [Warner, Matiana; Trask, Henry; Washburne Caroline].
Census San Pasqual. 1886. By Atkins, John. Director
    Office of Indian Affairs.

Census San Pasqual Valley [Indian]. 1909.
    Mission Indians.
Census San Diego County [Indian]. 1910. Trask,
    Frank household. San Diego County. Mesa Grande
    Reservation. pp. 218-B. SD 8. ED 136. Dwelling 22.
    Family 22. Images 11-12.
Census San Pasqual [Indian]. 1923. Mission Agency.
    By Ellis, C. L. Superintendent.
Census San Pasqual [Indian]. 1924. Mission Agency.
    By Ellis, C. L. Superintendent.
Census San Pasqual [Indian]. 1925. By Ellis, C. L.
    Superintendent.
Census San Pasqual [Indian]. 1926. Mission Agency.
    By Ellis, C. L. Superintendent.
Census San Pasqual [Indian]. 1929.
*Census San Pasqual [Indian].*1932.
*Census San Pasqual [Indian].*1933.
Census of the San Pasqual Reservation of the Mission
    Jurisdiction. April 1, 1934. Taken by District
    Superintendent John W. Dady.
Census San Pasqual [Indian]. 1936. Mission Jurisdiction.
    By Dady, John W. District Superintendent.
Census Santa Ysabel. 1852.
Census June 30, 1908 Santa Ysabel #2, Mesa Grande,
    Indian Census, by Thomas M. Games.
Census Volcan [Indian]. 1906. Harrington, John Peabody.
    Approval of Enrollment for Trask/La Chappa family,
    Pursuant to the authority delegated to the Solicitor by
    the Secretary of the Interior (210 DM 2.2A (4) (b), 24 F.
    R. 1348), and redelegated to the Associate Solicitor by
    the Solicitor (Solicitor's Regulation 19, 29 F.R. 6449),
    July 1965.
City Directory for Los Angeles. 1896. Publisher Maxwell,
    George W. San Francisco Chronicle Vol. 64 No. 59.
Cline, Lora L. 1979. *The Kwaaymii: Reflections on a Lost
    Culture.* El Centro: IVC Museum Society. Occasional
    Paper No. 5.
Commissioner of Indian Affairs Annual Report. 1868.
Commissioner of Indian Affairs Annual Report. 1869.
Commissioner of Indian Affairs Annual Report. 1871.
    Confession of Antonio Garra. 1852. National Archives.
Confession of William Marshall. N.d. Beattie Collection.
    Huntington Library.
Congress. 1849. Senate Document 4. 33rd Congress Special
    Session: *Luke Lea to Adam Johnson.* Washington DC.
Congress, Senate. 1851. 33rd Congress, Special Session, S.
    Ex. Doc. No. 4 (Serial 688). *Property taken or destroyed
    by Indians on or about 23rd November, 1851, at the
    rancho of the undersigned.*
Connolly Miskwish, Michael. 2007. *KUMEYAAY:
    A History Textbook, Volume 1, Precontact to 1893.*
    El Cajon: Sycuan Press.

Cook, Sherburne F. 1939. "Smallpox in Spanish and Mexican California, 1770-1845." *Bulletin of the History of Medicine.* 7:153-191.

Costo, Rupert and Costo, Jeanette Dulce Henry. 1987. *The Missions of California: A Legacy of Genocide.* San Francisco: The Indian Historian Press.

County of San Diego. N.d. *Book of Deeds: Rancho Pauba.* Book 1.

Couro and Langdon, Margaret. 1975. *Let's Talk Iipay: An Introduction to the Mesa Grande Language.* Malki Museum Press.

Culin, Stewart. 1903. *American Indian Games.* American Anthropologist (ns) 5.

Curtis, Edward S. 1926. *The North American Indian: Southern California Shoshoneans. The Diegueños. Plateau Shoshoneans. The Washo.* Norwood, Massachusetts: Plimpton Press.

Curtis, Edward. 1907. *The North American Indian.* Vol. XV:16.

Cuyamaca Rancho State Park. 1981. *A Cultural Resources Inventory and Management Plan for Prescribed Burning.* Vol. 2:1.

Cuyamaca Village National Register Form 2013.

Daily Alta California. 13 November 1868.

Davis, Edward H. 1936. San Diego Historical Society.

Death Certificate of San Diego County. 1929. Antonio La Chappa.

Death Record for Adolph Scholder of San Diego County. 1941. Ancestry.com accessed 2013.

Death Record for Ramon Ames of San Diego County. 1956. Ancestry.com accessed 2013.

Death Record for Pete La Chappa of San Diego County. 1983. Ancestry.com accessed 2013.

Department of the Interior patent No. 142190. May 26, 1910.

Dickason, Olive. 1997. *Canada's First Nations: A History of the Founding Peoples from the Earliest Times.* Toronto: Oxford University Press.

Dortch, J. H. 1910. *Department of the Interior, Office of Indian Affairs, to Amos R. Frank, Superintendent of Indian School and Special Disbursing Agent Mesa Grande.* Education Appointments. HVB. Positions of Judges. SC-4 9087 IN Shipek, Florence Dr. Accessed 2012. Archival Records at Kumeyaay Community College. Sycuan.

Dozier, Deborah. 2005. *Standing Firm: The Mission Indian Fight for Basic Human Rights.* Banning: Ushkana Press.

DuBois, Constance Goddard. 1901. "The Mythology of the Diegueños." *Journal of American Folklore.* Vol. XIV No.54.

DuBois, Constance. 1904. "The Mesa Grande Chaup Story." *Journal of American Folk-Lore* Vol. xvii.

DuBois, Constance Goddard. 1906. "The Mythology of the Mission Indians." *Journal of American Folklore Society.* Vol. LXXIII.

DuBois, Constance Goddard. 1909. *Huntington Free Library.* Bronx: New York.

Dunne, William D. 1907. *History of San Diego 1542-1907: An Account of the Rise and Progress of the Pioneer Settlement on the Pacific Coast of the United States.* San Diego: The History Company.

Dyke, A. S. and V. K. Prest. 1986. *Late Wisconsonian and Holocene Retreat of the Larentide Ice Sheet.* Geological Survey of Canada Map 1702A.

Ebbeling, Vanessa. 2010. *A Look Back: The Temecula Massacre.* Accessed from www.pe.com/localnews/-rivcountystories.

Engelhardt, Father Zephyrin. 1913. *The Missions and Missionaries of California* Vol. III, *Upper Californi, Part II, General History.* San Francisco: The James H. Barry Co.

Engelhardt, Father Zephyrin. 1922. *San Diego Mission.* San Francisco: James H. Barry Co.

Escobar, Lorraine. 2011. Genealogical Research of the Trask Family. California.

Evans, William Edward. 1966. "The Garra Uprising: Conflict Between San Diego Indians and Settlers in 1851." *California Historical Society Quarterly* 45.

Ewiiaapaayp Band of Kumeyaay Indians. 2004. *Reservation Location and Land Status.* Retrieved June 5, 2010.

Ewiiaapaayp Band of Kumeyaay Indians. 2004. *Tribal Government.* Retrieved June 5, 2010.

Ewiiaapaayp Band of Kumeyaay Indians. *Ewiiaayaap Tribal Culture and History.* 2004. Retrieved June 5, 2010.

Eyre, Eric. 1989. "For Mary Matteson, Indian Problems Mean Personal Investigation." *Times Advocate.*

Farris, Glenn J. 1994. "Jose Panto, *Capitan* of the Indian Pueblo of San Pascual." *Journal of California and Great Basin Anthropology* Vol. 16 No. 2.

Farris, Glenn. 1997. "Captain Jose Panto and the San Pascual Indian Pueblo in San Diego County 1835-1878." Crawford, Richard W. Editor. San Diego: *San Diego Historical Society Quarterly* Vol. 43 No. 2.

Fetzer, Leland and Jennifer Redmond. 2009. *Cuyamacas: The Story of San Diego's High Country.*

Fine, Gary Alan. 1993. "Ten Lies of Ethnology: Moral Dilemmas of Field Research." *Journal of Contemporary Ethnography.*

Fisher, Walter L. 1911. *Letter to John A. Francis, Attorney General, September 6, 1911.* Washington, D.C.: NARA.

Forbes, Jack D. 1967. *The Indians in America's Past.* New Jersey: Englewood Cliffs.

Foster, Daniel G. 1981. *The Granville Martin Interview: His Knowledge of the Cultural Resources, the History, and the Pre-History of Cuyamaca Rancho State Park*. Sacramento: Manuscript on file at California Department of Parks and Recreation.

Frank, Amos R. Dept. of the Interior U. S. Indian Service. Mesa Grande. *Report of January 13, 1911 to Thomas M. Games*. Supt.Volcan School. Reproduced from the Holdings of the National Archives at Riverside.

Gallegos, Dennis R., Monica Guerrero, Steve Bouscaren, and Susan Bugbee 2002 Otay/Kuchamaa Cultural Resource Background Study, San Diego County, California. Carlsbad, CA: Gallegos and Associates.

Games, Thomas M. 1902. Superintendent Mesa Grande. *Report of Student Leaving Phoenix Indian School.*

Games, Thomas M. 1907. *Report of the Superintendent of the Volcan Indian School Santa Ysabel.*

Games, Thomas M. 1907. *Report of the Superintendent of Mesa Grande.*

Garcia, Orlando. 1957. Report to San Pasqual Enrollment Committee.

Geiger, Maynard. 1969. *Franciscan Missionaries in Hispanic California 1769-1848*. Biographical Dictionary. San Marino: Huntington Library.

General Land Office San Diego County. 1909. Proclamation Creating Cleveland National Forest T12S R.1W S. B. M.

Gifford, E. W. 1918. *Handbook of the Indians of California* IN Carrico, Richard. 2010. *The San Pasqual Valley.*

Gifford, E. W. 1919-1920. *Abstracts from Notes on the Northern Diegueño*. Berkeley: Bancroft Library.

Gifford, E. W. 1931. The *Kamia of Imperial Valley*. Smithsonian Institution. Bureau of American Ethnology Bulletin 97.

Glum, William. 2012.*"The Man from Tennessee."* Accessed from www.coutsfamily.com.

Gorman, Tom. 1988. "Bad Blood: Money Seekers Claiming San Pasqual Indian Ancestry Reopen Rift." *Los Angeles Times*, July 3. http://articles.latimes.com/1988-07-03/local/me-8816_1_san-pasqual-valley accessed Jan 15, 2015.

Griffin, Clinton R. 1994. *Mission San Diego de Alcala: Baptisms for the Mission and Vicinity* 1769-1850. Self-published by author Glenn Farris 1994.

Griffin, John Strother. 1846. *Journal MSS-CE 76*. Berkeley: Bancroft Library.

Griswold del Castillo, Richard. 1990. *The Treaty of Guadalupe Hidalgo: A Legacy of Conflict*. Norman: University of Oklahoma Press.

Guinn, J. M. 1907. *A History of California*, Volume 2. Los Angeles.

Gunn, Guard D. 2010. *Clipping in the San Pasqual File*. San Diego Historical Society IN Carrico, Richard. 2010. *The San Pasqual Valley.*

Haas, Theodor. 1957. The Legal Aspects of Indian Affairs from 1887 to 1957. American Academy of Political and Social Science. 12-22.

Haas, Theodore H. 1947. *Ten Years of Tribal Government Under the Indian Reorganization Act*. 48 Stat. 984. US Indian Service: Haskell Institute Printing Department.

Hallaran, Kevin; Archibald, Allene; Bean, Lowell J.; Vane, Sylvia B. N.d. *The Indian Cemetery at Old Temecula.*

Hanna, David C., Jr. 1982. *Malcolm J. Rogers: The Biography of a Paradigm*. Masters thesis, Department of Anthropology, San Diego State University.

Harlow, Neal. 1987. Maps of the Pueblo Lands of San Diego 1602-1874. Los Angeles: Dawson's Book Shop.

Harrington, John P. 1925. *Field Notes, Maps, and Photographs from the Field Work Among the Mission Indians of California*. Notebooks on file at the Smithsonian Institution. Microfilm Reels No. 169 and 170 Diegueño. Riverside: University of California.

Harrington, John Peabody. 1908. "A Yuma Account of Origens." *Journal of American Folklore* 21.

Harrington, John Peabody. 1913-1933. *California Publications in American Archaeology and Ethnology: Southern California/Basin*. Vol. 11 No.2.

Harrington, Mark Raymond and Ruth DeEtte Simpson. 1961. *Southwest Museum Papers, Tule Springs, Nevada: With Other Evidences of Pleistocene Man in North America*. Los Angeles.

Harwood Caughey. 1974. John Walton. 1952. *The Indians of Southern California in 1852: The B. D. Wilson Report and a Selection of Contemporary Comments*, San Marino: Huntington Library.

Hauke, C.F. N.d. *Report from C.F. Hauke 2nd Assistant of Office of Indian Affairs noting location of Maria Antonia Waters.*

Hayes, Benjamin 1934: 140.

Hayes, Benjamin J. 1873. *Pueblo of San Pascual, Missions of Alta California: Extracts and Copies from Archives Volume 1 part 2*. Berkeley: Bancroft Library.

Hayes, Benjamin J. *Emigrant Notes of Benjamin Hayes 1850-1875*. Berkeley: Bancroft Library N.d. No. 39.

Hayes, Benjamin. 1929. *Pioneer Notes from the Diaries of Judge Benjamin Hayes 1849-1875*. Ed: Hubert Howe Bancroft. Los Angeles.

Hayes, Benjamin. N.d. "Confession of William Marshall," newspaper article Hayes IN Hayes, Benjamin. *"Scrapbooks"* Vol. 38.

Hedges, Ken. 1970. An Analysis of Diegueño Pictographs. Master's thesis on file at San Diego State University IN Carrico, Richard. 2010. San Pasqual Valley.

Hedges, Ken. 1975. "Notes on the Kumeyaay: A Problem of Identification." *Journal of California Anthropology* Vol. 2 No.1.

Heizer, Robert F. (ed.). 1976. *Some Last Century Accounts of the Indians of Southern California.* Ramona: Ballena Press Publications in Archaeology, Ethnology, and History No. 6.

Herrera, Eleanor. Interview. San Pasqual Reservation. May 2011.

Hickey, Bessie Lawson. 1992. *Memoirs of the Lawson Family.* Self-published.

Hill, Leonard. 1966. Certification of San Pasqual Indian Reservation Valley Center Tribal Roll.

Hinton, Leanne, and Lucille J. Watahomigie. 1984. Spirit Mountain: An Anthology of Yuman Story and Song. Tucson, AZ: University of Arizona Press.

Historical Society of Pennsylvania. 2009. Indian Rights Association Records 1830-1986. Collection 1523.

History of San Bernardino and San Diego Counties. 1965. Riverside Museum Press: Rubidoux Printing Co., p. 27.

Hohenthal, William D., Jr. 2001.Tipai Ethnographic Notes: A Baja California Indian Community at Mid-Century. Menlo Park, CA: Ballena Press and the Institute for Regional Studies of the Californias.

Holder, Julie. Interview. Rincon Reservation. May 2011.

Hudson, Millard E. 1976. Moss, James E., Editor. "The Pauma Massacre." *Journal of San Diego History. San Diego Historical Society Quarterly* Vol. 22 No. 1.

Hyden, H. E., 1965. *Letter to an area director of the Bureau of Indian Affairs, July 1965.* Sacramento, California.

Hyer, Joel R. 2001. *We are Not Savages: Native Americans in Southern California and the Pala Reservation 1840-1920.* Michigan State University Press.

Indian Reorganization Act. 1935. 48 stat. 984. Adopted June 18, 1934. Went into effect May 1935.

Indian Roll for California Applications. 1928.

Irving, Malcolm.1978. Phone interview with Welda Johnson. Escondido. 1978.

Jackson, Robert H. and Castillo, Edward. 1995. *Indians, Franciscans and Spanish Colonization: The Impact of the Mission System on California Indians.* Albuquerque: New Mexico.

Jackson, Helen Hunt & Abbot Kinney. 1883. *A Report on the Condition and Needs of the Mission Indians.*

Jayme, Luis, O.F. M. 1970. *Letter of Luis Jayme. O.F.M.* San Diego, *October 17, 1772* IN Geiger, Maynard. 1970. *Baja Travel Series.* Los Angeles: Dawson's Book Shop.

Johnson, Kenneth M. 1966. *K-344 or The Indians of California v. the United States.* Los Angeles: Dawson's Book Shop.

Jones. 2002. *Historical Dictionary of the Civil War A-L.* Rowman Littlefield.

Kappler, Charles J., 1913. Indian Affairs Laws and Treaties Vol. 3 (Laws). Oklahoma State University. http://hdl.handle.net/11244/10469 Accessed on March 12, 2015.

Kappler, Charles, ed. 1929. *Indian Affairs: Laws and Treaties* 5. Washington: Government Printing Office IN Carrico, Richard L. 1980. *San Diego Indians and the Federal Government: Years of Neglect 1850-1865.* San Diego: San Diego Historical Society Quarterly.

Kappler, Charles J. 1904. *Indian Affairs: Laws and Treaties.* Washington : Government Printing Office.

Kelsey, Charles E. 1906. *Report of Special Agent C. E. Kelsey for California Indians to the Commissioner of Indian Affairs.* Carlisle Indian School.

Kelsey, Charles E. 1906. *Census of Non-reservation Indians 1905-1906.* Heizer, Robert F. Ed. and *University of California Publications in American Archaeology and Ethnology.* 1957. Vol. 47 No. 2.

Kelsey, Charles E. 1909. *Letter to the Commissioner of Indian Affairs December 28, 1909.* Washington D.C.: NARA.

Kelsey, Charles E. Special Agent to the California Indians. 1910. *Report of San Pasqual Indian Reservation, April 7, 1910 to the Commissioner of Indian Affairs.* Washington D.C.

Kelsey, Charles E. 1911. *Report of May 4, 1911 to Commissioner of Indian Affairs.* Washington, D. C.

Kelsey, C. E. 1913. *Publications in Archaeology, Ethnology and History.* No. 13.

Kelsey, C. E. *Report of Special Agent for the California Indians.* Reprinted in Robert F. Heizer (Ed). *Federal Concern About Conditions of California Indians 1853-1913.* Eight Documents: Ballena Press.

Kelsey, Charles E., Special Agent to the Indians of California. 1913. *Letter to the Commissioner of Indian* Affairs October 4, 1913: Final Report on the Indians of California July 25, 1913. Washington, D. C.: NARA.

Kelsey, Harry. 1985. *European Impact on the California Indians 1530-1830.* "The Americas 41."

KPBS. 2012. Leroy Elliot: Native American Heritage Month 2012 Honoree. http://www.kpbs.org/news/2012/oct/02/leroy-elliott/ accessed February 2, 2015.

Kroeber, Alfred, L. 1925. *Handbook of the Indians of California* IN Carrico, Richard. 2010. *The San Pasqual Valley.*

Kroeber, Alfred. 1956. *Handbook of the Indians of California.* Reprint of Bulletin 18. Bureau of American Ethnology. Berkeley: California Book Company.

Kroeber, A. L. 1970. *Handbook of the Indians of California*. Berkeley: California Book Company.

Lane, F. K. 1905. Letter #2 attached to Senate Document of 32 Congress 1ˢᵗ Session. *Message from the President of the United States: Communicating Eighteen Treaties Made with Indians in California, of the Following Tribes.*

Lawson, Jr. Allen. Interview. San Pasqual Indian Reservation. May 2011.

Lawson, Hugh Jr. Interview. San Pasqual Reservation. May 2011.

Laylander, Don. 1995. "The Question of Prehistoric Agriculture Among the Western Yumans." *Estudios Fronterizos* 35-36:187-203.

1997. "Inferring Settlement Systems for the Prehistoric hunter-Gatherers of San Diego County, California." *Journal of California and Great Basin Anthropology.* Malki Museum. Morongo, California.

Lepper, Ruth. 2005. "Ballena Rancher Was a True Cowboy." *San Diego Union Tribune.* June 26, 2005.

Leupp, Francis E. 1909. *Approval Frank Trask Allotment at San Pasqual Indian Reservation Valley Center.*

Lightfoot, Kent G., and Otis Parrish. 2009. California Indians and their Environment: An Introduction. Berkeley: University of California Press.

Lipps, Oscar H. 1920. *Report on the Mission Indians.* Laguna Niguel: National Archives IN Carrico, Richard. 2010. *The San Pasqual Valley.*

Lockwood, Herbert. 1967. *Fallout from the Skeleton's Closet.* San Diego: San Diego Independent.

Lucas, Carmen. 2004. *Legacy of the Kwaaymii*: Introduction at www.americanindiansource.com.

Lucas, Tom. 1975. Interview with Richard Carrico at Laguna Ranch. Carrico, Richard Ed. 1983. "Brief Glimpse of the Kumeyaay Past: An Interview with Tom Lucas, Kwaaymii, of Laguna Ranch." *The Journal of San Diego History.* Scharf, Thomas L. Managing Editor. *San Diego Historical Society Quarterly.* 1983. Vol. 29 No. 2.

Luomala, Katharine. 1963. *Tipai-Ipai in California edited by Robert F. Heizer: Handbook of North American Indians.* William C. Sturtevant, General Ed. Vol 8. Washington DC..: Smithsonian Institution.

Luomala, Katharine. 1978. *Tipai-Ipai in California.* Ed. *Robert F. Heizer. Handbook of North American Indians.* Washington DC.: Smithsonian Institution.

MacMullen, Jerry. 1963. *The Journal of San Diego History.* Vol 9 No. 4.

Magante, Maurice, and Amago, Marvin. 1987. "*Families Were Separated*" IN Costo, Rupert and Costo, Jeanette Dulce Henry. *The Missions of California: A Legacy of Genocide.* San Francisco:The Indian Historian Press.

Mariner, Fray Juan. 1795. *The Discovery of Valle de San Jose: Diary of Fray Juan Mariner* in *The History of Warner's Ranch and Its Environs.* Los Angeles: William Reese Company.

Marriage Certificate for Lucretia Rios and Frank Trask. 1889. San Diego County. Justice of the Peace Thomas J. Cox Officiating.

Martinez, Diana. Interview. San Pasqual Reservation. May 2011.

Marvin Amago. *Families Were Separated* in Costo and Costo. 1987. *The Missions of California: A Legacy of Genocide.* San Francisco: The Indian Historian Press.

Matthews, Glenna. 2012. *The Golden State in the Civil War: Thomas Starr King, the Republican Party, and the Birth of Modern California.* New York: Cambridge University Press.

Mazzetti, Bo. Interview. Rincon Reservation. May 2011.

McGrew, Clarence Alan. 1922. *City of San Diego and San Diego County: The Birthplace of California.* New York: American Historical Society.

McGroarty, John S. 1911. *California: Its History and Romance.* Los Angeles: Grafton Publishing.

McHenry Petei. 1998. *The History of Valley Center, California: The Homestead Years 1860-1900.* Escondido: GP Marketing.

McIntire, John L. 1866. *A Report of the California State Agricultural Society.* San Diego.

McIntire, John L. 1892. *City Directory Los Angeles.*

Merriam Webster. 1991.

Miller, Anne J. PhD. *Temecula Massacre.* Accessed 2012 from www.cityoftemecula.org/Temecula/history.

Miskwish, Michael Connelly. 2007. *Kumeyaay: A History Textbook, Volume 1, Precontact to 1893, First Edition.* El Cajon: Sycuan Press.

Mission Baptismal Records, San Diego Mission, 06899 IN Carrico, Richard. 2010. *The San Pasqual Valley.*

Molto, E., J. D. Stewart, and P. Reimer. 1998. "The Chronology of Las Palmas Culture: New Radiocarbon Dates on Non-human Terrestrial Materials from William Massey's Cave Burial Sites." *Pacific Coast Archaeological Society Quarterly.* 34(4):1-19.

Moncada in Burrus. 1776. *Diario del Capitan*, Vol. 1.

Morales, Anna and Mendez, Helen and Frank. Interview. San Pasqual Reservation. May 2011.

Moyer, Cecil C. 1969. *Historic Ranchos of San Diego.* San Diego: Union Tribune Publishing IN Hyer, Joel R. 2001. *We are Not Savages: Native Americans in Southern California and the Pala Reservation 1840-1920.* Michigan State University Press.

National Archives Microfilm Publications. 1958. *Letters Received by the Office of Indian Affairs.* Washington: National Archives Microfilm Publications.

National Park Service. Accessed 2007. A *History of American Indians in California: 1934-1964.* 2004.

Newcomb, Steven T. 2008. *Pagans in the Promised Land: Decoding the Doctrine of Christian Discovery*. Golden: Fulcrum Publishing.

Official Register of the United States. Vol. 2. U.S. Dept. of the Interior. Post Offices and Post Masters' Compensation. 1891.

Olberg, Charles R. 1914-1929. *Irrigation Report for San Pasqual Indian Reservation Valley Center*.

Orfield, Gary, 1964. *A Study of the Termination Policy*. Denver: National Congress of American Indians.

Orosco, Frankie. Interview. San Pasqual Reservation. May 2011.

Palou. 1769. *Historical Memoirs Vol. 2* IN Carrico, Richard. 2010. *The San Pasqual Valley*.

Pancoast, Henry Spackman. 1884. The Indians Before the Law: The Indian Rights Association. Philadelphia: Kessenger Legacy Reprints.

Parker, Horace. N.d. *The Historic Valley of Temecula: The Temecula Massacre*. California: Paisano Press.

Parks Canada—L'Anse aux Meadows Nathional Historic Site of Canada. 2009. Retrieved July 29, 2009 Pc.gc.ca.

Patterson, Alex. 1992. *A Field Guide to Rock Art Symbols of the Greater Southwest*. Boulder: Johnson Books.

Peet, Mary Rockwood. 1949. *San Pasqual: A Crack in the Hills*. Culver City: The Highland Press.

Peet, Mary Rockwood. 1973. *San Pasqual: A Crack in the Hills*. Ramona: Ballena Press.

Phillips, George Harwood. 1974. *Indians and the Breakdown of the Spanish Mission System in California*. Los Angeles: University of California Los Angeles.

Pierce, Frank. 1910. *Notice of $200 payment to Woods for right-of-way at San Pasqual Indian Reservation Valley Center*. Washington DC.

Pierce, Frank. 1910. First Assistant Secretary of the Interior. "Regarding Illegal Occupancy of Indian Lands: General Land Office Descriptions Woods Lawsuit.

Pigniolo, Andrew. 2000. *Points, Patterns and People: Distribution of the Desert Side-Notched Point in San Diego*. Proceedings of the Society for California Archaeological Annual Meetings.

Pourade, Richard F. 1963. Editor emeritus of the *San Diego Union. The History of San Diego: The Silver Dons 1835-1865*. San Diego: Copley Press.

Property taken or destroyed by Indians on or about 23rd November, 1851, at the rancho of the undersigned: "U.S. Congress, Senate, 33rd Congress, Special Session*, S. Ex. Doc. No. 4 (Serial 688). 290-291.

Quinion and Hanks (accessed 2013 1928 California Indian Rolls as #2481 Jose Domingo Yanke)

Quinn, Charles Russell. 1962. *Mesa Grande Country*. Downey: Elena Quinn.

Quisquis, Felix. 1965. Report to Enrollment Committee San Pasqual.

Rawls, James J. 1986. *Indians of California: The Changing Image*. University of Oklahoma Press.

Regional Water Quality Control Board. 1998. *New River Pollution in Mexico: An Historical Overview*. Retrieved February 16, 2007.

Rios, Francisco. 1851. *Francisco Rios to Abel Stearns Collection*. San Marino: Huntington Library.

Rivera y Moncada, Fernando de. 1967. Ernest J. Burrus, ed. *Diario del capitán comandante Fernando de Rivera y Moncada*. Madrid: Ediciones J. Porrúa Turanzas.

Roberts, Elizabeth Judson. 1994. *Indian Stories of the Southwest*. San Francisco: Harr Wagner Publishing Company.

Robertson, Rosalie. 1987. *"The Crying Rock—Where They Killed the Children,"* IN Costo, Rupert and Costo, Jeanette Dulce Henry. *The Missions of California: A Legacy of Genocide*. San Francisco: The Indian Historian Press.

Rustvold, Marjorie M. 1968. *San Pasqual Valley: Rancheria to greenbelt*. Unpublished MA thesis. Social Sciences. San Diego State College.

Ryan, Frances Bevan. 1980. *Yes Escondido, There Was a Felicita*. No publisher shown.

San Diego County Land Records. 1877. *Document 548/ CACAA087465*. Washington D.C.: NARA.

San Diego Courthouse. 1975. Deposition in the death of Roswell Trask.

San Diego Herald. 1851. 11 – 14 December.

San Diego Herald. 1851. 18 December.

San Diego Herald. 1851. 25 December.

San Diego Herald. 1852. 10 January.

San Diego Historical Society. 2014.

San Diego Union. 1870. 17 February.

San Diego Union. 1870. 22 February.

San Diego Union. 1874.

San Diego Union. 1877.

San Diego Union. 1884. 23 October.

San Diego Union, 30 October 1915.

San Diego Union. 1938.

San Diego Union, May 1, 1938.

San Diego Union-Evening Tribune Obituary. 18 January 1962.

San Francisco Chronicle. 1896. Vol. 64. No. 59.

Schleuss, Heinz. 1984. "Local Indian Reservations Struggle to Become Self Sufficient." *Times Advocate*.

Schurr, Theodore. 2012. www.dailymail.co.,uk/ sciencetech/article-2092258/Native-Americans-actually-came.

Senate Document of January 19, 1905. *Message from the President of the United States, Communicating*

Eighteen Treaties Made with Indians in California. 32nd Congress, 1st Session.

Senate Interim Termination Hearings Transcripts. 1954. Palm Springs.

Sequoyah League Bulletin 4. 1907. *The Scattered Sheep of Mission Flocks* IN Carrico, Richard L. 2010. *The San Pasqual Valley.*

Shell, Charles E. Superintendent of the Indian School and Special Disbursing

Shipek, Florence C. 1982. "Kumeyaay Socio-Political Structure." *Journal of California and Great Basin Anthropology.*

Shipek, Florence, Dr. Accessed 2012. Handwritten manuscript from Shipek Archives at Kumeyaay Community College. Sycuan.

Shipek, Florence, Dr. Accessed 2012. Typed manuscript from Shipek Archives at Kumeyaay Community College. Sycuan.

Shipek, Florence, PhD. 1994. *Affidavit accessed 2012.* Sycuan: Kumeyaay Community College.

Shipek, Florence, PhD. Accessed 2012. "Letter to District Irrigation Superintendent, June 24, 1926." Sycuan: Kumeyaay Community College.

Shipek, Florence. 1987. *Pushed into the Rocks: Southern California Indian Land Tenure 1769-1986.* Lincoln: University of Nebraska Press.

Simon, John Y. 1967. *Papers of Ulysses S. Grant Vol. 1.* Southern Illinois University Press.

Smiley Commission. 1891. (26 Stat., L., 712).

Smith, Brian Frederick. 1982. *"The San Diego of Judge Benjamin F. Hayes: Excerpts from the Emigrant Notes 1850-1875."* MA in History: University of San Diego.

Smythe, William E. 1908. *History of San Diego 1542-1908: An Account of the Rise and Progress of the Pioneer Settlement on the Pacific Coast of the United States, Vol. I.* Old Town: The San Diego History Company.

Sparkman, Philip Stedman. 1908. *The Culture of the Luiseño Indians.* American Archaeology and Ethnology VIII No. 4. Berkeley: University of California Publications.

Spier, Leslie. 1923. *Southern Diegueño Customs.* Berkeley: University of California Publications in American Archaeology and Ethnology 20.

Stewart, Robert. Interview. San Pasqual Reservation. May 2011.

Stirling, Larry. 2007. "Did We Ever Thank Chemuctah?" *The Daily Transcript* at www.sddt.com/commentary/article.-cfm.

Superintendent San Pasqual Jurisdiction. 1942. *Report for San Pasqual Indian Reservation.*

Superior Court Files. 1878. San Diego Historical Society.

Sutton, Imre. 1994. *Land Claims in Native America in the Twentieth Century: An Encyclopedia.* Davis, Mary Ed. New York: Garland Publishing Company.

Table 1-1. 2002. *Terminology for Cultural History in the San Diego Area.* Adapted from Gallegos.

Cuyamaca Village National Register Form. 2013. *Sections 7, 8, 9.*

Taylor, Nelda Campagnoli. Interview by Welda Johnson. Escondido. November 2013.

Thorne, Tanis. 2012. *El Capitan: Adaptation and Agency on a Southern California Indian Reservation 1850-1937.* Banning: Malki Ballena Press.

Thornton, Russell. 1994. *American Indian Holocaust and Survival: A Population History since 1492.* Norman: University of Oklahoma Press.

Tofflemier, G. and Luomala, K. 1936. "Dreams and Dream Interpretation of the Diegueño Indians of Southern California." *Psychoanalytic Quarterly* Vol. 5.

Toler, Audrey Lawson. Interview. San Pasqual Reservation. May 2011.

Toler, Dave. Interview. San Pasqual Reservation. May 2011.

Toler, Dave. Personal Communication. 2014.

Toler, David L. III. Interview. San Pasqual Reservation. May 2011.

Trefousse, Hans L. 1989. *Andrew Johnson: A Biography.* Norton Publishing.

True, Delbert. 1970. *Investigation of a Late Prehistoric Complex in Cuyamaca Rancho State Park.* Monograph Series of the Archaeological Survey. Los Angeles: University of California.

Trust Patent for San Pasqual Indian Reservation Valley Center. 1910. *Patent Number 142190.*

Tyson, Rose. 2003. Footsteps Through Time: Four Million Years of Human Evolution. San Diego Museum of Man.

University of California Publications in American Archaeology and Ethnology. 1957. Vol. 47 No. 2.

US government report L-80665-16. N.d. *Character of Wilburn Reed.*

US House of Representatives Resolution 108. 83rd Congress. 1953. (U.S. Statutes at Large, 67: B132) OSU Library Electronic Publishing Center (1953-08-01). Retrieved on 2007-05-01.

Van Horn, Kurt. 1974. "Tempting Temecula." *Journal of San Diego History. San Diego Historical Society Quarterly* Vol. 20 No. 1.

Von Werlhof, Jay 2004 *That They May Know and Remember Volume 2: Spirits of the Earth.* Imperial Valley College Desert Museum Society. Self-published, Ocotillo, California.

Wade, Sue. 2011. *Record of California Troops: Company G, 4th Infantry Regiment.* 2011. Borrego Springs: California Dept. of Parks & Recreation.

Warren and True. 1961. *The San Dieguito Complex and Its Place in California Prehistory*. Vol. 2.

Warren, Claude N. and True, D. L. 1960-1961. *The San Dieguito Complex and Its Place in California Prehistory*. Archaeological Survey Annual Reports. Los Angeles: University of California.

Warren, Claude N., Gretchen Siegler and Frank Dittmer. 1998. *Paleo Indian and Early Archaic Periods. Prehistoric and Historic Archaeology of Metropolitan San Diego: A Historic Properties Background Study*. San Diego Metropolitan Wastewater Public Works.

Waterman, T. T. 1910. *The Religious Practices of the Diegueño Indians*. Los Angeles: University of California Publications in American Archaeology and Ethnology Vol. 8 No. 6.

Weber, David J. 1992. *The Spanish Frontier in North America*. New Haven: Yale University Press.

Wells, Spencer and Read, Mark. *The Journey of Man— A Genetic Odyssey*. Random House.

Whipple, A. W. 1961 *The Whipple Report: Journal of an Expedition from San Diego, California, to the Rio Colorado, from Sept. 11 to Dec. 11, 1849*. Los Angeles: Westernlore Press.

Whiting, B. C. 1869. *Annual Report: California for the Fiscal Year Ending June 30, 1869*. San Francisco: Frances and Valentine Commercial Printing House.

Wilken, Michael. 2012. *An Ethnobotany of the Baja California's Kumeyaay Indians*. Master's Thesis. San Diego State University. San Diego, California.

Woodward, Arthur. 1934. *Notes on the Indians of San Diego County from the Manuscripts of Judge Benjamin Hayes: The Masterkey*. Vol. 8 No. 5. Los Angeles: Southwest Museum. Note: In 1984 this book became *Just Before Sunset* (revised and expanded). Cline, Lora L. 2008. *Just Before Sunset*. Ramona: Sunbelt Publishers.

Woodward, Arthur. 1947. "Lances at San Pasqual." *California Historical Society Quarterly* Volume 20 No. 1.

Wozencraft, O. M. 1852. "*A Treaty of Peace and Friendship Between the United States Indian Agent O.M. Wozencraft, and the captains and headmen of the nation of Dieguino* [sic] *Indians*" IN U.S. Congress House of Representatives. 1857. Document No. 76, 4th Congress 3rd Session, Indian Affairs on the Pacific.

Index